Mark Alan Stewart

Frederick J. O'Toole

ARCO
Teach Yourself
the GRE
in 24 Hours

MACMILLAN • USA

GRE is a registered trademark of the Graduate Record Examinations Council, which does not endorse this book.

First Edition

Macmillan General Reference
A Simon & Schuster Macmillan Company
1633 Broadway
New York, NY 10019

Macmillan Publishing books may be purchased for business or sales
promotional use. For information please write: Special Markets
Department, Macmillan Publishing USA, 1633 Broadway, New York,
NY 10019.

An ARCO book

MACMILLAN is a registerd trademark of Macmillan, Inc.
ARCO is a registered trademark of Prentice-Hall, Inc.

Educational Testing Service, ETS Graduate Record Examinations, and
GRE are registered trademarks of Educational Testing Service.

ISBN: 0-02-862690-7 (book only)
ISBN: 0-02-862864-0 (book with CD-ROM)

Manufactured in the United States of America

10–9–8–7–6–5–4–3–2–1

About This Book

Congratulations! You have in your hands the best fast-track GRE self-study course available today! *ARCO Teach Yourself the GRE in 24 Hours* gives you a structured, step-by-step tutorial program that can help you master all the basics—no matter how limited your study time. In just 24 hour-long lessons, it cuts straight to the essentials, covering all the key points and giving you the practice you need to make each minute count. Even if the test is just days away, this *ARCO Teach Yourself* course will help you learn everything it takes to get the high GRE score you want.

In your very first hour-long lesson, you'll get an overview of everything that's on the test and how it's scored. Then you'll examine every test subject and question type, and in practically no time you'll be sailing through confidence-building workshops, quizzes, and full-length sample exams, sharpening your skills and building your confidence so that when test day comes, you'll be ready!

Who Should Use This Book

ARCO Teach Yourself the GRE in 24 Hours is written for students who want to prepare for the GRE the smartest way—but whose study time is limited. This book is for you if:

- You know that you'll get the most out of a structured, step-by-step tutorial program that takes the guesswork out of test prep

- You want to prepare on your own time, at your own pace—but you don't have time for a preparation program that takes weeks to complete

- You want a guide that covers all the key points—but doesn't waste time on topics you don't absolutely have to know for the test

- You want to avoid taking risks with this all-important test by relying on those "beat the system" guides that are long on promises—but short on substance

Overview

Contents

About the Authors

Mark Alan Stewart is an attorney (J.D., University of California at Los Angeles) and private test preparation consultant based in Southern California. He is one of today's leading authorities in the field of standardized exam preparation, bringing to this publication more than a decade of experience in coaching college students as they prepare for the GRE. His other Macmillan (ARCO) publications for graduate-level admissions include:

GMAT CAT: Answers to the Real Essay Questions

Teach Yourself the GMAT CAT in 24 Hours

30 Days to the LSAT

Perfect Personal Statements—Law, Business, Medical, Graduate School

Words for Smart Test-Takers

Math for Smart Test-Takers

GRE-LSAT Logic Workbook

GRE-LSAT-GMAT-MCAT Reading Comprehension Workbook

Frederick J. O'Toole (Ph.D. Philosophy, University of California) is a Professor of Philosophy at California State Polytechnic University, San Luis Obispo. His areas of specialization include Critical Thinking, Symbolic Logic, and History and Philosophy of Science. He brings to this publication over two decades of experience teaching students critical thinking concepts and skills. His other Macmillan (ARCO) publications for graduate-level admissions include:

GMAT CAT: Answers to the Real Essay Questions

Teach Yourself the GMAT CAT in 24 Hours

30 Days to the LSAT

Authors' Acknowledgments

The authors wish to thank Linda Bernbach and Cindy Kitchel at ARCO for their assistance. Mark Stewart also wishes to thank Kirk Taylor, Eva Anda, Judy Flynn, and Patrick Cunningham for their contributions; and Annette, Cinder, and Little Boo for their moral support. Fred O'Toole would like to thank his beautiful ladies, Joyce Connelly and Oona O'Toole, for their patience and support. Thanks also to Pearl, Tina and Boo Bear.

Credits

Introduction

Welcome to *ARCO Teach Yourself the GRE in 24 Hours*. By working your way through these pages, you'll get a fast-paced cram course on all the key points you need to know to raise your GRE score. In just 24 one-hour lessons, you'll review all of the topics and concepts that are tested on the GRE, and you will learn powerful strategies for answering every question type.

How to Use This Book

This book has been designed as a 24-hour teach-yourself training course complete with examples, workshops, quizzes, and full-length sample test sections. It is expected that you can complete each lesson in about an hour. However, you should work at your own rate. If you think you can complete more than one lesson in an hour, go for it! Also, if you think that you should spend more than one hour on a certain topic, spend as much time as you need.

How This Book Is Organized

Part I, "Start with the Basics," gives you a quick overview of important facts you need to know about the GRE. You'll learn how to register for the test, how the test is structured, how it's scored—and some general test-taking tips that will help you score higher on test day.

Part II, "Learn to Answer GRE Quantitative Questions," starts in Hours 2 and 3 with an overview of the math areas covered on the GRE and an in-depth look at each quantitative question type. Then, in Hours 4 – 9 you'll teach yourself the arithmetic, algebra and geometry concepts you'll need to score high on the GRE. At the end of each hour, you'll practice applying the concepts you learned by working through a GRE-style quiz.

Part III, "Learn to Answer GRE Verbal Questions," focuses on the concepts and strategies you'll need to know for the GRE Verbal section. In Hour 10 you'll concentrate on Verbal Analogies, in Hour 11 on Sentence Completions and Antonyms, and in Hours 12 and 13 on the Reading Comprehension skills you'll need for GRE success. Once again, you'll sharpen your skills with a GRE-style quiz.

Part IV, "Learn to Answer GRE Analytical Questions," provides everything you need to know about logic for the GRE. In Hours 14–16 you'll teach yourself strategies for handling all the most common GRE logic games. Then, in Hours 17 and 18 you'll examine the logical reasoning skills you'll need to critique arguments and recognize reasoning errors. Here, too, you'll have plenty of opportunites to try out your new skills on the GRE-style quiz at the end of each hour.

Part V, "Practice with Sample Exams," contains two practice GREs—one just like the paper-based test, and the other modeled on the computer-based GRE. Take each one under timed conditions, and you'll experience just how it feels to take the actual exam. Once you've finished each sample exam, check your answers against the Answer Key and read the explanation (see Appendix A) for each question you missed. Once you've finished, you will have completed this entire intensive, superconcentrated preparation program— and you'll be ready to get your best score on the real GRE.

Special Features of This Book

This book contains the following special features to help highlight important concepts and information.

A **Note** presents interesting pieces of information related to the surrounding discussion.

A **Tip** offers advice or teaches you an easier way to do something.

A **Time Saver** tells you about a faster way to answer a question or solve a problem.

A **Caution** advises you about potential problems and helps you steer clear of disaster.

An **Online** tells you where to look online to find additional information about a particular subject.

ACTION PLAN   The **Action Plan** icon identifies the steps to follow in answering each type of test question.

Part I

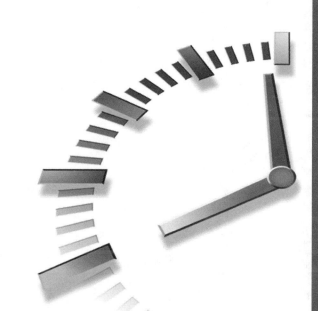

Start with the Basics

Hour 1

Get to Know the GRE

To start your preparation for the GRE, you'll spend this first hour familiarizing yourself with the format of the test and with the computerized testing environment. You'll also learn some basic test-taking strategies that you can use for all sections of the GRE. Here are your goals for this hour:

- Become familiar with the format of the GRE
- Learn how the GRE is scored and evaluated, and learn how your scores are reported to graduate schools
- Familiarize yourself with the computer-based version of the GRE
- Learn general strategies for performing your best on the exam

The GRE at a Glance

There are two versions of the GRE: the paper-based test and a computer-based test (CBT). Both versions include the same types of questions and measure the same abilities; but they differ in these respects:

- total exam time
- number of sections

- number of questions per section
- time allowed for each section

Here's the basic format for each version.

 NOTE | On both the paper-based test and the CBT, the exam sections can appear in *any* order. But the breaks always appear as shown here.

FORMAT OF THE PAPER-BASED GRE

Section	No. of Questions	Time Allowed
Quantitative	30	30 minutes
Quantitative	30	30 minutes
Verbal	38	30 minutes
Verbal	38	30 minutes
Break	Not applicable	10–15 minutes
Analytical	25	30 minutes
Analytical	25	30 minutes
Unscored	25–38	30 minutes
(Total testing time, excluding break)		$3\frac{1}{2}$ hours

FORMAT OF THE COMPUTER-BASED GRE

Section	No. of Questions	Time Allowed
Computer Tutorial	Not applicable	Not applicable
Quantitative	28	45 minutes ($1\frac{3}{4}$ minutes per question, on average)
Verbal	30	30 minutes (1 minute per question, on average)
Break (optional)	Not applicable	10 minutes
Analytical	35	60 minutes (about 2 minutes per question, on average)
Unscored Section	28–35	30–60 minutes
(Total testing time, excluding break)		$2\frac{3}{4} - 3\frac{1}{4}$ hours

1

> If you take the GRE before Fall of 1999, a *research* section might also be
> included—in addition to the four exam sections indicated above. The
> research section will be clearly identified, and it will not be scored. So don't
> expend too much brain power on it. This fifth section will involve either
> *mathematical reasoning* or a *writing measurement* (you compose an essay).
> Beginning in the Fall of 1999, the GRE will include both types of sections as
> *scored* sections.

TYPICAL DISTRIBUTION OF QUESTIONS

Question Format	Number of Questions Paper-Based Test	Number of Questions CBT
Quantitative Comparison	15	14
Problem Solving	15	14
Sentence Completion	7	6
Analogies	9	9
Antonyms	11	7
Reading Comprehension	11 (2 sets)	8 (3 sets)
Analytical Reasoning	19	26
Logical Reasoning	6	9

The Quantitative Section(s)

Quantitative questions measure your basic mathematical skills, your understanding of
basic math concepts, and your ability to reason quantitatively, to solve quantitative
problems, and to interpret graphical data.

Each Quantitative question conforms to one of two formats:

- Problem Solving
- Quantitative Comparison

Problem Solving questions require you to solve a mathematical problem and then select
the correct answer from among five answer choices.

Quantitative Comparison problems each consist of two quantitative expressions. Your
task is to compare the two quantities to determine which is greater, if either.

NOTE   To see examples of each format, take a peek at one of the Quantitative sample tests toward the back of this book (Hours 19 and 22).

The Verbal Section(s)

You'll encounter four different types of Verbal questions on the GRE:

- Sentence Completion
- Analogies
- Antonyms
- Reading Comprehension

Sentence Completion questions test your vocabulary, your ability to recognize proper (and improper) word usage, and your ability to understand a sentence's intended meaning. Each sentence includes one or two blanks. Your task is to fill in the blanks with the best of five choices.

Analogies test your vocabulary and your ability to understand relationships between two words in a pair. For each question, you're given a word pair, and asked to choose which word pair among five others provides the closest analogy to the original pair.

Antonyms test your vocabulary head on. In each antonym question, your task is to determine which word among five choices is most nearly opposite in meaning to a given word.

Reading Comprehension questions are designed to measure your ability to read carefully and accurately, to determine the relationships among the various parts of the passage, and to draw reasonable inferences from the material in the passage. Questions are divided into sets; each set pertains to the same passage. The passages are drawn from a variety of subjects, including the humanities, social sciences, and physical sciences.

NOTE   To see examples of each question type, take a peek at one of the Verbal sample tests toward the back of this book (Hours 20 and 23).

The Analytical Section(s)

Analytical questions come in two varieties:

- Analytical Reasoning
- Logical Reasoning

Analytical Reasoning questions test your ability to understand and draw conclusions from a system of relationships, to assimilate and organize information efficiently, and to visualize spatial relationships. The questions appear in sets (4–7 questions per set). Each set presents a distinct puzzle or *logic game* (our term).

Logical Reasoning questions are designed to evaluate your ability to understand, criticize, and draw reasonable conclusions from arguments. Each argument consists of a brief one-paragraph passage.

> To see examples of each question type, take a peek at one of the Analytical sample tests toward the back of this book (Hours 21 and 24).

The Unscored Section

No score is tabulated or reported for this exam section. The test-makers include this section in order to assess the integrity, fairness, and difficulty of questions, some of which may show up on future versions of the GRE in the scored sections.

Your unscored section will either be Quantitative, Verbal, or Analytical. By the end of the exam, you'll know which type of unscored section appeared on your exam—because you will have taken one extra section of that type.

Although your unscored section will look very much like one of the other three types of sections, it might also include so-called "experimental" questions. If you notice some odd questions that are a bit different from what you encounter in this book, it's a good bet you're looking at the unscored section.

> Even if you're convinced a particular section is the unscored section, do the best you can on it anyway. Why? If you slack off during the section, but your judgment turns out to be wrong, you've made a costly error in terms of your score! It's not worth the risk, is it?

The 10-Minute Break

During the paper-based exam, you'll take a 10-minute break after the third exam section. During the CBT, you can take up to a 10-minute break between the second and third section. The CBT break is optional; if you wish, you can take a shorter break or proceed immediately to the next section.

> During the CBT, the clock continues to run during the break. After 10 minutes, the next exam section starts—with or without you! Also, if you wait too long to begin answering questions once the next section has begun, the exam session automatically terminates and no responses or scores are tabulated or reported.

How the Computer-Based GRE Works

For each test-taker, the CBT system builds a customized test, by drawing on questions from a large pool. The CBT continually tailors its difficulty level to your level of ability. The initial few questions are average in difficulty level. As you respond *correctly* to questions, the CBT steps you up to more difficult questions. Conversely, as you respond *incorrectly* to questions, the CBT steps you down to easier ones.

We've experimented during the CBT by intentionally responding incorrectly, as well as correctly, to consecutive questions. Here's what we've observed: Early in the exam section the CBT can shift from the easiest level to a very challenging level (or vice versa) in as few as 3 or 4 successive questions. But later in the section, when your ability level is well established, the difficulty level will not vary as widely.

What You Should Know About the CBT System

The CBT does not let you skip questions. Given the interactive design of the test, this makes sense. The computer-adaptive algorithm cannot determine the appropriate difficulty level for the next question without a response (correct or incorrect) to each question presented in sequence.

The CBT does not let you return to any question already presented (and answered). Why? The computer-adaptive algorithm that determines the difficulty of subsequent questions depends on the correctness of prior responses. For example, suppose that you answer question 5 incorrectly. The CBT responds by posing slightly easier questions. Were the CBT to let you return to question 5 and change your response to the correct one, the questions following question 5 would be easier than they should have been, given your amended response. In other words, the process by which the CBT builds your score would be undermined.

One useful strategy for the paper-based exam is to cross-check different responses for consistency (especially helpful in the Reading Comprehension sets). Of course, you can't use this strategy on the CBT.

The CBT does not require you to finish each section. The CBT gives you the *opportunity* to respond to a total of 93 scored multiple-choice questions (28 Quantitative, 30 Verbal, and 35 Analytical). But the CBT does *not* require you to finish any section. The CBT will calculate a score based on the questions you've answered.

The CBT requires you to do some work on every section. In order to generate a score report, the CBT requires a minimum number of responses during each section. (ETS has not disclosed this minimum number, but it's probably *very* low—perhaps just 1.)

During each section, the CBT provides a 5-minute warning. When 5 minutes remain during each timed section, the on-screen clock (in the upper left corner of the screen) will blink silently several times to warn you. This 5-minute warning will be your only reminder.

Beepers and alarms aren't allowed in the testing room, although silent timing devices are permitted.

The GRE CBT Interface

The screen shot on page 11 shows the GRE CBT interface. (The upper screen shows a Reading Comprehension question; the lower screen shows a Problem Solving Quantitative question). Let's examine the features of the interface that are common to all exam sections.

The CBT Title Bar

A dark title bar will appear across the top of the computer screen at all times during all test sections. You can't hide this title bar, which displays three items:

> **left corner:** time remaining for the current section (hours and minutes)
>
> **middle:** the name of the test
>
> **right corner:** the current question number and total number of questions in the current section

The CBT Toolbar

A series of six buttons appear in a "toolbar" across the bottom of the computer screen at all times (you cannot hide the toolbar) during all test sections.

QUIT TEST

Click on this button to stop the test and cancel your scores for the entire test. If you click here, a dialog box will appear on the screen, asking you to confirm this operation.

EXIT SECTION

Click on this button if you finish the section before the allotted time expires and wish to proceed immediately to the next section. A dialog box will appear on the screen, asking you to confirm this operation.

TIME

Click on this button to display the time remaining to the nearest *second*. By default, the time remaining is displayed (in the upper left corner) in hours and minutes, but not to the nearest second.

HELP

Click on this button to access the directions for the current section, as well as the general test directions and the instructions for using the toolbar items.

NEXT and CONFIRM ANSWER

Click on the NEXT button when you're finished with the current question. When you do so, the current question will remain on the screen until you click on CONFIRM ANSWER. Until you confirm, you can change your answer as often as you wish. But once you confirm, the question disappears forever and the next one appears in its place.

Whenever the NEXT button is enabled (appearing dark gray), the CONFIRM ANSWER button is disabled (appearing light gray), and vice versa.

Stay away from the QUIT TEST button, unless you're absolutely sure you wish your GRE score for the day to "vaporize" and you're willing to throw away your exam registration fee. Also stay away from the EXIT SECTION button, unless you've already answered every question in the current section and don't feel you need a breather before starting the next one!

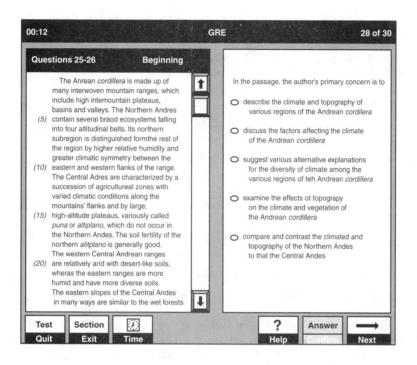

00:12   GRE   28 of 30

Questions 25-26   **Beginning**

The Anrean *cordillera* is made up of many interwoven mountain ranges, which include high intemountain plateaus, basins and valleys. The Northern Andres
(5) contain several braod ecosystems falling into four altitudinal belts. Its northern subregion is distinguished formthe rest of the region by higher relative humidity and greater climatic symmetry between the
(10) eastern and western flanks of the range. The Central Adres are characterized by a succession of agricultureal zones with varied climatic conditions along the mountains' flanks and by large,
(15) high-altitude plateaus, variously called *puna* or *altiplano*, which do not occur in the Northern Andes. The soil fertility of the northern *alitplano* is generally good. The western Central Andrean ranges
(20) are relatively arid with desert-like soils, wheras the eastern ranges are more humid and have more diverse soils. The eastern slopes of the Central Andes in many ways are similar to the wet forests

In the passage, the author's primary concern is to

○ describe the climate and topography of various regions of the Andrean *cordilera*

○ discuss the factors affecting the climate of the Andrean *cordillera*

○ suggest various alternative explanations for the diversity of climate among the various regions of teh Andrean *cordillera*

○ examine the effects ot topograpy on the climate and vegetation of the Andrean *cordillera*

○ compare and contrast the climated and topography of the Northern Andes to that the Central Andes

| Test | Section | 🕮 | | ? | Answer | → |
| Quit | Exit | Time | | Help | Confirm | Next |

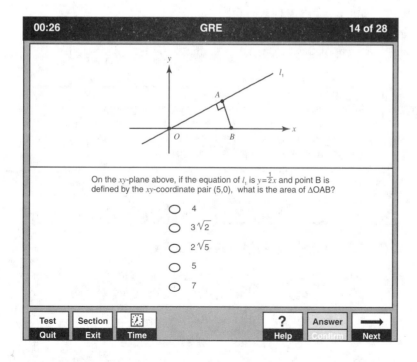

00:26   GRE   14 of 28

On the *xy*-plane above, if the equation of l_1 is $y=\frac{1}{2}x$ and point B is defined by the *xy*-coordinate pair (5,0), what is the area of $\triangle$OAB?

○ 4

○ $3\sqrt{2}$

○ $2\sqrt{5}$

○ 5

○ 7

| Test | Section | 🕮 | | ? | Answer | → |
| Quit | Exit | Time | | Help | Confirm | Next |

What You'll See on the Screen During the CBT

To respond to the questions, just click your mouse on one of the ovals next to the answer choices. You can't use the keyboard to select answers.

NOTE   On the CBT, the answer choices are *not* lettered (you'll click on blank ovals). But on the paper-based GRE, and in the sample questions throughout this book, the answer choices are lettered.

Split screens. For some questions, the screen splits either horizontally or vertically.

Reading Comprehension: The screen splits vertically. The left side displays the passage; the right side displays the question and answer choices.

Quantitative questions that include figures: The screen splits horizontally. The figure appears at the top; the question and answer choices appear at the bottom.

Vertical Scrolling. For some questions, you'll have to scroll up and down (using the vertical scroll bar) to view all the material that pertains to the current question.

Reading Comprehension: Passages are too long for you to see on the screen in their entirety; you'll have to scroll.

Quantitative questions that include figures: Some figures—especially charts and graphs—won't fit on the screen in their entirety; you'll have to scroll.

CAUTION   In Quantitative questions that include charts or graphs, be sure to scroll up and down to view not only the entire chart or graph, but also the information above and below it. Important numbers or other information you should know can sometimes hide just below the horizontal split!

Key Differences and Similarities Between the Paper-Based Test and the CBT

Here's a list of the key differences and similarities between the two versions of the GRE. Some of the differences might help you decide which version to take.

Key Features of the CBT

- The CBT is shorter than the paper-based test—93 vs. 186 scored questions, and $2\frac{3}{4} - 3\frac{1}{4}$ hours vs. $3\frac{1}{2}$ hours. So endurance is not quite as significant a factor.

> **NOTE** Also, if you finish one or more CBT sections early, you can go on to the next one right away, thereby reducing testing time even further.

- The CBT eliminates the chance of putting the right answer in the wrong place on the answer sheet.

- The CBT reduces the possibility of cheating. It's impossible to return to previous sections, work ahead to other sections, work beyond the expiration of an allotted time period, or copy a neighbor's responses.

- The interactive feature of the CBT allows for accurate assessment with fewer questions.

- If you finish an exam section early, you don't have to wait to proceed to the next section.

- The CBT is available at any time during the year, you don't have to register as far in advance as for the paper-based test, and you can schedule an appointment by telephone.

- You can see your scores *immediately* on competition of the test.

- Official scores are available to you and to the schools within two weeks after testing (paper-based test scores are available six weeks after testing).

Key Features of the Paper-Based Test

- Within each section, later questions are more difficult than earlier ones.

- As you work on a section, you can skip questions and return to them later if you have time.

- You can return to questions in order to reconsider your responses, as well as "cross-check" different responses for consistency. Cross-checking is especially helpful for Reading Comprehension and Analytical Reasoning sets.

- You can write directly in the test booklet. This is especially helpful for crossing out answer choices as you eliminate them and for annotating Reading Comprehension passages. The downside is that no scratch paper is allowed for the paper-based test, so you must do all scratchwork in the test booklet itself.

- You'll have an opportunity later to review your test (not just your answers, but also the test questions themselves) in order to assess your strengths and weaknesses—in case you plan to repeat the test.

- You might be more comfortable taking a traditional pencil-and-paper test, because you've been taking tests this way nearly your whole life.

- You don't have to worry about certain technical problems (hardware, software, and network problems, as well as power failures).

Don't hasten to register for the paper-based test just because you can skip questions, return to questions in the current section, and write in the test booklet. In designing the CBT, ETS has accounted for these inherent differences between the two versions. So you don't hold an automatic advantage by taking one version instead of the other.

Key Similarities Between the Two Versions

- The content areas and question types are the same for both versions.

- No calculators or audible alarms are allowed for either version.

- No food or drinks are allowed in the testing room. (During the paper-based test, you'll stow your personal belongings under your seat; at the CBT center you're provided a locker—free of charge.)

- The time factor is the same on both versions, even though the average time per question differs.

The average time per question in each CBT section is greater than in the corresponding paper-based section. But you'll probably feel just as much time pressure on the CBT as you would on the paper-based test. Why? Primarily because you'll use your scratch paper extensively, and looking back and forth between the computer screen and paper eats up time—more time than you might think.

- The registration fee is the same for both versions.

DO's and DON'Ts During the Exam

Do	DON'T

DO shop around for easier questions (paper-based test only).

DON'T resort to random guessing, unless you've run out of time.

DO find your optimal pace and stay on it.

DON'T be a perfectionist.

DO maintain an active mind set.

DO use your pencil.

DO move the keyboard to one side (CBT only).

DON'T waste time reading directions while the clock is running; make sure you already know them inside and out.

DO step through the computer tutorial as quickly as possible (CBT only).

DO take advantage of the optional 10-minute break, but don't exceed the 10-minute limit (CBT only).

DO read each question in its entirety, and read every answer choice.

DO take your time with the first few questions during each section (CBT only).

DO shop around for easier questions (paper-based test only). On the paper-based test, keep in mind that all questions are weighted equally. In each section, later questions are generally more difficult than earlier ones. So scan the current section for easier questions, and make sure you answer those first. It'll build your confidence, reduce anxiety, and help guard against a disastrous score.

DON'T resort to random guessing, unless you've run out of time. If you must guess, always try to eliminate obvious wrong-answer choices first, then go with your hunch. Eliminating even one choice improves your odds. But if you're out of time on a section, your strategy should differ, depending on whether you're taking the paper-based exam or the CBT.

Paper-based strategy: No penalty is assessed for incorrect responses. So always fill in the bubbles on your answer sheet for every question in each section—even if you're guessing randomly. Otherwise, you're cheating yourself out of at least a 20% chance that you'll get the answer right.

CBT strategy: If you're running out of time on the CBT, there's no advantage to guessing randomly on the remaining questions. Why not? You might luck out and guess correctly. But incorrect responses move you down the ladder of difficulty to easier questions, and correct responses to easier questions aren't worth as much as correct responses to more difficult ones. So on balance, there's no net advantage or disadvantage to guessing randomly.

Time is most definitely a factor on each section of the GRE (paper-based exam and CBT alike). Expect to work at a quicker pace than is comfortable for you. Try to check your pace after every 10 questions or so. Adjust your pace accordingly so that you have time to at least consider every question in the section. But try not to be a constant clock watcher, or you'll disrupt your own concentration.

The best way to avoid the time squeeze is to practice under timed conditions, so that you get a sense for your optimal pace.

DON'T be a perfectionist. You might find yourself reluctant to leave a question until you're sure your answer is correct. The design of the CBT contributes to this mind set, because your reward for correct responses to difficult questions is greater than your reward for easier questions. But a stubborn attitude will only defeat you, because it reduces the number of questions that you attempt, which in turn can lower your score. As you take the quizzes and sample tests in this book, get comfortable with a quick pace by adhering strictly to the time limits imposed. Set aside your perfectionist tendencies, and remember: You can miss quite a few questions and still score high. Develop a sense of your optimal pace—one that results in the greatest number of correct responses.

DO maintain an active mind set. During the GRE it's remarkably easy to fall into a passive mode—one in which you let your eyes simply pass over the words while you hope that the correct response jumps out at you as you scan the answer choices. Fight this tendency by interacting with the test as you read it. Keep in mind that each question on the GRE is designed to measure a specific ability or skill. So try to adopt an active, investigative approach to each question, in which you ask yourself:

- What skill is the question measuring?
- What is the most direct thought process for determining the correct response?
- How might a careless test-taker be tripped up on this type of question?

Answering these three questions is in large part what the rest of this book is all about.

DO use your pencil. Doing so helps keep you in an active mode. Making brief notes or drawing diagrams and flow charts will help keep your thought process clear and straight.

DO move the keyboard to one side (CBT only). You won't use the keyboard at all during the CBT. So put your scratch paper right in front of you, and get the keyboard out of the way.

DON'T waste time reading directions while the clock is running; make sure you already know them inside and out. On both the paper-based exam and the CBT, each new section begins with the directions for that section. Also, on the CBT, just before the first question of each type (e.g., Quantitative Comparison or Reading Comprehension) appears for the first time, the CBT will display additional directions for that specific question type. Keep in mind that whenever the CBT is showing you directions, the clock will be running! So dismiss the directions as quickly as you can by clicking on the DISMISS DIRECTIONS button—without taking any time to read them. (This advice presupposes that you already know the directions—which of course you will.)

DO step through the computer tutorial as quickly as possible (CBT only). Although the tutorial is not timed, the longer you spend on it, the more fatigued you'll be for the actual exam. The tutorial isn't worth more attention or eye strain than absolutely necessary. So get past it as quickly as possible.

DO take advantage of the optional 10-minute break, but don't exceed the 10-minute limit (CBT only). Remember: The CBT clock is always running, even during the scheduled 10-minute break. By all means, take advantage of this optional break. Leave the room, perhaps grab a quick snack from your locker, and do some stretching or relaxing. But don't get too relaxed! 10 minutes goes by very quickly, and the test will begin after that time has elapsed—with or without you!

| TIP | Be sure you find out before you start the CBT where the nearest restroom is located. You don't want to spend your "relaxing" 10-minute break frantically searching for a much-needed restroom. I know: It happened to me during my CBT break! |

DO read each question in its entirety, and read every answer choice. You'll discover during the hours ahead that the test-makers love to bait you with tempting wrong answer choices. This applies to every type of question on the exam. So unless you're quickly running out of time, never hasten to select and confirm an answer until you've read all the choices! This blunder is one of the leading causes of incorrect responses on the GRE.

DO take your time with the first few questions during each section (CBT only). The CBT uses your responses to the first few questions to move you either up or down the ladder of difficulty. Of course, you want to move up the ladder, not down. So take great care with the initial questions—perhaps moving at a somewhat slower pace initially.

Otherwise, you'll have to answer several questions just to reverse the trend by proving to the CBT that you're smarter than it thinks you are.

The CBT Test-Taking Experience

When you take a test as important as the GRE, it's a good idea to minimize test anxiety by knowing exactly what to expect on exam day. So lets walk through the pre-test and post-test procedures for the CBT. You'll also learn about the CBT testing environment.

When You Arrive at the Test Center

Here's what you can expect when you arrive at the test center:

- The supervisor will show you a roster, which includes the names of test-takers scheduled for that day, and will ask you to initial the roster next to your name, and indicate on the roster your arrival time.

- The supervisor will ask you to read a two-page list of testing procedures and rules. (We'll cover all these rules in the pages immediately ahead.)

- The supervisor will give you a "Nondisclosure Statement." You're to read the printed statement, then *write* the statement (in the space provided on the form) and sign it. In the statement, you agree to the testing policies and rules, and you agree not to reproduce or disclose any of the actual test questions. The supervisor will not permit you to enter the exam room until you've written and signed the statement.

- You'll probably have to sit in a waiting room for a while—until the supervisor calls your name. A 5–10 minute wait beyond your scheduled testing time is not uncommon. (Taking the GRE CBT is a lot like going to the dentist—in several respects!)

- The supervisor will check your photo identification. (You won't be permitted to take the test unless you have one acceptable form of photo identification with you.)

- The test center will provide a secure locker (free of charge) for stowing your personal belongings during the test.

- To help ensure that nobody else takes any part of the exam in your place, the supervisor will take a photograph of you.

- The supervisor might give you some rudimentary tips about managing your time during the exam. Just ignore the supervisor's tips, because they might not be good advice for you!

- Before you enter the testing room, you must remove everything from your pockets—except your photo I.D. and locker key.

- The supervisor will provide you with exactly six pieces of scratch paper (stapled together), along with two pencils. These are the only items you'll have in hand as you enter the testing room.

Testing Procedures and Rules

1

- If you want to exit the testing room for any reason, you must raise your hand and wait for the supervisor to come in and escort you from the room. (You won't be able to pause the testing clock for any reason.)
- No guests are allowed in the waiting room during your test.
- No food or drink is allowed in the testing room.
- No hats are allowed.
- You must sign out whenever you exit the testing room.
- You must sign in whenever you re-enter the testing room (the supervisor will ask to see your photo I.D. each time).
- If you need more scratch paper during the exam, just raise your hand and ask for it. The supervisor will happily replace your six-piece bundle with a new batch.
- The supervisor will replace your tired pencils with fresh, sharp ones upon your request anytime during the exam (just raise your hand).

What You Should Know About the CBT Testing Environment

- Individual testing stations are like library carrels; they're separated by half-walls.
- The height of you chair's seat will be adjustable, and the chair will swivel. Chairs at most testing centers have arms.
- Computer monitors are of the 14-inch variety. You can adjust contrast. If you notice any flickering, ask the supervisor to move you to another station. (You won't be able to tell if you monitor has color capability, because the GRE is strictly a black-and-white affair.)

 NOTE

> You can't change the size of the font on the screen, unless you specifically request before the exam begins that a special ZOOMTEXT function be made available to you.

- If your mouse has two buttons, you can use either button to click your way through the exam (both buttons serve the same function). Don't expect that nifty wheel between buttons for easy scrolling, because you're not going to get it. For all you gamers and laptop users, trackballs are available, but only if you request one before you begin the test.

- Testing rooms are not soundproof. During your test, expect to hear talking and other noise from outside the room.
- Expect the supervisor to escort other test-takers in and out of the room during your test—and to converse with them while doing so. This can be distracting!
- If the testing room is busy, expect to hear lots of mouse-clicking during your test. Because the room is otherwise fairly quiet, the incessant mouse-clicking can become annoying!
- Earplugs are available upon request.
- Expect anything in terms of room temperature, so dress in layers.
- You'll be under continual audio and video surveillance. To guard against cheating, and to record any irregularities or problems in the testing room as they occur, the room is continually audio-taped and videotaped. (Look for the cameras or two-way mirrors, then smile and wave!)

Before You Begin the Test— The Computer Tutorial

Okay, the supervisor has just escorted you into the inner sanctum and to your station, and has wished you luck. (My supervisor also encouraged me to "have fun!") Before you begin the test, the CBT system will lead you through a tutorial which includes four sections (each section steps you through a series of "screens"):

1. How to use the mouse (6 screens)
2. How to select and change an answer (6 screens)
3. How to scroll the screen display up and down (6 screens)
4. How to use the toolbars (21 screens); here you'll learn how to

   - Quit the test
   - Exit the current section
   - Access the directions
   - Confirm your response and move to the next question

 NOTE

If you want to see what some of the tutorial screens look like, ETS provides a variety of samples in its official GRE *Bulletin*.

Here's what you need to know about the CBT tutorial:

- You won't be able to skip any section or any screen during the tutorial

- As you progress, the system requires that you demonstrate competency in using the mouse, selecting and confirming answer choices, and accessing the directions. So you can't begin taking the actual test unless you've shown that you know how to use the system. (Don't worry: no test-taker has ever flunked the CBT system competency test.)

- At the end of each tutorial section (series of screens), you can repeat that section, at your option. But once you leave a section you can't return to it.

Don't choose to repeat any tutorial section. Why not? If you do, you'll be forced to step through the entire sequence of screens in that section again (an aggravating time-waster, especially for the 21-screen section!)

- You won't see any *true* GRE-style questions during the tutorial. Instead, again and again you'll encounter the same insipid sample question: "What is the capital of the United States of America?"

- If you carefully read all the information presented to you, expect to spend about 20 minutes on the tutorial.

On test day, you'll already know how the CBT system works. So step through the tutorial as quickly as you can, reading as little as possible. You can easily dispense with the tutorial in 5–10 minutes this way. Remember: The less time you spend with the tutorial, the less fatigued you'll be during the exam itself.

Post-Test CBT Procedures

Okay, it's been about 4 hours since you first entered the testing center, and you've just completed the fourth and final CBT section. You may think you've finished the CBT, but the CBT has not quite finished with you yet! There are yet more hoops to jump through before you're done.

1. **Respond to a brief questionnaire.** The CBT will impose on you a brief questionnaire (a series of screens) about your test-taking experience (believe it or not, these questions are multiple-choice, just like the exam itself). The questionnaire will ask you, for example:

- whether your supervisor was knowledgeable and helpful
- whether the testing environment was comfortable
- how long you waited after you arrived at the testing site to begin the test
- whether you were distracted by noise during your exam

2. **Cancel your test, at your option.** The most important question you'll answer while seated at your testing station is this next one. The CBT will ask you to choose whether to:

- cancel your scores (no scores are recorded; partial cancellation is not provided for) *or*
- see your scores immediately

Once you elect to see your scores, you can no longer cancel them—ever! So you should take a few minutes to think it over. The CBT gives you 5 minutes to choose. If you haven't decided within 5 minutes, the CBT will automatically show you your scores (and you forfeit your option to cancel.)

> If you click on the CANCEL SCORES button, the CBT will then give you yet another 5 minutes to think over your decision. So you really have 10 minutes altogether to make up you mind.

3. **View and record your scores.** If you elect to see your scores, you should write them down on your scratch paper. When you leave the testing room, the supervisor will allow you to transcribe them onto another sheet of paper (one that you can take home with you), so that you don't have to memorize them.

4. **Direct your scores to the schools of your choice.** Once you've elected to see your scores, the CBT will ask you to select the schools you wish to receive your score report (the CBT provides a complete list of schools).

> You can select as many as four schools at this time—without incurring an additional fee. This is your last chance for a freebie, so you should take full advantage of it. So compile your list of schools—before exam day.

1

Before You Leave the Testing Center

Upon your exiting the testing room for the final time:

- The supervisor will collect your pencils and scratch paper, and will count the number of sheets of paper to make sure you aren't trying to sneak out with any. (Then, if you're lucky you'll be allowed to watch while the supervisor ceremoniously rips up your scratch paper and drops it in the trash basket!)

- The supervisor will remind you to collect your belongings from your locker (if you used one), and turn in your locker key.

- The supervisor will provide you with an ETS pamphlet that explains how to interpret your test scores (you can take this home with you).

- The supervisor will provide you with a postcard-sized invitation to "blow the whistle" on anybody you suspect of cheating on the exam (the invitation ends with the assurance: "Confidentiality guaranteed").

Scoring, Evaluation, and Reporting

You'll receive three scaled scores (on a scale of 200–800) for the General GRE—one for each scored section. The GRE scoring system is simpler for the paper-based exam than for the CBT.

Paper-based exam: scaled scores are computed based solely on the number of correct responses (no penalty is assessed for incorrect responses).

CBT: Your score for each section of the CBT is based on two factors:

- *how many* questions you answer correctly
- the *difficulty level* of the questions you've answered

So even if you don't answer every question available in a section, you can still achieve a high score for that section if a high percentage of your responses are correct. (Remember: As you respond correctly to questions, subsequent questions become more difficult.)

NOTE

> The CBT system's algorithms for moving you from one level of difficulty to another and for calculating your scores are well-guarded ETS secrets. But knowing exactly how the system works wouldn't affect your exam preparation or test-taking strategy, anyway.

Percentile Rank. For each of your three GRE scores, you'll also receive a percentile rank (0–99%). A percentile rank of 60%, for example, indicates that you scored higher than

60% of all test-takers (and lower than 40% of all test-takers). Percentile ranks reflect your performance relative to the entire GRE test-taking population during the most recent three-year period.

NOTE   For a sample score-conversion table, see Appendix B.

Score Reporting. Official scores for the paper-based exam are mailed to test-takers and to schools approximately six weeks after testing. (You can obtain them a few weeks earlier by telephone.) Official CBT scores are mailed 10–15 days after testing. Score reports are "cumulative"; they include scores from *all* GRE exams you've taken during the last 5 years. Exam absences and cancellations also appear on your official report, but they will not adversely affect your chances of admission.

NOTE   You may choose to send only General Test scores, only Subject Test scores, or all scores. Also, your score report will indicate all your designated recipients. So each school will know which other schools you've considered applying to!

Evaluation of Scores. Graduate departments develop and implement their own individual policies for evaluating GRE scores. Also, some programs require GRE Subject Test scores, either instead of or in addition to, GRE General Test scores. Since policies vary widely among schools and programs, you should contact the schools' academic departments directly for specific information.

DO's and DON'Ts for GRE Preparation

Do	Don't

DO take the GRE early to allow yourself the option of retaking it.

DO wait until at least your junior or senior year to take the GRE.

DON'T be too confident about your test-taking prowess.

DON'T obsess about scores.

DON'T cram for the GRE, but don't over prepare either.

DO be realistic in your expectations.

DO take at least one of the sample tests in this book as you would the real exam—with only a few short breaks between sections.

DO take the real GRE once—just for practice.

Registering to Take the GRE

For detailed information about GRE registration procedures, consult the official GRE website (*http://www.gre.org*) or refer to the printed *GRE Information and Registration Bulletin*, published annually by ETS. This free bulletin is available directly from ETS as well as through career-planning offices at most four-year colleges and universities.

To obtain the *Bulletin* or other information about the GRE, you can contact ETS by any of these methods:

Telephone:	1-609-771-7670 (general inquiries)
	1-800-537-3160 (to request publications)
E-mail:	gre@ets.org
World Wide Web:	http://www.gre.org
	http://www.ets.org (the ETS home page)
Mail:	GRE
	ETS
	P.O. Box 6000
	Princeton, NJ 08541-6000

TIP

The GRE *Bulletin* is published only once a year, so for the most up-to-date official information you should check the ETS Web site.

Part II

Learn to Answer GRE Quantitative Questions

HOUR 2

Teach Yourself Quantitative Skills I

This hour you'll take a close-up look at the Quantitative section, and you'll learn some basic strategies for handling questions in the Problem Solving format. Here are your goals for this hour:

- Familiarize yourself with the directions and ground rules for the Quantitative section
- Learn what areas of math are covered on the GRE
- Learn what Problem Solving questions look like and how to answer them
- Learn some DOs and DON'Ts for handling Problem Solving questions
- Apply what you learn to some GRE-style Quantitative questions

The Quantitative Section—At a Glance

Time limit:

Paper-based: Two 30-minute sections
CBT: 45 minutes

Number of questions:

Paper-based: 30 questions in each section|
CBT: 28

Basic format:

- All questions are multiple-choice
- About half the questions are word problems (in a "real world" setting)
- Every question conforms to one of two formats:

  (1) Quantitative Comparison

  (2) Problem Solving
- Each paper-based Quantitative section includes 15 questions in each format
- The CBT Quantitative section includes 14 questions in each format

Ground rules:

- Calculators are prohibited
- Scratch paper is allowed and provided

Abilities tested:

- proficiency in arithmetical operations
- proficiency at solving algebraic equations
- ability to convert verbal information to mathematical terms
- ability to visualize geometric shapes and numerical relationships
- ability to devise intuitive and unconventional solutions to conventional mathematical problems

Areas covered:

The following provides a breakdown of the areas covered on the Quantitative section:

Properties of Numbers and Arithmetical Operations

- linear ordering (positive and negative numbers, absolute value)
- properties of integers (factors, multiples, prime numbers)
- arithmetical operations
- laws of arithmetic
- fractions, decimals, and percentages
- ratio and proportion
- exponents (powers) and roots
- basic descriptive statistics (mean, median, mode, range, standard deviation)
- basic probability

Algebraic Equations and Inequalities

- simplifying linear and quadratic algebraic expressions
- solving equations with one variable (unknown)
- solving equations with two variables (unknowns)
- solving factorable quadratic equations
- inequalities

Geometry, Including Coordinate Geometry

- intersecting lines and angles
- perpendicular and parallel lines
- triangles
- quadrilaterals (4-sided polygons)
- circles
- rectangular solids (three-dimensional figures)
- cylinders
- pyramids
- coordinate geometry

Interpreting Statistical Charts, Graphs, and Tables

- pie charts
- bar graphs
- line charts
- tables

Areas not covered:

- complex calculations involving large and/or unwieldy numbers
- advanced algebra concepts
- formal geometry proofs
- trigonometry
- calculus
- advanced statistics concepts and methods

Directions: Certain instructions apply to *all* Quantitative questions. Most of these instructions are actually assumptions for interpreting figures:

- All numbers used are real numbers.
- All figures lie on a plane unless otherwise indicated.
- All angle measures are positive.
- All lines shown as straight are straight. On the CBT, lines that appear "jagged" can also be assumed to be straight (lines can look somewhat jagged on the computer screen).
- Figures are intended to provide useful information for answering the questions. However, except where a figure is accompanied by a "Note" stating that the figure is drawn to scale, solve the problem using your knowledge of mathematics, *not* by visual measurement or estimation.

 NOTE

On the paper-based test, these instructions are listed at the very beginning of the Quantitative section. On the CBT, they will appear on your screen whenever you click on the HELP button.

Terminology you should know: Although the GRE is not designed as a vocabulary test, you'll need to know what the basic math terms mean. Don't worry: The list of "Areas

Covered" (on pages 31 and 32) includes most of the vocabulary you'll need to know, and we'll define these and any other terms you should know during the hours ahead.

The Problem Solving Format

Problem Solving questions require you to work to a solution (a numerical value or other expression), then find that solution among the five answer choices.

How Many:

> *Paper-based exam:* 15 questions (out of 30 altogether) in each Quantitative section
> *CBT:* 14 questions (out of 28 altogether)

Where:

> *Paper-based exam:* Questions 16–30 in both Quantitative sections
> *CBT:* Interspersed with Quantitative Comparison questions

What's covered:

> Any of the Quantitative areas listed on pages 31 and 32 is fair game for a Problem Solving question.

Directions:

> There are no special directions for Problem Solving questions. You'll simply be instructed to solve the problem and indicate the best answer choice. (See page 32 for instructions that apply to all Quantitative questions.)

What Problem Solving Questions Look Like

Let's look at two typical Problem Solving questions. Take a minute or two to attempt each one. We'll analyze them a few pages ahead. Question 1 is a word problem involving the concept of *percent decrease*. (Word problems account for about half of the Quantitative questions.)

QUESTION 1. If Susan drinks 10% of the juice from a 16-ounce bottle immediately before lunch and 20% of the remaining amount with lunch, approximately how many ounces of juice are left to drink after lunch?

(A) 4.8

(B) 5.5

(C) 11.2

(D) 11.5

(E) 13.0

Question 2 involves the concept of *arithmetic mean* (simple average).

 2. The average of 6 numbers is 19. When one of those numbers is taken away, the average of the remaining 5 numbers is 21. What number was taken away?

(A) 2

(B) 8

(C) 9

(D) 11

(E) 20

What You Should Know About the Problem Solving Format

Numerical answer choices are listed in order—from smallest in value to greatest in value. Notice in our first sample question that the numerical values in the answer choices got *larger* as you read down from (A) to (E). That's the way it is with every Problem Solving question whose answer choices are all numbers.

NOTE

> There is one exception to this pattern. If a question asks you which answer choice is greatest (or smallest) in value, the answer choices will not necessarily be listed in ascending order of value—for obvious reasons.

Expect word problems to account for about half of your Problem Solving questions. This is true not just on the paper-based GRE but also on the CBT, since word problems are not necessarily more difficult than other Problem Solving questions.

Some Problem Solving questions will include figures (geometry figures, graphs, and charts). Most of the 5–8 geometry questions will be accompanied by some type of figure. Also, each Data Interpretation question will be accompanied by a chart or graph. On the paper-based exam, a typical set of Data Interpretation questions will involve 2–3 separate graphs or charts.

Figures are not necessarily drawn to scale. Accompanying figures are intended to help you, not to mislead or trick you by their visual appearance. Nevertheless, don't rely on them to solve the problem, since visual features such as line segments and angles aren't necessarily drawn to scale. (If a figure is drawn to scale, you'll see this note near the figure: "*Note:* Drawn to scale.")

> **NOTE** The fact that figures are not necessarily drawn to scale comes into play more often in Quantitative Comparison questions, as you'll see next hour.

How to Approach a Problem Solving Question

Here's a 5-step approach that will help you to handle any Problem Solving question. Just a few pages ahead, we'll apply this approach to our three sample Problem Solving questions.

ACTION PLAN
1. **Size up the question.**
2. **Size up the answer choices.**
3. **Look for a shortcut to the answer.**
4. **Set up the problem and solve it.**
5. **Verify your response before moving on.**

Let's Apply the 5-Step Action Plan

It's time to go back to the two sample questions you looked at a few pages back. Let's walk through them—one at a time—using the five-step approach you just learned.

QUESTION 1. If Susan drinks 10% of the juice from a 16-ounce bottle immediately before lunch and 20% of the remaining amount with lunch, approximately how many ounces of juice are left to drink after lunch?

(A) 4.8

(B) 5.5

(C) 11.2

(D) 11.5

(E) 13.0

ANALYSIS The correct answer is (**D**). This is a relatively easy question. Approximately 80% of test-takers respond correctly to questions like this one. Here's how to solve the problem with the 5-step approach:

1. This problem involves the concept of *percent*—more specifically, *percentage decrease*. The question is asking you to perform two computations—in sequence. (The result of the first computation is used to perform the second one.) Percent questions tend to be relatively simple. All that is involved here is a two-step computation.

2. The five answer choices in this question provide two useful clues:

   - Notice that they range in value from 4.8 to 13.0. That's a wide spectrum, isn't it? But what general size should we be looking for in a correct answer to this question? Without crunching any numbers, it's clear that most of the juice will still remain in the bottle, even after lunch. So you're looking for a value much closer to 13 than to 4. Eliminate (A) and (B).

   - Notice that each answer choice is carried to exactly one decimal place, and that the question asks for an *approximate* value. These two features are clues that you can probably round off your calculations to the nearest "tenth" as you go.

3. You already eliminated (A) and (B) in step 1. But if you're on your toes, you can eliminate all but the correct answer without resort to precise calculations. Look at the question from a broader perspective. If you subtract 10% from a number, then 20% from the result, that adds up to *a bit less* than a 30% decrease from the original number. 30% of 16 ounces is 4.8 ounces. So the solution must be a number that is *a bit larger than 11.2* (16 – 4.8). Answer choice (D), 11.5, is the only choice that fits the bill!

 TIP

> GRE Problem Solving questions are designed to reward you for recognizing easier, more intuitive ways of narrowing down the choices to the correct answer. Don't skip over step 3. It's well worth your time to look for a more intuitive solution to any problem.

4. If your intuition fails you, go ahead and crunch the numbers. First, determine 10% of 16, then subtract that number from 16:

   $16 \times .1 = 1.6$
   $16 - 1.6 = 14.4$

   Susan now has 14.4 ounces of juice. Now perform the second step. Determine 20% of 14.4, then subtract that number from 14.4:

   $14.4 \times .2 = 2.88$
   Round off 2.88 to the nearest tenth: 2.9
   $14.4 - 2.9 = 11.5$

5. 11.5 is indeed among the answer choices. Before moving on, however, ask yourself whether your solution makes sense—in this case, whether the size of our number (11.5) "fits" what the question asks for. If you performed step 2, you should already realize that 11.5 is in the right ballpark. If you're confident that your calculations were careful and accurate, confirm your response and move on to the next question.

QUESTION 2. The average of 6 numbers is 19. When one of those numbers is taken away, the average of the remaining 5 numbers is 21. What number was taken away?

    (A) 2

    (B) 8

    (C) 9

    (D) 11

    (E) 20

2

ANALYSIS The correct answer is **(C)**. This question is average in difficulty level. Approximately 60% of test-takers respond correctly to questions like this one. Here's how to solve the problem with the 5-step approach:

1. This problem involves the concept of *arithmetic mean* (simple average). To handle this question, you need to be familiar with the formula for calculating the average of a series of numbers. But notice that the question does not ask for the average, but rather for one of the numbers in the series. This curve-ball makes the question a bit tougher than most arithmetic mean problems.

2. Take a quick look at the answer choices for clues. Notice that the middle three are clustered closely together in value. So take a closer look at the two aberrations: (A) and (E). Choice (A) would be the correct answer to the question: "What is the difference between 19 and 21?" But this question is asking something entirely different, so you can probably rule out (A) as a "sucker bait" answer choice. (E) might also be a sucker bait choice, since 20 is simply 19 + 21 divided by 2. If this solution strikes you as too simple, you've got good instincts! The correct answer is probably either (B), (C), or (D). If you're pressed for time, guess one of these, and move on to the next question. Otherwise, go to step 3.

TIP

> In complex questions, don't look for easy solutions. Problems involving algebraic formulas generally aren't solved simply by adding (or subtracting) a few numbers. Your instinct should tell you to reject easy answers to these kind of problems.

3. If you're on your "intuitive toes," you might recognize a shortcut to the answer here. You can solve this problem quickly by simply comparing the two *sums*. Before the sixth number is taken away, the sum of the numbers is 114 (6×19). After taking away the sixth number, the sum of the remaining numbers is 105 (5×21). The difference between the two sums is 9, which must be the value of the number taken away.

4. Lacking a burst of intuition (step 3), you can solve this problem in a conventional (and slower) manner. The formula for arithmetic mean can be expressed this way:

$$AM = \frac{a + b + \dots}{N}$$

In this formula, each term in the numerator is a different number in the series, and N is the number of terms altogether. In the question, we started with six terms, so letting f equal the number that is taken away:

$$19 = \frac{a + b + c + d + e + f}{6}$$
$$114 = a + b + c + d + e + f$$
$$f = 114 - (a + b + c + d + e)$$

Here's the arithmetic mean formula for the remaining five numbers:

$$21 = \frac{a + b + c + d + e}{5}$$
$$105 = a + b + c + d + e$$

Substitute 105 for $(a + b + c + d + e)$ in the first equation:

$$f = 114 - 105$$
$$f = 9$$

5. If you have time, check to make sure you got the formula right, and check your calculations. Also make sure you didn't inadvertently switch the numbers 19 and 21 in your equations. (It's remarkably easy to commit this careless error under time pressure!) If you're satisfied that your analysis is accurate, confirm your answer and move on to the next question.

 CAUTION   Take heed: On the GRE, careless errors—such as switching two numbers in a problem—are far and away the leading cause of incorrect responses.

DO's and DON'Ts for Problem Solving

Here's a useful list of DO's and DON'Ts for Problem Solving questions. Some of these tips we've already touched on during our sample question walk-through. Others are mentioned here for the first time.

You'll learn how to apply these DOs and DON'Ts in this hour's Workshop.

Do	DON'T

2

DO use your pencil and scratch paper.

DO look for simple solutions to simple problems, but complex solutions to complex problems.

DON'T split hairs with word problems; instead, accept the premise at face value.

DON'T rely on accompanying diagrams to solve the problem (except for data interpretation questions).

DON'T do more work than needed to get to the answer.

DO narrow down answer choices by sizing up the question.

DO check the answer choices for clues.

DO start with what you know, and ask yourself what else you know.

DO use trial-and-error if you're stuck (plug in numbers in place of variables).

DO answer the precise question being asked.

DON'T be fooled by "sucker bait" answer choices.

Workshop

For this hour's Workshop, we've hand-picked 10 Problem Solving questions which illustrate the DO's and DON'Ts you just learned. (The problems get tougher as you go along.) For each question, you'll see one or two hints to help you focus on those DO's and DON'Ts. Don't worry if you come across some mathematical concepts you don't understand. You'll learn them during the next several hours. Right now, focus on the art of the GRE.

Additional Quantitative questions are available on-line, at the authors' Web site: *http://www.west.net/~stewart/gre*

(Answers and explanations begin on page 42.)

DIRECTIONS: Attempt the following 10 questions. Try to limit your time to 15 minutes. Be sure to read the explanations that follow. They're just as important as the questions themselves, because they explain how the DO's and DON'Ts come into play.

Quiz

1. Which of the following fractions is equal to $\frac{1}{4}\%$?

    (A) $\dfrac{1}{400}$ (B) $\dfrac{1}{40}$ (C) $\dfrac{1}{25}$

    (D) $\dfrac{4}{25}$ (E) $\dfrac{1}{4}$

    (Hint: Look for simple solutions to simple problems.)

    (Hint: Look out for sucker-bait answer choices.)

2. Jill is now 20 years old and her brother Gary is now 14 years old. How many years ago was Jill three times as old as Gary was at that time?

    (A) 3
    (B) 8
    (C) 9
    (D) 11
    (E) 13

    (Hint: Use the trial-and-error method if you're stuck.)
    (Hint: Be sure to answer the precise question that's asked.)

3. Which of the following is nearest in value to $\sqrt{664} + \sqrt{414}$?

    (A) 16
    (B) 33
    (C) 46
    (D) 68
    (E) 126

    (Hint: Don't do more work than needed to get to the answer.)
    (Hint: Look out for sucker-bait answer choices.)

4. At ABC Corporation, five executives earn $150,000 each per year, three executives earn $170,000 each per year, and one executive earns $180,000 per year. What is the average salary of these executives?

    (A) $156,250
    (B) $160,000
    (C) $164,480
    (D) $166,670
    (E) $170,000

    (Hint: Complex questions call for complex solutions.)
    (Hint: Narrow down the answer choices by making a common-sense estimate.)

5. If $2x + 1$ is a multiple of 5, and if $2x + 1 <$ 100, how many possible values for x are prime numbers?

(A) 5
(B) 6
(C) 7
(D) 8
(E) 9

(Hint: Don't do more work than needed to get to the answer.)
(Hint: Use your pencil and scratch paper to plug in numbers.)

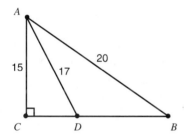

6. In the figure above, what is the length of DB?

(A) $5\sqrt{21} - 8$
(B) 12
(C) $8\sqrt{3}$
(D) $5\sqrt{7} - 8$
(E) $18 - 2\sqrt{6}$

(Hint: Check the answer choices for clues.)
(Hint: Don't rely on a figure's visual proportions to solve the problem.)

7. If a train travels $r + 2$ miles in h hours, which of the following represents the number of miles the train travels in one hour and 30 minutes?

(A) $\dfrac{3r + 6}{2h}$ (B) $\dfrac{3r}{h + 2}$ (C) $\dfrac{r + 2}{h + 3}$

(D) $\dfrac{r}{h + 6}$ (E) $\dfrac{3}{2}(r + 2)$

(Hint: Check the answer choices for clues.)
(Hint: Look out for "sucker bait" answer choices.)

8. A container holds 10 liters of a solution which is 20% acid. If 6 liters of pure acid are added to the container, what percent of the resulting mixture is acid?

(A) 10
(B) 20
(C) $33\dfrac{1}{3}$
(D) 40
(E) 50

(Hint: Estimate the size of the answer you're looking for in order to narrow down the answer choices and to check your work.)

2

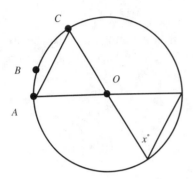

9. If O is the center of the circle in the figure above, and if arc ABC measures 85°, what is the value of x?

   (A) 45
   (B) 47.5
   (C) 65
   (D) 85
   (E) 95

   (Hint: In dealing with complex problems, start with what you know, and ask yourself what else you know.)
   (Hint: Don't rely on a figure's visual proportion to solve the problem.)

10. Two water hoses feed a 40-gallon tank. If one of the hoses dispenses water at the rate of 2 gallons per minute, and the other hose dispenses water at the rate of 5 gallons per minute, how many minutes does it take to fill the 40-gallon tank, if the tank is empty initially?

   (A) $2\dfrac{5}{8}$

   (B) $5\dfrac{5}{7}$

   (C) 7

   (D) 12

   (E) 28

   (Hint: Narrow down answer choices by sizing up the question.)
   (Hint: Look out for sucker-bait answer choices.)

Answers and Explanations

1. **(A)** This is a relatively simple *percent-fraction conversion* problem (one of the topics for hour 4). To solve the problem, divide the fraction by 100, dropping the percent sign:

   $$\frac{1}{4}\% = \frac{\frac{1}{4}}{100} = \frac{1}{4} \cdot \frac{1}{100} = \frac{1}{400}$$

   Remember: Don't assume a question is more complex than it appears to be. This sort of thinking can waste time and can lead you down the wrong path.

   Notice the sucker bait answer choices here. Here's the common mistake:

   $$\frac{1}{4} = 25\%$$

   So maybe the correct answer will include some form of the number 25.

   So the correct answer is probably either (C) or (D).

   Wrong!

2. **(D)** This problem involves setting up and solving a *linear equation*. (You'll learn all the skills you need to handle problems like this one during hours 6 and 7). There are two ways to solve this problem: (1) the conventional way, and (2) by trial-and-error.

The conventional way:

Set up and solve an equation. Jill's age x years ago can be expressed as $20 - x$. At that time, Gary's age was $14 - x$. The following equation emerges:

$$20 - x = 3(14 - x)$$
$$20 - x = 42 - 3x$$
$$2x = 22$$
$$x = 11$$

Jill was three times as old as Gary 11 years ago. (Jill was 9 and Gary was 3.)

By trial-and-error:

Try each answer choice, one at a time. Start with (A):

$$20 - 3 = 17$$
$$14 - 3 = 11$$

Is 17 three times greater than 11? No.

Go on to answer choice (B).

Eventually, you'll get to the correct answer (D):

$$20 - 11 = 9$$
$$14 - 11 = 3$$

Is 9 three times greater than 3? Yes!

Notice the sucker bait answer choice here. 11 years ago, Jill was 9 years old. A test-taker who forgets exactly what the question asks for might look for *Jill's age* among the answer choices, and choose (C).

3. **(C)** This problem involves the *square root* concept (one of the topics for hour 5). There's no need to calculate either root since the question asks for an approximation. 664 is slightly greater than 625, which is 25^2. 414 is slightly greater than 400, which is 20^2. Thus the sum of the terms is just over 45 (approximately 46).

Notice the sucker-bait answer choice here. Here's the common mistake:

$$644 + 414 = 1078$$
$$\sqrt{1078} \approx 33$$

The correct answer must be (B).

Wrong!

4. **(B)** This question covers the concept of *weighted average* (one of the topics for hour 7). The salaries range from $150,000 to $180,000. Since 5 of the 8 executives earn the lowest salary in the range, common sense should tell you that the average salary is <u>not</u> midway between these figures (the midway point is near $166,000), but rather closer to $150,000. The problem is too complex to solve simply by calculating a simple average of three numbers. So you can eliminate (D) and (E). Now here's how to solve the problem. Assign a "weight" to each of the three salary figures, then

determine the weighted average of the nine salaries:

$$5(150{,}000) = 750{,}000$$
$$3(170{,}000) = 510{,}000$$
$$1(180{,}000) = 180{,}000$$
$$750{,}000 + 510{,}000 + 180{,}000 = 1{,}440{,}000$$
$$1{,}440{,}000 \div 9 = 160{,}000$$

5. **(A)** This problem involves integers, factors, and prime numbers. (You'll explore these concepts during hour 5.) Don't waste time trying to reason through this problem in a purely abstract manner. Instead, start plugging in numbers for x, and keep going until you see a pattern that allows you to get to the answer as quickly as possible. And use you pencil! Here's how to do it. A prime number is a positive integer that is not divisible by any integer other than itself and 1. The smallest prime number is 2. Since the question asks for prime numbers, x must be positive. To check for a pattern (read: shortcut), start scratching out some equations, working your way up from the lowest possible value for x:

$$2(2) + 1 = 5$$
$$2(4.5) + 1 = 10$$
$$2(7) + 1 = 15$$
$$2(9.5) + 1 = 20$$
$$2(12) + 1 = 25$$

Notice that as the sum increases in multiples of 5 the value of x in *every other equation* is an integer that also increases in multiples of 5, and that ends with either 2 or 7. This makes the rest of your job much easier. No integer ending in 2 (other the integer 2) is a prime

number. So you know that, in addition to the integer 2, you need only consider values for x ending in 7 that are less than 49 (because $2x + 1 < 100$):

$$\{2, 7, 17, 27, 37, 47\}$$

Five of these integers—2, 7, 17, 37, and 47—are prime numbers.

6. **(D)** This problem involves the Pythagorean Theorem, which applies to all right triangles—triangles with one 90° angle. (You'll learn all about the Theorem during hour 8.) Notice that all but one of the answer choices include a square root, and that three of them indicate a difference (one term is subtracted form another). These features provide a clue that you need to find the difference between two lengths ($CB - CD$), and that you'll probably be using the Pythagorean Theorem to do it.

To find DB, you subtract CD from CB. Thus, you need to find those two lengths first. ACD is a right triangle with sides 8, 15, and 17 (one of the Pythagorean triplets you'll learn about during hour 8). Thus, $CD = 8$. CB is one of the legs of ABC. Determine CB by applying the Theorem:

$$15^2 + (CB)^2 = 0^2$$
$$225 + (CB)^2 = 400$$
$$(CB)^2 = 175$$
$$CB = \sqrt{25 \cdot 7} = 5\sqrt{7}$$

Accordingly, $DB = 5\sqrt{7} - 8$

If you had tried to answer the question *visually* by comparing the length of DB to the other lengths in the figure, then estimating the numerical values of the answer choices, you no doubt would have chosen the wrong answer. *DB* appears to be approximately 15, yet its actual length (based on the numbers provided) is just over 5!

7. **(A)** This is an algebraic word problem involving the concept of rate. (You'll explore more problems like this one during hour 7). Notice that all of the answer choices contain fractions. This is a clue that you should try to create a fraction as you solve the problem. Here's how to do it. Given that the train travels $r + 2$ miles in h hours, you can express its rate in miles per hour as $\frac{r+2}{h}$. In $\frac{3}{2}$ hours, the train would travel $\frac{3}{2}$ this distance:

$$\frac{3}{2}\left(\frac{r+2}{h}\right) = \frac{3r+6}{2h}$$

Look out for answer choice (E). It has all the elements of a correct answer, except that it omits h! Common sense should tell you that the correct answer must include both r and h.

8. **(E)** This is an algebraic word problem involving the concept of mixture. (You'll explore more problems like this one during hour 7). Your common sense should tell you that when you add more acid to the solution, the percent of the solution that is acid will increase. So you're looking for an answer that's greater than 20—either (C), (D), or (E). If you need to guess at this point, your odds are 1 in 3. Here's how to solve the problem. The original amount of acid is (10)(20%) = 2 liters. After adding

6 liters of pure acid, the amount of acid increases to 8 liters, while the amount of total solution increases from 10 to 16 liters. The new solution is 8/16 (or 50%) acid.

9. **(B)** Don't try to measure the size of the angle in question by eye; you might choose (C)—and you'd be wrong! To solve this problem, you need to know a variety of geometry rules involving triangles and circles. (You'll explore these rules during hours 8 and 9.) Your starting point in this problem is with what you know: arc *ABC* measures 85°. Here's how to solve the problem, step by step (the symbol ≅ signifies "congruent to," which means the same size and shape):

1. Since O is the circle's center, $\angle AOC$ must also be 85°.

2. Since AO and CO are each equal in length to the circle's radius, they are equal in length to each other ($AO \cong CO$).

3. Since $AO \cong CO$, the angles opposite those sides (in ACO) must also be congruent. $\angle CAO \cong \angle ACO$.

4. Since the sum of all three angles of a triangle is 180°, the sum of angles $\angle CAO$ and $\angle ACO$ is 95. Each of the two angles = 47.5°

5. Since O is the circle's center, the other triangle (the one with the angle in question) is congruent to $\triangle OCA$. Thus, $x = 47.5$

2

10. **(B)** In order to solve this problem, you need to know the algebraic formula for combining rates of work. (You'll learn algebraic formulas during hour 7.) Letting A equal the aggregate (combined) time, you can express the portion of the job that each hose performs per minute as $\frac{A}{20}$ and $\frac{A}{8}$. The sum of the two portions is 1 (the entire job):

$$\frac{A}{20} + \frac{A}{8} = 1$$

$$\frac{2A + 5A}{40} = 1$$

$$\frac{7A}{40} = 1$$

$$7A = 40$$

$$A = \frac{40}{7}, \text{ or } 5\frac{5}{7}$$

Looking for a shortcut or a quick way of checking your work? You can probably narrow down the answer choices by estimating the *size* of the number you're looking for. Use common sense. The *second* hose alone would obviously take 8 minutes to fill the tank (a 40 gallon tank is filled at the rate of 5 gallons per minute). The *first* hose speeds up the process, but just a little. So you're looking for an answer that's a bit less that 8. (B) and (C) are the only viable answer choices. The number 7—choice (C)— is simply the sum of the two rates. So (C) should strike you as far too easy a solution to this complex problem. That leaves (B), which happens to be the correct answer!

Notice the sucker-bait answer choices in this question. Here are two common mistakes:

1. The first hose alone can fill the tank in 20 minutes.

   The second hose alone can fill the tank in 8 minutes.

       Subtract: $20 - 8 = 12$.

   Thus the correct answer choice is (D). Wrong!

2. The first hose alone can fill the tank in 20 minutes.

   The second hose alone can fill the tank in 8 minutes.

       Add: $20 + 8 = 28$.

   Thus the correct answer choice is (E). Wrong!

Hour 3

Teach Yourself
Quantitative Skills II

This hour you'll continue to take a close-up look at the Quantitative section. Specifically, you'll learn some basic strategies for handling the Quantitative Comparison format and for tackling Data Interpretation (charts and graphs) questions. Here are your goals for this hour:

- Learn what Quantitative Comparison questions look like and how to answer them
- Learn some DO's and DON'Ts for handling Quantitative Comparison questions
- Learn what Data Interpretation questions look like, and learn a 5-step approach for handling them
- Learn some DO's and DON'Ts for handling Data Interpretation questions
- Apply what you learn to some GRE-style Quantitative questions

The Quantitative Comparison Format

Along with Problem Solving questions, you'll also find peculiar questions called *Quantitative Comparisons* on the GRE. This unusual question format appears on only two standardized tests: the GRE and the SAT.

How Many:

Paper-based exam: 15 questions (out of 30 altogether) in each Quantitative section

CBT: 14 questions (out of 28 altogether)

Where:

Paper-based exam: Questions 1–15 in both Quantitative sections (all Quantitative Comparisons appear before all Problem Solving questions)

CBT: Interspersed with Problem Solving questions

What's covered:

Quantitative Comparisons cover the same mix of arithmetic, algebra, and geometry as Problem Solving questions.

Directions:

In addition to the instructions that apply to all Quantitative questions (see page 32), the following instructions apply only to Quantitative Comparison questions.

Directions: Each question of this type consists of two quantities, one in Column A and one in Column B. Compare the two quantities select:

(A) if the quantity in Column A is greater

(B) if the quantity in Column B is greater

(C) if the quantities are equal

(D) if the relationship cannot be determined from the information given.

Notes:

- Since there are only four choices, NEVER MARK (E).

- In some questions, additional information pertaining to one or both of the quantities to be compared is centered above the two columns.

- Any symbol appearing in both columns represents the same thing in one column as in the other.

NOTE The paper-based and CBT directions are the same, except that on the CBT you won't be instructed to choose a lettered answer choice—because you'll select (click on) one of four blank ovals (instead of marking an answer sheet).

What Quantitative Comparison Questions Look Like

Let's take a look at three typical Quantitative Comparisons. At the risk of giving away the answers up front, the correct answer (A, B, C or D) is different for each question. (We'll analyze all four questions a few pages ahead.)

3

 NOTE On the paper-based exam, the four answer choices are indicated at the top of each page. On the CBT, the answer choices always appear on the screen along with each question (you click on one of four blank ovals to choose an answer).

	Column A	Column B
QUESTION 1.	$\frac{1}{4} + \frac{13}{52} + \frac{5}{6}$	$\frac{1}{5} + \frac{3}{10} + \frac{10}{12}$

(A) The quantity in Column A is greater
(B) The quantity in Column B is greater
(C) The quantities are equal
(D) The relationship cannot be determined from the information given.

	Column A	Column B

QUESTION

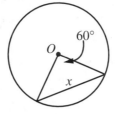

O lies at the center of the circle.

2.	$6x$	The circumference of circle O

(A) The quantity in Column A is greater.
(B) The quantity in Column B is greater.
(C) The quantities are equal.
(D) The relationship cannot be determined from the information given.

QUESTION	Column A	Column B

$$xy \neq 0$$

3. $x^2 + y^2$ $(x + y)^2$

(A) The quantity in Column A is greater.
(B) The quantity in Column B is greater.
(C) The quantities are equal.
(D) The relationship cannot be determined from the information given.

Some Quantitative Comparisons will include diagrams (geometry figures, graphs, and charts), but most won't. Also, expect to see fewer word problems among Quantitative Comparison questions than among Problem Solving questions.

What You Should Know About the Quantitative Comparison Format

There are only four answer choices: (A), (B), (C), and (D). Part of what makes Quantitative Comparison format unique among the various types of GRE questions is that there are only four answer choices: A, B, C, and D. If you're taking the paper-based GRE, don't mark choice (E) on your answer sheet for any Quantitative Comparison question! If you're taking the CBT, there's no danger of making this mistake, since you'll only see four ovals (signifying A through D) on the screen.

The answer choices are the same for all Quantitative Comparison questions. Another feature that makes Quantitative Comparisons unique among other types of GRE questions is that the answer-choice format is fixed—that is, the choices are the same for all Quantitative Comparison questions.

All information centered above the columns applies to both columns. But remember that some Quantitative Comparisons include centered information, while others don't.

Variables signify the same thing in both expressions. If you see any variable—such as x—in both columns, you can assume that x signifies the same value in both expressions.

Figures are not necessarily drawn to scale. If a comparison is accompanied by a figure, the figure will not necessarily be drawn to scale. So don't rely solely on the visual appearance of a figure; rely instead on your knowledge of mathematics and on the other centered information along with the expressions in Columns A and B.

Quantitative Comparisons can vary widely in difficulty level. These questions are not inherently easier or tougher than Problem Solving questions. The level of difficulty and complexity can vary widely, just as with Problem Solving questions.

Quantitative Comparisons get tougher as you go along (on the paper-based GRE). If you're taking the paper-based exam, Quantitative Comparisons will increase in difficulty as you progress from Question 1 to 15. But on the CBT, there's no set order. Instead, difficulty level is determined by your responses to previous questions (see Hour 1 for details).

Calculating is not what Quantitative Comparison is primarily about. Expect to do far less number crunching and equation solving for Quantitative Comparisons than for Problem Solving questions. What's being tested here is your ability to recognize and understand principles more than your ability to work step-by-step toward a solution. (That's what Problem Solving is about.)

How to Approach a Quantitative Comparison Question

Here's a 6-step approach that you should follow for every Quantitative Comparison question. Just ahead we'll apply the 6 steps to each of our four sample Quantitative Comparisons.

ACTION PLAN

1. **Size up the question.**
2. **Check both quantities for possible shortcuts and for clues as to how to proceed.**
3. **Deal with each quantity.**
4. **Consider all possibilities for any "unknowns" (variables).**
5. **Compare the two quantities (Columns A and B).**
6. **Check your answer if you have time.**

Let's Apply the 6-Step Action Plan

Now let's revisit our three sample questions. We'll walk through each one, applying the 6-step approach you just learned. (From now on, we won't list the four answer choices; you should know them by now.)

62341_

	Column A	Column B
QUESTION 1.	$\frac{1}{4} + \frac{13}{52} + \frac{5}{6}$	$\frac{1}{5} + \frac{3}{10} + \frac{10}{12}$

ANALYSIS The correct answer is (**C**). This is a relatively easy question. Approximately 85% of test-takers respond correctly to questions like this one. Here's how to compare the two quantities, using the 6-step approach:

1. Both quantities involve numbers only (there are no variables), so this comparison appears to involve nothing more than combining fractions by adding them. Since the denominators differ, then what's probably being covered is the concept of "common denominators." Nothing theoretical or tricky here.

2. You can cancel $\frac{5}{6}$ from quantity A and $\frac{10}{12}$ from quantity B, because these two fractions have the same value. You don't affect the comparison at all by doing so. Canceling across quantities before going to step 3 will make that step far easier!

3. For each of the two quantities, find a common denominator, then add the two fractions:

$$\frac{1}{4} + \frac{13}{52} = \frac{1}{4} + \frac{1}{4} = \frac{1}{2}$$

$$\frac{1}{5} + \frac{3}{10} = \frac{2}{10} + \frac{3}{10} = \frac{5}{10} = \frac{1}{2}$$

4. There are no variables, so go on to step 5.

5. Since $\frac{1}{2} = \frac{1}{2}$, the two quantities are equal.

6. Check your calculations (you should have used pencil and paper). Did you convert all numerators properly? If you're satisfied that you're calculations are correct, confirm your response (C) and move on.

	Column A	Column B
QUESTION		

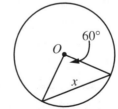

O lies at the center of the circle.

	Column A	Column B
2.	$6x$	The circumference of circle *O*

ANALYSIS The correct answer is (**B**). This is a moderately difficult question. Approximately 45% of test-takers respond correctly to questions like this one. Here's how to compare the two quantities, using the 6-step approach:

1. One quick look at this problem tells that you need to know the formula for finding a circle's circumference, and that you should look for a relationship between the triangle and the circle. If you recognize the circle's radius as the key, then you shouldn't have any trouble making the comparison.

2. A quick glance at the two quantities should tell you to proceed by finding the circumference of the circle in terms of x (quantity B), then comparing it to quantity A.

3. Because the angle at the circle's center is 60°, the triangle must be equilateral. All three sides are equal, and they are all equal in length to the circle's radius (r). Thus, $x = r$. A circle's circumference (distance around the circle) is defined as $2\pi r$, and $\pi \approx 3.1$. Since $x = r$, the circumference of this circle equals approximately $(2)(3.1)(x)$, or a bit over $6x$.

4. You've already determined the value of the variable x to the extent possible. Its value equals r (the circle's radius). The comparison does not provide any information to determine a precise value for x.

5. Since the circumference of this circle must be greater than $6x$, quantity B is greater than quantity A. There's no need to determine the circumference any more precisely. As long as you're confident it's greater than $6x$, that's all the number crunching that's required.

6. Check your calculation again (you should have used pencil and paper). Make sure you used the correct formula. (It's surprisingly easy to confuse the formula for a circle's area with the one for its circumference—especially under exam pressure!). If you're satisfied your analysis is correct, confirm your response (B) and move on.

	Column A	Column B

$$xy \neq 0$$

	Column A	Column B
3.	$x^2 + y^2$	$(x + y)^2$

ANALYSIS The correct answer is (**D**). This is a relatively difficult question. Approximately 30% of test-takers respond correctly to questions like this one. Here's how to compare the two quantities, using the 6-step approach:

1. This question involves quadratic expressions and factoring. Since there are two variables here (x and y), but no equations, you won't be calculating precise numerical values for either variable.

2. On their face, the two quantities don't appear to share common terms that you can simply cancel across quantities. But they're similar enough that you can bet on revealing the comparison by manipulating one or both expressions.

3. Quantity A is not factorable, so leave it as is—at least for the time being. Factor quantity B:

   $$(x + y)^2 = x^2 + 2xy + y^2.$$

   Notice this is the same as the expression in quantity A—with the addition of the middle term $2xy$. Now you can cancel common terms across columns, so you're left to compare 0 (quantity A) with $2xy$ (quantity B).

4. The terms x and y are variables that can be either positive or negative. Be sure to account for different possibilities. For example, if x and y are either both positive or both negative, quantity B is greater than 0—and thus greater than quantity A. However, if one variable is negative while the other is positive, then quantity B is less than 0—and thus less than quantity A.

5. You've done enough work already to determine that the correct answer must be (D). You've proven that which quantity (A or B) is greater depends on the value of at least one variable. There's no need here to try plugging in fractions—or any specific numbers. The answer is (D): The relationship cannot be determined from the information given.

6. Check your work in step 3, and make sure your signs (plus and minus) are correct. If you're satisfied that your analysis is correct, confirm your response (D) and move on.

DO's and DON'Ts for Quantitative Comparisons

Do	Don't

DO memorize the answer choices.

DON'T select (E) as your answer choice.

DON'T perform endless calculations.

DO only as much work as you need to do to make the comparison.

DO the math if it's not difficult.

DON'T rely on the appearance of figures to make the comparison.

DON'T choose (D) if a comparison does not involve variables or figures.

DO consider all the possibilities when it comes to unknowns.

DO manipulate one quantity to make it look more like the other one.

DO perform arithmetic across columns to simplify the comparison.

DON'T multiply or divide across columns unless you know that the quantity you're using is positive.

DO solve centered equations for values you need in order to make the comparison.

DO check your calculations.

Data Interpretation (Statistical Graphs and Charts)

Data Interpretation questions require you to analyze information presented graphically in statistical charts, graphs, and tables.

How many:

Paper-based exam: 1 set of 5 questions

CBT: 4 questions (2 sets of 2 questions)

Where:

Paper-based exam: Questions 21–25 on each of the two 30-question Quantitative sections.

CBT: Interspersed with other Quantitative questions (look for the first and second sets to appear, respectively, about one-third and two-thirds of the way through the section)

Format:

- Data Interpretation questions always appear in the Problem Solving format.
- Each question in a set pertains to the same graphical data.
- On the paper-based exam, a set may involve anywhere from *one to four* distinct displays (tables, charts, graphs). On the CBT, each set involves either *one or two* distinct displays (the size of the computer screen does not allow for more than two displays).

What's covered: Four types of graphical displays appear most frequently:

1. pie charts
2. tables
3. bar graphs
4. line graphs

 NOTE

On the CBT, you're more likely to encounter tables and pie charts than the other two display types. Why? On the computer screen, it's difficult to make visual measurements required for interpreting bar and line graphs. But visual measurements aren't required for pie charts and tables. Nevertheless, all four types are fair game, so be ready for them all!

Skills tested: Your ability to calculate percentages, ratios, and fractions based on the numbers you glean from graphical data.

What Data Interpretation Sets Look Like

Let's take a look at a Data Interpretation set. This one involves two related *pie charts*, and it includes three questions.

 NOTE

On the paper-based exam, this set would include 5 questions altogether. On the CBT, it would probably include 2 questions.

Questions 1–2 refer to the following two charts.

INCOME AND EXPENSES–DIVISIONS A, B, C AND D
OF XYZ COMPANY (YEAR X)

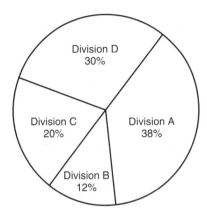

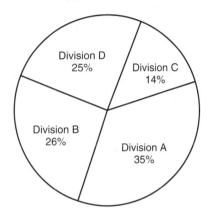

INCOME
(Total Income = $1,560,000)

EXPENSES
(Total Expenses = $495,000)

QUESTION 1. By approximately what percent did Division A's expenses exceed Division B's expenses?

(A) 9%

(B) 26%

(C) 35%

(D) 45%

(E) 220%

QUESTION 2. With respect to the division whose income exceeded its expenses by the greatest percent among the four divisions, by approximately what amount did the division's income exceed its own expenses?

(A) $69,000

(B) $90,000

(C) $150,000

(D) $185,000

(E) $240,000

What You Should Know About Data Interpretation

Data Interpretation questions always appear in the Problem Solving format. You won't see any peculiar format like Quantitative Comparisons here.

Data Interpretation questions can be long and wordy. Data Interpretation questions are notoriously difficult to understand. (Question 2 in our sample set is a good example.) Get used to it; that's the way the test-makers design them. You'll probably find that you have more trouble interpreting the questions than the figures.

On the CBT, you'll probably have to scroll (vertically) to see the entire display. Graphical displays usually appear at the top of the screen (above the question) rather than to one side of the question. Some vertical scrolling may be necessary to view the entire display, including the information above and below the chart, graph, or table.

Tougher questions require interpreting across figures. In a set with two or more figures, you'll have to combine data from two or more figures to answer the more difficult questions (as with Question 2 in our sample set).

Data Interpretation questions get tougher as you go (paper-based exam). On the paper-based exam, expect the first one or two questions to be fairly simple—possibly involving only one figure, and requiring only one or two steps to get to the answer. (Question 1 in our sample set is a good example.) Later questions are more complex.

Some figures are drawn to scale; others are not. If a figure is drawn to scale, you might see the following note below it: "*Note:* Drawn to scale." Keep in mind:

- Bar graphs will be drawn to scale
- Line charts will be drawn to scale
- Pie charts will not be drawn to scale
- Visual scale is irrelevant with tables

You don't see a Note with the pie charts in our sample set, do you? That's because you answer the pie-chart questions based on the numbers and the text information, *not* based on the visual proportions of the various pie segments.

Important assumptions will be provided. Any additional information that you might need to know to interpret the figures will be indicated above and below the figures. (Be sure to read this information.)

Most questions ask for an approximation. You'll see some form of the word *approximate* in almost every Data Interpretation question. This is because the test-makers are trying to gauge your ability to interpret graphical date, not your ability to crunch numbers to the "n-th" decimal place. (Notice that all three questions in our sample sets include the word "approximately").

Many of the numbers used are almost round. This feature relates to the previous one. The GRE rewards test-takers who recognize that rounding off numbers (to an appropriate extent) will suffice to get to the right answer. So they pack Data Interpretation figures with numbers that are close to "easy" ones. (The numbers in our pie chart set serve as good examples. $1,560,000 is close to $1,500,000 million and $495,000 is close to $500,000.)

Figures are not drawn to deceive you or to test your eyesight. In bar graphs and line charts, you won't be asked to split hairs to determine values. These figures are designed with a comfortable margin for error in visual acuity. Just don't round up or down too far. (You'll see an example of a line chart in this hour's Workshop.)

How to Approach Data Interpretation Questions

Follow these 5 steps to handle any Data Interpretation set.

1. **Look at the "big picture" first.**
2. **Read the entire Data Interpretation question very carefully.**
3. **Perform the steps needed to get to the answer.**
4. **Check choices (A) through (E) for your answer.**
5. **Check your calculations, and make sure the size and form (number, percentage, total, etc.) of your solution conforms with what the question asks.**

Let's Apply the 5-Step Action Plan

Now let's apply this 5-step approach to each of the sample questions you saw earlier. We'll walk through each question in detail for you.

1. Size up the two charts, and read the information above and below them. Notice that we're only dealing with one company during one year here. Notice also that dollar totals are provided, but that the pie segments are all expressed only as percentages. That's a clue that your main task in this set will be to calculate dollar amounts for various pie segments. Now read the first question.

QUESTION 1. By approximately what percent did Division A's expenses exceed Division B's expenses?

    (A) 9%

    (B) 26%

    (C) 35%

    (D) 45%

    (E) 220%

ANALYSIS The correct answer is **(C)**. This is a relatively easy question; approximately 75% of test-takers respond correctly to questions like this one. Here's how to solve the problem, using the 5-step approach:

1. You already performed step 1.

2. This question requires two steps: (1) locate the numbers you need on the appropriate chart, and (2) calculate the percentage asked for. The key to handling this question quickly is to recognize that since the two percentages—35% and 26%—relate to the *same total*, you can compare these percentages without converting them into dollar figures. The ratio is the same either way. So don't do more pencil work than you have to.

3. The question essentially asks:

   35% is greater than 26% by what percent?

   The quickest way to estimate the percentage difference is to first consider the difference between 35 and 26 (9), then ask yourself: "Approximately what percent of 26 is 9?" As it turns out, 9 is exactly one-third of 27, so you're looking for a percentage that's just a bit larger than 33% (one-third). Don't worry: this sort of rounding off and approximating works perfectly well for GRE Data Interpretation questions.

4. The only answer choice that is "just a bit larger" than 33% is (C). The nearest alternative, 26%, is not close enough to worry that our approximations were too rough. If you have time, go to Step 5.

5. Make sure you got your numbers from the right segments of the right chart. (It's remarkably easy to grab the wrong numbers by mistake, especially under exam conditions!) Also make sure you calculated a percentage difference (not a *dollar* difference, and not a *sum*). If you're satisfied with your analysis, move on to the next question.

QUESTION 2. With respect to the division whose income exceeded its own expenses by the greatest percent among the four divisions, by approximately what amount did the division's income exceed its own expenses?

(A) $69,000

(B) $90,000

(C) $150,000

(D) $185,000

(E) $240,000

ANALYSIS The correct answer is **(E)**. This is a difficult question; approximately 20% of test-takers respond correctly to questions like this one. Here's how to solve the problem, using the 5-Step approach:

1. You already performed step 1.

2. This is a very complex question. First you need to compare profitability—in dollar amount—among the four divisions. You can rule out Division B, since its expenses exceeded its income. That leaves Divisions A, C, and D. Be careful: you're not being asked to compare percentage profitability, but rather dollar amounts.

3. For Divisions A, C, and D, compare two dollar figures in terms of percent:

   Division A: 38% of total income and 35% of total expenses

   Division C: 20% of total income and 14% of total expenses

   Division D: 30% of total income and 25% of total expenses

   Division C's income was a bit more than $300,000 (20% of $1,500,000). Division C's expenses were a bit less than $75,000 (15% of $500,000). Perform similar calculations for Divisions A and D, and you'll discover that Division C was the most profitable one in percentage terms. Division C's income exceeded it's expenses by a bit more than $225,000.

4. Answer choice (E), $240,000, is the only one close to our approximation.

5. If you have time, rethink step 3. Make sure you're convinced that Division C's profit was greater than either A's or D's. Also, ask yourself if $240,000 in the right ballpark? If you're confident about your analysis, move on to the next question.

3

DO's and DON'Ts for Data Interpretation Questions

Do	**DON'T**

DON'T confuse percentages with raw numbers.

DON'T go to the wrong chart (or portion of a chart) for your numbers.

DO save time and avoid computation errors by rounding off.

DON'T distort numbers by rounding off inappropriately.

DO handle lengthy, confusing questions one part at a time.

DON'T split hairs in reading line charts and bar graphs.

DO formulate a clear idea as to the overall size of number the question is calling for.

DO scroll vertically to see the entire display (on the CBT).

Workshop

For this hour's workshop, we've hand-picked 7 Quantitative Comparison questions and 3 Data Interpretation questions which illustrate the DO's and DON'Ts you just learned. For each question, you'll see one or two hints to help you focus on those DO's and DON'Ts. Don't worry if you come across some mathematical concepts you don't understand. You'll learn them during the next several hours. Right now, focus on the <u>art</u> of the GRE.

Additional Quantitative questions are available on-line, at the authors' Web site: *http://www.west.net/~stewart/gre*

Quiz

(Answers and explanations begin on page 65.)

DIRECTIONS: Attempt the following 10 questions. Try to limit your time to 15 minutes. Be sure to read the explanations that follow. They're just as important as the questions themselves, because they explain how the DO's and DON'Ts come into play.

Column A	Column B

1.   The toll on a certain highway is $1.20 for the first mile and 35 cents for each additional mile.

The toll for a 7-mile drive on the highway	$3.30

(Hint: Be sure to use the right numbers for computing the toll.)

2.

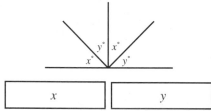

x	y

(Hint: Unless you're told that it's drawn to scale, don't rely on the visual proportions of a figure.)

3. $x > y$

x^2y	xy^2

(Hint: Don't multiply or divide across columns unless you know that the quantity you're using is positive.)

4.

The sum of all integers from 19 to 50, inclusive	The sum of all integers from 21 to 51, inclusive

(Hint: Don't choose D if a comparison does not involve variables and is not accompanied by visual figures.)
(Hint: Perform arithmetic across columns to simplify the comparison.)

Column A	Column B

5.

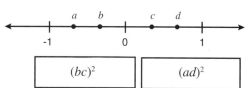

$(bc)^2$	$(ad)^2$

(Hint: Don't rely on the visual proportions of a figure to analyze the comparison.)
(Hint: Try plugging in some simple "test" numbers in place of variables.)

6. $x \neq 0$

$\dfrac{x^2 + 6x}{2}$	$3x$

(Hint: Perform arithmetic across columns to simplify the comparison.)

7.

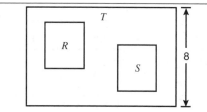

R and S are each rectangular carpets, 3 feet by 4 feet. R and S cover 20% of the larger carpet T as shown.

48	The perimeter of T

(Hint: The correct answer to a question involving numerical quantities is never D.)
(Hint: Start with what you know, and ask yourself what else you know.)

Questions 8–10 refer to the following two charts.

WORLDWIDE SALES OF THREE XYZ MOTOR COMPANY
MODELS, 1996-1997 MODEL YEAR

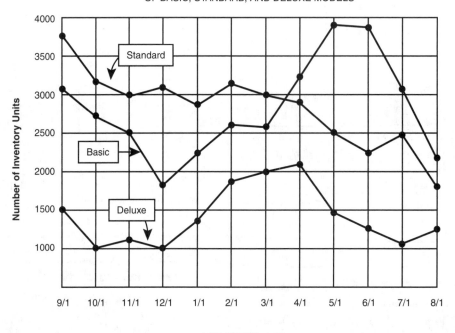

		Automobile Model	
	Basic	Standard	Deluxe
U.S. institutions	3.6	8.5	1.9
U.S. consumers	7.5	11.4	2.0
Foreign institutions	1.7	4.9	2.2
Foreign consumers	1.0	5.1	0.8

(Purchaser category)

<u>Note</u>: All numbers are in thousands.

TOTAL WORLDWIDE DEALER INVENTORY
OF BASIC, STANDARD, AND DELUXE MODELS

1996-1997 Model Year
(by month)

<u>Note</u>: Drawn to scale.

8. Of the total number of units sold to institutions during the 1996–97 model year, which of the following most closely approximates the percentage that were NOT standard models?

   (A) 24%
   (B) 36%
   (C) 41%
   (D) 59%
   (E) 68%

   (Hint: It's okay to approximate, but don't distort numbers by rounding off inappropriately.)

9. During the month in which total dealer inventory of all three models combined increased by the greatest number, by approximately what percent did the worldwide inventory of the standard model increase?

   (A) 5
   (B) 10

   (C) 15
   (D) 20
   (E) 25

   (Hint: A quick visual inspection can help narrow down your choices.)
   (Hint: Don't confuse percentages with raw numbers.)

10. With respect to the model that experienced that largest percentage change in inventory during any single month, how many units of that model were sold to consumers during the 1996–97 model year?

    (A) 2800
    (B) 3200
    (C) 3900
    (D) 8500
    (E) 16,500

    (Hint: A quick visual inspection can help narrow down your choices.)
    (Hint: Don't confuse percentages with raw numbers.)

Answers and Explanations

1. **(C)** Because the question includes no variables and no figures, you can safely eliminate answer choice (D). Why? Two numerical values can always be compared—it's just a matter of doing it. Notice that quantity A is a verbal description, while quantity B is simply a numerical value. Your dealing with a Problem Solving question in disguise, and you should proceed by working from the verbal expression to a solution, then comparing that solution with the quantity B ($3.30). Determine the value of quantity A (be sure not to inadvertently multiply $.35 by 7 instead

of 6; it's surprisingly easy to make this careless mistake when you're under pressure):

The toll for a 7-mile drive is $1.20 + (6)($.35) = $1.20 + $2.10 = $3.30.

Quantity A ($3.30) is exactly the same as quantity B, so the correct answer is (C).

2. **(D)** Based on the figure, you would think the answer to this question is (C). Although each of the four angles appears to be the same size, the figure is not necessarily drawn to scale. To make the

comparison, rely on your understanding of geometry principles and your ability to visualize angles, not on the figure. The correct answer is (D). This diagram makes the answer clear:

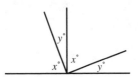

3. **(D)** Should you divide both columns by x and by y? NO! Although you know that x is greater than y, you don't know whether x and y are positive or negative. You cannot multiply or divide by a quantity unless you're certain that the quantity is positive. If you forget this, here is what could happen. Divide both sides by xy:

Column A	Column B
$x > y$	
x	y

Based on this simple comparison, you would select (A), wouldn't you? But the correct answer to this comparison is (D). For example, let $x = 1$ and $y = 0$. On this assumption, both quantities have the value 0. Or let $x = 1$ and $y = -1$. On this assumption, quantitiy A is -1 and quantitiy B is 1. This proves that the correct choice is (D).

4. **(B)** When you first see this comparison, you may be tempted to start adding each string of numbers. But Quantitative Comparisons never *require* this much number crunching. There is an easier way. But before we show it to you, assume you

have to take a guess. Don't guess (D)! You know that it is possible to make the comparison; you just don't have time to do it. Now, here's the shortcut. The two number strings have in common integers 21 through 50. So you can subtract (or cancel) all of these integers from both sides of the comparison. That leaves you to compare $(19 + 20)$ to 51. You can now see clearly that quantity B is greater.

5. **(B)** The product ad is a negative fractional number greater than a and approaching zero. Similarly, the product bc is a negative fractional number greater than b and approaching zero. But ad must be less (further to the left on the number line) than bc. Try a few simple fractions is you have trouble reasoning through the problem abstractly. Let $a = -\frac{2}{3}$, $b = -\frac{1}{3}$, $c = \frac{1}{3}$, and $d = \frac{2}{3}$. $\left(-\frac{2}{3}\right)\left(\frac{2}{3}\right) < \left(-\frac{1}{3}\right)\left(\frac{1}{3}\right)$. Given that $ad < bc$, since both products are negative, squaring them reverses the inequality, and $(ad)^2 > (bc)^2$.

6. **(A)** Given the complexity of the expression in Column A, it's difficult to make a judgment about which quantity is greater. So try to simplify the expression by multiplying both quantities by 2. Here's the result:

Column A	Column B
$x \neq 0$	
$x^2 + 6x$	$6x$

Aha! Notice that each column includes the term $6x$. You can subtract $6x$ from both columns:

Column A	Column B
$x \neq 0$	
x^2	0

Now you should see the comparison. Any non-zero number squared is positive (greater than zero), so the correct answer is (A).

7. **(A)** This is a Problem Solving question in disguise. Apply the centered information to determine the verbal quantity B—the perimeter of T. Then compare that solution with quantity A (48). You're given the combined area of R and S is 24 feet, so start there. This area is 20% of 120. Thus, the area of T is 120. Given that one dimension of T is 8, the other dimension must be 15 ($8 \times 15 = 120$). The perimeter of $T = 2(8) + 2(15) = 16 + 30 = 46$. Since $46 < 48$, quantity A is greater.

8. **(C)** Answering this question requires two steps. First, the total number of product units sold to institutions = $(3.6 + 8.5 + 1.9) + (1.7 + 4.9 + 2.2) = 22.8$. The number of these units that were not standard versions = $(3.6 + 1.9) + (1.7 + 2.2) = 9.4$. No go on to the second step. Ask yourself: "9.4 is approximately what percent of 22.8?" This question is the same as asking the percent equivalent of $\frac{9.4}{22.8}$. Here's a quick way to approximate the percentage. Round down *both* the numerator and denominator to give you the fraction $\frac{8}{20}$. It is clear now that you're looking for an answer choice that's around 40% ($\frac{8}{20} = \frac{40}{100}$). Only (C) fits the bill.

9. **(C)** This question deals exclusively with the line chart. First, look at the overall trend during each month. Notice that January was the only month during which inventory for all three models increased. Although a substantial net increase occurred during December as well, visual inspection should convince you that January is the month during which total inventory increased the most. During January, basic model inventory increased from 2250 to 2600, an increase of 350. Now compute the percent increase: $\frac{350}{2250} \approx \frac{5}{32}$, or just over 15%. Only answer choice (C) fits the bill.

10. **(A)** First, inspect the line chart for the steepest drop or rise over a one-month period. During January the deluxe model inventory increased by more than 50%, the greatest monthly percentage change for any of the models.

Now go on to the second step. Based on the sales table, the number of deluxe models sold to consumers was 2800 (2.0K + .8K).

HOUR **4**

Teach Yourself
Arithmetic I

This hour you'll begin to teach yourself the arithmetic you'll need for the GRE. You'll focus on four of the test-makers' favorite topics: simple average, fractions, percents, and ratios/proportion. In this hour you will learn:

- The formula for arithmetic mean (average), and how to apply it to GRE questions
- How to handle fractions effectively on the GRE
- How to deal with GRE problems involving percent
- The concepts of ratio and proportion, and how these concepts are covered on the GRE
- How to apply the concepts you learn this hour to some exercises and to a GRE-style Quiz

Problems Involving Descriptive Statistics

First up this hour is what the test-makers call *descriptive statistics*. This area includes many concepts, but here are the only five you need to know for the GRE (in order by frequency of appearance on the exam):

> **arithmetic mean (average):** In a set of *n* measurements, the sum of the measurements divided by *n*
>
> **median:** The middle measurement after the measurements are ordered by size (or the average of the two middle measurements if the number of measurements is odd)
>
> **mode:** the measurement that appears most frequently in a set
>
> **range:** the difference between the greatest measurement and the smallest measurement
>
> **standard deviation:** a measure of dispersion among members of a set

We'll focus here on *mean* and *median* because these two concepts are covered on the GRE far more frequently than the others. But first, here's a simple example that illustrates each of the five concepts:

Example: Given a set of six measurements, {8,–4,8,3,2,7}:

mean = 4	$(8 - 4 + 8 + 3 + 2 + 7) \div 6 = 24 \div 6 = 4$
median = 5	The average of 3 and 7—the two middle measurements in the set ordered in this way: {–4,2,3,7,8,8}
mode = 8	8 appears twice (more frequently than any other measurement)
range = 12	The difference between –4 and 8
standard deviation	(see below)

On the GRE, you probably won't need to calculate standard deviation (it's a complex process). More likely, you'll be asked to *compare* standard deviations. And you'll probably be able to do this informally by simply remembering the general rule that *the greater the data are spread away from the mean, the greater the standard deviation.* Consider these two distributions:

Distribution A: {1,2.5,4,5.5,7}
Distribution B: {1,3,4,5,7}

In both sets, the mean and median is 4, and the range is 6. But the standard deviation of A is greater than that of B, because 2.5 and 5.5 are further away than 3 and 5 from the mean.

Arithmetic Mean (Simple Average)

Calculating a simple average of a series of numbers is pretty easy, and the test-makers know it. So GRE simple-average questions are always a bit more complex than the simple calculation in our example on page 70.

QUESTION Dan scored an average of 72 on his first four math tests. After taking the next test, his average dropped by 2. Which of the following is his most recent test score?

(A) 60

(B) 62

(C) 64

(D) 66

(E) 68

ANALYSIS The correct answer is **(B)**. Dan's average after the fifth test was 72 – 2, or 70. Set up the formula for arithmetic mean, plugging in the information you already know (let x equal Dan's most recent test score):

$$A = \frac{(\text{score } 1 + \text{score } 2 + \text{score } 3 + \text{score } 4) + \text{score } 5}{5}$$

$$70 = \frac{4(72) + x}{5}$$

$$70 = \frac{288 + x}{5}$$

$$350 = 288 + x$$

$$62 = x$$

4

> **TIP** When you're facing any arithmetic-mean problem, just plug the information that the question provides into the formula, and you'll be able to handle the problem with no sweat.

Median

In a set of numbers arranged from lowest to highest in value, the *median* is:

- the middle value, if the set includes an *odd* number of terms
- the average of the two middle values, if the set includes an *even* number of terms

Here's an example in the Quantatative Comparison format.

Column A	Column B

Set Q: {8,4,–3,6,–7,5}

The median of all numbers in Set Q	The mean (average) of all numbers in Set Q

The correct answer is **(A)**. To determine quantity A, rearrange the numbers in order of value: {–7,–3,4,5,6,8}. Since the set includes 6 terms (an even number), the median is the average of the two middle terms: $\frac{4+5}{2}$, or $\frac{9}{2}$. To determine quantity B, add the digits, then divide by 6: $\frac{8 + 4 - 3 + 6 - 7 + 5}{6} = \frac{13}{6}$. Since $\frac{9}{2} > \frac{13}{6}$, quantity A is greater.

> For the same set of values, the mean (simple average) and the median can be, but are not necessarily, the same. For example:
>
> The set {3,4,5,6,7} has both a mean and median of 5.
>
> The set {–2,0,5,8,9} has a mean of 4 but a median of 5.

Percent, Fraction, and Decimal Conversions

Many GRE questions will require you to convert percents, fractions, and decimals back and forth from one form to another. You should know how to make any conversion quickly—without stopping to think how to do it.

> Percents are usually less than 100, but they can be 100 or greater as well. Percents greater than one hundred convert to numbers greater than 1:
>
> $140\% = 1.40 = 1\frac{4}{10}$, or $1\frac{2}{5}$
>
> $5893\% = 58.93 = 58\frac{93}{100}$

How many fifths are in 280%?

(A) 1.4

(B) 2.8

(C) 14

(D) 28

(E) 56

ANALYSIS The correct answer is **(C)**. Convert 280% to a fraction, then reduce to lowest terms:

$$280\% = \frac{280}{100} = \frac{28}{10} = \frac{14}{5}.$$

TIP

> To guard against conversion errors, keep in mind the general size of the number you are dealing with. For example, think of .09% as just under .1%, which is one-tenth of a percent, or a thousandth (a pretty small number). Think of $\frac{4}{5}$ as just under $\frac{5}{5}$, which is obviously $\frac{1}{10}$, or 10%. Think of 668% as more than 6 times a complete 100% or between 6 and 7.

Problems Involving Fractions

You'll find 4 basic types of "pure" fraction problems on the GRE:

1. Adding or subtracting fractions
2. Multiplying fractions
3. Dividing fractions
4. Comparing fractions

You'll probably encounter at least one or two "pure" fraction problems on the GRE. But you'll also apply all four skills over and over in working conversion problems (like the one you just looked at) as well as more complex GRE problems.

TIME SAVER

> Just as in multiplication, when you divide fractions, always combine and factor terms within each fraction, where possible, before you actually do the division.

QUESTION $\dfrac{4\frac{1}{2}}{1\frac{1}{8}} - 3\frac{2}{3} =$

(A) $-\dfrac{1}{8}$

(B) $\dfrac{1}{12}$

(C) $\dfrac{5}{24}$

(D) $\dfrac{1}{3}$

(E) $\dfrac{2}{5}$

ANALYSIS   The correct answer is **(D)**. First, convert all mixed numbers into fractions:

$$\dfrac{\frac{9}{2}}{\frac{9}{8}} - \dfrac{11}{3}$$

Eliminate the complex fraction as follows:

$$\dfrac{9}{2} \cdot \dfrac{8}{9} - \dfrac{11}{3} = \dfrac{8}{2} - \dfrac{11}{3}$$

express each fraction using the common denominator 6, then combine:

$$\dfrac{8}{2} - \dfrac{11}{3} = \dfrac{24}{6} - \dfrac{22}{6} = \dfrac{2}{6}, \text{ or } \dfrac{1}{3}$$

QUESTION   Which of the following fractions is greatest in value?

(A) $\dfrac{3}{5}$

(B) $\dfrac{21}{32}$

(C) $\dfrac{11}{16}$

(D) $\dfrac{5}{8}$

(E) $\dfrac{7}{11}$

The correct answer is **(C)**. To compare (B), (C), and (D), you can use a common denominator of 32:

$$\frac{21}{32} \qquad \frac{11}{16} = \frac{22}{32} \qquad \frac{5}{8} = \frac{20}{32}$$

The largest of these is $\frac{11}{16}$. Compare $\frac{11}{16}$ to $\frac{7}{11}$ using the cross-product method. $11 \cdot 11 > 16 \cdot 7$. Finally, compare $\frac{11}{16}$ to $\frac{3}{5}$ using the cross-product method. $11 \cdot 5 > 16 \cdot 3$. Thus, $\frac{11}{16} > \frac{3}{5}$.

NOTE

In this particular type of problem, the answer choices won't necessarily be listed in ascending value, since doing so would give the answer away.

Operations with Decimal Points

GRE problems involving decimal numbers sometimes require you to combine these numbers by either multiplying or dividing.

Multiplying decimal numbers. The number of decimal places (digits to the right of the decimal point) in a product should be the same as the total number of decimal places in the numbers you multiply. So to multiply decimal numbers quickly:

1. Multiply, but ignore the decimal points
2. Count the total number of decimal places among the numbers you multiplied
3. Include that number of decimal places in your product

Here are two simple examples:

(23.6)(.07)	3 decimal places altogether
(236)(7) = 1652	Decimals temporarily ignored
(23.6)(.07) = 1.652	Decimal point inserted
(.01)(.02)(.03)	6 decimal places altogether
(1)(2)(3) = 6	Decimals temporarily ignored
(.01)(.02)(.03) = .000006	Decimal point inserted

Dividing decimal numbers. When you divide (or compute a fraction), you can move the decimal point in both numbers by the same number of places either to the left or right without altering the quotient (value of the fraction). Here are three related examples:

$$11.4 \div .3 \left(\text{or } \tfrac{11.4}{.3} \right) = \tfrac{114}{3} = 38$$

$$1.14 \div 3 \left(\text{or } \tfrac{1.14}{3} \right) = \tfrac{114}{300} = .38$$

$$114 \div .03 \left(\text{or } \tfrac{114}{.03} \right) = \tfrac{11400}{3} = 3800$$

| TIP | Removing decimal points from a fraction helps you to see the general size (value) of the fraction you're dealing with. |

Problems Involving Percent

On the GRE, you might find any one of four types of "pure" percent problems:

1. Finding a % of a number
2. Finding a number when a % is given
3. Finding what % one number is of another
4. Finding percent increase or decrease

The last type is by far the most likely of the four to appear on the GRE.

QUESTION A clerk's salary is $320.00 after a 25% raise. Before the clerk's raise, the supervisor's salary was 50% greater than the clerk's salary. If the supervisor also receives a raise in the same amount as the clerk's raise, what is the supervisor's salary after the raise?

(A) $370

(B) $424

(C) $448

(D) $480

(E) $576

ANALYSIS The correct answer is **(C)**. $320 is 125% of the clerk's former salary. Expressed algebraically:

$$
\begin{aligned}
320 &= 1.25x \\
32000 &= 125x \\
\$256 &= x \text{ (clerk's salary before the raise).}
\end{aligned}
$$

Thus, the clerk received a raise of $64 ($320 – $256). The supervisor's salary before the raise was:

$256 + 50% of $256 = $256 + $128 = $384

The supervisor received a $64 raise. Thus, the supervisor's salary after the raise is $448 ($384 + $64).

CAUTION

Semantics is important in problems of percent. Be sure you understand the distinction between these two statements:

6 is 100% greater than 3.

6 is 200% of 3.

If you confuse their meaning, you're asking for trouble on the GRE!

Problems Involving Ratio and Proportion

GRE ratio problems sometimes involve a *whole* divided into two or more *parts*, where your task is to determine either (1) the size of one of the parts (2) the size of the whole. You can solve these problems by setting up algebraic equations. But there's another approach that is usually quicker more intuitive.

Think about a ratio as a whole made up of different parts—like a whole pie divided into pieces. Let's use a male-to-female ratio of 12:16 (3:4) as an example. The "whole pie" consists of 28 equal slices—the total number; the whole equals the sum of its slices:

16 slices (males) + 12 slices (females) = the whole pie (28 students)

$$\frac{16}{28} + \frac{12}{28} = \frac{28}{28} \text{ (the whole pie)}$$

QUESTION Three lottery winners—X, Y and Z—are sharing a lottery jackpot. X's share is $\frac{1}{5}$ of Y's share and $\frac{1}{7}$ of Z's share. If the total jackpot is $195,000, what is the dollar amount of Z's share?

(A) $15,000

(B) $35,000

(C) $75,000

(D) $105,000

(E) $115,000

ANALYSIS The correct answer is (**D**). Think about these shares as slices of a whole pie—the whole jackpot. First, express the winners' proportionate shares as ratios. The ratio of X's share to Y's share is 1 to 5. Similarly, the ratio of X's share to Z's share is 1 to 7. The jackpot share ratio is as follows:

$$X : Y : Z = 1 : 5 : 7$$

4

X's winnings account for 1 of 13 equal parts (1 + 5 + 7) of the total jackpot. $\frac{1}{13}$ of $195,000 is $15,000. Accordingly, *Z*'s share is 7 times that amount, or $105,000.

Setting Up Proportions (Equal Ratios)

A proportion is simply a statement that two ratios are equal. Since you can express ratios as fractions, you can express a proportion as an equation—for example, $\frac{16}{28} = \frac{4}{7}$. If one of the four terms is missing from the proportion, you can solve for the missing term using algebra.

QUESTION At *c* cents per pound, what is the cost of *a* ounces of candy?

    (A) $\dfrac{c}{a}$

    (B) $\dfrac{a}{c}$

    (C) ac

    (D) $\dfrac{ac}{16}$

    (E) $\dfrac{16c}{a}$

ANALYSIS The correct answer is **(D)**. This question is asking: "*c* cents is to one pound as *how many cents* is to *a* ounces?" Set up a proportion, letting *x* equal the cost of *a* ounces. Because the question asks for ounces, convert 1 pound to 16 ounces. Use the cross-product method to solve quickly:

$$\frac{c}{16} = \frac{x}{a}$$
$$16x = ca$$
$$x = \frac{ca}{16}, \text{ or } \frac{ac}{16}$$

 NOTE

On the GRE, you'll also see more complex word problems involving proportion (for example, problems involving motion, direct and inverse variation, and mixtures). These problems involve specific formulas, which you'll learn during hour 7.

Altering a Ratio

A GRE question might ask you alter a ratio, by adding or subtracting from one (or both) terms in the ratio. The number added or subtracted might be either known or unknown.

QUESTION Among registered voters in a certain district, the ratio of men to women is 3:5. If the district currently includes 24,000 registered voters, how many additional men must register to make the ratio 4:5?

(A) 2000

(B) 3000

(C) 4000

(D) 5000

(E) 6000

ANALYSIS The correct answer is **(B)**. This question involves three steps. First, set up a proportion to determine the current number of registered male voters and female voters:

$$\frac{3}{8} = \frac{x}{24,000}$$
$$8x = 72,000$$
$$x = 9,000$$

Of the 24,000 voters, 9000 are men, and 15,000 are women.

Next, determine the number of male voters needed altogether for a 4:5 men/women ratio, given that the number of female voters remains unchanged (15,000):

$$\frac{4}{5} = \frac{x}{15,000}$$
$$5x = 60,000$$
$$x = 12,000$$

Since the district currently includes 9000 male voters, 3000 more are needed to make the ratio 4:5.

4

In the question above, the numbers are simple enough that you can probably use intuition instead of resorting to algebra. In the first step, it should be clear enough to you that $\frac{3}{8} = \frac{9}{24}$. In the second step, it should be equally clear that $\frac{4}{5} = \frac{12}{15}$.

Workshop

In this Workshop, you'll tackle a 10-question GRE-style quiz, designed for you to review and apply the concepts and question types you learned about this hour.

 Additional Quantitative questions are available on-line, at the authors' Web site: *http://www.west.net/~stewart/gre*

Quiz

Directions: Attempt the following 10 GRE-style questions. Try to limit your time to 15 minutes. For each question, you'll see one or two hints to help you if you're having trouble.

(Answers and explanations begin on page 82.)

1. A number p equals $\frac{3}{2}$ the average of 10, 12, and q. What is q in terms of p?

    (A) $\frac{2}{3}p - 22$

    (B) $\frac{4}{3}p - 22$

    (C) $2p - 22$

    (D) $\frac{1}{2}p - 22$

    (E) $\frac{9}{2}p - 22$

    (Hint: Plug the information you know into the formula for arithmetic mean.)

2. If $a \neq 0$ or 1, $\dfrac{\frac{1}{a}}{2 - \frac{2}{a}} =$

    (A) $\dfrac{1}{2a - 2}$

    (B) $\dfrac{2}{a - 2}$

    (C) $\dfrac{1}{a - 2}$

    (D) $\dfrac{1}{a}$

    (E) $\dfrac{2}{2a - 1}$

    (Hint: You can divide by multiplying instead.)

3. The temperature at 12:00 noon is 66 degrees. If the temperature increases by 25% during the afternoon, then decreases by 25% during the evening, what is the temperature, in degrees, at the end of the evening?

(A) $61\frac{7}{8}$

(B) $62\frac{1}{4}$

(C) $62\frac{3}{8}$

(D) 63

(E) 66

(Hint: Compute percent change with the number before the change.)
(Hint: Convert decimal numbers to fractions.)

4. Diane receives a base weekly salary of $800 plus a 5% commission on sales. In a week in which her commission totaled $8000, the ratio of her total weekly earnings to her commission was

(A) 1:3

(B) 5:8

(C) 2:1

(D) 5:2

(E) 3:1

(Hint: Be sure not to confuse total earnings with commission, and be sure not to reverse the ratio.)

5. Machine X, Machine Y and Machine Z each produce widgets. Machine Y's rate of production is $\frac{1}{3}$ that of Machine X, and Machine Z's production rate is twice that of Machine Y. If Machine Y can produce 35 widgets per day, how many widgets can the three machines produce per day working simultaneously?

(A) 105

(B) 164

(C) 180

(D) 210

(E) 224

(Hint: Convert ratios to fractional parts that add up to 1.)

6. There is enough food at a picnic to feed either 20 adults or 32 children. All adults eat the same amount, and all children eat the same amount. If 15 adults are fed, how many children can still be fed?

(A) 4

(B) 6

(C) 8

(D) 12

(E) 24

(Hint: Set up a proportion, or approach the question intuitively.

7. What number must be subtracted from the denominator of the fraction $\frac{7}{16}$ to change the value of the fraction to $\frac{4}{9}$?

(A) $\frac{1}{16}$

(B) $\frac{1}{4}$

(C) $\frac{7}{9}$

(D) $\frac{3}{2}$

(E) $\frac{5}{2}$

(Hint: Set up a proportion, then solve for the number.)

4

(Questions 8–10 are Quantitative Comparison problems.)

8.

Column A	Column B
The arithmetic mean (average) of a, b, c, and d	$\dfrac{a}{4}+\dfrac{b}{4}+\dfrac{c}{4}+\dfrac{d}{4}$

(Hint: Apply the arithmetic-mean formula.)

9.

Column A	Column B
$\dfrac{7}{11}+\dfrac{2}{3}$	$\dfrac{1}{2}+\dfrac{5}{6}$

(Hint: Determine lowest common denominators.)

10.

Column A	Column B
10% of 11, increased by 10%	11% of 10, increased by 11%

(Hint: Don't jump at the obvious answer without thinking. You may be falling for sucker-bait!)

Answers and Explanations

1. **(C)** Apply the arithmetic-mean formula, solving for q:

$$p = \frac{3}{2}\left(\frac{10+12+q}{3}\right)$$

$$p = \frac{10+12+q}{2}$$

$$2p = 22 + q$$

$$2p - 22 = q$$

2. **(A)** Combine terms in the denominator, then multiply the numerator fraction by the reciprocal of the denominator fraction:

$$\frac{\frac{1}{a}}{\frac{2a-2}{a}} = \frac{1}{a}\cdot\frac{a}{2a-2} = \frac{1}{2a-2}$$

3. **(A)** 25% of 66 is 16.5. Thus, the temperature increased to 82.5 degrees during the afternoon. 25% of 82.5 ($\frac{1}{4}$ of 82.5) is

20.625, or $20\frac{5}{8}$. Thus, the temperature decreased to $61\frac{7}{8}$ degrees during the evening.

4. **(E)** Diane's commission can be expressed as: $(.05)(8,000) = \$400$. Adding her commission to her base salary: $\$800 + \$400 = 1,200$ (total earnings). The ratio of $\$1,200$ to $\$400$ is 3:1.

5. **(D)** The ratio of X's rate to Y's rate is 3 to 1, and the ratio of Y's rate to Z's rate is 1 to 2. You can express the ratio among all three as 3:1:2 (x:y:z). Accordingly, Y's production accounts for $\frac{1}{6}$ of the total widgets that all three machines can produce per day. Given that Y can produce 35 widgets per day, all three machines can produce $(35)(6) = 210$ widgets per day.

6. **(C)** You can set up the proportion $\frac{15}{20} = \frac{x}{32}$, where x equals the number of children that can be fed instead of 15 adults. Solve for x:

$$\frac{15}{20} = \frac{x}{32}$$
$$\frac{3}{4} = \frac{x}{32}$$
$$4x = 96$$
$$x = 24$$

32 – 24, or 8 children can still be fed. You can also approach this question intuitively. $\frac{15}{20}$, or $\frac{3}{4}$, of the food is gone. The $\frac{1}{4}$ of the food that remains will feed $\frac{1}{4}$ of the 32 children—8 children.

7. **(B)** Set up a proportion, then solve for x by cross-multiplying:

$$\frac{7}{16 - x} = \frac{4}{9}$$
$$4(16 - x) = (7)(9)$$
$$64 - 4x = 63$$
$$-4x = -1$$
$$x = \frac{1}{4}$$

8. **(C)** According to the arithmetic mean formula, the average of the four variables is $\frac{a + b + c + d}{4}$. You can distribute the denominator 4 to each variable in the numerator. Thus, the two quantities are the same.

9. **(B)** Combine each pair of fractions:

Column A: $\frac{7}{11} + \frac{2}{3} = \frac{21}{33} + \frac{22}{33} = \frac{43}{33}$

Column B: $\frac{1}{2} + \frac{5}{6} = \frac{3}{6} + \frac{5}{6} = \frac{8}{6}$, or $\frac{4}{3}$

To compare the two fractions, use the common denominator 33:

$$\frac{4}{3} = \frac{44}{33} > \frac{43}{33}.$$

10. **(B)** Numbers such as these would tempt many test-takers to choose (C). But the values are not the same. 10% of 11 = 11% of 10 = 1.10. Thus, increasing 1.10 by 11% must yield a greater number than increasing it by 10%.

4

HOUR 5

Teach Yourself
Arithmetic II

This hour you'll broaden your arithmetical horizon by dealing with numbers in more abstract, theoretical settings. You'll examine a variety of relationships and patterns among numbers—just the sort of stuff the test-makers love to cover on the GRE! Here are your goals for this hour:

- Understand the concept of absolute value
- Determine factors and multiples of numbers
- Recognize prime numbers
- Know the impact of exponents and radicals on the size and sign of numbers
- Know the ways you can and cannot combine base numbers and exponents
- Know the ways you can and cannot combine terms under radical signs
- Learn to recognize numerical progressions
- Learn quick ways to compare large sets of numbers
- Know how to deal with simple probability questions

Absolute Value

The absolute value of a real number refers to the number's distance from zero (the origin) on the number line. The symbol for absolute value is a pair of vertical lines—for example, the absolute value of x is $|x|$. Although any negative number is less than any positive number, the absolute value of a negative number can be less than, equal to, or greater than a positive number. Here's one instance of each:

$$|-7| = 7 < |8| \qquad\qquad |-7| = 7 = |7| \qquad\qquad |-7| = 7 > |6|$$

QUESTION

Column A	Column B

$$ab \neq 0$$

$|-a|$	$-|b|$

ANALYSIS The correct answer is (**A**). The absolute value of any non-zero number must be a positive number. Therefore, $|-a|$ must be positive, while $-|b|$ must be negative. The quantity in column A is greater.

Shortcuts for Finding Factors

Determining all the factors of large integers can be tricky. The following rules can help you determine quickly whether one integer is a multiple of (is divisible by) another integer:

1. Any integer is a factor of itself.
2. 1 and –1 are factors of all integers (except 0).
3. The integer zero has no factors and is not a factor of any integer.
4. A positive integer's largest factor (other than itself) will never be greater than one half the value of the integer.

Here are some shortcuts to determining divisibility by common numbers:

If the integer has this feature:	Then it is divisible by:
It ends in 0, 2, 4, 6 or 8	2
The sum of the digits is divisible by 3	3
The number formed by the last 2 digits is divisible by 4	4
The number ends in 5 or 0	5
The number meets the tests for divisibility by 2 and 3	6
The number formed by the last 3 digits is divisible by 8	8
The sum of the digits is divisible by 9	9

TIP

Memorize these shortcuts for the GRE; you'll be glad you did. A great way to learn them is to apply them to the numbers between 0 and 100 that are *not* included in the list of prime numbers on page X.

QUESTION

Column A	Column B
The number of positive factors of the integer 16	The number of positive factors of the integer 81

ANALYSIS The correct answer is **(C)**. There are 5 positive factors of 16: {1,2,4,8,16}. There are also 5 positive factors of 81: {1,3,9,27,81}.

Therefore, the two quantities are equal.

Prime Numbers

A *prime number* is a positive integer having only two positive factors: 1 and the number itself. In other words, a prime number is not divisible by (a multiple of) any positive integer other than itself and 1.

NOTE

Zero and 1 are not considered prime numbers. 2 is the first prime number.

Recognizing prime numbers is important when simplifying numbers on math exams. For example, if you know that 59 is a prime number, then you won't waste any time trying to reduce $\frac{9}{59}$ to a simpler fraction (a fraction with smaller numbers). Learn to recognize all the prime numbers between 0 and 100, without having to think about it. Here they are:

Prime numbers between zero (0) and 100.

2	11	23	41	53	61	71	83	91
3	13	29	43	59	67	73	89	97
5	17	31	47			79		
7	19	37						

5

QUESTION	Column A	Column B
	The number of prime numbers between 80 and 90	The number of prime numbers between 90 and 100

ANALYSIS The correct answer is **(C)**. There are two prime numbers between 80 and 90: 83 and 89. There are also two prime numbers between 90 and 100: 91 and 97. Therefore, the two quantities are equal.

Patterns to Look for When Combining Integers

What happens to integers when you combine them by adding, subtracting, multiplying, or dividing? Here are some useful observations:

Addition and subtraction:

integer ± integer = integer

even integer ± even integer = even integer (or zero, if the two integers are the same)

even integer ± odd integer = odd integer

odd integer ± odd integer = even integer (or zero, if the two integers are the same)

Multiplication and division:

integer − integer = integer

integer ÷ non-zero integer = integer, but only if the numerator is divisible by the denominator (if the result is a quotient with no remainder)

odd integer × odd integer = odd integer

even integer × non-zero integer = even integer

even integer ÷ 2 = integer

odd integer ÷ 2 = non-integer

QUESTION If $\frac{x}{y}$ is a negative integer, which of the following terms must also be a negative integer?

(A) $\dfrac{x^2}{y}$

(B) $-\dfrac{x^2}{y^2}$

(C) $\dfrac{x}{y^2}$

(D) $x + y$

(E) xy

ANALYSIS The correct answer is (**B**). Of the five expressions, only (B) must be a negative integer, even if x and y are not themselves integers. Because the overall fraction is an integer, $\frac{x^2}{y^2}$ must be an integer. Any number squared is positive, so $\frac{x^2}{y^2}$ must be positive. Accordingly, $-\frac{x^2}{y^2}$ must be negative.

(A) can be either a positive or negative integer, depending on whether y is positive or negative.

(C) can be a non-integer, since the denominator of the original expression is squared. Also, (c) can be either positive or negative, depending on the sign of x.

(D) must be an integer, but can be either positive or negative, depending on whether x is negative or y is negative.

(E) must be negative, but it is not necessarily an integer—for example:

$$\frac{-\frac{2}{3}}{\frac{2}{3}} = -1, \text{ but } -\frac{2}{3} \cdot \frac{2}{3} = -\frac{4}{9} \text{ (a non-integer)}$$

Exponents (Powers)

On the GRE, questions that focus on the concept of exponents come in two basic types (we'll look at both types just ahead):

- questions about the effect of exponents on the *size* and *sign* of a number (or other term)
- questions about *combining* terms that contain exponents

Exponents and the Real Number Line

Raising numbers to powers can have surprising effects on the size and/or sign (negative vs. positive) of the base number. This is one of the test-makers' favorite areas! The impact of raising a number to an exponent (power) depends on the region on the number line where the number and exponent fall. Here are the four regions you need to consider:

1. less than –1 (to the left of –1 on the number line)

2. between –1 and 0

3. between 0 and 1

4. greater than 1 (to the right of 1 on the number line)

5

QUESTION   If $-1 < x < 0$, which of the following expressions is smallest in value?

   (A) x^2

   (B) x^3

   (C) x^0

   (D) $-x$

   (E) $\dfrac{1}{x^3}$

ANALYSIS   The correct answer (**E**). From largest to smallest, the order is: (C), (D), (A), (B), (E). Here's an analysis of each answer choice:

(C) equals 1 (any non-zero term raised to the power of zero equals 1)

(D) is a positive number between 0 and 1

(A) is a positive number between 0 and $|x|$, which is the value of (D)

(B) is a negative non-integer between 0 and x

(E) is a negative number less than (to the left of) -1

Combining Base Numbers and Exponents

When you add or subtract terms, you cannot combine base numbers or exponents. It's as simple as that. Let's express this prohibition in terms of those intrepid variables a, b, and x:

$$a^x + b^x \neq (a + b)^x$$

It's a whole different story for multiplication and division. First, remember these two simple rules:

   1. You can combine base numbers first, but only if the exponents are the same.
   2. You can combine exponents first, but only if the base numbers are the same.

Let's assume first that exponents are the same:

General rule:	Examples:
$a^x \cdot b^x = (ab)^x$	$2^3 \cdot 3^3 = (2 \cdot 3)^3 = 6^3 = 216$
	$2^3 \cdot 3^3 = (8)(27) = 216$
$\dfrac{a^x}{b^x} = \left(\dfrac{a}{b}\right)^x$	$\dfrac{2^3}{3^3} = \left(\dfrac{2}{3}\right)^3 = \dfrac{2}{3} \cdot \dfrac{2}{3} \cdot \dfrac{2}{3} = \dfrac{8}{27}$

Now let's assume that base numbers are the same. When multiplying these terms, add the exponents. When dividing them, subtract the denominator exponent from the numerator exponent:

General rule:	*Examples:*
$a^x \cdot a^y = a^{x+y}$	$2^3 \cdot 2^2 = 2^{(3+2)} = 2^5 = 32$
$\dfrac{a^x}{a^y} = a^{x-y}$	$\dfrac{2^5}{2^2} = 2^{(5-2)} = 2^3 = 8$

QUESTION $\dfrac{9^{11} \cdot 11^9}{11^{11} \cdot 9^9} =$

(A) $\dfrac{1}{9}$

(B) $\dfrac{81}{121}$

(C) $\dfrac{9}{11}$

(D) 1

(E) 9

ANALYSIS   The correct answer is **(B)**. The key to this question is to recognize that since the base numbers 9 and 11 appear in both the numerator and denominator, you can factor out 9^9 and 11^9:

$$\frac{9^{11} \cdot 11^9}{11^{11} \cdot 9^9} = \frac{\left(9^9 \cdot 9^2\right) \cdot 11^9}{\left(11^9 \cdot 11^2\right) \cdot 9^9} = \frac{9^2}{11^2} = \frac{81}{121}$$

> **CAUTION**   Remember: You can't combine base numbers or exponents of two terms unless you're multiplying or dividing the terms *and* either the base numbers are the same or the exponents are the same.

5

Additional Exponent Rules

The only kind of exponents you're likely to see on the GRE are positive integers. Keep in mind, though, that exponents can also be *negative*, and they can also be *non-integers*. So remember these two rules—one for negative exponents and the other for fractional exponents—just in case:

1. Raising a number to a negative power is the same as "1 over" the same number but with a positive exponent.

$$n^{-2} = \frac{1}{n^2} \qquad 3^{-2} = \frac{1}{3^2} = \frac{1}{9}$$

2. The numerator of a fractional exponent becomes the number's exponent. The denominator becomes the root.

General rule:	Examples:
$n^{\frac{1}{2}} = \sqrt{n}$	$9^{\frac{1}{2}} = \sqrt{9} = 3$
$n^{\frac{2}{3}} = \sqrt[3]{n^2}$	$8^{\frac{2}{3}} = \sqrt[3]{8^2} = \sqrt[3]{64} = 4$
$n^{\frac{3}{2}} = \sqrt{n^3}$	$4^{\frac{3}{2}} = \sqrt{4^3} = \sqrt{64} = 8$

To cover all your bases, also keep in mind these two additional rules for exponents:

General rule:	Examples:
$(a^x)^y = a^{xy}$	$(2^2)^4 = 2^8 = 256$
$a^0 = 1 \ (a \neq 0)$	$34^0 = 1$

For the GRE, memorize the exponential values in the following table. You'll be glad you did, since these are the ones that you're most likely to see on the exam.

Base	Power and Corresponding Value						
	2	3	4	5	6	7	8
2	4	8	16	32	64	128	256
3	9	27	81	243			
4	16	64	256				
5	25	125	625				
6	36	216					

Roots and the Real Number Line

As with exponents, the root of a number can bear a surprising relationship to the size and/ or sign (negative vs. positive) of the number (another favorite area of the test-makers). Here are four observations you should remember:

1. If $n > 1$, then $1 < \sqrt[3]{n} < \sqrt{n} < n$ (the higher the root, the lower the value). However, if n lies between 0 and 1, then $n < \sqrt{n} < \sqrt[3]{n} < 1$ (the higher the root, the higher the value).

2. The square root of any negative number is an imaginary number, not a real number. Remember: you won't encounter imaginary numbers on the GRE.

3. Every negative number has exactly one cube root, and that root is a negative number. The same holds true for all other odd-numbered roots of negative numbers.

4. Every positive number has two square roots: a negative number and a positive number (with the same absolute value). The same holds true for all other even-numbered roots of positive numbers.

CAUTION

> Don't take this fourth observation too far! Every positive number has only one *cube* root, and that root is always a positive number. The same holds true for all other odd-numbered roots of positive numbers.

QUESTION If $x < -1$, which of the following is largest in value?

(A) $-\sqrt{\dfrac{.9}{x^3}}$

(B) $-\sqrt[3]{x}$

(C) $\sqrt[3]{x}$

(D) $\dfrac{1}{\sqrt[3]{x}}$

(E) x^3

ANALYSIS The correct answer is **(B)**. From largest to smallest (left to right on the number line), the order is: (B),(A),(D),(C),(E). Here's the analysis of each answer choice:

(B) must be a positive number greater than 1

(A) must be a positive non-integer between zero and 1.

(D) must be a negative non-integer between zero and –1

(C) must be greater than (to the right of) x, between x and –1 on the number line

(E) must be smaller than x (to the left of x on the number line)

If you wish to confirm this analysis, let $x = -2$, in each of the five expressions.

Combining Radicals

The rules for combining terms that include roots are quite similar to those for exponents. One rule applies to addition and subtraction, while a different rule applies to multiplication and division.

Addition and subtraction: If a term under a radical is being added to or subtracted from a term under a different radical, you cannot combine the two terms under the same radical.

General rule:	Examples:
$\sqrt{x} + \sqrt{y} \neq \sqrt{x+y}$	$\sqrt{4} + \sqrt{16} = 2 + 4 + 6$, but
	$\sqrt{4+16} = \sqrt{20} \approx 4.4$
$\sqrt{x} - \sqrt{y} \neq \sqrt{x-y}$	$\sqrt{25} - \sqrt{9} = 5 - 3 = 2$, but
	$\sqrt{25-9} = \sqrt{16} = 4$
$\sqrt{x} + \sqrt{x} = 2\sqrt{x}$ (not $\sqrt{2x}$)	$\sqrt{36} + \sqrt{36} = 2\sqrt{36} = 2(6) = 12$, but
	$\sqrt{2 \cdot 36} = \sqrt{72} \approx 8.5$

Multiplication and Division: Terms under different radicals can be combined under a common radical if one term is multiplied or divided by the other, but only if the root is the same. Here are three different cases:

General rule:	Examples:
$\sqrt{x}\sqrt{x} = x$	$\sqrt{33.9}\sqrt{33.9} = 33.9$
$\sqrt{x}\sqrt{y} = \sqrt{xy}$	$\sqrt{9}\sqrt{4} = \sqrt{9 \cdot 4} = \sqrt{36} = 6$
$\dfrac{\sqrt{x}}{\sqrt{y}} = \sqrt{\dfrac{x}{y}}$	$\dfrac{\sqrt[3]{125}}{\sqrt[3]{8}} = \sqrt[3]{\dfrac{125}{8}} = \dfrac{5}{2}$

Simplifying Radicals

On the GRE, always look for the possibility of simplifying radicals by moving part of what's inside the radical to the outside. Check inside your square-root radicals for factors that are squares of nice tidy numbers (especially integers).

QUESTION $\sqrt{\dfrac{x^2}{36} + \dfrac{x^2}{25}} =$

(A) $\dfrac{x^2}{11}$

(B) $\dfrac{x^2\sqrt{61}}{61}$

(C) $\dfrac{11x}{30}$

(D) $\dfrac{x^2}{15}\sqrt{\dfrac{x}{2}}$

(E) $\dfrac{x}{30}\sqrt{61}$

ANALYSIS The correct answer is **(E)**. You cannot move either term out of the radical without first combining them, using a common denominator:

$$\sqrt{\frac{x^2}{36} + \frac{x^2}{25}} = \sqrt{\frac{25x^2 + 36x^2}{(36)(25)}} = \sqrt{\frac{61x^2}{(36)(25)}} = \frac{x}{(6)(5)}\sqrt{\frac{61}{1}} = \frac{x}{30}\sqrt{61}$$

TIP

On the GRE, if you can reduce an expression under a radical sign by removing terms or factors, do it! Also, eliminate radicals from denominators. More than likely, these steps will be necessary to solve the problem at hand.

5

For the GRE, memorize the roots in the following table. You'll be glad you did, since these are the ones that you're most likely to see on the exam.

Common square roots:	*Common cube roots:*
$\sqrt{121} = 11$	$\sqrt[3]{8} = 2$
$\sqrt{144} = 12$	$\sqrt[3]{27} = 3$
$\sqrt{169} = 13$	$\sqrt[3]{64} = 4$
$\sqrt{196} = 14$	$\sqrt[3]{125} = 5$
$\sqrt{225} = 15$	$\sqrt[3]{216} = 6$
$\sqrt{625} = 25$	$\sqrt[3]{343} = 7$
	$\sqrt[3]{512} = 8$
	$\sqrt[3]{729} = 9$
	$\sqrt[3]{1000} = 10$

Problems Involving Sets

A *set* is simply a group of two or more numbers or other terms. GRE problems involving sets come in four different varieties:

- *descriptive statistics* (mean, median, mode, range, standard deviation)
- *progressions* (recognizing a pattern among a series of terms)
- *comparisons* (finding sums of and differences between different sets of numbers)
- *probability* (determining possible combinations of terms within sets as well as between sets)

The first variety you examined last hour along with other pure number-crunching concepts. Now you'll explore the other three types.

Progressions

You might encounter a GRE question involving a series of numbers (or other terms) in which the terms *progress* according to some pattern. Your task is to recognize the pattern and to identify unknown terms based on it.

 In the series $\{N_1, N_2, N_3 \ldots\}$, where $N_x = x^2 - 2x$, what is the value of $(N_{50} - N_{49}) - (N_{48} - N_{47})$?

(A) −16

(B) 4

(C) 9

(D) 22

(E) 49

ANALYSIS The correct answer is **(B)**. Don't try to solve this problem by crunching large numbers. Instead, look for a pattern. Apply the formula for N_x to the first several terms of the series: $N_1 = -1, N_2 = 0, N_3 = 3, N_4 = 8, N_5 = 15, N_6 = 24$. Notice the linear progression in which the difference between each successive term and the preceding one increases by 2. As a result, given four successive terms, the difference between the third and fourth terms will always be greater than the difference between the second and third terms by 2. It follows that the difference between the third and fourth terms will always be greater than the difference between the first and second terms by 4. Accordingly, $(N_{50} - N_{49}) - (N_{48} - N_{47}) = 4$. If you failed to see this pattern, you could have used some "test" numbers to discover it:

$$N_4 - N_3 - N_2 - N_1 = (8 - 3) - [0 - (-1)] = 4$$
$$N_5 - N_4 - N_3 - N_2 = (15 - 8) - (3 - 0) = 4$$
$$N_6 - N_5 - N_4 - N_3 = (24 - 15) - (8 - 3) = 4$$

Comparisons

The test-makers might also ask you to compare two sets of numbers. Always look for a pattern among the numbers which provides a shortcut to determining their sum.

QUESTION What is the difference between the sum of all positive even integers less than 102 and the sum of all positive odd integers less than 102?

(A) 0

(B) 1

(C) 50

(D) 51

(E) 101

ANALYSIS The correct answer is **(D)**. To see the pattern, compare the initial terms of each sequence:

even integers: {2,4,6,...100}
odd integers: {1,3,5,...99, 101}

For each successive term, notice that the odd integer is *one less* than the corresponding even integer. There are a total of 50 corresponding integers, so the difference between the sums of all these corresponding integers is 50. But the odd-integer sequence includes one additional integer: 101. So the difference is (–50 + 101), or 51.

 TIME SAVER Whenever you're about to tally up a long string of numbers, stop! Look for a pattern to shortcut the process. Your knack at recognizing these patterns is just what the test-makers are trying to gauge!

5

Probability

A GRE question might ask for the number of possible combinations in a set or the probability of selecting any one term or combination of terms from a set. By definition, the probability of an event occurring ranges from 0 to 1.

QUESTION Inside a hat are four tickets: a, b, c, and d. If two of the tickets are drawn randomly from the hat, what is the probability that tickets b and c have been drawn?

(A) $\dfrac{1}{9}$

(B) $\dfrac{1}{8}$

(C) $\dfrac{1}{6}$

(D) $\dfrac{1}{4}$

(E) $\dfrac{1}{3}$

ANALYSIS The correct answer is **(C)**. You can approach questions such as this one intuitively, without resort to formal mathematics. Ask yourself: How many possible combinations of two tickets are there? Tally up the possibilities methodically, working from left to right alphabetically:

Combinations with a: $\{ab\}$ $\{ac\}$ $\{ad\}$
Combinations with b (not already accounted for): $\{bc\}$ $\{bd\}$
Combinations with c (not already accounted for): $\{cd\}$
Combinations with d have all been accounted for

As you can see, there are six distinct two-ticket combinations. Accordingly, the probability of selecting any one combination is 1 in 6, or $\dfrac{1}{6}$.

Workshop

In this hour's Workshop, you'll tackle a 10-question GRE-style quiz, designed for you to review and apply the concepts and question types you learned about this hour.

Additional Quantitative questions are available on-line, at the authors' Web site: *http://www.west.net/~stewart/gre*

Quiz

(Answers and explanations begin on page 101.)

1. On the real number line, if the distance between x and y is 16.5, which of the following could be the values of x and y?

    (A) -11.5 and 5.5
    (B) 8.25 and -8.75
    (C) 14.5 and 30.5
    (D) -11 and 5.5
    (E) -16.5 and 16.5

    (Hint: Visualize the real number line, and think absolute value.)

2. If n is the first of two consecutive odd integers, and if the difference of their squares is 120, which of the following equations can be used to find their values?

    (A) $(n + 1)^2 - n^2 = 120$
    (B) $n^2 - (n + 2)^2 = 120$
    (C) $[(n + 2) - n]^2 = 120$
    (D) $(n + 2)^2 - n^2 = 120$
    (E) $n^2 - (n + 1)^2 = 120$

    (Hint: The difference between n and n + 2 must be positive.)

3. $\dfrac{\frac{3a^2c^4}{4b^2}}{6ac^2} =$

    (A) $\dfrac{ac^2}{8b^2}$

    (B) $\dfrac{ac^2}{4b^2}$

    (C) $\dfrac{4b^2}{ac^2}$

    (D) $\dfrac{8b^2}{ac^2}$

    (E) $\dfrac{ac^2}{6b^2}$

    (Hint: You can divide by multiplying instead.)

    (Hint: Look for common factors.)

4. What is the difference between the sum of the integers 15 through 33, inclusive, and the sum of the integers 11 through 31, inclusive?

    (A) 11
    (B) 15
    (C) 26
    (D) 32
    (E) 41

    (Hint: When comparing sets, sometimes you can cancel common terms.)

5

5. A sock drawer contains five pairs of socks: two black, two blue, and one white pair. If two pairs are randomly selected from the drawer, what is the probability that the white pair and a black pair have been selected?

(A) $\dfrac{1}{3}$

(B) $\dfrac{1}{4}$

(C) $\dfrac{1}{5}$

(D) $\dfrac{1}{6}$

(E) $\dfrac{1}{8}$

(Hint: Count each pair of the same color as a distinct term in the set.)

Questions 6–10 are Quantitative Comparisons.

Column A	Column B

6. $-1 < x < 0$

$\left|x^4\right|$ $\left|x^3\right|$

(Hint: Fractions get smaller as their exponents get bigger.)

Column A	Column B

7. The arithmetic mean (average) of all prime numbers less than 20 | The arithmetic mean (average) of all prime numbers less than 10 |

(Hint: If the math is not difficult, do it.)

8. $\dfrac{\sqrt{12}+\sqrt{18}}{\sqrt{12+18}}$ 1

(Hint: Don't jump at simple answers to complex problems.)

9. $n < 0$

The sixth term in the series: $\{n-1, n^2-2, n^3-3,...\}$ The fifth term in the series: $\{n+1, n^2+2, n^3+3,...\}$

(Hint: Consider all possible values for n.)

10. $0 < a < b < c < 1$

a^3b^2c ab^2c^3

(Hint: Cancel common terms across columns.)

(Hint: You can use your intuition, or you can plug in some numbers.)

Answers and Explanations

1. **(D)** Distance on the number line is always positive, so add 11 to 5.5. The difference between −11 and 5.5 is 16.5.

2. **(D)** The other integer is $n + 2$. Since the difference between n and $(n + 2)$ is positive, the term $(n + 2)$ must appear first in the equation.

3. **(A)** You can simplify by multiplying the numerator fraction by the reciprocal of the denominator:

$$\frac{3a^2c^4}{4b^2} \cdot \frac{1}{6ac^2}$$

Factor out 3, a, and c^2 from both the numerator and the denominator:

$$\frac{ac^2}{4b^2} \cdot \frac{1}{2} = \frac{ac^2}{8b^2}$$

4. **(B)** You need not add all the terms of each sequence. Instead, notice that the two sequence have in common integers 15 through 31, inclusive. Thus, those terms cancel out, leaving $32 + 33 = 65$ in the first sequence and $11 + 12 + 13 + 14 = 50$ in the second sequence. The difference is 15.

5. **(C)** There are ten possible two-pair combinations. Label the pairs Black A, Black b, Blue A, Blue b, and White. Two of these ten combinations (or 1 in 5) include a black pair and the white pair:

   Black A, Black B
   Black A, Blue A
   Black A, Blue B
   Black A, White
   Black B, Blue A
   Black B, Blue B
   Black B, White
   Blue A, Blue B
   Blue A, White
   Blue B, White

6. **(B)** The absolute value of any fraction between −1 and 1 decreases (approaching zero) as the fraction is raised to higher and higher powers.

7. **(B)** The average of all prime numbers less than 20 is $10\frac{2}{7}$.

   Quantity B = $2 + 3 + 5 + 7$

8. **(A)** The rules for combining terms under radicals should tell you immediately that the correct answer is *not* (C). A rough approximation of the three root values suffices here:

$$\frac{3^+ + 4^+}{5^+} \approx \frac{7}{5} > 1$$

9. **(D)** The sixth term in Column A's series is $n^6 - 6$. Given $n < 0$, n^6 must be positive, but it could be either less than 6 or greater than 6. Thus, $n^6 - 6$ could be either negative or positive (depending on the value of n). The fifth term in Column B's series is $n^5 + 5$. Given $n < 0$, n^5 must be negative, but $n^2 + 5$ might be either negative or positive (depending on the value of n). If n is a small fraction, such as $-\frac{1}{2}$, then quantity B is greater than quantity A. But if n is a larger number, such as −5, then quantity A is greater than quantity B.

10. **(B)** You can cancel out b^2, a, and c from both columns. So you're left to compare a^2 to c^2. Because $0 < a < c$, $a^2 < c^2$.

5

HOUR 6

Teach Yourself Basic Algebra

This hour you'll continue to prepare for the Quantitative section, by forging ahead to algebra. In this hour you will learn:

- How to solve a linear equation with one variable
- How to solve a system of two equations with two variables
- How to factor quadratic expressions and to find the roots of quadratic equations
- How to recognize unsolvable equations when you see them
- How to handle algebraic inequalities on the GRE

Linear Equations with One Variable

Algebraic expressions are usually used to form equations, which set two expressions equal to each other. Most equations you'll see on the GRE are *linear* equations, in which the variables don't come with exponents. To solve any linear equation containing one variable, your goal is always the same: isolate the unknown (variable) on one side of the equation. To accomplish this, you may need to perform one or more of the following operations on both sides, depending on the equation:

1. Add or subtract the same term from both sides
2. Multiply or divide the same term from both sides
3. Clear fractions by cross-multiplication
4. Clear radicals by raising both sides to the same power (exponent)

Performing any of these operations on *both* sides does not change the equality; it merely restates the equation in a different form.

 TIP

> If you don't remember anything else this hour, remember this key to solving any equation: Whatever operation you perform on one side of an equation you must also perform on the other side; otherwise, the two sides won't be equal!

Let's take a look at each of these four operations to see when and how to use each one.

1. Add or subtract the same term from both sides of the equation.

To solve for x, you may need to either add or subtract a term from both sides of an equation—or do both.

QUESTION   If $2x - 6 = x - 9$, then $x =$

    (A) −9

    (B) −6

    (C) −3

    (D) 2

    (E) 6

ANALYSIS   The correct answer is **(C)**. First, put both x-terms on the left side of the equation by subtracting x from both sides; then combine x-terms:

$$2x - 6 - x = x - 9 - x$$
$$x - 6 = -9$$

Next, isolate x by adding 6 to both sides:

$$x - 6 + 6 = -9 + 6$$
$$x = -3$$

2. **Multiply or divide both sides of the equation by the same non-zero term.**

   To solve for x, you may need to either multiply or divide a term from both sides of an equation.

   QUESTION   If $12 = \dfrac{11}{x} - \dfrac{3}{x}$, then $x =$

   (A) $\dfrac{3}{11}$

   (B) $\dfrac{1}{2}$

   (C) $\dfrac{2}{3}$

   (D) $\dfrac{11}{12}$

   (E) $\dfrac{11}{3}$

   ANALYSIS   The correct answer is **(C)**. First, combine the x-terms:

   $$12 = \dfrac{11 - 3}{x}$$

   Next, clear the fraction by multiplying both sides by x:

   $$12x = 11 - 3$$
   $$12x = 8$$

   Finally, isolate x (strip it of its coefficient 12) by dividing both sides by 12:

   $$x = \dfrac{8}{12}, \text{ or } \dfrac{2}{3}$$

6

3. If each side of the equation is a fraction, your best bet is to cross-multiply.

Where the original equation equates two fractions, use cross-multiplication to eliminate the fractions. Multiply the numerator from one side of the equation by the denominator from the other side. Set the product equal to the product of the other numerator and denominator. (In effect, cross-multiplication is a shortcut method of multiplying both sides of the equation by both denominators.)

QUESTION   If $\dfrac{7a}{8} = \dfrac{a+1}{3}$, then $a =$

(A) $\dfrac{8}{13}$

(B) $\dfrac{7}{8}$

(C) 2

(D) $\dfrac{7}{3}$

(E) 15

ANALYSIS   The correct answer is **(A)**. First, cross-multiply as we've described:

$$(3)(7a) = (8)(a + 1)$$

Next, combine terms (distribute 8 to both a and 1):

$$21a = 8a + 8$$

Next, isolate a-terms on one side by subtracting $8a$ from both sides; then combine the a-terms:

$$21a - 8a = 8a + 8 - 8a$$
$$13a = 8$$

Finally, isolate a by dividing both sides by its coefficient 13:

$$\frac{13a}{13} = \frac{8}{13}$$

$$a = \frac{8}{13}$$

4. Square both sides of the equation to eliminate radical signs.

Where the variable is under a square-root radical sign, remove the radical sign by squaring both sides of the equation. (Use a similar technique for cube roots and other roots.)

 If $3\sqrt{2x} = 2$, then $x =$

(A) $\dfrac{1}{18}$

(B) $\dfrac{2}{9}$

(C) $\dfrac{1}{3}$

(D) $\dfrac{5}{4}$

(E) 3

ANALYSIS The correct answer is **(B)**. First, clear the radical sign by squaring all terms:

$$(3)^2\left(\sqrt{2x}\right)^2 = 2^2$$
$$(9)(2x) = 4$$
$$18x = 4$$

Next, isolate x by dividing both sides by 18:

$$x = \frac{4}{18}, \text{ or } \frac{2}{9}$$

CAUTION Look out when you square both sides of an equation! In some instances, doing so will reveal that you're really dealing with a quadratic equation—perhaps with more than one solution. Don't panic; you'll learn all about quadratic equations a bit later this hour.

6

Linear Equations with Two Variables

What we've covered up to this point is pretty basic stuff. If you haven't quite caught on, you should probably stop here and consult a basic algebra workbook for more practice. On the other hand, if you're with us so far, let's forge ahead and add another variable. Here's a simple example:

$$x + 3 = y + 1$$

Quick...what's the value of x? It depends on the value of y, doesn't it? Similarly, the value of y depends on the value of x. Without more information about either x or y, you're stuck; well, not completely. You can express x in terms of y, and you can express y in terms of x:

$$x = y - 2$$

$$y = x + 2$$

Let's look at one more: $4x - 9 = \frac{3}{2}y$

Solve for x in terms of y:

$$4x = \frac{3}{2}y + 9$$

$$x = \frac{3}{8}y + \frac{9}{4}$$

Solve for y in terms of x:

$$\frac{4x - 9}{\frac{3}{2}} = y$$

$$\frac{2}{3}(4x - 9) = y$$

$$\frac{8}{3}x - 6 = y$$

To determine numerical values of x and y, you need a system of two linear equations with the same two variables. Given this system, there are two different methods for finding the values of the two variables:

1. the *substitution* method

2. the *addition-subtraction* method

Next we'll apply each method to determine the values of two variables in a two-equation system.

 NOTE   You can't solve one equation if it contains two unknowns (variables). You either need to know the value of one of the variables, or you need a second equation.

The Substitution Method

To solve a system of two equations using the substitution method, follow these steps (we'll use x and y here):

1. In *either* equation isolate one variable (x) on one side
2. Substitute the expression that equals x in place of x in the other equation.
3. Solve that equation for y.
4. Now that you know the value of y, plug it into *either* equation to find the value of x.

QUESTION   If $\frac{2}{5}p + q = 3q - 10$, and if $q = 10 - p$, then $\frac{p}{q} =$

(A) $\frac{5}{7}$

(B) $\frac{3}{2}$

(C) $\frac{5}{3}$

(D) $\frac{25}{6}$

(E) $\frac{35}{6}$

ANALYSIS   The correct answer is **(A)**. Don't let the fact that the question asks for $\frac{p}{q}$ (rather than simply p or q) throw you. Because you're given two linear equations with two unknowns, you know that you can first solve for p and q, then divide p by q. First thing's first: Combine the q-terms in the first equation:

$$\frac{2}{5}p = 2q - 10$$

Next, substitute $(10 - p)$ for q (from the second equation) in the first equation:

$$\frac{2}{5}p = 2(10 - p) - 10$$

$$\frac{2}{5}p = 20 - 2p - 10$$

$$\frac{2}{5}p = 10 - 2p$$

6

Move the *p*-terms to the same side, then isolate *p*:

$$\frac{2}{5}p + 2p = 10$$

$$\frac{12}{5}p = 10$$

$$p = \left(\frac{5}{12}\right)(10)$$

$$p = \frac{50}{12}, \text{ or } \frac{25}{6}$$

Substitute $\frac{25}{6}$ for *p* in either equation to find *q* (we'll use the second equation):

$$q = 10 - \frac{25}{6}$$

$$q = \frac{60}{6} - \frac{25}{6}$$

$$q = \frac{35}{6}$$

The question asks for $\frac{p}{q}$, so do the division:

$$\frac{p}{q} = \frac{\frac{25}{6}}{\frac{35}{6}} = \frac{25}{35}, \text{ or } \frac{5}{7}$$

The Addition-Subtraction Method

Another way to solve for two unknowns in a system of two equations is with the addition–subtraction method. Here are the steps:

1. Make the coefficient of *either* variable the same in both equations (you can disregard the sign)

2. Make sure the equations list the same variables in the same order

3. Place one equation above the other

4. Add the two equations (work down to a sum for each term), or subtract one equation from the other, to eliminate one variable

5. You can repeat steps 1–3 to solve for the other variable.

QUESTION If $3x + 4y = -8$, and if $x - 2y = \dfrac{1}{2}$, then $x =$

(A) -12

(B) $-\dfrac{7}{5}$

(C) $\dfrac{1}{3}$

(D) $\dfrac{14}{5}$

(E) 9

ANALYSIS The correct answer is **(B)**. To solve for x, you want to eliminate y. You can multiply each term in the second equation by 2, then add the equations:

$$3x + 4y = -8$$
$$2x - 4y = \;\;1$$
$$\overline{5x + 0y = -7}$$

$$x = -\frac{7}{5}$$

Since the question asked only for the value of x, stop here. If the question had asked for both x and y (or for y only), you could have multiplied both sides of the second equation by 3, then subtracted the second equation from the first:

$$3x + 4y = -8$$
$$3x - 6y = \frac{3}{2}$$

$$0x + 10y = -9\tfrac{1}{2}$$

$$10y = -\tfrac{19}{2}$$

$$y = -\tfrac{19}{20}$$

NOTE If a question requires you to find values of both unknowns, you can combine the two methods. For example, after using addition-subtraction to solve for x in the last question, you can then substitute $-\frac{7}{5}$, the value of x, into either equation to find y.

6

Factorable Quadratic Equations

Up to this point in our quest for the value of x, we've been avoiding those pesky exponents. But on the GRE, you'll be asked to solve not only linear equations but also quadratic equations, which include a "squared" variable, such as x^2. An equation is quadratic if you can express it in this general form:

$$ax^2 + bx + c = 0$$

Keep in mind that in this general form:

x is the variable

a, b, and c are constants (numbers)

$a \neq 0$

b can equal 0

c can equal 0

Let's look at four examples of a quadratic equation. Notice that the b-term and c-term are not essential; in other words, either b or c (or both) can equal zero:

Quadratic equation	Same equation, but in the form: $ax^2 + bx + c = 0$
$2w^2 = 16$	$2w^2 - 16 = 0$ (no b-term)
$x^2 = 3x$	$x^2 - 3x = 0$ (no c-term)
$3y = 4 - y^2$	$y^2 + 3y - 4 = 0$
$7z = 2z^2 - 15$	$2z^2 - 7z - 15 = 0$

Every quadratic equation has exactly two solutions. (These two solutions are called *roots*.) All quadratic equations on the GRE can be solved by *factoring*.

To solve any factorable quadratic equation, follow these three steps:

1. Put the equation into the standard form: $ax^2 + bx + c = 0$.
2. Factor the terms on the left side of the equation into two linear expressions (with no exponents).
3. Set each linear expression (root) equal to zero and solve for the variable in each one.

Some quadratic expressions are easier to factor than others. If either of the two constants b or c is zero, the expression will be easier to factor. Otherwise, factoring is a bit trickier.

Let's walk through the last of the four equations above to see how you factor and solve it.

First, put the equation into quadratic form:

$$2z^2 - 7z - 15 = 0$$

Notice that z^2 has a coefficient of 2. This complicates the process of factoring into two binomials. A bit of trial and error may be required to determine all coefficients in both binomials. Set up two binomial shells:

$$(2z\ )(z\ ) = 0$$

One of the two missing constants must be negative, since their product is –15. The possible integral pairs for these constants are:

$$(1,-15)\ (-1,15)\ (3,-5)\ (-3,5)$$

Substituting each value pair for the two missing terms in the shell equation reveals that 3 and –5 are the missing constants (remember to take into account that the first x-term includes a coefficient of 2):

$$(2z + 3)(z - 5) = 0$$

You can check your work by reversing the process:

$$2z^2 - 10z + 3z - 15 = 0$$
$$2z^2 - 7z - 15 = 0$$

Now, solve for z:

$$(2z + 3)(z - 5) = 0$$
$$2z + 3 = 0,\ z - 5 = 0$$
$$z = -\frac{3}{2},\ 5$$

TIP

> When dealing with a quadratic equation, your first step is usually to put it into the general form $ax^2 + bx + c = 0$. But keep in mind: The only essential term is ax^2.

6

Non-Linear Equations with Two Variables

In the "real" math world, solving non-linear equations with two or more variables can be *very* complicated, even for bona-fide, card-carrying mathematicians. But on the GRE, all you need to remember are these three general forms:

Sum of two variables, squared: $(x + y)^2 = x^2 + 2xy + y^2$

Difference of two variables, squared: $(x - y)^2 = x^2 - 2xy + y^2$

Difference of two squares: $x^2 - y^2 = (x + y)(x - y)$

Let's verify these equations using the FOIL method:

$$\left(x + y\right)^2$$
$$= (x + y)(x + y)$$
$$= x^2 + xy + xy + y^2$$
$$= x^2 + 2xy + y^2$$

$$\left(x - y\right)^2$$
$$= (x - y)(x - y)$$
$$= x^2 - xy - xy + y^2$$
$$= x^2 - 2xy + y^2$$

$$(x + y)\,(x - y)$$
$$= x^2 + xy - xy - y^2$$
$$= x^2 - y^2$$

QUESTION   If $x^2 - y^2 = 100$, and if $x + y = 2$, then $x - y =$

(A) –2

(B) 10

(C) 20

(D) 50

(E) 200

ANALYSIS   The correct answer is **(D)**. If you're on the lookout for the difference of two squares, you can handle this question with no sweat. Use the third equation you just learned:

$$x^2 - y^2 = (x + y)(x - y)$$
$$100 = (x + y)(x - y)$$
$$100 = 2(x - y)$$
$$50 = x - y$$

TIP   For the GRE, memorize the three equations listed here. When you see one form on the exam, it's a sure bet that your task is to convert it to the other form.

Equations that Can't be Solved

Never assume that one equation with one variable is solvable. Similarly, never assume that a system of two equations with two variables is solvable. The test-makers love to use the Quantatitative Comparison format to find out if you know an unsolvable equation when you see one. You need to be on the look out for three different types:

1. Identities

2. Quadratic equations in disguise

3. Equivalent equations

Identities

Be on the lookout for equations that you can reduce to $0 = 0$. You cannot solve any such equation. Here's an example in the Quantatative Comparison format.

QUESTION

Column A	Column B

$$3x - 3 - 4x = x - 7 - 2x + 4$$

$$x \qquad\qquad\qquad 0$$

ANALYSIS The correct answer is **(D)**. All terms on both sides cancel out:

$$3x - 3 - 4x = x - 7 - 2x + 4$$
$$-x - 3 = -x - 3$$
$$0 = 0$$

$\therefore$ x could equal any real number

Quadratic Equations in Disguise

Some equations that appear linear (variables include no exponents) may actually be quadratic. For the GRE, here are the two situations you need to be on the lookout for:

1. The same variable inside a radical also appears outside:

$$\sqrt{x} = 5x$$
$$\left(\sqrt{x}\right)^2 = (5x)^2$$
$$x = 25x^2$$
$$25x^2 - x = 0$$

2. The same variable that appears in the denominator of a fraction also appears elsewhere in the equation:

$$\frac{2}{x} = 3 - x$$
$$2 = x(3 - x)$$
$$2 = 3x - x^2$$
$$x^2 - 3x + 2 = 0$$

6

You can see that in both scenarios you're dealing with a quadratic (non-linear) equation!

QUESTION	Column A	Column B

$$6x = \sqrt{3x}$$

x	$\dfrac{1}{12}$

ANALYSIS The correct answer is **(D)**. An unwary test-taker might assume that the centered equation is linear—because x is not squared. Substituting $\frac{1}{12}$ for x satisfies the equation. But are the two quantities—x and $\frac{1}{12}$—necessarily equal? No! If you clear the radical by squaring both sides of the equation, then isolate the x-terms on one side of the equation, you'll see that the equation is quite quadratic indeed:

$$36\,x^2 = 3x$$
$$36x^2 - 3x = 0$$

To ferret out the two roots, factor out x, then solve for each root:

$$x(36x - 3) = 0$$
$$x = 0, \; 36x - 3 = 0$$
$$x = 0, \; \frac{1}{12}$$

Because $\frac{1}{12}$ is only one of two possible values for x, the correct answer to this Quantitative Comparison must be (D).

Equivalent Equations

In some cases, what appears to be a system of two equations with two variables is actually one equation expressed in two different ways.

QUESTION	Column A	Column B

$$a + b = 30$$
$$2b = 60 - 2a$$

a	b

ANALYSIS The correct answer is **(D)**. An unwary test-taker might waste time trying to find the values of a and b, because the centered data appears at first glance to provide a system of two linear equations with two unknowns. But you can easily manipulate the second equation so that it is identical to the first:

$$2b = 60 - 2a$$

$$2b = 2(30 - a)$$

$$b = 30 - a$$

$$a + b = 30$$

So you're really dealing with only one equation. You can't solve one equation in two unknowns, so the correct answer must be (D).

TIME SAVER

> When you encounter any Quantitative Comparison question that calls for solving one or more equations, stop in your tracks before taking pencil to paper. Size up the equation to see whether it's one of the three unsolvable animals you learned about here. If so, then unless you're given more information the correct answer must be (D).

Solving Algebraic Inequalities

You can solve algebraic inequalities in the same manner as equations. Isolate the variable on one side of the equation, factoring and canceling wherever possible. However, one important rule distinguishes inequalities from equations: Whenever you multiply or divide by a negative number, you must reverse the inequality symbol. Simply put: If $a > b$, then $-a < -b$. Here's an example:

$12 - 4x < 8$	original inequality
$-4x < -4$	12 subtracted from each side; inequality unchanged
$x > 1$	both sides divided by –4; inequality reversed

Workshop

In this hour's Workshop, you'll tackle a 10-question GRE-style quiz, designed for you to review and apply the concepts and question types you learned about this hour.

ONLINE

> Additional Quantitative questions are available on-line, at the authors' Web site: *http://www.west.net/~stewart/gre*

6

Quiz

(Answers and explanations begin on page 120.)

1. If $\dfrac{2y}{9} = \dfrac{y-1}{3}$, then $y =$

   (A) $\dfrac{1}{3}$

   (B) $\dfrac{4}{9}$

   (C) $\dfrac{9}{15}$

   (D) $\dfrac{9}{4}$

   (E) 3

   (Hint: You can cross-multiply to solve for y quickly.)

2. If $ax - b = cx + d$, then in terms of a, b, c, and d, $x =$

   (A) $-\dfrac{bd}{ac}$

   (B) $a - c + b + d$

   (C) $\dfrac{a-c}{b+d}$

   (D) $\dfrac{b+d}{a-c}$

   (E) $\dfrac{a+d}{b-c}$

   (Hint: Isolate the x-terms on one side of the equation, then factor.)

3. If $3x + 2y = 5a + b$, and if $4x - 3y = a + 7b$, then $x =$

   (A) $a + b$
   (B) $a - b$
   (C) $2a + b$
   (D) $4a - 6b$
   (E) $3a + 4b$

   (Hint: You can "line up" corresponding terms, then use addition-subtraction.)

4. If $x + y = 8$, $x + z = 7$, and $y + z = 6$, what is the value of x?

   (A) 3
   (B) 3.5
   (C) 4
   (D) 4.5
   (E) 5

   (Hint: Given three equations in three variables, you can solve for any variable.)

5. Which of the following is a factor of $x^2 - x - 20$?

   (A) $x - 10$
   (B) $x - 2$
   (C) $x - 4$
   (D) $x + 4$
   (E) $x + 5$

   (Hint: Use the FOIL method to factor the expression into two binomials.)

6. If $\dfrac{9b^3 - 15b^2 - 6b}{18b^2 + 6b} = 13b - 17$, then $b =$

(A) $-\dfrac{14}{5}$

(B) $\dfrac{5}{16}$

(C) $\dfrac{32}{25}$

(D) 3

(E) $\dfrac{7}{2}$

(Hint: Start by factoring out common terms in each expression.)

Questions 7–10 are Quantatative Comparisons.

	Column A	*Column B*
7.	$5x - 4y = 3$	
	$4y - 5x = 3$	
	x	y

(Hint: Notice that in both equations the right side is the same.)

	Column A	*Column B*
8.	$p + q = -4$	
	$p - q = 4$	
	$p^2 - q^2$	0

(Hint: Quantity A is a notorious quadratic.)

	Column A	*Column B*
9.	$\dfrac{2}{3x} = \dfrac{3}{2}x$	
	x	$\dfrac{2}{3}$

(Hint: Clear x from the denominator.)

	Column A	*Column B*
10.	$a = b$	
	$c = d$	
	$b > c$	
	$a + c$	$b + d$

(Hint: Use substitution to make one quantity look like the other one.)

6

Answers and Explanations

1. **(E)**
$$9(y - 1) = 2y(3)$$
$$9y - 9 = 6y$$
$$3y = 9$$
$$y = 3$$

2. **(D)** Isolate the x-terms, factor out x, then isolate x:
$$ax - b = cx + d$$
$$ax - cx = b + d$$
$$x(a - c) = b + d$$
$$x = \frac{b + d}{a - c}$$

3. **(A)** Multiply the first equation by 3, the second by 2, then add:
$$9x + 6y = 15a + 3b$$
$$\underline{8x - 6y = 2a + 14b}$$
$$17x + 0y = 17a + 17b$$
$$x = a + b$$

4. **(D)** This problem involves a system of three equations with three variables. The following solution employs both the substitution and addition-subtraction methods.

   Express x in terms of y: $x = 8 - y$. Substitute this expression for x in the second equation: $(8 - y) + z = 7$ or $-y + z = -1$. Add this equation to the third equation in the system.
$$-y + z = -1$$
$$\underline{y + z = 6}$$
$$2z = 5$$
$$z = 2.5$$

Substitute z's value for z in the second equation to find the value of x:
$$x + 2.5 = 7$$
$$x = 4.5$$

5. **(D)**
$$x^2 - x - 20$$
$$= x^2 - 5x + 4x - 20$$
$$= (x - 5)(x + 4)$$

6. **(C)** Here are the steps required to solve for b:
$$\frac{3b\left(3b^2 - 5b - 2\right)}{6b(3b + 1)} = 13b - 17$$
$$\frac{3b(3b + 1)(b - 2)}{6b(3b + 1)} = 13b - 17$$
$$\frac{b - 2}{2} = 13b - 17$$
$$b - 2 = 26b - 34$$
$$25b = 32$$
$$b = \frac{32}{25}$$

7. **(D)** In each equation, the right side is the same—the number 3. Thus, $5x - 4y = 4y - 5x$. Solve for x in terms of y:
$$5x - 4y = 4y - 5x$$
$$10x = 8y$$
$$x = \frac{8}{10}y$$

Which value, x or y, is greater depends on whether x and y are positive or negative numbers.

8. **(B)** $p^2 - q^2 = (p + q)(p - q) = (-4)(4) =$ -16, which is less than 0.

9. **(D)** Clearing x from the denominator reveals that this equation is quadratic, and that it has both a positive and a negative root.

$$\frac{2}{3} = \frac{3}{2}x^2$$

$$\frac{4}{9} = x^2$$

$$\pm\frac{2}{3} = x$$

10. **(C)** This problem is simpler than in might appear. In Column A, simply substitute b for a and d for c (because $a = b$ and $c = d$). The result is $b + d$, which is the same expression as the one in Column B.

6

HOUR 7

Teach Yourself Alegbra Word Problems

This hour you'll look at the various types of GRE word problems that involve setting up and solving algebraic equations. In this hour you'll learn to handle all the most common types of word problems including:

- Weighted average problems
- Currency (coin and bill) problems
- Motion problems
- Work problems
- Mixture problems
- Age problems
- Overlapping set problems
- Investment problems

On the GRE, most algebra word problems appear in the Problem Solving
format. So we'll use this format for the samples you'll see this hour (although
the Workshop includes some algebra problems in the Quantitative Comparison format as well.)

Weighted Average Problems

During hour 4, you examined the concept of simple average (arithmetic mean). Recall the
formula for determining the average (A) of a series of terms (numbers), where n equals the
number of terms (numbers) in the series:

$$A = \frac{a+b+c+...}{n}$$

Thus, the arithmetic mean of –2, 7, 22, and 19 is 11.5:

$$A = \frac{-2+7+22+19}{4} = \frac{46}{4} = 11.5$$

When some numbers among the terms to be averaged are given greater "weight" than
others, however, you have to make some adjustments to the basic formula to find the
average. As a simple illustration, suppose that a student receives grades of 80 and 90 on
two exams, but the former grade receives three times the weight of the latter exam. The
student's weighted-average grade is not 85 but rather some number closer to 80 than 90.
One way to approach this problem is to think of the first grade (80) as three scores of 80,
which added to the score of 90 and divided by 4 (not 2) results in the weighted average:

$$WA = \frac{80+80+80+90}{4} = \frac{330}{4} = 82.5$$

You can also approach this problem more intuitively (less formally). You're looking for a
number between 80 and 90 (a range of 10). The simple average would obviously lie
midway between the two. Given that the score of 80 receives three times the weight of the
score of 90, the weighted average is three times closer to 80 than to 90, or three-fourths of
the way from 90 to 80. Dividing the range into four segments, it is clear that the weighted
average is 82.5. Similarly, if 80 received twice the weight of 90, the weighted average is
$83\frac{1}{3}$, and if 80 received four times the weight of 90, the weighted average is 82.

QUESTION Mike's average monthly salary for the first four months that he worked was
$3000. What must his average monthly salary be for each of the next eight
months, so that his average monthly salary for the year is $3,500?

(A) $3600

(B) $3750

(C) $3800

(D) $3850

(E) $4000

ANALYSIS The correct answer is **(B)**. The $3000 salary receives a weight of 4, while the unknown salary receives a weight of 8. You can approach this problem in strict algebraic fashion:

$$3500 = \frac{4(3000) + 8x}{12}$$
$$(12)(3500) = 12,000 + 8x$$
$$30,000 = 8x$$
$$x = 3750$$

Mike's salary for each of the next eight months must be $3750 for Mike to earn an average of $3500 a month during the entire 12 months.

You can also approach this problem more intuitively. One-third of the monthly salary payments are "underweighted" (less than the desired $3500 average) by $500. Thus, to achieve the desired average with 12 salary payments, you must overweight the remaining two-thirds of the payments (exceeding $3500) by half that amount—that is, by $250.

 TIME SAVER Weighted average is a concept we can all relate to intuitively in our everyday lives. So use your common sense on GRE problems to quickly rule out answer choices that strike you as too high or low.

Currency (Coin and Bill) Problems

Currency problems are really quasi-weighted-average problems, because each item (bill or coin) in a problem is weighted according to its monetary value. Unlike weighted average problems, however, the "average" value of all the bills or coins is not at issue. In solving currency problems, remember the following:

- You must formulate algebraic expressions involving both *number* of items (bills or coins) and *value* of items.

7

- You should convert the value of all moneys to a common unit (that is, cents or dollars) before formulating an equation. If converting to cents, for example, you must multiply the number of nickels by 5, dimes by 10, and so forth.

QUESTION Jim has $2.05 in dimes and quarters. If he has four fewer dimes than quarters, how much money does he have in dimes?

(A) 20 cents

(B) 30 cents

(C) 40 cents

(D) 50 cents

(E) 60 cents

ANALYSIS The correct answer is (**B**). Letting x equal the number of dimes, $x + 4$ represents the number of quarters. The total value of the dimes (in cents) is $10x$, and the total value of the quarters (in cents) is $25(x + 4)$, or $25x + 100$. Given that Jim has $2.05, the following equation emerges:

$$10x + 25x + 100 = 205$$
$$35x = 105$$
$$x = 3$$

Jim has three dimes, so he has 30 cents in dimes.

You can also solve most GRE currency problems by trial-and-error. Plug each value into the problem to see if it works. Let's use trial-and-error for choices (A) and (B):

(A) 20 cents is 2 dimes, so Jim has 6 quarters. 20 cents plus $1.50 add up to $1.70. Wrong answer!

(B) 30 cents is 3 dimes, so Jim has 7 quarters. 30 cents plus $1.75 add up to $2.05. Correct answer!

Motion Problems

Motion problems involve the linear movement of persons or objects over time. Fundamental to all GRE motion problems is the following simple and familiar formula:

distance = rate × time

$d = r \cdot t$

Don't confuse *motion* problems with *work* problems. Although both involve rate, work problems do not involve movement over a distance but rather rate of work and results of production.

Nearly every GRE motion problem falls into one of three categories:

- Two objects moving in opposite directions
- Two objects moving in the same direction
- One object making a round trip

NOTE A fourth type of motion problem involves perpendicular (right-angle) motion—for example, where one object moves in a northerly direction while another moves in an easterly direction. However, this type is really just as much a geometry as an algebra problem, because you determine the distance between the two objects by applying the Pythagorean Theorem to determine the length of a triangle's hypotenuse. (The topic of triangles is one of the main courses on next hour's geometry menu.)

QUESTION Janice left her home at 11 a.m., traveling along Route 1 at 30 mph. At 1 p.m., her brother Richard left home and started after her on the same road at 45 mph. At what time did Richard catch up to Janice?

(A) 2:45 p.m.

(B) 3:00 p.m.

(C) 3:30 p.m.

(D) 4:15 p.m.

(E) 5:00 p.m.

ANALYSIS The correct answer is **(E)**. Notice that the distance that Janice covered is equal to the distance Richard covered—that is, distance is constant. Letting x equal Janice's time, you can express Richard's time as $x - 2$. Substitute these values for time and the values for rate given in the problem into the motion formula for Richard and Janice:

Formula: rate $\times$ time = distance

Janice: $(30)(x) = 30x$

Richard: $(45)(x - 2) = 45x - 90$

7

Because the distance is constant, you can equate Janice's distance to Richard's, then solve for x:

$$30x = 45x - 90$$
$$15x = 90$$
$$x = 6$$

Janice had traveled six hours when Richard caught up with her. Because Janice left at 11:00 a.m., Richard caught up with her at 5:00 p.m.

QUESTION How far can Scott drive into the country if he drives out at 40 mph, returns over the same road at 30 mph, and spends eight hours away from home including a one-hour stop for lunch?

(A) 105 miles

(B) 115 miles

(C) 120 miles

(D) 125 miles

(E) 130 miles

ANALYSIS The correct anwer is **(C)**. Scott's actual driving time is 7 hours, which you must divide into two parts: his time spent driving into the country and his time spent returning. Letting the first part equal x, the return time is what remains of the seven hours, or $7 - x$. Substitute these expressions into the motion formula for each of the two parts of Scott's journey:

Formula: rate $\times$ time = distance

Going: $(40)(x) = 40x$

Returning: $(30)(7 - x) = 210 - 30x$

Because the journey is round trip, the distance going equals the distance returning. Simply equate the two algebraic expressions, then solve for x:

$$40x = 210 - 30x$$
$$70x = 210$$
$$x = 3$$

Scott traveled 40 mph for 3 hours, so he traveled 120 miles.

TIP

Regardless of which type of motion problem you're dealing with, you should always start with the same task: set up *two* distinct equations patterned after the simple motion formula ($r \cdot t = d$).

Work Problems

Work problems involve one or more "workers" (people or machines) accomplishing a task or job. In work problems, there's an inverse relationship between the number of workers and the time that it takes to complete the job—in other words, the more workers, the quicker the job gets done. A GRE work problem might specify the rates at which certain workers work alone and ask you to determine the rate at which they work together, or vice versa. Here's the basic formula for solving a work problem:

$$\frac{A}{x} = \frac{A}{y} = 1$$

In this formula:

- x and y represent the time needed for each of two workers, x and y, to complete the job alone

- A represents the time it takes for both x and y to complete the job working in the *aggregate* (together).

So each fraction represents the portion of the job completed by a worker. The sum of the two fractions must be 1, if the job is completed. (If you don't understand this formula, don't worry about it. Just memorize it!)

NOTE

In the real world, teamwork often creates a synergy whereby the team is more efficient than the individuals working alone. But on the GRE, you can assume that no additional efficiency is gained by two or more workers working together.

7

QUESTION One printing press can print a daily newspaper in 12 hours, while another press can print it in 18 hours. How long will the job take if both presses work simultaneously?

(A) 7 hours, 12 minutes

(B) 9 hours, 30 minutes

(C) 10 hours, 45 minutes

(D) 15 hours

(E) 30 hours

ANALYSIS The correct answer is **(A)**. Just plug the two numbers 12 and 18 into our work formula, then solve for A:

$$\frac{A}{12} + \frac{A}{18} = 1$$

$$\frac{3A}{36} + \frac{2A}{36} = 1$$

$$\frac{5A}{36} = 1$$

$$5A = 36$$

$$A = \frac{36}{5}, \text{ or } 7\frac{1}{5} \text{ hours, or 7 hours, 12 minutes}$$

TIP Had you needed to guess the answer, you could have easily ruled out answer choices (D) and (E), which both nonsensically suggest that the aggregate time it takes both presses together to produce the newspaper is *longer* than the time it takes either press alone. Remember: In work problems, use your common sense to narrow down answer choices!

Now we're going to throw a "slowball" at you. Be ready for the GRE work problem in which one worker operates counter-productively to the other. You handle this scenario simply by subtracting one fraction from the other, instead of adding them together.

QUESTION A certain tank holds a maximum of 450 cubic meters of water. If a hose can fill the tank at a rate of 5 cubic meters per minute, but the tank has a hole through which a constant .5 cubic meters of water escapes each minute, how long does it take to fill the tank to its maximum capacity?

(A) 81 minutes

(B) 90 minutes

(C) 100 minutes

(D) 112 minutes

(E) 125 minutes

ANALYSIS The correct answer is **(C)**. In this problem, the hole (which is the is the second "worker") is acting counter-productively, so you must subtract its rate from the hose's rate to determine the aggregate rate of the hose and the hole. The hose alone takes 90 minutes to fill the tank. The hole alone empties a full tank in 900 minutes. Plug these values into our slightly modified formula, then solve for A:

$$\frac{A}{90} - \frac{A}{900} = 1$$

$$\frac{10A}{900} - \frac{A}{900} = 1$$

$$\frac{10A - A}{900} = 1$$

$$\frac{9A}{900} = 1$$

$$9A = 900$$

$$A = 100$$

It takes 100 minutes to fill the tank to its maximum capacity.

Mixture Problems

In mixture problems, you combine substances with different characteristics, resulting in a particular mixture or proportion. Here are some typical scenarios:

- *Wet mixtures* involving liquids, gases, or granules, which are measured and mixed by volume or weight, not by number (quantity).

- *Dry mixtures* involving a number of discreet objects, such as coins, cookies, or marbles, that are measured and mixed by number (quantity) as well as by relative weight, size, value, and so on.

Wet mixture problems usually involve percentages, while dry mixture problems involve raw numbers (quantities). But whether the mixture is dry or wet, you should use the same basic approach.

7

QUESTION How many quarts of pure alcohol must you add to 15 quarts of a solution that is 40% alcohol to strengthen it to a solution that is 50% alcohol?

(A) 2.5

(B) 3.0

(C) 3.25

(D) 3.5

(E) 4.0

ANALYSIS The correct answer is **(B)**. The original amount of alcohol is 40% of 15. Letting x equal the number of quarts of alcohol that you must add to achieve a 50% alcohol solution, $.4(15) + x$ equals the amount of alcohol in the solution after adding more alcohol. You can express this amount as 50% of $(15 + x)$. Thus, you can express the mixture algebraically as follows:

$$(.4)(15) + x = (.5)(15 + x)$$
$$6 + x = 7.5 + .5x$$
$$.5x = 1.5$$
$$x = 3$$

You must add three quarts of alcohol to achieve a 50% alcohol solution.

If you have difficulty expressing mixture problems algebraically, use a table such as the following to indicate amounts and percentages, letting x equal the amount or percentage that you're asked to solve for:

	# of quarts	×	% alchohol	=	amount of alchohol
original	15		40%		6
added	x		100%		x
new	$15 + x$		50%		$.5(15 + x)$

QUESTION How many pounds of nuts selling for 70 cents per pound must you mix with 30 pounds of nuts selling at 90 cents per pound to make a mixture that sells for 85 cents per pound?

(A) 8

(B) 10

(C) 11

(D) 14

(E) 15

ANALYSIS The correct answer is (**B**). The cost (in cents) of the nuts selling for 70 cents per pound can be expressed as $70x$, letting x equal the number that you're asked to determine. You then add this cost to the cost of the more expensive nuts ($30 \times 90 = 2{,}700$) to obtain the total cost of the mixture, which you can express as $85(x + 30)$. You can state this algebraically and solve for x as follows:

$$70x + 2700 = 85(x + 30)$$
$$70x + 2700 = 85x + 2550$$
$$150 = 15x$$
$$x = 10$$

You must add 10 pounds of 70-cent-per-pound nuts to make a mixture that sells for 85 cents per pound.

As with wet mixture problems, if you have trouble formulating an algebraic equation needed to solve the problem, indicate the quantities and values in a table such as the one shown in the figure below letting x equal the value that you're asked to determine.

	# of pounds	×	price per pound	=	total value
less expensive	x		70		$70x$
more expensive	30		90		2,700
mixture	$x + 30$		85		$85(x + 30)$

CAUTION Mixture problems often involve units of measurement—such as weight, price, and distance. This feature gives the test-makers a great opportunity to trap you by commingling ounces and pounds, cents and dollars, inches and feet, and so forth. Don't fall for this ploy! Once you set up your equation, always convert terms to the same unit of measurement. You'll be glad you did.

Age Problems

Age problems ask you to compare ages of two or more people at different points in time. In solving age problems, you might have to represent a person's age at the present time, several years from now, or several years ago. Any age problem allows you to set up an equation to relate the ages of two or more people, as in the following examples:

7

- If X is 10 years younger than Y at the present time, you can express the relationship between X's age and Y's age as $X = Y - 10$ (or $X + 10 = Y$).

- Five years ago, if A was twice as old as B, you can express the relationship between their ages as $2(B - 5) = A - 5$, where A and B are the present ages of A and B, respectively.

QUESTION Fred, Geri, and Holly were each born on May 15, but in different years. Fred is twice as old as Geri was 4 years ago, and Holly is five years older than Geri will be one year from now. If the total age of Fred, Geri, and Holly is 78, how old is Fred?

(A) 20

(B) 26

(C) 32

(D) 36

(E) 44

ANALYSIS The correct answer is **(C)**. Fred's age can be expressed in terms of Geri's, and Geri's age can be expressed in terms of Holly's:

$$F = 2(G - 4) = 2G - 8$$
$$H = G + 6$$

Given that the total age of F, G, and H is 78, substitute these two expressions for F and G in the equation $F + G + H = 78$, then solve for G:

$$(2G - 8) + G + (G + 6) = 78$$
$$4G - 2 = 78$$
$$4G = 80$$
$$G = 20$$

To find F, substitute 20 for G in the equation $F = 2G - 8$:

$$F = 2(20) - 8$$
$$F = 32$$

Problems Involving Overlapping Sets

Overlapping set problems involve distinct sets that share some number of members. Don't confuse these problems with the statistics problems you examined last hour. GRE overlapping set problems come in one of two varieties:

1. Single overlap (easier)
2. Double overlap (tougher)

QUESTION Each of the 24 people auditioning for a community-theater production is either an actor, a musician, or both. If 10 of the people auditioning are actors and 19 of the people auditioning are musicians, how many of the people auditioning are musicians but not actors?

(A) 10
(B) 14
(C) 19
(D) 21
(E) 24

ANALYSIS The correct answer is **(B)**. You can approach this relatively simple problem somewhat informally: The number of actors plus the number of musicians equals 29 (10 + 19 = 29); however, only 24 people are auditioning; thus, 5 of the 24 are actor-musicians, so 14 of the 19 musicians must not be actors.

Here's a more formal way to approach this problem. It includes three mutually exclusive sets:

1. actors who are not musicians
2. musicians who are not actors
3. actors who are also musicians

The total number of people among these three sets is 24. You can represent this scenario with the following algebraic equation (n = number of actors-musicians), solving for $19 - n$ to respond to the question:

$$(10 - n) + n + (19 - n) = 24$$
$$29 - n = 24$$
$$n = 5$$
$$19 - n = 14$$

7

There are 14 musicians auditioning who are not actors. To keep from getting confused when dealing with problems such as this one, try drawing a Venn diagram in which overlapping circles represent the set of musicians and the set of actors:

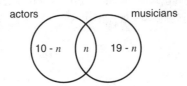

actors   musicians

$10 - n$ n $19 - n$

QUESTION The inventory at a certain men's clothing store includes 480 neckties, each of which is either 100% silk or 100% poyester. 40% of the ties are striped, and 130 of the ties are silk. 52 of the silk ties are striped. How many of the ties are polyester but are not striped?

(A) 180

(B) 210

(C) 240

(D) 350

(E) 400

ANALYSIS The correct answer is (**B**). This double overlap problem involves four distinct sets: striped silk ties, striped polyester ties, non-striped silk ties, and non-striped polyester ties. Set up a table representing the four sets, filling in the information given in the problem as shown in the figure (the value required to answer the question is indicated by the question mark).

	silk	polyester	
striped	52		40% (192)
non-striped		?	
	130	350	

Given that 130 ties are silk (see the left column), 350 ties must be polyester (see the right column). Also, given that 40% of the 480 ties (192 ties) are striped (see the top row), 140 of the polyester ties (192 – 52) must be striped. Accordingly, 350 – 140, or 210, of the ties are polyester and non-striped.

Investment Problems

GRE investment problems usually involve interest and require more than simply calculating interest earned on a given principal amount at a given rate. They usually call for you to set up and solve an algebraic equation, although sometimes you can solve these problems intuitively.

QUESTION Dr. Kramer plans to invest $20,000 in an account paying 6% interest annually. How much more must she invest at the same time at 3% so that her total annual income during the first year is 4% of her total initial investment?

(A) $32,000

(B) $36,000

(C) $40,000

(D) $47,000

(E) $49,000

ANALYSIS The correct answer is **(C)**. You can solve this problem intuitively—as a weighted average problem. Notice that 4% is exactly *one-third* of the way from 3% to 6%. So to reduce an overall 6% return to an overall 4% return, it makes sense that an additional investment earning 3% should be exactly twice the amount earning 6%, which is given as $20,000 (in other words, the ratio of the amount earning 3% to the amount earning 6% must be 2:1). Lacking this intuition, you can solve the problem algebraically. Letting x equal the amount invested at 3%, you can express Dr. Kramer's total investment as $20,000 + x$. The interest on $20,000 plus the interest on the additional investment equals the total interest from both investments. You can state this algebraically as follows:

$$.06(20,000) + .03x = .04(20,000 + x)$$

Multiply all terms by 100 to eliminate decimals, then solve for x:

$$6(20,000) + 3x = 4(20,000 + x)$$
$$120,000 + 3x = 80,000 + 4x$$
$$40,000 = x$$

She must invest $40,000 at 3% for her total annual income to be 4% of her total investment ($60,000).

7

TIP In solving GRE investment problems, it's best to eliminate percentage signs (or multiply by 100 to eliminate decimals).

Workshop

In this hour's Workshop, you'll tackle a 10-question GRE-style quiz, designed for you to review and apply the concepts and question types you learned about this hour.

 ONLINE | Additional Quantitative questions and exercises are available on-line, at the authors' Web site: *http://www.west.net/~stewart/gre*

Quiz

DIRECTIONS: Attempt the following 10 GRE-style questions. Try to limit your time to 20 minutes. For each question, you'll see one or two hints to help you if you're having trouble.

(Answers and explanations begin on page 140.)

1. Sue and Nancy have $4.00 in quarters, dimes, and nickels between them. If they have 35 coins, and if the number of quarters is half the number of nickels, how many quarters do they have?

   (A) 5
   (B) 10
   (C) 20
   (D) 3
   (E) 6

   (Hint: Express all money values in cents, then add them together)

2. Gina leaves home on her bicycle, riding at a rate of 12 mph. Twenty minutes after she leaves, Jim leaves home by automobile along the same route at 36 mph. How many miles must Jim drive before he catches up with Gina?

   (A) 6
   (B) 7.5

   (C) 9
   (D) 10.5
   (E) 12

   (Hint: Use the motion formula $(r \times t = d)$ to set up two motion equations, one for Gina and one for Jim)

3. Alfredo leaves his lodge at 11 a.m. and drives to the top of a mountain at an average rate of 24 miles per hour, arriving at the summit at 11:15 a.m. If he spends 50 minutes at the summit, then skies back to the lodge, arriving at 12:30 p.m., what is the average speed at which Alfredo skied?

   (A) 10.2 mph
   (B) 12.8 mph
   (C) 14.4 mph
   (D) 15.0 mph
   (E) 15.4 mph

   (Hint: First determine the distance from the lodge to the summit.)

4. Barbara invests $2,400 in the National Bank at a 5% annual rate of interest. How much additional money must she invest at 8% so that the total annual income will be equal to 6% of her entire initial investment?

   (A) $1,000
   (B) $1,200
   (C) $2,400
   (D) $3,000
   (E) $3,600

   (Hint: Let x equal the dollars that Barbara invests at 8%.)

5. How many ounces of soy sauce must be added to an 18-ounce mixture of peanut sauce and soy sauce consisting of 32% peanut sauce in order to create a mixture that is 12% peanut sauce?

   (A) 21
   (B) $24\frac{3}{4}$
   (C) $26\frac{2}{3}$
   (D) 30
   (E) $38\frac{2}{5}$

   (Hint: Equate the original amount of peanut sauce with the amount of peanut sauce after adding more soy sauce.)

6. Among all sales staff at Listco Corporation, college graduates and those without college degrees are equally represented. Each sales staff member is either a level 1 or level 2 employee. Level 1 college graduates account for 15% of Listco's sales staff. Listco employs 72 level 1 employees, 30 of whom are college graduates. How many sales staff members without college degrees are level 2 employees?

   (A) 29
   (B) 35
   (C) 42
   (D) 58
   (E) 64

   (Hint: Use a 4-quadrant table to help organize the information.)

Questions 7–10 are Quantitative Comparisons

Column A	Column B

7. Rick can eat an entire large pizza in 10 minutes. Kevin can eat the same large pizza in 8 minutes.

The time it takes Rick and Kevin together to eat a large pizza	$4\frac{1}{2}$ minutes

   (Hint: Find quantity A by applying the work formula.)

8. 32 sculptors at a craft fair are also painters. The number of painters and the number of sculptors at the fair total 44.

The number of the sculptors who are not painters	The number of sculptors who are not painters added to the number of painters who are not sculptors

   (Hint: Use a Venn diagram to help visualize each of three sets.)

7

	Column A	Column B		Column A	Column B

9. *P*'s age is twice *Q*'s age. One year ago *R*'s age was exactly half of *P*'s age at that time.

The difference between *P*'s age and *R*'s age	*Q*'s age

(Hint: If P were twice as old as R is now, then Q's age would equal R's age.)

10. The total price of five grocery items is $6.05. The price of one of the items is exactly fifty percent greater than the price of the other four items.

$1.65	The price of the most expensive grocery item

(Hint: It's quicker to start from quantity A and work toward the total.)

Answers and Explanations

1. **(B)** Let x = number of quarters, and express the other numbers in terms of x:

$2x$ = number of nickels
$35 - 3x$ = number of dimes

Express all money values in cents; the total is 400:

$$25(x) + 5(2x) + 10(35 - 3x) = 400$$
$$25x + 10x + 350 - 30x = 400$$
$$5x = 50$$
$$x = 10$$

2. **(A)** Set up two motion equations, one for Gina and one for Jim (change 20 minutes to $\frac{1}{3}$ hour):

Formula: Rate × Time = Distance

Gina: $12 \times x$

Jim: $36 \times (x - \frac{1}{3})$

Distance is constant, so equate Gina's distance with Jim's distance, then solve for x:

$$12x = 36(x - \frac{1}{3})$$
$$12x = 36x - 12$$
$$12 = 24x$$
$$x = \frac{1}{2}$$

Gina rode for $\frac{1}{2}$ hour at 12 mph, thereby traveling 6 miles. Accordingly, Jim also had traveled 6 miles when he caught up with her.

3. **(C)** It took Alfredo 25 minutes to ski back to the lodge. Set up two motion equations, one for Alfredo's drive up, the other for his skiing down. (The 15-minute drive $= \frac{1}{4}$ hour, and the 25-minute return trip $\frac{5}{12}$ hour):

Formula: Rate × Time = Distance

Drive Up: $24 \times \frac{1}{4} = 6$

Ski Down: $x \times \frac{5}{12} = \frac{5}{12}x$

The distances are equal:

$$6 = \frac{5}{12}x$$

$$x = \frac{72}{5}, \text{ or } 14\frac{2}{5}, \text{ or } 14.4$$

Alfredo skied down the mountain at an average rate of 14.4 mph.

4. **(B)** If Barbara invests x additional dollars at 8%, her total investment will amount to $2400 + x$ dollars.

$$.05(2400) + .08(x) = .06(2400 + x)$$
$$5(2400) + 8(x) = 6(2400 + x)$$
$$12000 + 8x = 14400 + 6x$$
$$2x = 2400$$
$$x = 1200$$

5. **(D)** Letting x equal the number of ounces of soy sauce added to the mixture, $18 + x$ equals the total amount of the mixture after the soy sauce is added. The amount of peanut sauce (5.76 ounces) must equal 12% of the new total amount of the mixture, which is $18 + x$. You can express this as an algebraic equation and solve for x:

$$5.76 = .12(x + 18)$$
$$576 = 12(x + 18)$$
$$576 = 12x + 216$$
$$360 = 12x$$
$$x = 30$$

30 ounces of soy sauce must be added to achieve a mixture that includes 12% peanut sauce.

6. **(D)** You can organize the information in this problem as shown in the following figure.

	Level 1	Level 2	
cg	30(15%)	70(35%)	50%
non-cg	42(21%)	58(29%)	50%
	72(36%)	128(64%)	

7. **(B)** Plug the values for Rick's rate and Kevin's rate into the work formula, then solve for A:

$$\frac{A}{10} + \frac{A}{8} = 1$$
$$\frac{4A}{40} + \frac{5A}{40} = 1$$
$$\frac{9A}{40} = 1$$
$$9A = 40$$
$$A = \frac{40}{9}, \text{ or } 4\frac{4}{9}$$

It takes $4\frac{4}{9}$ (less than $4\frac{1}{2}$) minutes for Rick and Kevin together to eat a large pizza.

8. **(D)** Quantity B must equal 12 (44 – 32). Quantity A could equal any number from 0 to 12. If every sculptor at the fair is also a painter, quantity A would equal zero (and B would be greater than A). At the other extreme, as many as 12 sculptors might not be painters, in which case B would equal A.

7

9. **(B)** You can approach this problem intuitively, without a written system of equations. If P were twice as old as R is now, then Q's age would equal R's age, and the correct answer would be (C). But R's current age must be greater than half of P's (because one year ago R's age was exactly half of P's). Given that Q's age is exactly half of P's age, R must be older than Q. Accordingly, $P - R < Q$.

10. **(C)** The conventional (longer) way to approach this comparison is to set up an equation that expresses the weighted average, letting x equal the price of the four less expensive items:

$$x + x + x + x + 1.5x = \$6.05$$
$$5.5x = \$6.05$$
$$x = \frac{\$6.05}{5.5}$$
$$x = \$1.10$$

The four items priced the same cost $1.10 each. Accordingly, the price of the most expensive item is $1.10 + .5($1.10), or $1.65. A quicker route to the correct answer is to start from quantity A and work toward the total:

$\frac{2}{3}$ of $1.65 = $1.10 (the price of each of the other items)

$1.10 × 4 = $4.40 (the total price of the other four items)

$4.40 + $1.65 = $6.05 (the total price of all five items)

HOUR 8

Teach Yourself Geometry I

This hour you'll continue your preparation for the Quantitative section, by forging ahead to geometry. You'll learn how to handle GRE geometry problems involving intersecting lines, triangles, and quadrilaterals. Here are your goals for this hour:

- Know the relationships among angles formed by intersecting lines
- Know the characteristics of any triangle
- Learn the Pythagorean Theorem and apply it to any right triangle
- Recognize Pythagorean triplets in order to quickly solve right triangle problems
- Know the relationship between area and perimeter of an equilateral triangle
- Know the distinguishing characteristics of squares, rectangles, parallelograms, rhombuses, and trapezoids
- Review the concepts and formulas you learn by applying them to a GRE-style quiz

Lines and Angles

Lines and line segments are the basic building blocks of all GRE geometry problems. In fact, some GRE geometry problems involve nothing more than intersecting lines—and the angles they form. Here are four basic rules you need to remember about angles formed by intersecting lines:

1. Opposite angles are equal in degree measure, or *congruent* ($\cong$). In other words, they're the same size.

2. If adjacent angles combine to form a straight line, their degree measures total 180. In fact, a straight line is actually a 180° angle.

3. If two lines are perpendicular [$\perp$] to each other, they intersect at right (90°) angles.

4. The sum of all angles formed by intersecting lines is 360°.

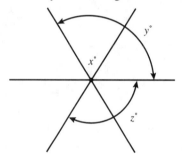

QUESTION In the figure above, if $y = 100$ and $z = 135$, what is the value of x?

    (A) 35

    (B) 40

    (C) 45

    (D) 50

    (E) 55

ANALYSIS The correct answer is (**E**). Angles y and z exceed 180° by the value of x; that is, $y + z - x = 180$. Substitute 100 and 135 for y and z, respectively, in order to solve for x.

$$100 + 135 - x = 180$$
$$55 = x$$

> **TIP**
>
> GRE "wheel spoke" problems almost always involve overlapping angles.
> Check opposite angles to determine the amount of the overlap.

GRE problems involving parallel lines also involve at least one *transversal*, which is a line that intersects each of two (or more) parallel lines. In this next figure, $l_1 \parallel l_2$, and l_3 transverses l_1 and l_2.

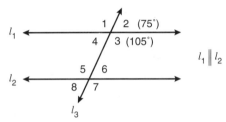

In this figure, because $l_1 \parallel l_2$, the upper cluster of angles (created by the intersection of l_1 and l_3) is identical to, or mirrors, the lower cluster (created by the intersection of l_2 and l_3). For example, $\angle 1$ is congruent (equal in size or degree measure) to $\angle 5$. Because opposite angles are congruent:

- All the *odd*-numbered angles are congruent (equal in size) to one another.
- All the *even*-numbered angles are congruent (equal in size) to one another.

QUESTION

Column A	*Column B*

In the figure above, $l_1 \parallel l_2$.

$q + z$ $y + r$

ANALYSIS The correct answer is **(D)**. Because the two lines are parallel, $q = z$ and $y = r$. However, the relationship between supplementary angles cannot be determined. The two quantities are equal only if both lines are perpendicular to the transversal (forming eight 90° angles).

CAUTION   In transversal problems, you can substitute one angle for a corresponding angle (in another cluster), but *only* if the problem indicates that they're congruent *or* if you know for sure that you're dealing with parallel lines.

Angles and Sides

Here are three basic characteristics—or properties—that apply to *all* triangles, regardless of shape or size. (There's a fourth property as well, involving a triangle's *area*. You'll examine that one separately, just a few pages ahead.)

1. *Length of the sides.* In any triangle, each side is shorter than the sum of the lengths of the other two sides.

2. *Angle measures.* In any triangle, the sum of the three interior angles is 180°.

3. *Angles and opposite sides.* In any triangle, the relative angle sizes correspond to the relative lengths of the sides opposite those angles. In other words, the smaller the angle, the smaller the side opposite the angle (and vice versa). Accordingly, if two angles are equal in size, the sides opposite those angles are of equal length (and vice-versa).

CAUTION   Don't take rule 3 too far! The ratio among angle sizes does not necessarily correspond precisely to the ratios among the lengths of the sides opposite those angles. For example, if a certain triangle has angle measures of 30°, 60°, and 90°, the ratio of the angles is 1:2:3. However, this does *not* mean that the ratio of the lengths of opposite sides is also 1:2:3 (it is *not*, as you will soon learn!).

QUESTION

Column A	Column B

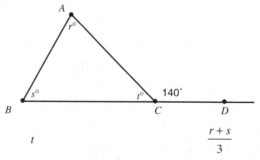

t	$\dfrac{r+s}{3}$

ANALYSIS   The correct answer is (**B**). Given that $\angle ACD = 140°$, $t = 40$ (because the sum of the two angles is $180°$). Because the sum of the three angles of $\triangle ABC$ is $180°$, $r + s = 140$. $\dfrac{140}{3} > 40$. Thus, quantity B is greater than quantity A.

8

TIP

The measure of an exterior angle of a triangle (such as $\angle ACD$ in the last question) is equal to the sum of the measures of the two remote interior angles.

Area of a Triangle

Here's a fourth property that applies to any triangle:

The area of any triangle is equal to $\frac{1}{2}$ the product of its base and its height (height is also called the *altitude*):

$$\text{Area} = \frac{1}{2} \cdot \text{base} \cdot \text{altitude (height)}$$

$$A = \frac{1}{2}(b)(h)$$

You can use any side as the base to calculate area.

CAUTION

Do not equate altitude (height) with the length of any particular side. Instead, imagine the base on flat ground, and drop a plumb line straight down from the top peak of the triangle to define height or altitude. The only types of triangles in which the altitude equals the length of one side are *right* triangles—as you'll see next.

Right Triangles

The only case where a triangle's altitude (height) equals the length of any of its sides is with a right triangle, in which one angle measures 90° and, of course, each of the other two angles measures less than 90°. The two sides forming the 90° angle are commonly referred to as the triangle's *legs* (*a* and *b* in the figure below), whereas the third (and longest side) is referred to as the *hypotenuse* (*c* in the figure below).

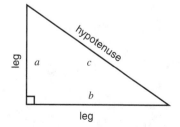

The *Pythagorean Theorem* expresses the relationship among the sides of any right triangle (*a* and *b* are the two legs, and *c* is the hypotenuse):

$$a^2 + b^2 = c^2$$

With any right triangle, if you know the length of two sides, you can determine the length of the third side with the Theorem.

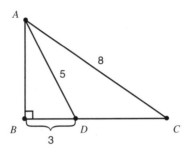

In the figure above, what is the area of $\triangle ABC$?

(A) $4\sqrt{3}$

(B) $\dfrac{15\sqrt{2}}{2}$

(C) $8\sqrt{3}$

(D) 14

(E) 16

The correct answer is (**C**). Don't be intimidated by complex problems such as this one. You already have the tools to solve the problem. First determine what values you need to know to answer the question, then perform the steps to find each of those values. To calculate the area of $\triangle ABC$, you need to know its base (*BC*) and its height (*AB*). Determine *AB* by applying the Pythagorean Theorem to $\triangle ABD$:

$$3^2 + (AB)^2 = 5^2$$
$$(AB)^2 = 25 - 9$$
$$(AB)^2 = 16$$
$$AB = 4$$

8

Now find *BC* by applying the Theorem again, this time to $\triangle ABC$:

$$4^2 + (BC)^2 = 8^2$$
$$(BC)^2 = 64 - 16$$
$$(BC)^2 = 48$$
$$BC = \sqrt{48}, \text{ or } 4\sqrt{3}$$

Now you can find the area of $\triangle ABC$:

$$\text{Area of } \triangle ABC = \frac{1}{2} \cdot 4\sqrt{3} \cdot 4 = 8\sqrt{3}$$

 CAUTION

> The Pythagorean Theorem applies only to *right* triangles, not to any others. Never apply the Theorem unless you're sure the triangle includes a 90° angle; and never try to calculate a triangle's area using the length of one side as the altitude unless you're sure the side is one of two that forms a right angle!

Pythagorean Triplets

A Pythagorean triplet is a specific ratio among the sides of a triangle that satisfies the Pythagorean Theorem. In each of the following triplets, the first two numbers represent the relative lengths of the two legs, whereas the third—and largest—number represents the relative length of the hypotenuse (the first four appear far more frequently on the GRE than the last two):

ratio:	Theorem
$1:1:\sqrt{2}$	$1^2 + 1^2 = (\sqrt{2})^2$
$1:\sqrt{3}:2$	$1^2 + (\sqrt{3})^2 = 2^2$
3:4:5	$3^2 + 4^2 = 5^2$
5:12:13	$5^2 + 12^2 = 13^2$
8:15:17	$8^2 + 15^2 = 17^2$
7:24:25	$7^2 + 24^2 = 25^2$

Each triplet above is expressed as a *ratio* because it represents the relative proportion of the triangle's sides. All right triangles with sides having the same ratio or proportion have the same shape. For example, a right triangle with sides of 5, 12, and 13 is smaller but exactly the same shape (proportion) as a triangle with sides of 15, 36, and 39.

To save valuable time on GRE right triangle problems, learn to recognize given numbers (lengths of triangle sides) as multiples of Pythagorean triplets. In the previous Problem Solving question, for instance, you could have saved time by recognizing that △*ABD* is a 3:4:5 triangle.

QUESTION Two boats leave the same dock at the same time, one traveling at 10 miles per hour and the other traveling due north at 24 miles per hour. How many miles apart are the boats after three hours?

(A) 68

(B) 72

(C) 88

(D) 98

(E) 110

ANALYSIS The correct answer is **(D)**. The distance between the two boats after three hours forms the hypotenuse of a triangle in which the legs are the two boats' respective paths. The ratio of one leg to the other is 10:24, or 5:12. So you know you're dealing with a 5:12:13 triangle. The slower boat traveled 30 miles (10 mph × 3 hours). 30 corresponds to the number 5 in the 5:12:13 ratio, so the multiple is 6 (5 × 6 = 30). 5:12:13 = 30:72:98.

Other Special Right Triangles

In two (and only two) of the unique triangles we've identified as Pythagorean triplets, *all degree measures are integers:*

1. The corresponding angles opposite the sides of a $1{:}1{:}\sqrt{2}$ triangle are 45°, 45°, and 90°.

2. The corresponding angles opposite the sides of a $1{:}\sqrt{3}{:}2$ triangle are 30°, 60°, and 90°.

This next figure shows these two angle triplets and their corresponding side triplets.

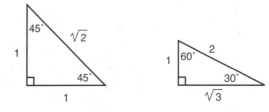

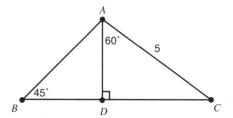

QUESTION In the figure above, what is the length of *AB*?

(A) $\dfrac{3\sqrt{3}}{2}$

(B) $\dfrac{7}{3}$

(C) $\dfrac{5\sqrt{2}}{3}$

(D) $2\sqrt{2}$

(E) $\dfrac{7}{2}$

ANALYSIS The correct answer is (**C**). To find the length of *AB*, you first need to find *AD* and *BD*. The angles of $\triangle ADC$ are 30°, 60°, and 90°. So you know that the ratio among its sides is $1 : \sqrt{3} : 2$. Given that $AC = 5$, $AD = \dfrac{5}{2}$ ($1:2 = \dfrac{5}{2}:5$). Next, you should recognize $\triangle ABD$ as a 45°–45°–90° triangle. The ratio among its sides is $1 : 1 : \sqrt{2}$. You know that $AD = \dfrac{5}{2}$. Accordingly, $AB = \dfrac{5\sqrt{2}}{3}$

NOTE Two 45°-45°-90° triangles pieced together form a square, and two 30°-60°-90° triangles together form an equilateral triangle. This amazing phenomenon fascinates the test-makers, so it should interest you as well. (We'll look closer at equilateral triangles and at squares in just a bit.)

Isosceles Triangles

An *isosceles* triangle has the following two special properties:

1. Two of the sides are congruent (equal in length).
2. The two angles opposite the two congruent sides are congruent (equal in size, or degree measure).
3. A line that bisects the angle formed by the equal sides bisects the opposite side.

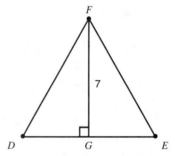

QUESTION   If the area of $\triangle DEF$ in the figure above is 21, and if $\triangle FDG$ has the same area as $\triangle FEG$, what is the length of *EF*?

(A) $\dfrac{10\sqrt{2}}{3}$

(B) $\dfrac{7\sqrt{3}}{2}$

(C) $\sqrt{51}$

(D) $4\sqrt{3}$

(E) $\sqrt{58}$

ANALYSIS   The correct answer is (**E**). The area is given as 21, and the height is 7. To find *EF*, first determine *DE* (the triangle's base, or *b*):

$$A = \frac{1}{2}(b)(h)$$
$$21 = \frac{1}{2}(b)(7)$$
$$b = 6$$

Because the triangle is isosceles, *FG* bisects *DE*. So use $\frac{1}{2}b$ as a leg of either of two right triangles, *DFG* or *FEG*, and apply the Pythagorean Theorem to find *EF*.

8

$(EF)^2 = 3^2 + 7^2$

$(EF)^2 = 9 + 49 = 58$

$EF = \sqrt{58}$

Equilateral Triangles

An equilateral triangle has the following three properties:

1. All three sides are congruent (equal in length)

2. All three angles are 60°

3. The area = $\dfrac{s^2 \sqrt{3}}{4}$ (s = any side)

Any line bisecting one of the 60° angles divides an equilateral triangle into two right triangles with angle measures of 30°, 60°, and 90°; in other words, into two 1:$\sqrt{3}$:2 triangles. (Remember the Pythagorean angle triplet a few pages back?)

	Column A	Column B

QUESTION

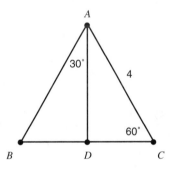

The area of △*ABC* $4\sqrt{3}$

ANALYSIS   The correct answer is (**D**). The area of △*ABC* = $4\sqrt{3}$ if the triangle is equilateral. However, you don't know whether the two smaller triangles are both 30°-60°-90° (1:$\sqrt{3}$:2) triangles. If you were informed that ∠*DAC* were 30°, or that ∠*ABC* were 60°, or that *AD* ⊥ *BC*, then △*ABC* would be equilateral, and the two quantities would be equal. But the problem does not provide any such information.

NOTE   On the GRE, you might also encounter equilateral triangles in problems involving *circles* (one of next hour's topics).

Quadrilaterals

A *quadrilateral* is a four-sided figure. Here are the specific types of quadrilaterals you should know for the GRE:

1. square
2. rectangle
3. parallelogram
4. rhombus
5. trapezoid

Each of these five figures has its own properties (characteristics) that should be second nature to by the time you take the GRE. The two most important properties are:

Area (the surface covered by the figure on a plane)

Perimeter (the total length of all sides)

 NOTE   All quadrilaterals share one important property: The sum of the four interior angles of any quadrilateral is 360°.

The Square

This next figure shows a square. All squares share these properties:

1. All four sides are equal in length
2. All four angles are right angles (90°)
3. The sum of all four angles is 360°
4. Perimeter = $4s$
5. Area = s^2

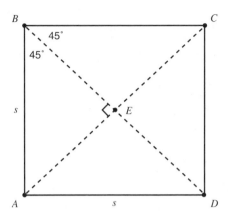

When you add diagonals to a square (dotted lines above), you create these additional relationships:

1. Diagonals are equal in length ($AC = BD$).

2. Diagonals are perpendicular; their intersection creates four right angles.

3. Diagonals bisect each 90° angle of the square; that is, they split each angle into two equal (45°) angles.

4. Divide the square of either diagonal by 2 to obtain square's area:

    $$\text{Area of square} = \frac{(AC)^2}{2} \text{ or } \frac{(BD)^2}{2}$$

    This formula applies only to squares, not to other quadrilaterals!

5. Diagonals create four distinct congruent (the same shape and size) triangles, each having an area $\frac{1}{2}$ the area of the square: $\triangle ABD$, $\triangle ACD$, $\triangle ABC$, and $\triangle BCD$. Each triangle is a $1{:}1{:}\sqrt{2}$ triangle, with 45°-45°-90° angles.

6. Diagonals create four distinct congruent triangles, each having an area $\frac{1}{4}$ the area of the square: $\triangle ABE$, $\triangle BCE$, $\triangle CDE$, and $\triangle ADE$. Each triangle is a $1{:}1{:}\sqrt{2}$ triangle, with 45°–45°–90° angles.

Rectangles

This next figure shows a rectangle. All rectangles share these properties:

1. Opposite sides are equal in length

2. All four angles are right angles (90°)

3. The sum of all four angles is 360°

4. Perimeter $= 2l + 2w$

5. Area $= l \times w$

6. The maximum area of a rectangle with a given perimeter is a square

7. The minimum perimeter of a rectangle with a given area is a square

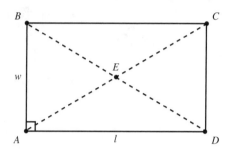

Here's what happens when you add diagonals to a rectangle (refer to the figure above):

1. Diagonals are equal in length ($AC = BD$)

2. Diagonals bisect each other ($AE = BE = CE = DE$)

3. Diagonals are *not* perpendicular (unless the rectangle is a square)

4. Diagonals do *not* bisect each 90° angle of the rectangle (unless the rectangle is a square)

5. Diagonals create four distinct congruent triangles, each having an area $\frac{1}{2}$ the area of the rectangle: $\triangle ABD$, $\triangle ACD$, $\triangle ABC$, and $\triangle BCD$

6. $\triangle ABE$ is congruent to $\triangle CDE$; both triangles are isosceles (but they are right triangles *only* if the rectangle is a square)

7. $\triangle BEC$ is congruent to $\triangle AED$; both triangles are isosceles (but they are right triangles *only* if the rectangle is a square)

8. The area of each of the four small triangles is $\frac{1}{4}$ the area of the rectangle

Diagonals of rectangles are *not* perpendicular and do *not* bisect each 90° angle of the rectangle—*unless* the rectangle is a square (in which case they do both).

A typical GRE rectangle question will also involve one or more triangles.

QUESTION A farmer uses 140 feet of fencing to enclose a rectangular field. If the ratio of length to width is 3 : 4, what is the distance in feet from one corner of the field diagonally to the opposite corner?

(A) 40

(B) $25\sqrt{3}$

(C) 45

(D) 50

(E) $\dfrac{65\sqrt{3}}{2}$

ANALYSIS The correct answer is (**D**). Given a 3:4 ratio, you can express the perimeter of the field in this manner:

$$2(3x) + 2(4x) = 140$$
$$14x = 140$$
$$x = 10$$

The field's dimensions are 30' × 40'. You should recognize each triangle created by the diagonal as a 3:4:5 right triangle, with a diagonal (hypotenuse) of 50.

Parallelograms

The next figure shows a parallelogram. All parallelograms share these properties:

1. Opposite sides are parallel

2. Opposite sides are equal in length

3. Opposite angles are congruent (the same size, or equal in degree measure)

4. The sum of all four angles is 360°

5. All four angles are congruent *only* if the parallelogram is a rectangle—that is, if the angles are right angles

6. Perimeter = $2l + 2w$

7. Area = base (b) × altitude (a)

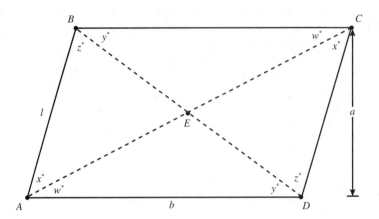

Here's what happens when you add diagonals to a parallelogram (refer to the figure above):

1. Diagonals bisect each other (*BE = ED*, *CE = AE*)
2. Diagonals (*AC* and *BD*) are *not* equal in length (unless the figure is a rectangle)
3. Diagonals are *not* perpendicular (unless the figure is a square or rhombus)
4. Diagonals do *not* bisect each angle of the parallelogram (unless it is a square or rhombus)
5. Diagonals create two pairs of congruent triangles, each having an area $\frac{1}{2}$ the area of the parallelogram: $\triangle ABD$ is congruent to $\triangle BCD$, and $\triangle ACD$ is congruent to $\triangle ABC$
6. $\triangle ABE$ is congruent to $\triangle CED$ (they are mirror-imaged horizontally *and* vertically); the triangles are isosceles only if the quadrilateral is a rectangle
7. $\triangle BEC$ is congruent to $\triangle AED$ (they are mirror-imaged horizontally *and* vertically); the triangles are isosceles only if the quadrilateral is a rectangle
8. The area of each of the small triangles is $\frac{1}{4}$ the area of the parallelogram.

| CAUTION | Diagonals of a parallelogram are not perpendicular and do *not* bisect each angle of the parallelogram—*unless* the parallelogram is either a square or rhombus (in which case they do both). |

The Rhombus

The next figure shows a rhombus. All rhombuses share these properties:

1. All sides are equal in length.
2. Opposite sides are parallel.
3. The sum of all four angles is $360°$
4. No angles are right angles (angle measures $\neq 90°$).
5. Perimeter $= 4s$.
6. Area $=$ side $(s) \times$ altitude (a).

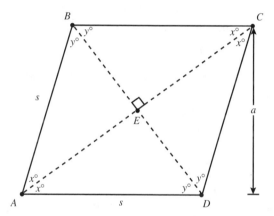

Here's what happens when you add diagonals (AC and BD) to a rhombus (refer to the figure above):

1. Area of the rhombus $= \frac{AC \times BC}{2}$ ($\frac{1}{2}$ the product of the diagonals); this formula applies to a rhombus and a square, but not to any other quadrilaterals!
2. Diagonals bisect each other ($BE = ED$, $AE = EC$)
3. Diagonals are perpendicular (their intersection creates four right angles)
4. Diagonals are *not* equal in length ($AC \neq BD$)
5. Diagonals bisect each angle of the rhombus
6. Diagonals create four *congruent* (the same shape and size) isosceles triangles, each triangle having an area $\frac{1}{2}$ the area of the rhombus; none of these four triangles are right triangles
7. Diagonals create four congruent (the same shape and size) triangles, each with an area $\frac{1}{4}$ the area of the rhombus.

> **TIP**
>
> Every square is a rhombus, so if you know the diagonal of a square, you can apply the rhombus formula (the diagonals of a square are equal):
>
> Area of a square = $\left(\frac{1}{2}\right)$(diagonal)(diagonal)

Trapezoids

This next figure shows a trapezoid. All trapezoids share these properties:

1. Only one pair of opposite sides are parallel ($BC \parallel AD$)
2. The sum of all four interior angles is $360°$
3. Perimeter $= AB + BC + CD + AD$
4. Area $= \dfrac{BC + AD}{2} \times$ altitude (a)

   (one-half the sum of the two parallel sides multiplied by the altitude)

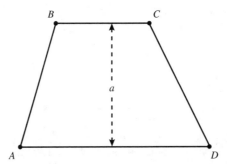

No predictable patterns emerge from the addition of two diagonals to a trapezoid.

8

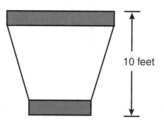

10 feet

QUESTION To cover the floor of an entry hall, a strip of carpet one foot wide and twelve feet long is cut into two pieces, shown as the shaded strips in the figure above, and each piece is connected to a third carpet piece as shown. If the two strips run parallel to each other, what is the total area of the floor?

(A) 44

(B) 48

(C) 54

(D) 56

(E) 60

ANALYSIS The correct answer is (**E**). The altitude of the trapezoidal piece is 8. The sum of the two parallel sides of this piece is 12' (the length of the 1' × 12' strip before it was cut). You can apply the trapezoid formula to determine the area of this piece:

$$A = (8)\left(\frac{12}{2}\right) = 48$$

The total area of the two shaded strips is 12, so the total area of the floor is 60.

Workshop

In this hour's Workshop, you'll tackle a 10-question GRE-style quiz, designed for you to review and apply the concepts and question types you learned about this hour.

Additional Quantitative questions are available on-line, at the authors' Web site: *http://www.west.net/~stewart/gre*

Quiz

(Answers and explanations begin on page 165.)

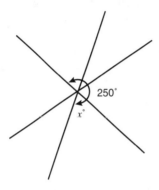

1. In the figure above, what is the value of *x*?

   (A) 50
   (B) 55
   (C) 60
   (D) 70
   (E) 80

   (Hint: The total degree measure of all angles with a common vertex is 360°.)

2. In triangle *ABC*, *AB* is the same length as *BC*. If the degree measure of the interior angle at point *B* is *b*°, which of the following represents the degree measure of the interior angle at point *A*?

   (A) *b*
   (B) $180 - b$
   (C) $180 - \dfrac{b}{2}$

   (D) $90 - \dfrac{b}{2}$
   (E) $90 - b$

   (Hint: The triangle is isosceles.)

3. In a parallelogram with an area of 15, the base is represented by $x + 7$ and the altitude is $x - 7$. What is the length of the parallelogram's base?

   (A) 1
   (B) 5
   (C) 8
   (D) 15
   (E) 34

   (Hint: The area of a parallelogram is the product of its base and altitude.)

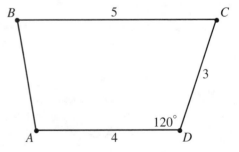

4. What is the area of trapezoid *ABCD* in the above figure?

(A) $5\sqrt{2}$

(B) $\dfrac{9\sqrt{3}}{2}$

(C) $\dfrac{27\sqrt{3}}{4}$

(D) $13\dfrac{1}{2}$

(E) 16

(Hint: The area of a trapezoid is $\frac{1}{2}$ the product of the sum of the two parallel sides.)

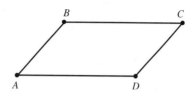

5. In parallelogram *ABCD* in the figure above, ∠*B* is 5 times as large as ∠*C*. What is the degree measure of ∠*B*?

   (A) 30
   (B) 60
   (C) 100
   (D) 120
   (E) 150

   (Hint: The sum of the four interior angles of any parallelogram is 360°.)

Questions 6–10 are Quantatative Comparisons.

Column A	Column B

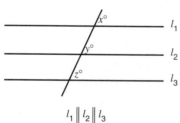

$l_1 \parallel l_2 \parallel l_3$

6.　　　$x + y$　　　　　$y + z$

(Hint: corresponding angles formed by a transversal are congruent if the other two lines are parallel.)

Column A	Column B

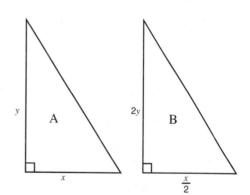

7.　Area of triangle A　　Area of triangle B

(Hint: Apply the formula for the area of a triangle to each quantity.)

Column A	Column B

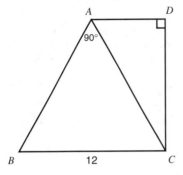

8. 12 side *CD*

(Hint: The relative lengths of a triangle's sides correspond to relative sizes of angles opposite the sides.)

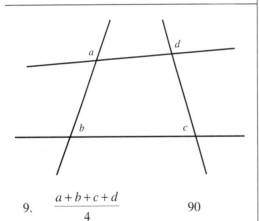

9. $\dfrac{a+b+c+d}{4}$ 90

(Hint: Opposite angles are congruent.)

Column A	Column B

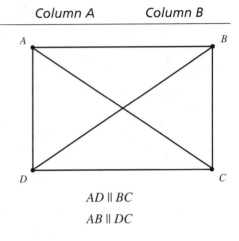

AD ∥ *BC*

AB ∥ *DC*

10. one fourth the area of *ABDC* one half the area of △*ADC*

(Hint: Recall the properties that distinguish a rectangle from other parallelograms.)

Answers and Explanations

1. **(D)** The two angles not part of the 250° arc total 110°. Together with angle x, these two angles form a straight line. Thus, $x = 70$.

2. **(D)** The triangle is isosceles, so $\angle A = \angle C$. Letting a, b, and c represent the degree measures of $\angle A$, $\angle B$, and $\angle C$, respectively, solve for a:

$$a + c + b = 180$$
$$a + b = 180 \ [a = c]$$
$$a = \frac{180}{2} - \frac{b}{2}$$
$$a = 90 - \frac{b}{2}$$

3. **(D)** The area of a parallelogram = (base)(altitude):

$$(x + 7)(x - 7) = 15$$
$$x^2 - 49 = 15$$
$$x^2 = 64$$
$$x = 8$$
$$\text{base} = x + 7 = 15$$

4. **(C)** The area of a trapezoid is $\frac{1}{2}$ the product of the sum of the two parallel sides $(BC + AD)$ and the trapezoid's height. To determine the trapezoid's height, form a right triangle, as shown in the figure below. This right triangle conforms to the 30-60-90 Pythagorean angle triplet. Thus, the ratio of the three sides is $1 : \sqrt{3} : 2$. The hypotenuse is given as 3, so the height is

$\frac{3\sqrt{3}}{2}$. Calculate the area of the trapezoid is as follows:

$$\frac{1}{2}(4 + 5) \cdot \frac{3\sqrt{3}}{2} = \frac{9}{2} \cdot \frac{3\sqrt{3}}{2} = \frac{27\sqrt{3}}{4}$$

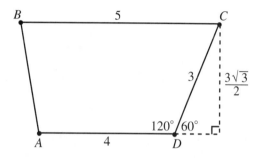

5. **(E)** The sum of the angles in a parallelogram is 360°. $\angle B$ and $\angle C$ together account for half the sum, or 180°. Letting x equal the degree measure of angle C:

$$5x + x = 180$$
$$6x = 180$$
$$x = 30$$
$$\angle B = 5x = (5)(30) = 150$$

6. **(C)** Since there are three parallel lines, the corresponding angles are equal. If x, y and z are all the same, then $x + y$ must equal $y + z$.

7. **(C)** Triangle B has a height that is double that of Triangle A; it has a base that is half that of Triangle A. This will result in the two triangles having the same area.

8. (**A**) Notice the right angle at $\angle BAC$. Side *BC* must be the longest side since it is opposite the largest angle. Since $\angle ADC$ is also a right angle, side *AC* must be longer than *CD*.

9. (**C**) Since the opposite angles are the same size, angles *a* and *d* can be moved inside the quadrilateral. All quadrilaterals contain 360 degrees. 360 divided by 4 is 90.

10. (**C**) Since *ABCD* is a parallelogram, the area of $\triangle ADC$ must be half that of *ABCD*. It follows that one half the area of $\triangle ADC$ equals one fourth the area of *ABCD*.

HOUR 9

Teach Yourself Geometry II

This hour you'll continue to teach yourself geometry, focusing on problems involving polygons with five or more sides, circles, three-dimensional figures, and the coordinate plane. In this hour you will learn:

- How to determine angle sizes of any polygon
- The characteristics of any circle, and the relationship between a circle's radius, diameter, circumference, and area
- How to apply the area and circumference formulas to GRE circle questions
- How to handle hybrid problems, which combine circles with other geometric figures
- How to determine surface area and volume of rectangular solids, cubes, and right cylinders
- The relationship between the edges, faces, and volume of any rectangular solid
- How to solve coordinate geometry problems

Polygons

Last hour you concentrated on three-sided polygons (triangles) and four-sided polygons (quadrilaterals). Now let's look at polygons having more than four sides. Consider these two:

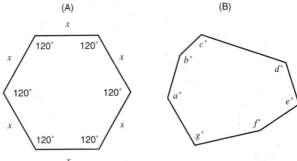

In polygon (A), which has six sides, notice that all angles are congruent (the same size) and that all sides are congruent (the same length). For the GRE, remember these two rules about sides and angles of polygons:

1. If all angles of a polygon are congruent (the same size), then all sides are congruent (equal in length).

2. If all sides of a polygon are congruent (the same length), then all angles are congruent (equal in size).

 NOTE   A polygon in which all sides are congruent and all angles are congruent is called a *regular* polygon. A regular triangle is equilateral; a regular quadrilateral is square. (For the GRE, you don't need to know the terminology—just the principle.)

You can use the following formula to determine the sum of all interior angles of *any* polygon, regular or otherwise (n = number of sides):

$(n - 2)(180°)$ = sum of interior angles

This formula applies to irregular polygons, such as (B) above, as well as regular polygons such as (A) above. You can find the average size of the angles by dividing the sum by the number of sides. For regular polygons, the average angle size is also the size of every angle.

QUESTION

Column A	Column B

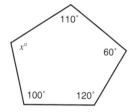

x 140

ANALYSIS The correct answer is (**A**). Since the figure has 5 sides, it contains 540 degrees:

$180(5 - 2) = 540$

The sum of the five angles is 540, so solve for x:

$540 = x + 110 + 60 + 120 + 100$

$540 = x + 390$

$150 = x$

Circles

A *circle* is the set of all points that lie equidistant from the same point (the circle's *center*) on a plane. For the GRE, you should know the following terms involving circles:

radius: the distance from a circle's center to any point on the circle

diameter: the greatest distance from one point to another on the circle

chord: a line segment connecting two points on the circle

circumference: the distance around the circle (its "perimeter")

arc: a segment of a circle's circumference (an arc can be defined either as a length or as a degree measure)

Properties of a Circle

There are 6 properties of any circle that you should know for the GRE:

1. Every point on a circle's circumference is equidistant from the circle's center.
2. The total number of degrees of all angles formed from the circle's center is 360.
3. Diameter is twice the radius

4. Circumference $= 2\pi r$, or πd

5. Area $= \pi r^2$, or $\frac{\pi d^2}{4}$

6. The longest possible chord of a circle passes through its center and is the circle's diameter.

With the area and circumference formulas, you can determine a circle's area, circumference, diameter, and radius, as long as you know just one of these four values.

 NOTE The value of π is approximately 3.14, or $\frac{22}{7}$. On the GRE, you probably won't have to work with a value for π any more precise than "a little over 3". In fact, in most circle problems, the solution is expressed in terms of π rather than numerically.

GRE circle problems almost always involve other geometric figures as well, as you're about to see.

Circles with Triangles Inside of Them

One common type of GRE circle problem is a "hybrid" involving a circle and a triangle. Look for any of the following three varieties on the GRE:

1. A *right* triangle with one vertex at the circle's center and the other two on the circumference ($\triangle ABO$ in the next figure).

   Given either that $\angle AOB = 90°$ or that $AB = r\sqrt{2}$, here's what else you know about $\triangle ABO$ (r = radius):

   - $AO = r$, and $OB = r$ (OA and OB each equal the circle's radius)
   - $AO = OB$ ($\triangle ABO$ is a right isosceles triangle)
   - $\angle OAB = \angle OBA = 45°$
   - AB (the hypotenuse) $= r\sqrt{2}$, because the ratio of the triangle's sides is $1:1:\sqrt{2}$
   - Area of $\triangle ABO = \frac{r^2}{2}$

2. An *equilateral* triangle with one vertex at the circle's center and the other two on the circumference ($\triangle ODC$ in the next figure).

   Given either that $\angle DOC = 60°$ or that $DC = r$, you know that $\triangle ODC$ is equilateral ($OD = OC = DC = r$, all angles are $60°$)

3. A triangle *inscribed* inside a circle (all three vertices lie on the circle's circumference) in which one side equals the circle's diameter ($\triangle FGH$ in the next figure).

   $\triangle FGH$ must be a right triangle (it must include one 90° angle)—regardless where point G lies on the circle's circumference. If you don't believe it, go ahead and draw some more triangles, moving G around the circumference. (We know you will, anyway.)

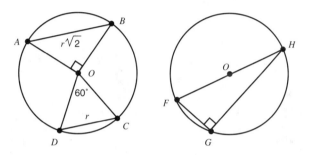

9

QUESTION

Column A	Column B

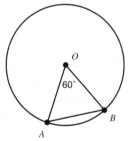

Point O lies at the center of the circle.

The length of AB The radius of circle O

ANALYSIS The correct answer is **(C)**. $\triangle OAB$ is equilateral (all angle measures are equal, and all sides are equal). OA, as well as OB, is the length of the circle's radius. Thus, AB must be the same length as the radius.

Squares Inside Circles (and Vice Versa)

Another common type of GRE circle problem is a hybrid involving a circle and a square. Look for either:

1. A circle with an *inscribed* square (left-hand figure below)
2. A circle with a *circumscribed* square (right-hand figure below)

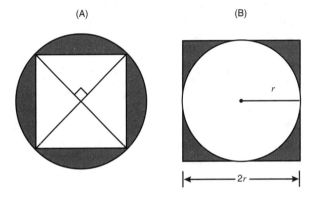

In either case, the square touches the circle at four and only four points. Here are the characteristics that emerge in each of these two figures:

In the left-hand figure:

   Each of the four small triangles formed by the diagonals is a $1:1:\sqrt{2}$ triangle.

   In each of the four small triangles, the ratio of the hypotenuse (same as the side of the square) to the legs (same as circle's radius) is $\sqrt{2}:1$.

   The area of a square inscribed in a circle is $\left(r\sqrt{2}\right)^2$, or $2r^2$.

   The ratio of the inscribed square's area to the circle's area is $2:\pi$.

   The *difference* between the two areas—the total shaded area—is $\pi r^2 - 2r^2$.

   The area of each crescent-shaped shaded area is $\frac{1}{4}\left(\pi r^2 - 2r^2\right)$.

In the right-hand figure:

   Each side of the square is $2r$ in length.

   The square's area is $(2r)^2$, or $4r^2$.

   The ratio of the square's area to that of the inscribed circle is $\frac{4}{\pi}:1$.

   The *difference* between the two areas—the total shaded area—is $4r^2 - \pi r^2$, or $r^2(4-\pi)$

The area of each separate (smaller) shaded area is $\frac{1}{4}$ of the difference identified above. Because each side of the square is tangent to the circle, it is *perpendicular* to a line segment from the tangent point (where the line segment touches the circle) to the circle's center.

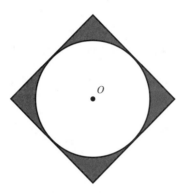

QUESTION If the area of circle O in the figure above is 64π, what is the perimeter of the square?

(A) 16

(B) 32

(C) 64

(D) 32π

(E) 64π

ANALYSIS The correct answer is **(C)**. The area of the circle = $64\pi = r^2\pi$. Thus, the radius of the circle = 8. The side of the square is 16—twice the circle's radius. Therefore, the perimeter of the square is $4 \times 16 = 64$.

Comparing Circles

A third type of circle problem calls for you to compare circles. The relationship between a circle's radius and area is exponential, not linear (because $A = \pi r^2$). So if one circle's radius is *twice* that of another's (as in the left-hand figure on page 174), the ratio of the circles' areas is 1:4 $\left(\pi r^2 : \pi (2r)^2\right)$. If the larger circle's radius is *three* times the length of that of the smaller circle (as in the right-hand figure on page 174), the ratio is 1:9 $\left(\pi r^2 : \pi (3r)^2\right)$. A 1:4 ratio between radii results in a 1:16 area ratio (and so forth).

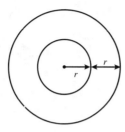 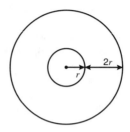

 QUESTION If a circle whose radius is x has an area of 4, what is the area of a circle whose radius is $3x$?

   (A) $\sqrt{13}$

   (B) $4\sqrt{13}$

   (C) 12

   (D) 36

   (E) 144

ANALYSIS The correct answer is **(D)**. The area of a circle is πr^2. The area of a circle with a radius of x is πx^2, which is given as 4. The area of a circle with radius $3x$ is $\pi (3x)^2 = 9\pi x^2$. Therefore, the area of the larger circle is 9 times the area of the smaller circle.

> **TIP**
>
> A GRE question might call for you to determine the difference in area, a segment of the area, or circumference of two circles, given their radii. No sweat! Just calculate each area (or circumference), then subtract.

Solids

If you understand how to determine areas of two-dimensional figures such as rectangles, triangles, and circles, you won't have any trouble handling problems involving three-dimensional objects—or *solids*. For the GRE, you should know these three basic shapes:

1. Rectangular solids (boxes)
2. Cubes
3. Cylinders (tubes)

The following figure summarizes the formulas for determining surface area (*SA*) and volume (*V*). Memorize these formulas!

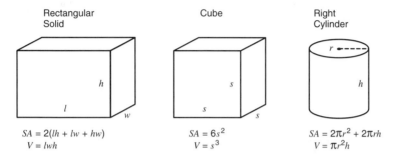

Rectangular Solid

$SA = 2(lh + lw + hw)$
$V = lwh$

Cube

$SA = 6s^2$
$V = s^3$

Right Cylinder

$SA = 2\pi r^2 + 2\pi rh$
$V = \pi r^2 h$

 NOTE

On the GRE, pyramids appear occasionally as well, but far less frequently than the other three solids. Also, notice that globes (balls) and cones are missing from this list; that's because they're not covered on the GRE.

Rectangular Solids

The volume (*V*) of any rectangular solid (the left-hand solid in the figure above) is the product of its three dimensions: length, width, and height.

Volume = length × width × height

$V = lwh$

Each of three pairs of opposing faces are identical; in other words, they have the same dimensions and area. So the surface area of any rectangular solid can be expressed as follows:

Surface Area = $2lh + 2lw + 2hw = 2(lh + lw + hw)$

QUESTION A rectangular box with a square base contains 24 cubic feet. If the height of the box is 18 inches, how long is each edge of the base?

(A) 4

(B) 6

(C) 8

(D) 12

(E) 16

ANALYSIS The correct answer is **(A)**. The volume of a rectangular box is the product of its length, width, and height. Since the height is 18 inches, or $1\frac{1}{2}$ feet, and the length and width of the square base are the same, we can use the same variable (such as x) to represent l and w in the volume formula, then solve for x:

$$x \cdot x \cdot 1\frac{1}{2} = 24$$
$$x^2 = 16$$
$$x = 4$$

Cubes

A *cube* (the middle solid in the preceding figure) is a special type of rectangular solid in which all six faces, or surfaces, are square. Because all six faces of a cube are identical in dimension and area, given a length s of one of a cube's sides—or edges—its surface area is six times the square of s, and its volume is the cube of s:

Surface Area = $6s^2$

Volume = s^3

Here's the relationship between the area of each square face of a cube and the cube's volume:

$$\text{Volume} = \left(\sqrt{\text{Area}}\right)^3$$
$$\text{Area} = \left(\sqrt[3]{\text{Volume}}\right)^2$$

QUESTION Find the edge, in inches, of a cube whose volume is equal to the volume of a rectangular solid 2 inches by 6 inches by 18 inches.

(A) 4

(B) 6

(C) 8

(D) 9

(E) 12

ANALYSIS The correct answer is **(B)**. First, determine the volume of the rectangular solid:

$$V = l \cdot w \cdot h = 2 \cdot 6 \cdot 18 = 216$$

Equate this volume with the volume of the cube and solve for s (the length of any edge of the cube):

$$V = s^3$$
$$216 = s^3$$
$$6 = s$$

Cylinders

The right-hand solid in the figure on page 175 is a "right" circular cylinder (the tube is sliced at 90° angles). This is the only kind of cylinder you need to know for the GRE. The *surface area* of a right cylinder can be determined by adding together three areas:

1. the circular base
2. the circular top
3. the rectangular surface around the cylinder's vertical face (visualize a rectangular label wrapped around a soup can)

The area of the vertical face is the product of the circular base's circumference (i.e., the rectangle's width) and the cylinder's height. Thus, given a radius r and height h of a cylinder:

$$\text{Surface Area } (SA) = 2\pi r^2 + (2\pi r)(h)$$

Given a cylinder's radius and height, you can determine its *volume* by multiplying the area of its circular base by its height:

$$V = \pi r^2 h$$

QUESTION A certain cylindrical pail has a diameter of 14 inches and a height of 10 inches. If there are 231 cubic inches in a gallon, which of the following most closely approximates the number of gallons the pail will hold?

(A) 4.8

(B) 5.1

(C) 6.7

(D) 14.6

(E) 44

ANALYSIS The correct answer is **(C)**. The volume of the cylindrical pail is equal to the area of its circular base multiplied by its height:

$$V = \pi r^2 h = \left(\frac{22}{7}\right)(49)(10) = 1540 \text{ cubic inches}$$

The gallon capacity of the pail $= \frac{1540}{231}$, or about 6.7.

Coordinate Geometry

On the GRE, you're likely to encounter one or two *coordinate geometry* questions, which involve the rectangular *coordinate plane* (or *xy*-plane) defined by two axes—a horizontal *x*-axis and a vertical *y*-axis. You can define any point on the coordinate plane by using two coordinates: an *x-coordinate* and a *y-coordinate*. A point's *x*-coordinate is its horizontal position on the plane, and its *y*-coordinate is its vertical position on the plane. You denote the coordinates of a point with (*x,y*), where *x* is the point's *x*-coordinate and *y* is the point's *y*-coordinate.

Coordinate Signs and the Four Quadrants

The center of the coordinate plane—the intersection of the *x* and *y* axes—is called the *origin*. The coordinates of the origin are (0,0). Any point along the *x*-axis has a *y*-coordinate of 0 (*x*,0), and any point along the *y*-axis has an *x*-coordinate of 0 (0,*y*). The coordinate signs (positive or negative) of points lying in the four quadrants I–IV in this next figure are as follows:

Quadrant I (+,+)

Quadrant II (–,+)

Quadrant III (–,–)

Quadrant IV (+,–)

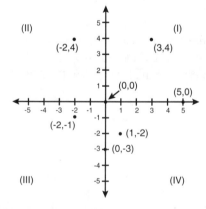

Notice that we've plotted seven different points on this plane. Each point has its own unique coordinates. Before you read on, make sure you understand why each point is identified (by two coordinates) as it is.

Coordinate Triangle Problems

GRE coordinate geometry problems can involve any 2-dimensional geometric figures you examined in this hour or the last one. But they usually involve either triangles, circles, or both. In triangle problems, your task is usually to determine the length of a sloping line segment (by forming a right triangle and applying the Pythagorean Theorem).

QUESTION On the *xy*-plane, what is the length of a line segment with end points defined by the (*x,y*) coordinate pairs (−2,−1) and (3,4)?

(A) 4

(B) 5

(C) $4\sqrt{2}$

(D) 6

(E) $5\sqrt{2}$

9

ANALYSIS The correct answer is **(E)**. On the coordinate plane, construct a right triangle with the line segment as the hypotenuse. The length of the horizontal leg is 5 (the horizontal distance from −2 to 3). The length of the vertical leg is also 5 (the vertical distance from −1 to 4). So you're dealing with an isosceles right triangle. The ratios of the lengths of the three sides is $1:1:\sqrt{2}$. Since each leg (either of the short sides) is 5 in length, the length of the hypotenuse is $5\sqrt{2}$. The upper triangle in the following diagram illustrates the solution:

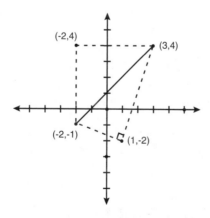

QUESTION On the *xy*-plane, what is the area of a triangle whose three vertices are defined by the (*x*,*y*) coordinate pairs (–2,–1), (3,4), and (1,–2)?

(A) 8

(B) 9

(C) 10

(D) 12

(E) 13

ANALYSIS The correct answer is (C). The information in this question establishes the lower triangle in the preceding diagram. The angle at point (1, –2) measures 90° because the slopes of the two dotted line segments are $-\frac{1}{3}$ and 3, so the segments are perpendicular. The base and height of the triangle are represented by the dotted lines. The area of the triangle is, of course, $\frac{1}{2}bh$. So we need to determine *b* and *h*. Think of *b* as the hypotenuse of a right triangle, this time with legs of 1 and 3 in length. Similarly, think of *h* as the hypotenuse of a right triangle whose legs are 2 and 6 in length. Do any of the convenient Pythagorean triplets allow us to shortcut applying the Pythagorean Theorem to determine each hypotenuse (the dotted line segments in the lower triangle)? No, not in either of these cases. So we need to find *b* and *h* the "long" way:

$$b^2 = 1^2 + 3^2$$
$$b^2 = 10$$
$$b = \sqrt{10}$$

$$h^2 = 2^2 + 6^2$$
$$h^2 = 40$$
$$h = \sqrt{40}, \text{ or } 2\sqrt{10}$$

We're not quite done. Now we need to plug these values into our formula for the area of a triangle:

$$\text{Area} = \frac{1}{2}\left(\sqrt{10}\right)\left(2\sqrt{10}\right)$$
$$\text{Area} = 10$$

Coordinate Circle Problems

In circle problems, your task is usually to determine the circumference or area of a circle lying on the plane. By now you know that triangles pervade the area of geometry, and coordinate-plane circle problems are no exception.

QUESTION   On the *xy*-plane, what is the area of a circle whose center is located at the point defined by the (*x*,*y*) coordinates (2,–1), if the point (–3,3) lies on the circle's circumference?

(A) 9π

(B) 75

(C) 25π

(D) 81

(E) 41π

ANALYSIS   The correct answer is (**C**). Construct a right triangle with the circle's radius as the hypotenuse. The length of the triangle's horizontal leg is 5 (the horizontal distance from –3 to 2), and the length of its vertical leg is 4 (the vertical distance from –1 to 3).

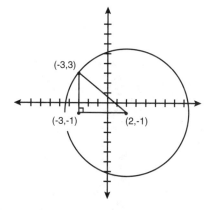

Be careful: These numbers do *not* conform to the Pythagorean triplet 3:4:5, because 4 and 5 are the lengths of the two *legs* here! Instead, you must calculate the length of the hypotenuse (the circle's radius) by applying the Pythagorean Theorem:

$$4^2 + 5^2 = r^2$$
$$16 + 25 = r^2$$
$$41 = r^2$$
$$\sqrt{41} = r$$

Now you can find the area of the circle:

$$\text{Area} = \pi\left(\sqrt{41}\right)^2$$
$$\text{Area} = 41\pi$$

Defining a Line on the Coordinate Plane

You can define any line on the coordinate plane with the following algebraic equation:

$y = mx + b$

In this equation:

    m is the slope of the line

    b is the y-intercept

    x and y are the coordinates of any point on the line

Any (x,y) pair defining a point on the line can substitute for the variables x and y in this equation. The constant b represents the line's *y-intercept* (the point on the y-axis where the line crosses that axis). The constant m represents the line's *slope*.

TIP

> Think of the slope of a line as a fraction in which the numerator indicates the vertical change from one point to another on the line (moving left to right) corresponding to a given horizontal change, which the fraction's denominator indicates. The common term used for this fraction is "rise-over-run."

Problems involving the algebraic equation for defining a line do *not* appear as frequently as the types we've already looked at. But you should be ready for one—just in case.

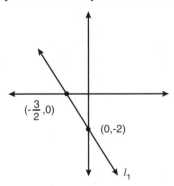

QUESTION Which of the following points lies on l_1 on the xy-plane pictured above?

(A) $\left(-\frac{3}{2}, -2\right)$

(B) $(4,6)$

(C) $\left(\frac{3}{8}, -\frac{3}{2}\right)$

(D) $\left(-\frac{8}{3}, 2\right)$

(E) $\left(-2, -\frac{3}{2}\right)$

ANALYSIS The correct answer is **(D)**. One way to handle this problem is to first determine the slope by using the two coordinate pairs $\left(-\frac{3}{2},0\right)$ and $(0,-2)$, then compare either point to each answer choice in turn to determine which choice gives you the same slope. An easier way, though, is to substitute each value pair into the equation $y = -\frac{3}{2}x - 2$. The only (x,y) pair that satisfies the equation is $\left(-\frac{8}{3},2\right)$, which is answer choice (D).

Workshop

In this hour's Workshop, you'll tackle a 10-question GRE-style quiz, designed for you to review and apply the concepts and question types you learned about this hour.

ONLINE | Additional Quantitative questions are available on-line, at the authors' Web site: *http://www.west.net/~stewart/gre*

Quiz

DIRECTIONS: Attempt the following 10 GRE-style questions. Try to limit your time to 15 minutes. For each question, you'll see one or two hints to help you if you're having trouble.

(Answers and explanations begin on page 186)

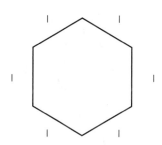

1. What is the area of the hexagon in the figure above?

   (A) $\dfrac{2\sqrt{3}}{3}$

   (B) $\sqrt{3}$

   (C) $\dfrac{3\sqrt{3}}{2}$

   (D) 4

   (E) $2\sqrt{2}+1$

   (Hint: Divide the polygon into rectangles and triangles.)

2. The length of an arc of a certain circle is one fifth the circumference of the circle. If the length of the arc is 2π, what is the radius of the circle?

(A) 1
(B) 2
(C) $\sqrt{10}$
(D) 5
(E) 10

(Hint: You can find the radius if you know the circumference.)

3. If the volume of one cube is 8 times greater than that of another, what is the ratio of the area of one square face of the larger cube to that of the smaller cube?

(A) 2:1
(B) 4:1
(C) 8:1
(D) 12:1
(E) 16:1

(Hint: The relationship between volume and area is not linear.)

4. In a particular 4-sided pyramid, each side of the square base is 50 feet in length. If the apex of the pyramid is 60 feet from the ground, what is the total surface area of the pyramid, excluding the base? (Assume that all triangular faces are equal in area.)

(A) 1625
(B) 1475 $\sqrt{10}$
(C) 5250
(D) 2500 $\sqrt{5}$
(E) 6500

(Hint: First find the sloping height of each face.)
(Hint: Look for Pythagorean triplets.)

5. On the coordinate plane, how many units is the point $\left(-4, -\frac{15}{2}\right)$ from the origin, point (0,0)?

(A) $\frac{29}{4}$
(B) 8
(C) $\frac{17}{2}$
(D) 9
(E) $6\sqrt{3}$

(Hint: Look for a Pythagorean triplet.)

Questions 6–10 are Quantatative Comparisons.

Column A	Column B
6. Area of a circle with a radius of $\frac{2r}{3}$	Area of a circle with a circumference of $\frac{4\pi r}{3}$

(Hint: Find the circumference of the circle in Column A.)

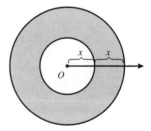

7.   The center of both circles is O.

| The area of the shaded region | Three times the area of the smaller circle |

(Hint: You can use ratios as a shortcut.)

Column A	Column B

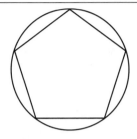

8. In the figure above, a pentagon whose sides are all equal in length touches a circle at exactly five points.

The length of any side of the pentagon	The radius of the circle

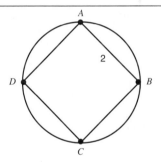

9. ABCD is a square.

The length of minor arc AD	$\pi \sqrt{2}$

(Hint: First determine the circle's radius.)

Column A	Column B
10. The number of $\frac{1}{2}$-inch cubes that would fit into a rectangular box having the dimensions $3'' \times 4'' \times 5''$.	The number of 1-inch cubes that would fit into a rectangular box having the dimensions $6'' \times 8'' \times 10''$.

(Hint: Look for similarities between the two boxes.)

9

Answers and Explanations

1. **(C)** Each angle in the hexagon is 120°. You can divide up the figure as indicated here:

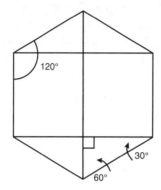

Each of the four triangles is a 30-60-90 triangle, so the ratio of the sides of each is $1:\sqrt{3}:2$. The hypotenuse is 1, so the other two sides are $\frac{1}{2}$ and $\frac{\sqrt{3}}{2}$. The area of each triangle $= \left(\frac{1}{2}\right)\left(\frac{1}{2}\right)\left(\frac{\sqrt{3}}{2}\right) = \frac{\sqrt{3}}{8}$. The hexagon includes four such triangles, so the total area is $\frac{\sqrt{3}}{2}$. The area of each of the two rectangles is $(1)\left(\frac{\sqrt{3}}{2}\right)$, so the area of both rectangles combined is $\sqrt{3}$. The total of all triangles and both rectangles is $\sqrt{3} + \frac{\sqrt{3}}{2}$, or $\frac{3\sqrt{3}}{2}$

2. **(D)** The circumference is five times the length of the arc:

$$5(2\pi) = 10\pi = \pi d$$

$$d = 10, \text{ and } r = 5$$

3. **(B)** The answer is 4:1. The ratio of the two volumes is 8:1. Thus, the linear ratio of the cubes' edges is the cube root of this ratio: $\sqrt[3]{8}$, or 2:1. The area ratio is the square of the linear ratio, or 4:1.

4. **(E)** The altitude of the pyramid (60) and one-half the length of a side (25) form the legs of a right triangle whose hypotenuse is the sloping (angular) height of each face. This triangle is a 5:12:13 right triangle whose sides are 25, 60, and 65. (The sloping height of each triangular face is 65.) You can now determine the area of each triangular face:

$$A = \left(\frac{1}{2}\right)(50)(65)$$

$$A = 1625$$

Accordingly, the total surface area of the pyramid is 4 times this amount, or 6500 square feet.

5. **(C)** Plotting the points reveal a 8-15-17 triangle $\left(4^2 + \left(\frac{15}{2}\right)^2 = \left(\frac{17}{2}\right)^2\right)$, in which the x-axis and y-axis serve as the two legs of the triangle.

6. **(C)** The circumference of a circle is $2\pi r$, so the circumference of the circle in Column A is $2\pi \frac{2r}{3}$, or $\frac{4\pi r}{3}$. Therefore, the two quantities are equal.

7. **(C)** The area of a circle $= \pi r^2$. Given that the radius of the larger circle is twice that of the smaller one, the area ratio is 4:1. Accordingly, the area of the shaded region is 3 times the area of the smaller circle (4 times the area of the smaller circle minus the area of the smaller circle).

8. **(A)** Because the pentagon is regular (all five sides are equal in length), each angle measures 108°. A line segment from the circle's center to any of the pentagon's angles bisects that angle into two 54° angles. The figure below shows the triangle formed by two such line segments. The angle at the circle's center (*O*) must measure 72° (54 + 54 + 72 = 180). Accordingly, the side opposite that angle (any side of the pentagon) must be greater in length than the circle's radius.

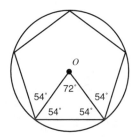

9. **(B)** Given that $AB = 2$, the circle's radius is $\sqrt{2}$, and the circle's circumference is $2\pi\sqrt{2}$. The length of arc AD is exactly $\frac{1}{4}$ that circumference, or $\frac{1}{2}\pi\sqrt{2}$. Quantity B is twice the value of Quantity A.

10. **(C)** Because each dimension is doubled in the cube size as well as in the box size, the number of cubes that will fit is the same in both cases. (480 cubes will fit into the box.)

9

Part III

Learn to Answer GRE Verbal Questions

Hour

HOUR 10

Teach Yourself Analogies

This hour you'll learn how to handle Analogy questions, which appear in the Verbal section of the GRE. Here are your goals for this hour:

- Learn what Analogy questions look like and how to answer them
- Learn tips for avoiding common Analogy pitfalls and traps
- Learn to recognize the types of word relationships that appear most frequently on the exam.
- Review the concepts you learn today by attempting a GRE-style quiz

GRE Analogies—At a Glance

Where: In the Verbal section, mixed in with Sentence Completions, Antonyms, and Reading Comprehension questions

How Many:

Paper-based test: 9 questions (of 38 altogether)

CBT: 9 questions (of 30 altogether)

What's Covered: Analogy questions test (1) your ability to understand the relationship between the meaning of two words and (2) your vocabulary.

The directions for Analogies are essentially the same for the paper-based test as for the CBT:

> **DIRECTIONS:** In this question, a numbered word pair in capital letters is followed by five lettered word pairs. Choose the lettered pair that expresses a relationship most similar to the relationship expressed in the numbered pair.

What GRE Analogies Look Like

Let's take a look at two typical Analogy questions. Take a minute or so to try each one. (We'll analyze these two questions a few pages ahead.) Start by reading the questions as follows:

"*Scribble* is to *write* as — is to —."

"*Adjudication* is to *trial* as — is to —."

QUESTION   1. SCRIBBLE : WRITE : :

(A) mutter : shout

(B) dispatch : send

(C) tattle : inform

(D) stagger : walk

(E) worry : please

QUESTION   2. ADJUDICATION : TRIAL : :

(A) postlude : symphony

(B) forecast : weather

(C) footnote: report

(D) misdemeanor : felony

(E) prognosis : surgery

What You Should Know About GRE Analogies

Analogy questions include words only (no phrases). Unlike Antonym questions, in which answer choices can be either words or short phrases, you won't see any phrases among GRE Analogies.

The first words in the six pairs all match in their part of speech (noun, verb, or adjective); the same is true of the second words. For example, if the first word of the original pair is a verb, the first word in each answer choice will also be a verb (or should be considered a verb, if the word can be of more than one part of speech).

Tougher vocabulary makes for a tougher question. Most words you'll encounter in Analogy questions will be common, everyday ones. But also expect to see some more advanced vocabulary. Tougher words make for tougher questions, because you can't tell a relationship between two words if you don't know what the words mean!

10

> **NOTE**
>
> On the CBT, you're more likely to encounter tougher vocabulary if you've responded correctly to previous Analogy questions.

Analogy questions in which all the individual words are easy can be surprisingly tough. Just because you know the meaning of all twelve words in an Analogy question, don't assume the question will be a piece of cake. Distinctions between the quality of different answer choices can be subtle, regardless of the vocabulary involved!

Analogy questions get tougher as you go along (paper-based test). On the paper-based test, expect the first one or two questions to be "no-brainer" confidence builders. But you might have to resort to a reasoned guess on a few of the later ones. On the CBT, of course, there's no set pattern in difficulty level.

Analogy questions can be more time-consuming than you might think. Unless you limit your time strictly, you can easily find yourself pondering a more difficult Analogy question for two or three minutes—without settling on an answer. Analogy questions are designed with subtle "shades of gray" between competing answer choices. Get used to it.

How to Approach GRE Analogies

Here's a 5-step approach that will help you to handle any Analogy question.

ACTION PLAN   1. **Determine the meaning of each word in the original pair.**

2. **Determine how the two words are related, and make up a sentence that expresses that relationship.**

3. **Try out your sentence with each answer choice, eliminating the choices that clearly don't work.**

4. **If you're left with more than one answer—or no answer at all—go back and make your sentence fit better.**

5. **Choose the best answer; if none of the choices fits exactly, choose the one that works best.**

Let's Apply the 5-Step Action Plan

Let's revisit the two GRE-style Analogies you attempted a few minutes ago. This time around, we'll walk through each one using the 5-step approach you just learned.

QUESTION   1. SCRIBBLE : WRITE : :

(A) mutter : shout

(B) dispatch : send

(C) tattle : inform

(D) stagger : walk

(D) worry : please

ANALYSIS   The correct answer is **(D)**. This question is easier than average. One feature that makes this analogy easy is that you're probably familiar with all the words. Another feature that makes this analogy easy is that the relationship between the words in the original pair is rather straightforward. Let's walk through this question, using the 5-step approach:

1. The meaning of the two words is obvious. Go on to Step 2.

2. Here's a sentence that describes the relationship between the original pair:

> "To *scribble* is to *write* in a careless or sloppy manner"
>
> or "*Scribbling* is a careless or sloppy manner of *writing*."

3. Try out each answer choice to see which ones fit in our sentence as substitutes for the original word pair.

(A) Is *muttering* a careless or sloppy manner of *shouting*? No. Muttering might be careless or sloppy, but its relationship to shouting has to do with volume, not degree of care—muttering is quiet, whereas shouting is loud. Eliminate (A).

(B) Is *dispatching* a careless or sloppy manner of *sending*? No. To dispatch is to send; in other words, the two words are synonymous. (*Dispatch* can also be used as an adjective—meaning "haste" or "speed." But since the first words in the other pairs are all verbs, you should analyze *dispatch* as a verb here.) Eliminate (B).

(C) Is *tattling* a careless or sloppy manner of *informing*? Perhaps. To tattle is to "tell on" or "disclose a secret." In many instances, tattling might be considered careless in the sense that the tattler doesn't care about the person he or she is tattling on. But is tattling necessarily careless? No. Let's not eliminate (C) yet, though. It's not a perfect match, but it is somewhat analogous.

(D) Is *staggering* a careless or sloppy manner of *walking*? Yes! To stagger is to walk in a clumsy, teetering manner.

10

(E) Is *worrying* a careless or sloppy manner of *pleasing*? No. The two words are unrelated to each other. Eliminate (E).

4. We've narrowed down our choices to (C) and (D). Since (D) is such a good fit, we can eliminate (C). There's no need to go back and revise our sentence.

5. Choose (D), and move on to the next question.

QUESTION   2. ADJUDICATION : TRIAL : :

    (A) postlude : symphony

    (B) forecast : weather

    (C) footnote: report

    (D) misdemeanor : felony

    (E) prognosis : surgery

ANALYSIS   The correct answer is (**E**). This Analogy question falls squarely into the "difficult" category. One feature that makes this a toughie is that it's packed with words that might look somewhat familiar to you but that you might have trouble defining precisely. Another feature that makes this analogy tough is that the relationship between the words in the original pair is a bit abstract (and the same can be said for some of the other pairs as well). Here's how to tackle the question, using the 5-step action plan:

1. If *adjudication* is a new word to you, take it apart and look for clues. The root *jud* appears at the beginning of more common words such as *judge* and *judicial*. The prefix *ad* means "to or toward." So a good guess would be that the verb *adjudicate* means "to

judge." In fact, that's exactly correct! An *adjudication* is a decree or pronouncement, such as a verdict, usually made by a judge at the conclusion of a *trial*.

> **TIP**
>
> If you don't know the meaning of a word, try to guess based on its root and/ or prefix. Also, the other word in the pair might provide a clue.

2. Start by expressing the relationship simply, without getting too specific or abstract:

   "An *adjudication* occurs at the conclusion of a *trial*."

3. Try out each answer choice to see which ones fit in our sentence as substitutes for the original word pair.

   (A) Does a *postlude* occur at the conclusion of a *symphony*? Yes. A postlude is a concluding piece or movement of a symphony.

   (B) Does a *forecast* occur at the conclusion of *weather*? No. By definition, a forecast precedes a weather event. Eliminate (B).

   (C) Does a *footnote* occur at the conclusion of a *report*? Generally not. Footnotes usually appear at the bottom (or "foot") of the page on which they are referenced (although they can be grouped as endnotes at the end of a report). (C) is a weak analogy, so eliminate it.

   (D) Does a *felony* occur at the conclusion of a *misdemeanor*? No. The words *felony* and *misdemeanor* describe types of crimes. (By definition, a felony is a more serious crime than a misdemeanor.) By the way, (D) is classic sucker bait; it involves the same general topic as the original pair. But the relationship between *felony* and *misdemeanor* is not even close to the one between *adjudication* and *trial*. Eliminate (D).

   (E) Does a *prognosis* occur at the conclusion of *surgery*? Yes, it can. A prognosis is a prediction of the chances of recovery from illness or surgery; a prognosis may very well occur just after surgery is completed.

4. We've narrowed down the choices to (A) and (E). We need another sentence that is either more specific or that focuses on a different aspect of the relationship between *adjudication* and *trial*. Consider the *purpose* or *function* of an adjudication (now we're getting a bit more abstract):

   "An *adjudication* is a pronouncement of the outcome—or result—of a *trial*."

5. (A) doesn't fit the bill at all, does it? But (E) is a very close fit. A *prognosis* is a pronouncement (by the physician) as to the result of *surgery*—the surgery might have been successful, for example, and the chances of recovery good. Sure, the analogy isn't perfect. But it's the closest match among the five choices.

DO's and DON'Ts for Tackling GRE Analogies

Do	**DON'T**

DO create a sentence that includes the two capitalized words.

DON'T be too general or too specific with your sentence.

DO eliminate any answer choice in which the two words are unrelated to each other.

DON'T give up if you know only one of the two words in an answer choice; you can always take an educated guess, even with just one of the words.

DO eliminate answer choices that don't match the original word pair in their "charge"—positive, negative, or neutral.

DO look for familiar roots and prefixes to help you guess the meaning of unfamiliar words.

DON'T fall for sucker-bait answer choices that involve the same subject as the original pair.

10

Nine Analogy Categories You Should Know

Most GRE Analogies fall into one of nine categories, which we've identified here by sample sentences (in each sentence, the two blanks indicate where you plug in the two words):

"——— is a key characteristic of ———."

"——— is a function or use of ———."

"——— runs contrary in meaning to ———."

"——— operates against ———."

"——— is a type, form, or example of ———."

"——— is a place or environment for ———."

"——— is a condition or ingredient for ———."

"——— is a part, element, or aspect of ———."

"——— is evidence or a result of ———."

Knowing these categories will help make your task easier—and, in fact, may produce instant answers to the easier analogies on your test. But you won't be able to solve every GRE Analogy simply by plugging the word pair into one of these nine sentences. For most analogies you'll have to refine the relationship further to get the correct answer.

In the pages ahead, you'll learn that each category includes at least two distinct variations—or *patterns*. For each category, you'll find sentences and illustrative word pairs to help you recognize each *pattern* when you see it on the exam.

These nine categories are the ones you're most likely to encounter on the GRE. But not every Analogy question fits neatly into one of these categories; you'll probably encounter one or two oddballs as well. So try to be flexible as you tackle the Analogies on your test.

"Key Characteristic of" Analogies

In this type of relationship, one word helps explain the meaning of the other word. Look for one of two distinct patterns to help you refine the relationship.

1. **Defining characteristic**

   "— is a characteristic that defines what a — is."

   "By definition, a — is —."

   BRAVE : HERO

   NOVEL : INVENTION (*novel* means "original or new")

   ALTRUISM : PHILANTHROPIST (a *philanthropist* is a generous humanitarian; *altruism* means "good will or benevolence")

2. **Ideal (but not necessary) characteristic**

   "An effective — must be —."

   "An ideal — should be —."

   SWORD : SHARP

   FOUNDATION : STRENGTH

   SURGEON : DEXTEROUS (*dexterous* means "skillful with one's hands")

 In handling "key characteristic of" Analogies, keep in mind the two words must bear some similarity in meaning. So you can quickly eliminate any answer choice in which the two words are even the least bit contrary in flavor.

"Function or Use of" Analogies

In this relationship, one word is essentially a *tool*, while the other word is a *function* or *use* of the tool. Look for one of two distinct patterns to help you refine the relationship.

1. Inherent purpose (function)

"A — is a tool designed to —."

"The chief purpose of — is to —."

KEY: UNLOCK

LOOM : WEAVE

BUTTRESS : REINFORCE (a *buttress* is a type of supporting structure)

2. One of several possible uses or applications

"A — can, but need not, be used to —."

"A — can serve several functions, one of which is to —"

"A — can —, although it isn't designed for this purpose.

FINGER : POINT

SPEECH : INSPIRE

EDIFICE : MEMORIALIZE (an *edifice* is an imposing structure, typically a monument)

"Contrary Meaning" Analogies

In this type of relationship, the two words run *contrary* or are *opposed* to each other in meaning. On the exam, you're unlikely to see two capitalized words that are perfect opposites (e.g., HOT : COLD). The test-makers prefer to hide the ball. Instead, learn to distinguish among three patterns.

1. Impossible characteristic

"By definition, — cannot be characterized by —."

"— describes precisely what — is not."

MINERAL : ORGANIC

FRUCTOSE : SOUR

FIXTURE : MOMENTUM

2. Mutually exclusive conditions

"Something that is — would probably not be described as —."
"A — person cannot also be —."

PURE : SOILED
TIMID : EXPERIMENTAL
OBVIOUS : CLANDESTINE (*clandestine* means "secretive")

3. Lack or absence is part of the definition

"— describes a lack or absence of —."
"If something is —, it lacks —."

DEFLATED : AIR
DIZZY : EQUILIBRIUM
IMPENITENT : REMORSE (*impenitent* means "lacking remorse")

 TIP

Whenever you encounter two words that first strike you as contrary in
meaning, keep in mind that they might involve different *degrees* instead.
There's a difference! For instance, a *demand* isn't the opposite of (or the lack
of) a *request*. And *ripeness* isn't the opposite (or the lack of) *freshness*.

"Operates Against" Analogies

In this type of relationship, the two words run contrary to each other, and their contrary
nature involves *function* or *purpose*. Look for one of four distinct patterns to help you
refine the relationship.

1. Correction, reversal, elimination

"— serves to correct/reverse/eliminate —."

SUSTENANCE : MALNUTRITION : (*sustenance* means "food or nourishment")
LOOSEN : STRANGULATED
INUNDATED : SCARCE (*inundated* means "flooded or deluged")

NOTE In the correct/reverse/eliminate pattern, one word usually carries a positive connotation, while the other is negatively charged.

2. Lessening (decrease) in degree, extent, amount, quantity

"— serves to lessen the degree/extent/amount of —."

BRAKE : SPEED
COMPRESSION : AMPLITUDE (*amplitude* means "fullness or breadth")
FILTER : SPECTRUM

3. Prevention

"— serves to prevent — from occurring."

BLOCKADE : PROGRESS
CORRAL : DISPERSE
UMBRELLA : DRENCH

4. Opposing functions

"— and — serve opposing functions."
"— and — work at cross-purposes."

FERTILIZER : SICKLE
ANCHOR : CORK
EPOXY : MILLSTONE

"Type, Form, or Example of" Analogies

In this type of relationship, one word is a type, example, form, or variety of the other word. Look for one of these three distinct patterns to help you refine the relationship.

1. Specific example or category

"A — is one category of —."
"A — is an example of —."

WOODWIND : INSTRUMENT

ANTHOLOGY : COLLECTION (an *anthology* is a *collection* of writings)

CALORIE : MEASUREMENT (a *calorie* is a unit of *measurement* for heat)

2. Neutral vs. negative form

"To — is to — in an unlawful/immoral/harmful manner."

"— is a negative/bad/poor form of —.

"To — is to —, but with an improper purpose.

SCRIBBLE : WRITE (Remember this pair from earlier in the hour?)

MOCK : MIMIC (to *mock* is to ridicule, typically through mimicry)

PEDANT : SCHOLAR (a *pedant* makes an excessive show of learning)

3. Difference in degree, scale, extent, amount, quantity

"— takes — to an extreme."

"— is a faster/larger/stronger form of —."

"— is the same as — but on a larger scale."

SOLICIT : CANVASS (to *canvass* is to solicit orders from a group)

COUNSEL : ADMONISH (to *counsel* is to advise; to *admonish* is to urge strongly)

MALAISE : DISTRAUGHT (*malaise* means "uneasiness"; *distraught* means "troubled or distressed")

 CAUTION | Be careful to distinguish patterns 2 and 3. A negatively charged word is not necessarily an extreme word.

"Place or Environment for" Analogies

In this type of relationship, one word describes a *place* (location, environment, forum, setting); the other word describes an *object* or *event* associated with that place. Look for one of two distinct patterns to help you refine the relationship.

1. **The only place generally associated with the object or event**

"— usually occurs in a —."

"A — is the only place you'll find —."

COOK : KITCHEN

HONEYCOMB: HIVE

ELEGY : FUNERAL (an *elegy* is a song of mourning)

2. **One of many places associated with the object or event**

"— is one activity that might occur at a —."

"— is one place where — might be found."

OBSERVE : LABORATORY

EXTRACTION : QUARRY

POACH : LAKE (to *poach* is to illegally remove fish or game)

"Condition for or Ingredient of" Analogies

In this relationship, one word is a *condition* or *ingredient* associated with the other word. Look for one of these two distinct patterns to help you refine the relationship.

1. **Necessary condition or ingredient**

"— is needed in order to —."

"— can't happen without —."

"— is a necessary ingredient for —."

WIND : SAIL

VOTERS : ELECTION

EGO : CONCEIT

2. **Helpful condition, but not a necessary one**

"— promotes/assists —."

"— thrives in conditions described as —."

"— is one possible ingredient for producing a —."

QUIET : CONCENTRATE
TAILWIND : RACER
ANONYMITY : SURVEILLANCE

"Part, Element, or Aspect of" Analogies

In this type of relationship, one word is an *element*, *part*, *facet*, or *aspect* of the other word. Look for one of four distinct patterns to help you refine the relationship.

1. Intrinsic aspect or quality

"— is one intrinsic aspect of a —, and it can't be separated from the whole."

" Every — includes some kind of —, which can't be separated from the whole."

TEMPERATURE : CLIMATE
TEXTURE : WOOD
ATTITUDE : PERSONALITY

2. Part-to-whole (essential part)

"A — is a distinct physical component/part of every —."

WALL : HOUSE
SCREEN : TELEVISION
WHEEL : AUTOMOBILE

3. Part-to-whole (non-essential part)

"A — is one possible component/part of a —."

SHOES : OUTFIT
CODA : COMPOSITION (a *coda* is an distinctive ending of a musical composition)
ADJUDICATION : TRIAL (Remember this pair from earlier in the hour?)

4. Individual-to-group

"Several —s make up a —."

"A group of —s is called a —.

PATRON : CLIENTELE (a *patron* is a customer; *clientele* refers to a business' customers as a group)

LION : PRIDE (a *pride* is a community of *lions*)

PATCH : MOSAIC (a *mosaic* is an assemblage of pieces to form a larger artwork)

"Evidence or Result of" Analogies

In this relationship, one word provides *evidence* of the other one. Look for three distinct patterns to help you refine the relationship.

1. **Cause-and-effect (natural or likely outcome or consequence)**

   "If — occurs, so will —."

   "— is a byproduct of —."

   BOREDOM : MONOTONY

   OBSOLESCENCE : INNOVATION

   INJURY : REMISS (*remiss* means "negligent or neglectful")

2. **Process and product (the result is intentional)**

   "You create a — by the process of —."

   "— is the intentional result of —."

   SMOOTH : SHAVE

   COFFEE : BREW

   DEAL : NEGOTIATE

3. **Symptom, sign, or manifestation**

   "— is an indication that — has occurred."

   "— is one possible symptom of —."

   TUMOR : CANCER

   BLUSH : EMBARRASSED

   ISOLATION : MISANTHROPE (a *misanthrope* is a person who hates or distrusts humankind)

10

In "Evidence or Result of" Analogies, if the two original words bear some similarity in meaning, you can easily eliminate any answer choice in which the two words are the least bit contrary in meaning to each other.

Workshop

In this Workshop, you'll apply what you just learned about handling GRE Analogies to a 10-question GRE-style quiz.

Additional Analogy questions are available on-line, at the authors' Web site: *http://www.west.net/~stewart/gre*

Quiz

(Answers and explanations begin on page 208.)

1. DECREE : INFORM : :

   (A) fascinate : interest
   (B) gallop : canter
   (C) resign : quit
   (D) endure : persist
   (E) shout : whisper
   (Hint: This analogy involves a synonym with a slant.)

2. WEAPON : INTIMIDATE : :

   (A) icebox : preserve
   (B) donor : give
   (C) memory : recall
   (D) sun : shine
   (E) meal : serve
   (Hint: Some tools do more than one job.)

3. SENSATION : PARALYSIS : :

   (A) sincerity : dishonesty
   (B) verbosity : shyness
   (C) insult : injury
   (D) apathy : curiosity
   (E) scarcity : surplus
   (Hint: Be careful not to define "paralysis" too broadly.)

4. CARETAKER : ATTENTIVE : :

   (A) writing : legible
   (B) hair : curly
   (C) mule : obstinate
   (D) mansion : spacious
   (E) meat : broiled
   (Hint: The capitalized words are related in two ways.)

5. EXTORT : INFLUENCE : :

   (A) spice : flavor
   (B) plummet : descend
   (C) rifle : borrow
   (D) abet : gamble
   (E) omit : forget
   (Hint: This analogy is more than just a matter or degree.)

6. FALLOW : PRODUCTIVITY : :

   (A) handsome : attraction
   (B) friendly : allegiance
   (C) bitter : taste
   (D) obscure : clarity
   (E) poisonous : protection
   (Hint: Farmers sometimes intentionally leave their fields fallow.)

10

7. WAR : OFFENSIVE : :
    (A) school : student
    (B) waterfall : river
    (C) night : sleep
    (D) stadium : soccer
    (E) game : poker
    (Hint: This is an "environment for" analogy)

8. COUNTERPOINT : MELODY : :
    (A) pane : window
    (B) masonry : brick
    (C) coffee : bean
    (D) sketch : pencil
    (E) biography : book
    (Hint: "Counterpoint" is the art of combining melodies.)

9. DEBACLE : DAM : :
    (A) blood : artery
    (B) pitchfork : hay
    (C) knowledge : education
    (D) contest : referee
    (E) disease : nutrient
    (Hint: Violent flooding would be considered a debacle.)

10. NATAL : GESTATION : :
    (A) conclusive : premise
    (B) wealthy : investment
    (C) humble : conceit
    (D) truthful : proof
    (E) feeble : cowardice
    (Hint: "Gestation" means "pregnancy.")
    (Hint: You've probably heard the term "nativity scene.")

Answers and Explanations

1. **(C)** This is a "degree of" analogy. A *decree* is a pronouncement or declaration. A decree *informs*, but it's a distinctively official or formal way of doing so. Similarly, *resigning* is a formal way of *quitting*.

2. **(A)** This is a "possible use of" analogy." A *weapon* is a tool which might be used to *intimidate*. Similarly, an *icebox* is a tool which might be used to *preserve* (by means of freezing).

3. **(B)** This is a "symptom of" analogy, turned upside down. One sign of *paralysis* is the lack of *sensation* (feeling). Similarly, one sign of *shyness* is the lack of *verbosity*. As for (A) and (E), the two words in each pair are antonyms. The same can't be said for *sensation* and *paralysis*. Paralysis is not defined by a lack of sensation, but rather by lack of ability to move.

4. **(D)** This is an "ideal characteristic of" analogy. A good *caretaker* is *attentive*; in fact, "attending to" is the function of a caretaker. Similarly, good *writing* is *legible*; in fact, the purpose of writing is to be read.

5. **(C)** This is a "degree of" analogy. To *extort* is to force from a person by violence or intimidation. So it's both a heightened

and a negative slant on *influencing*. Similarly, to *rifle* is to loot or steal—both a heightened and a negative slant on *borrowing*.

6. **(E)** This is an "inherent purpose of" analogy. *Fallow* means "to leave a field uncultivated for the purpose of restoring *productivity*." Similarly, the reason some animals are *poisonous* is to *protect* themselves from predators and other enemies.

7. **(C)** This is an "environment for" analogy. An *offensive* (a noun here) is a planned attack and is used in the context of a battle or *war*. In other words, an offensive is an event that usually occurs during a war. Similarly, *sleep* is an event that usually occurs during the *night*. As for (D), soccer is an event that *might* take place in a stadium. But to say that soccer usually occurs in a stadium would be an overstatement. Also, a stadium is a physical *place*, whereas *war* and *night* are not.

8. **(B)** This is a "component of" analogy. *Counterpoint* refers to the interplay of two or more *melodies*. So each melody is a distinct and necessary component of counterpoint. Similarly, each *brick* is a distinct and necessary component of *masonry* (brick or stone work, such as a chimney). As for (C), *beans* are ingredients which are combined to make *coffee*, but the bean as a distinct unit is not part of the product.

9. **(E)** This is an "operates against" analogy. A *debacle* is a destructive flood or other disaster. The function of a *dam* is to control the flow of water, thereby preventing floods. Similarly, the purpose of a *nutrient* is to provide and maintain health, thereby preventing *disease*.

10. **(A)** This is a "necessary condition" analogy. *Gestation* means "pregnancy"; *natal* means "pertaining to birth." (The birth of Christ is depicted in a "nativity scene.") Thus, gestation is a necessary condition for and must precede a birth. Similarly, a *premise* is a necessary condition for and must precede a *conclusion*.

10

Hour 11

Teach Yourself Sentence Completions and Antonyms

This hour you'll teach yourself how to handle Sentence Completion and Antonym questions—two of the four question types that appear on the Verbal section. Here are your goals for this hour:

- Learn what Sentence Completion questions look like and how to answer them
- Learn what Antonym questions look like and how to answer them
- Learn tips for avoiding common Sentence Completion and Antonym pitfalls and traps
- Practice what you learned this hour by attempting a GRE-style Quiz

Sentence Completion—At a Glance

Where: In the GRE Verbal section, mixed in with Antonyms, Analogies, and Reading Comprehension questions

How Many:

Paper-based test: 7 questions (of 38 altogether)

CBT: 6 questions (of 30 altogether)

What's Covered: GRE Sentence Completions are designed to measure a variety of verbal abilities, including

1. your ability to understand the intended meaning of a sentence
2. your ability to distinguish between a sentence that makes sense and one that lacks sense
3. your ability to recognize proper (and improper) use of words
4. your ability to recognize proper (and improper) written expression
5. your vocabulary

Directions: The directions for Sentence Completions are essentially the same on the paper-based test as on the CBT:

This sentence contains either one or two blanks. A blank indicates that a word or brief phrase has been omitted. Select among the five choices the word or phrase for each blank that *best* fits the meaning of the sentence as a whole.

What GRE Sentence Completions Look Like

Here are two GRE-style Sentence Completions questions. Notice that the first sentence contains one blank, while the second sentence contains two. Take a few minutes to complete these two sentences. (We'll analyze them a few pages ahead.)

QUESTION Sleep researchers now view sleep as involving degrees of detachment from the surrounding world, a ------- whose rhythm is as unique and as consistent as a signature.

(A) realm

(B) progression

(C) science

(D) restfulness

(E) condition

QUESTION Throughout the twentieth century, African American members of Congress have not only ------- their respective constituencies but also served as proxies in the democratic process for all African Americans; yet the biographies of certain of those members seem to ------- their struggle to extend the ideals of the nation's founders to encompass all citizens.

(A) served..describe

(B) abandoned..affirm

(C) promoted..criticize

(D) represented..belie

(E) influenced..discredit

What You Should Know about Sentence Completions

Most Sentence Completions will contain two blanks. Expect no more than two of your Sentence Completions to contain single blanks. The rest will contain two.

Your task is always the same: fill in either one or two blanks. You won't see three or more blanks in a GRE Sentence Completion question. That's not how the test-makers build them.

Sentence Completion sentences are long and complex; each one will look like something from a GRE Reading Comprehension passage. You won't find short, snappy sentences here; that would make your task too easy. Expect all of your sentences to run at least 25 or 30 words in length and to be complex in structure. Also, Sentence Completion sentences are strictly academic in content and style, just like GRE Reading Comprehension passages.

Blanks usually call for single words. To fill in most blanks, you'll choose among single words. But you might encounter one or two blanks in which you choose among brief phrases (typically, prepositional phrases).

The emphasis on vocabulary isn't as strong in Sentence Completions as in Analogies and Antonyms. You might find a few challenging words among Sentence Completions questions. But unlike Analogies and Antonyms, the emphasis here is on *word usage* and *sense* (whether the word is the right one to convey the intended meaning of the sentence), not on vocabulary.

You'll typically encounter both a best and second-best answer choice. Except for the easiest Sentence Completions, you'll see at least two choices that seem to fit—at least at first glance. But one answer will more effectively convey the intended meaning of the sentence as a whole.

The correct answer will make for an "excellent" sentence. The best answer will provide words that make for a clear, effective, and eloquent sentence. Although the official instructions don't tell you so, if there's anything wrong with an answer choice, it can't be the correct one.

Sentence Completions increase in difficulty as you go (paper-based test). On the paper-based test, later questions are generally tougher than earlier ones. (On the CBT, there's no set pattern.)

How to Approach GRE Sentence Completions

Here's a 5-step Action Plan for tackling any Sentence Completions. After reviewing these steps, you'll apply them to the examples you encountered a few pages back.

1. **Read the sentence in its entirety, just to get the gist of it.**
2. **Read the sentence again, and fill in the blanks with your own words.**
3. **Test each answer choice, eliminating ones that are obviously wrong.**
4. **Compare the remaining choices by reading the entire sentence again with each version.**
5. **Confirm your choice by reading that version of the sentence one more time.**

Let's Apply the 5-Step Action Plan

Let's revisit the two Sentence Completions questions you attempted a few pages back. This time around, we'll walk through each one using the 5-step approach you just learned.

QUESTION Sleep researchers now view sleep as involving degrees of detachment from the surrounding world, a ------- whose rhythm is as unique and as consistent as a signature.

(A) realm
(B) progression
(C) science
(D) restfulness
(E) condition

ANALYSIS **1.** The sentence as a whole seems to suggest that sleep is a dynamic process involving a series of different stages defined by degree of detachment. Notice that the purpose of the second clause to describe what sleep is. This observation is key in getting to the correct answer.

2. If you were filling in the blank yourself (without the aid of the answer choices), what word would you use? The missing word refers to "sleep," so perhaps a word such as *state* or *condition* might occur to you as a good completion.

 CAUTION

> Notice that our "home-grown" completion is among the answer choices. Does this mean we can confidently choose (E) and move on to the next question without another thought? No! Another choice might be better than (E). In Sentence Completions, always give some thought to each answer choice!

3. First, let's eliminate answer choices that are obviously wrong. The correct answer must make sense as a characterization of sleep. (C) and (D) make no sense as characterizations of sleep. Eliminate them. Notice also that "rhythm" is mentioned as a feature or trait of the missing word ("— whose rhythm..."). So the correct answer must make sense in this way as well. To describe a "realm" as having a rhythm makes no sense. Eliminate (A).

4. We've narrowed the choices down to (B) and (E). Read the sentence with each word in turn. Ask yourself which word is more appropriate and effective in conveying the thrust of the sentence—that sleep is a dynamic process involving a series of different stages. The word *progression* clearly drives home this notion more pointedly and effectively than the word *condition*.

5. The best answer is (B). If you're still undecided, take your best guess among the viable choices and move on. On the paper-based test, you can come back to the question later if you have time.

QUESTION Throughout the twentieth century, African American members of Congress have not only ------- their respective constituencies but also served as proxies in the democratic process for all African Americans; yet the biographies of certain of those members seem to ------- their struggle to extend the ideals of the nation's founders to encompass all citizens.

(A) served..describe

(B) abandoned..affirm

(C) promoted..criticize

(D) represented..belie

(E) influenced..discredit

11

ANALYSIS   **1.** In reading this sentence, you should have noticed that it changes direction midway through. This change is signaled by the key word *yet*, which provides a clue that the second part of the sentence sets up a contrast or contradiction to the first part. You can bet that this structural clue will be crucial to determine the best answer.

2. (first blank): Let's read the sentence again, filling in the first blank with our own word (ignoring the answer choices for now). The words "not only...but also" are important clues that the first blank must complement the phrase "served as prox-ies...." (*proxy* means "substitute.") A negatively charged word such as *harmed*, *ignored*, or *disagreed with* would make no sense in the first blank, would it? But a word such as *served*, *represented*, or *aided* would fit nicely.

2. (second blank): Now let's fill in the second blank with our own word—one that makes sense together with the first word. During Step 1, we determined that the meaning of second clause should reflect a contrast to that of the first one. So a word such as *ignore*, *de-emphasize*, or *trivialize* would make sense here. Here's a good paraphrase of the sentence that shows the idea that it is probably trying to convey:

In doing their jobs, these members of Congress have helped (*aided*) all African Americans, yet some biographies don't reflect (they *ignore*) the efforts of these members.

3. Let's take a first pass at each answer choice. Because this question includes two blanks, don't try to shortcut the process by scanning for key words that might signal obvious winners and losers. Dual-blank Sentence Completions are not designed to be solved this easily. Let's consider each answer choice in turn:

(A) *Served* fits nicely, but *describe* fails to establish the necessary contrast between the two parts of the sentence. Eliminate (A).

(B) *Abandoned* doesn't fit, because it doesn't complement "served as proxies...." You can eliminate (B) even without considering the second word (*affirm*).

(C) *Promoted* and *criticize* each seem to make sense in context, and together they set up a sense of contrast between the two clauses. So (C) is in the running.

(D) *Represented* fits nicely. If you don't know what *belie* means, perhaps you can guess based on its root *lie* (falsehood), which provides the sort of contrast between the two clauses we're looking for. So (D) is in the running. (We'll define *belie* in Step 4.)

(E) *Influenced* establishes a different meaning for the first clause than the one we've been inferring. But *influenced* does make some sense in the first clause. *Discredit* makes sense as well and sets of the necessary contrast between the two clauses. So (E) is in the running.

4. We've narrowed down our choices to (C), (D), and (E). Now read the sentence again with each of these three pairs, in turn.

(C) This answer choice suffers from two subtle defects. First, it is the *goals* or *interests* of a constituency, not the constituency itself, that an elected representative promotes. So *promoted* sets up an improper idiomatic expression. Second, for the word *criticize* to establish a clear contrast, the first clause should at least suggest the opposing notion of *approval*; but it doesn't. So even though the "flavor" of *criticize* is in the right direction, it is not a perfect fit in the context of the sentence as a whole.

(D) To *belie* is to misrepresent or contradict. For example, a smile belies sadness. Similarly, a biography can belie the struggle described in the sentence—perhaps by misdescribing it as an easier effort than it has in fact been. So (D) appears to be a good answer choice.

(E) This answer choice suffers from two subtle defects. First, this version of the sentence inappropriately *discredits* a *struggle*; but it makes better sense to discredit the *strugglers*. You can eliminate (E) based on this defect alone. Second, although the word *influence* makes sense in context, it doesn't establish the close parallel in ideas that the correlative phrases "not only...but also..." call for. (D) is better in this respect.

5. The best answer is (D). If you're still undecided, take your best guess among the viable choices and move on. On the paper-based test, you can come back to the question later if you have time.

DO's and DON'Ts for Handling Sentence Completions

Do	Don't

DO look for key words in the surrounding sentence that offer clues to the missing word(s).

DO think up your own answer as a way to start.

DON'T choose an answer to a dual-blank question just because one of the words is a perfect fit.

DON'T choose an answer just because it contains a tough word.

DO check for usage and idiom problems if you're having trouble getting to the best answer.

DO test every answer choice.

11

GRE Antonyms—At a Glance

Where: In the GRE Verbal section, mixed in with Sentence Completions, Analogies, and Reading Comprehension questions

How Many:

Paper-based test: 11 questions (of 38 altogether)

CBT: 7 questions (of 30 altogether)

What's Covered: GRE Antonyms are designed to measure your vocabulary

Directions: The directions for Antonyms are essentially the same on the paper-based test as on the CBT:

> Select the word or phrase among the five choices that is most nearly *opposite* in meaning to the word in capital letters. *Note:* This question might require you to distinguish fine shades in meaning, so you should carefully consider all five choices.

What GRE Antonyms Look Like

Here are three GRE-style Antonym questions. Notice that the original word is in capital letters. That's the word for which you find the antonym. Take a few minutes to attempt all three. (We'll analyze each one a few pages ahead.)

NOTE From now on, we'll refer to the words in capital letters as *headwords*.

 QUESTION LOQUACIOUS:

    (A) rational

    (B) abrasive

    (C) agitated

    (D) compact

    (E) articulate

QUESTION TABLE:

    (A) proceed

    (B) flatten

    (C) raise

    (D) conform

    (E) stall

QUESTION RETRIBUTION:

    (A) delightful experience

    (B) forgiveness for an offense

    (C) control over a destructive urge

    (D) return to normality

    (E) generous donation

What You Should Know about Antonyms

11

Each answer choice is of the same part of speech (noun, verb, or adjective) as the original. If a particular word could be considered as one of two or more parts of speech, the other words in the question will reveal which part of speech you should assume.

Headwords are always single words (no phrases; hyphenated words appear only rarely); but answer choices can be either single words or short phrases. Most answer choices will be single words, but you'll encounter at least a few phrases as well. Questions that include phrases as answer choices are not necessarily tougher or easier than other questions—just a bit wordier.

All words are part of the modern English language. You won't be tested on informal or slang uses of words. You won't encounter archaic words that aren't used at all today (for some examples of archaic words, check out some Shakespeare). And you won't encounter non-English words that have not been adopted as part of the English language.

Common, everyday words probably have uncommon alternative meanings. One way the test-makers try to throw you off track is with headwords that have both common and uncommon meanings. Whenever you encounter a headword that is a common, everyday one, it probably takes more than one part of speech (noun, verb, or adjective) and more than one meaning (you'll need to know the less common one to get the question right). Here are some examples from previous exams:

tack: direction

fell: chop

rent: rip or tear

pan: criticize severely

list: sway from side to side

shoulder: bear a burden or responsibility

ape: imitate

appropriate: acquire

temper: adapt or make suitable

host: throng, swarm, or gathering

The best choice isn't always a perfect opposite. Your task is to figure out which word (or phrase) is *most nearly* opposite in meaning to the word in capital letters. Some best answers will be near-perfect opposites, but others won't.

The second-best answer can come very close indeed. The official directions warn you that some questions may require you to "distinguish fine shades of meaning." It's true.

Vocabulary is what GRE Antonyms are all about. Expect GRE Antonyms to include tougher words on average than GRE Analogies. That's because the test-makers design Antonyms as a pure, unadulterated test of your vocabulary (unlike Analogies and Sentence Completions, which call for other abilities as well).

Easier words make for easier questions; tough words make for tough questions. Expect to see a broad spectrum of words—from everyday ones to ones that look like they're part of the Martian language. Easier words make for easier questions, of course. Here's a brief list of some of the most ordinary and the most off-the-wall headwords from previous exams.

Some easy headwords:	Some headwords from Mars:
begin	stygian (adj.): devilish
secure (verb)	repine (verb): meditate morbidly
asset	cadge (verb): mooch or borrow
evacuate	inveigle (verb): lure or entice
shallow	chary (adj.): careful or cautious
balloon (verb)	prolixity (noun): wordiness or verbosity
send	fatuity (noun): foolishness or folly
harmony	macerate (verb): moisten
press (verb)	grouse (verb): complain
dominant	sidereal (adj.): pertaining to the stars

CAUTION Just because a particular headword is a common, everyday word, doesn't mean that getting the answer right will be a piece of cake. Antonym questions with easier words often require you to distinguish "fine shades of meaning" between answer choices.

Unfamiliar headwords often contain familiar roots or resemble more familiar words. You can take advantage of this feature to make reasoned guesses. For example, here are some headwords that are uncommon words but that look like familiar ones:

Headword and definition:	Familiar word that looks similar:
AGGRANDIZE: make more important	grand (large)
EVINCE: demonstrate convincingly	convince
FORESTALL: hinder from advancing	stall (to delay)
FUNEREAL: sorrowful	funeral
LARGESS: generous donation	large
NEXUS: connection	next
PERENNIAL: enduring	annual (occurring every year)
QUIESCENCE: calmness	quiet
URBANE: refined or elegant	urban
VENAL: corrupt	venom (poison)

A headword might be difficult to deal with simply because its part of speech (noun, verb, or adjective) is not commonly used. Turning the word into a more familiar form can help. Here are some examples that have appeared on previous exams:

uncommon form:	more familiar form:
aphoristic (obvious)	aphorism (proverb or cliché)
canonical (authorized)	canon (rule)
congruity (unity)	incongruous (incompatible)
digressive (winding or meandering)	digression (deviation)
estimable (honorable)	esteem (honor)
gleanable (gatherable or discoverable)	glean (to gather or to discovery through patient investigation)
improbity (dishonesty)	probity (honesty)
obstinacy (stubbornness)	obstinate (stubborn)
precursory (preceding)	precursor (predecessor)

continues

continued

uncommon form:	more familiar form:
profundity (depth)	profound (deep)
sagacity (wisdom)	sage (a wise person)
teetotalism (abstinence)	teetotaler (one who abstains form drinking)
testiness (irritability)	testy (irritable)
zenithal (upright or vertical)	zenith (highest point)

Antonyms increase in difficulty as you go (paper-based test). On the paper-based test, later questions are generally tougher than earlier ones. (On the CBT, there's no set pattern.)

How to Approach GRE Antonyms

Let's face it: Approaching GRE Antonyms does not involve rocket science. It's a pretty straightforward process. After reviewing the following five steps, you'll apply them to the three examples you encountered a few pages back.

1. **Determine the headword's part of speech.**
2. **Define the headword.**
3. **Compare each answer choice with your definition of (or synonym for) the headword.**
4. **Compare the quality of the remaining choices.**
5. **Confirm your selection by comparing it to the headword.**

Let's Apply the 5-Step Action Plan

It's time to look again at the three GRE-style Antonyms you encountered a few pages back. This time around, we'll walk through each one using the 5-step approach you just learned.

QUESTION LOQUACIOUS:

(A) rational

(B) abrasive

(C) agitated

(D) compact

(E) articulate

ANALYSIS 1. The first three answer choices can be adjectives only. Thus, *loquacious* must be an adjective.

2. *Loquacious* carries two similar but distinct meanings: "talkative" (more common) and "wordy" (less common). These are good synonyms as well. Keep them both in mind.

3. (A), (B), and (C) bear no clear relationship to either *talkative* or *wordy*. Eliminate them!

4. (D) and (E) are the only two viable answer choices. Let's examine each one in turn:

(D) *Compact* (an adjective here) means "condensed or compressed." Wordy speech is characterized by the opposite of compactness. So compact is clearly contrary in meaning to *loquacious*.

(E) *Articulate* (an adjective here) means "well-spoken, eloquent, or fluent." But does an articulate person necessarily speak in a brief, concise manner (the opposite of *wordy*)? Not necessarily. Brevity or conciseness is not part of the job description for an articulate person. Accordingly, *articulate* is not nearly as opposite in meaning to *loquacious* as *compact*.

5. (D) appears to be the best answer. Let's verify our decision. Is *loquacious* contrary in meaning to *compact*? Yes.

QUESTION TABLE:

(A) proceed

(B) flatten

(C) raise

(D) conform

(E) stall

ANALYSIS 1. *Table* is such a common word that you can bet there's an uncommon definition that's up the test-makers' sleeves here. All the answer choices are verbs. So *table* must also be a verb.

2. *Table* means "to lay aside a proposal for an indefinite period of time." Two everyday words that are contrary in meaning to *table* are *proceed* or *act*.

3. (B), (C), and (D) are completely unrelated to *act* (and to *table*). Eliminate them.

4. *Proceed* (D) is contrary in meaning to *table*. *Stall* (E) means "to delay or procrastinate." *Stall* is a synonym for *table*, so (E) gets it backwards. Eliminate it!

5. (D) appears to be the best answer. Let's verify our decision. Is *proceed* contrary in meaning to *table*? Yes.

11

NOTE   If you think definitions as offbeat as the one for *table* here are too obscure for the test-makers, think again! The verb *table* has indeed appeared as an Antonym headword on the GRE.

QUESTION   RETRIBUTION:

(A) delightful experience

(B) forgiveness for an offense

(C) restraint in behavior

(D) return to normality

(E) generous donation

ANALYSIS   1. All of the answer choices define nouns. So *retribution* must be a noun.

2. *Retribution* means "revenge or vengeance"—in other words, "getting even with someone." Both *revenge* and *vengeance* are good synonyms.

3. Let's consider each answer choice. We'll compare each one to the homey phrase "getting even":

(A) Is *a delightful experience* a good definition of what "getting even" is not? No. In fact, vengeance might actually be a delightful experience, at least for the avenger. Eliminate (A).

(B) Is *forgiveness for an offense* a good definition of what "getting even" is not? Yes! A person who seeks to get even with another has not forgiven the other person. So (B) is indeed part of the definition of what retribution is not.

(C) Is *restraint in behavior* a good definition of what "getting even" is not? Perhaps. "Getting even" is indeed characterized by a lack of restraint in behavior. But is restraint part of the definition of what "getting even" is not? Perhaps not. Let's "table" answer choice (C) for now, and move on to (D) and (E).

(D) Is *return to normality* a good definition of what "getting even" is not? No. "Getting even" results in a return to equilibrium, but it may or may not result in a return to a "normal" relationship between the avenger and avenged. The connection is not clear enough, so eliminate (D).

(E) Is *a generous donation* a good definition of what "getting even" is not? No. "Getting even" is certainly contrary to making a gift; but it isn't part of the definition. Eliminate (E).

4. (B) and (C) are the only two viable candidates. Notice that (C) describes the *lack of* vengeance, but (C) doesn't describe what vengeance is not. This distinction is crucial; in fact, it's the reason why (B) is a better answer choice than (C). If you're still not convinced, try the reverse route: What word is the opposite of "restraint in behavior"? Impulsiveness or spontaneity. These are hardly good synonyms for *vengeance*, are they?

5. Let's verify our decision. Is "forgiveness for an offense" a good definition of what retribution (vengeance) is not? Yes.

TIP

> If the answer choices are phrases, it's a good bet that one of them will provide a good definition of what the headword is not. So think of answer choice phrases as possible *definitions*, not just potential antonyms.

DO's and DON'Ts for Handling GRE Antonyms   11

Do	DON'T

DON'T expect to find a perfect opposite.

DO think of a common synonym (either a word or short phrase) for an uncommon headword.

DON'T give up just because a word is unfamiliar.

DO start with the answer choice in order to gain insight.

DON'T assume the question is easy just because the headword is easy.

DO use intuitive techniques to narrow down the choices.

DO convert a word to another part of speech if you're stuck.

DO resolve close judgment calls in favor of the more specific antonym.

Workshop

In this Workshop, you'll apply what you just learned about handling Sentence Completions and Antonyms to a GRE-style quiz that includes 15 questions.

 Additional Sentence Completion and Antonym questions are available on-line, at the authors' Web site: *http://www.west.net/~stewart/gre*

Quiz

Directions: Attempt the following 15 GRE-style questions. 1–5 are Sentence Completions; 6–15 are Antonyms. Try to limit your time to 15 minutes altogether. We've included hints to help you if you're having trouble.

(Answers and explanations begin on page 228.)

1. The main advantage of inertial guidance systems in modern aircraft, spacecraft, and submarines is that they are ------- and are able to function without ------- data.

   (A) reliable..additional
   (B) automatic..external
   (C) scientific..losing
   (D) computerized..processing
   (E) internal..vital
   (Hint: The two phrases with the blanks convey complementary ideas.)

2. Hong Kong prospered as the center of trade with China, ------- until it fell to the Japanese in 1941.

   (A) increasing
   (B) succeeding
   (C) languishing

   (D) retreating
   (E) burgeoning
   (Hint: The missing word must complement the idea expressed in the first clause.)

3. One aim of educational technology should be to ------- instruction more precisely to the individual needs of students, because vast differences in the ways students learn are ------- when they are taught the same thing.

   (A) adapt..discovered
   (B) direct..reinforced
   (C) design..acknowledged
   (D) adjust..overlooked
   (E) retrofit..undermined
   (Hint: The second part of the sentence explains the first clause; it flows in the same direction.)

4. Proponents of urban development oppose the popular notion that social-psychological mechanisms leading to criminal and other antisocial activity are more likely to ------- if ------- such as population density, spatial immobility, and anonymity are found.

(A) function..cities
(B) react..factors
(C) disappear..problems
(D) fail..criminals
(E) emerge..traits

(Hint: The two missing words must help convey an idea that proponents of urban development would naturally oppose.)

5. The science of astronomy is widely viewed today as ------- at least as much as theoretical, in that sooner or later what astronomers detect finds its way into theory, or the theory is modified to ------- it.

(A) observational..disprove
(B) beneficial..accept
(C) empirical..embrace
(D) practical..demonstrate
(E) important..supersede

(Hint: The sentence sets up a contrast between "theoretical" and the first missing word.)

6. EXACERBATE:

(A) prevent from occurring
(B) lessen in degree
(C) withhold praise
(D) smooth over
(E) treat condescendingly

(Hint: Words that look similar often have similar meanings.)

7. CURSIVE:

(A) polite
(B) thorough
(C) disjointed
(D) straight
(E) unadorned

(Hint: Be prepared to make fine distinction between the quality of answer choices.)

8. ACCESSION:

(A) aloofness
(B) usurpation
(C) severance
(D) privacy
(E) passivity

(Hint: Perhaps you've heard the headword's verb form "accede.")

9. SANGUINE:

(A) destitute
(B) exuberant
(C) volatile
(D) tardy
(E) forlorn

(Hint: Look out for second-best answers, which are just a bit off the mark.)

10. PRESCIENCE:

(A) ignorance
(B) omen
(C) innocence
(D) refuse
(E) evidence

(Hint: Word parts (prefixes and roots) can help give you a flavor for what a word means.)

11

11. SATIATE:

    (A) crave deeply

    (B) apply forcefully

    (C) be repelled by

    (D) deplete entirely

    (E) enjoy thoroughly

    (Hint: This headword looks a lot like "saturate.")

    (Hint: Traits associated with each other are not necessarily related by definition.)

12. LICENTIOUS:

    (A) seemly

    (B) sacred

    (C) resolute

    (D) stalwart

    (E) blithe

    (Hint: You might be more familiar an antonym for the correct answer.)

13. ACCLAIM:

    (A) disbelieve

    (B) controvert

    (C) betray

    (D) taunt

    (E) proscribe

    (Hint: This question involves a close call between three choices.)

14. VITRIOLIC:

    (A) humble

    (B) agreeable

    (C) thoughtful

    (D) pure

    (E) complicated

    (Hint: Many words convey a sense of their meaning just by the way they sound.)

15. TAUT:

    (A) immersed

    (B) sedate

    (C) overly refined

    (D) easily fooled

    (E) circular

    (Hint: If you're stuck, try thinking of antonyms for the answer choices, then ask yourself whether the headword sounds right.)

Answers and Explanations

1. **(B)** Notice that the word "advantage" is singular (not plural). This suggests that the two phrases "they are —" and "they are able to..." must express nearly the same idea. (B) fits the bill; an *automatic* system is by definition one that functions without *external* help. (In the digital realm, the words "data" and "help" can carry essentially the same meaning.) None of the other answer choices establishes as

close a relationship between these two phrases. A *reliable* system does not by definition function without *additional* data, and a *scientific* system does not by definition function without *losing* data. So you can eliminate (A) and (C). A *computerized* system cannot function without *processing* data, so (D) makes no sense. Any system requires *vital* information to function, so (E) makes no sense.

2. **(E)** In this sentence, the second clause should continue in the same direction as the first. You're looking for a word that complements *prospered*. You can eliminate (C) and (D), both of which contradict the first clause. (*Languish* means "weaken.") Now consider the remaining choices. (A) makes for a vague sentence; what was Hong Kong increasing? (B) also makes for a vague sentence; what was Hong Kong succeeding in? As for (E), *burgeoning* means "blossoming or growing"—a good complement to the idea of *prospering*. So (E) provides the best completion.

3. **(D)** The first part of the sentence suggests that instructional methods need to be modified in some way to alleviate a problem. *Adapt* and *adjust* both make sense here. The second part of the sentence suggests that the problem is that when students are taught the same thing their individual needs are not adequately accounted for. In other words, these needs are *overlooked*, at least to some extent. (D) is the only choice that makes sense for both blanks.

4. **(E)** Proponents of urban development would oppose the idea that urban development fosters crime. So the "mechanism" referred to in the sentence might either *function*, *react*, or *emerge*, but not disappear or fail. You can eliminate (C) and (D). As for the second blank, population density, ethnic heterogeneity, and anonymity are all examples of the second missing word. It makes no sense to characterize these examples either as "cities" or "criminals." So you can eliminate (A) and (D) on this count. As for the two remaining choices, (B) is weaker than (E) on two counts. First, the sentence as a whole does not strongly support the use of the word *react*; what the mechanisms might react to is neither stated nor inferred in the sentence. Second, while a trait is properly referred to as "found," a factor is not (factors typically "come into play"). So (B) makes for an improper idiomatic expression.

5. **(C)** The phrase "at least as much as" sets up a comparison between *theoretical* and the first missing word. This word should express an idea that opposes theoretical. (A), (C), and (D) are the only viable choices. The transitional phrase "in that" signals that the first missing word should be a synonym for *detect*. This narrows the choices to (A) and (C). Now consider the second word in each of these two answer choices. *Disprove* runs contrary to the intended meaning of the sentence as a whole. Thus, (C) provides the best completion.

6. **(B)** *Exacerbate* has two common meanings: "provoke" and "intensify or

11

heighten." (*Exacerbate* is similar in meaning to *exaggerate*.) To *lessen in degree* is to do the opposite of intensify.

7. **(C)** *Cursive* refers to a flowing, continuous style of printing or writing. *Disjointed* means "disconnected or separated." Cursive printing is curved (the opposite of straight), but curvature isn't what defines *cursive*. It's a close call, but (C) is better than (D). As for (E), *unadorned* (plain or simple) is not clearly opposed to *cursive* in meaning; cursive printing may or may not be fancy.

8. **(C)** *Accession* means "inauguration or installation," as in the common phrase "accede to the throne." Accession marks the beginning of a term of office or career. *Severance* is a disconnection, usually marking the end of a job or career. *Usurpation* (B) means "taking over or assuming, usually by force." So the meaning of *usurpation* is in the same direction as the meaning of *accession*. As for (D), lack of *privacy* might characterize the result of an accession, but it is not a defining characteristic of it.

9. **(E)** *Sanguine* means "hopeful or optimistic." *Forlorn* means "despairing or despondent." *Destitute* (impoverished) is the second-best answer. A destitute person is typically desperate. But financial poverty is part of what defines *destitution*. *Sanguine* is not defined by financial well-being. As for (B), the meaning of *exuberant* (enthusiastic) is in the same direction as the meaning of *sanguine*.

10. **(A)** *Prescience* means "foreknowledge of future events." (*Pre* means "before"; *scien-* means "knowledge.") *Ignorance* means "lack of knowledge."

11. **(D)** *Satiate* means "to fill to capacity." To *deplete entirely* is to use up completely. *Crave* (long for) is related to *satiate*—a person who has become satiated doesn't crave anymore. But lack of craving is not part of the definition of *satiate*.

12. **(A)** *Licentious* means "indecent or obscene." *Seemly* means "appropriate or decent." (The word *unseemly* is more common than its antonym *seemly*.) What about (B)? *Sacred* means holy. A licentious person might be considered immoral, but not unholy (unblessed). Besides, *sacred* is used to refer to an object or place, not a person. So (B) is a weaker antonym than (A).

13. **(D)** To *acclaim* is to approve enthusiastically. It's a close call between (D), (B), and (E). To *taunt* is to insult or ridicule. To *controvert* (B) is to oppose or argue against. A person who controverts might also disapprove, but opposing is not the same as disapproving. To *proscribe* (E) is to prohibit or forbid. Two good antonyms for *proscribe* are "allow" and "permit"—not quite the same as "approve."

14. **(B)** *Vitriolic* means "caustic, sarcastic, or scathing"—a near opposite of *agreeable*. The word *vitriolic* sounds like it describes something that's disagreeable, doesn't it?

15. **(B)** *Taut* means "tense or rigid." *Sedate* (an adjective here) means "calm or relaxed."

Hour 12

Teach Yourself Reading Comprehension I

This hour (as well as the next) you'll teach yourself how to handle the Reading Comprehension questions that appear in the Verbal Ability section of the GRE. Here are your goals for this hour:

- Teach yourself what Reading Comprehension questions look like and how to deal with them
- Teach yourself about some common problems and how to avoid them
- Teach yourself some techniques to help you follow the author's train of thought
- Review what you learned this hour by attempting a GRE-style quiz

GRE READING COMPREHENSION AT A GLANCE

Where: In the GRE Verbal section, mixed in with the Analogy, Antonym, and Sentence Completion questions

How Many:

Paper-Based Test: 11 questions based on 2 passages

CBT: 8 questions based on 3 passages

Basic Format:

Paper-Based Test: 1 short passage (150-200 words) with 3-4 questions, 1 long passage (450-500 words) with 7-8 questions.

CBT: 2 short passages (150-200 words) with 2 questions each, 1 long passage (450-500 words) with 4 questions.

Ground Rules:

- Scratch paper is provided.
- Pencils are permitted and provided.
- Consider each question independently of all others.

What's Covered: You will be tested on some or all of the following Reading Comprehension skills:

- Recognizing the main point or primary purpose of the passage
- Recalling information explicitly stated in the passage
- Making inferences from specific information stated in the passage
- Interpreting, assimilating, or recognizing the purpose of specific information in the passage
- Recognizing the author's tone or attitude as it is revealed in the language of the passage

Directions: Here are sample directions for Reading Comprehension. On both the paper-based exam and the CBT, you'll encounter the directions just before your first group of Reading Comprehension questions:

Paper-based exam:

Each passage in this group is followed by questions or incomplete statements about its content. After reading a passage, select the best answer to each question from the five lettered choices. Answer all the questions following a passage on the basis of what the passage states or implies.

CBT:

The questions in this group are based upon a reading passage. After reading the passage, select the best answer to each question from the five choices. Answer all the questions following the passage on the basis of what the passage states or implies.

What Reading Comprehension Questions Look Like

A Reading Comprehension set consists of a 200-500 word passage followed by 2-8 questions (depending on the test version) each of which has five answer choices. Here's an example of a typical GRE reading comprehension set (we'll analyze this example just a few pages ahead):

NOTE

In both versions of the GRE, passage lines are numbered as they are below, because questions occasionally refer to portions of the passage by line number.

12

The encounter that a portrait records is most tangibly the sitting itself. The sitting may be brief or extended, collegial or confrontational. Cartier-Bresson has

(5) expressed his passion for portrait photography by characterizing it as "a duel without rules, a delicate rape." Such metaphors contrast quite sharply with Richard Avedon's conception of a sitting. While

(10) Cartier-Bresson reveals himself as an interloper and opportunist, Avedon confesses—perhaps uncomfortably—to a role as diagnostician and (by implication) psychic healer: not as someone who necessarily

(15) transforms his subjects, but as someone

who reveals their essential nature. Both photographers, however, agree that the fundamental dynamic in this process lies squarely in the hands of the artist.

(20) A quite-different paradigm has its roots not in confrontation or consultation but in active collaboration between the artist and sitter. This very different kind of relationship was formulated most vividly by

(25) William Hazlitt in his essay entitled "On Sitting for One's Picture" (1823). To Hazlitt, the "bond of connection" between painter and sitter is most like the relationship between two lovers. Hazlitt fleshes

(30) out his thesis by recalling the career of

Sir Joshua Reynolds. According to Hazlitt, Reynold's sitters were meant to enjoy an atmosphere that was both comfortable for them and conducive to the enterprise (35) of the portrait painter, who was simultaneously their host and their contractual employee.

1. Which of the following best expresses the passage's main idea?

    (A) The success of a portrait depends largely on the relationship between artist and subject.
    (B) Portraits, more than most other art forms, provide insight into the artist's social relationships.
    (C) The social aspect of portraiture sitting plays an important part in the sitting's outcome.
    (D) Photographers and painters differ in their views regarding their role in portrait photography.
    (E) The paintings of Reynolds provide a record of his success in achieving a social bond with his subjects.

2. The author quotes Cartier-Bresson in order to

    (A) refute Avedon's conception of a portrait sitting.
    (B) provide one perspective of the portraiture encounter.
    (C) support the claim that portrait sittings are, more often than not, confrontational encounters.
    (D) show that a portraiture encounter can be either brief or extended.
    (E) distinguish a sitting for a photographic portrait from a sitting for a painted portrait.

3. Which of the following best characterizes the portraiture experience as viewed by Avedon?

    (A) a collaboration
    (B) a mutual accommodation
    (C) a confrontation
    (D) an uncomfortable encounter
    (E) a consultation

NOTE

There are no *lettered* answer choices on the GRE-CBT. Instead, you'll select your answer by clicking on the blank oval that precedes your answer choice.

What You Should Know About Reading Comprehension Questions

Reading Comprehension questions are not designed simply to measure your ability to remember what you read. Rather, they are designed to gauge your ability to assimilate and understand the ideas presented.

Most questions require you to draw information from various parts of the passage. Although it might be possible to analyze some questions based on an isolated sentence or two, for most questions you need to bring together information from various parts of the passage to reach your answer.

Questions focusing on information appearing early in the passage usually come before other questions.

Questions vary in difficulty. Some require close judgment calls, whereas for others the "best" response is far better than any other choice. Questions requiring you simply to recall one or two specific bits of information are easier than those requiring you to assimilate and assess an entire paragraph or the entire passage.

Reading Comprehension questions are not designed to test your vocabulary. Where a passage introduces but does not define a technical term, the passage supplies all that you need to know about the term to respond to the questions.

Reading Comprehension passages draw from a variety of subjects, including the humanities, social sciences, the physical sciences, ethics, philosophy, and law. Specific sources include professional journals and periodicals, dissertations, as well as periodicals and books that deal with sophisticated subjects of intellectual interest.

Prior knowledge of the subject matter of Reading Comprehension passages is not important. The testing service is careful to ensure that all questions can be answered based solely on the information that the passage provides. The exam includes passages from a variety of disciplines, so it is unlikely that any particular test-taker knows enough about two or more of the areas included on the test to hold a significant advantage over other test-takers.

How to Tackle a Reading Comprehension Question

Here's a 5-step approach to help you handle the Reading Comprehension questions.

1. **Read the first question stem carefully.**
2. **Read the passage carefully.**
3. **Read *all* of the answer choices carefully.**
4. **Select the choice that best answers the question on the basis of the information provided.**
5. **Repeat Steps 1-4 for each of the remaining questions.**

12

Analyzing a Sample Reading Comprehension Problem

Go back to the sample reading comprehension set involving portraits on page 233-234. Try to answer the questions using the 5-step approach you just learned. Then read the explanation that follows. (Take your time; you're just getting started, so work through the problem deliberately step by step.)

 Here are the answers and explanations:

Question 1. The best response is **(C)**. Although it is difficult to articulate a single "main idea" or thesis of this passage, the author seems to be most concerned with emphasizing that a portrait sitting is a social encounter, not just an artistic exercise, and that artists consider their relationship with their sitters to be somehow significant. For this reason, response (C) is a good statement of the author's main point.

> **TIP**
>
> In many cases the main idea can be identified by simply considering what the author is most concerned with or spends most time talking about.

> **TIME SAVER**
>
> Answer choices that distort, confuse, or depart from the information in the passage, or that introduce information not contained in the passage can be eliminated immediately.

Question 2. This question is a typical "purpose-of-detail" question (you learn more about question types later). **(B)** is the best response. In the passage, the author compares and contrasts three different perspectives of the portraiture encounter: Avedon's view, Cartier-Bresson's view, and Reynold's view as interpreted and reflected by Hazlitt.

Question 3. This is a typical example of a question in which your job is to assimilate and interpret specific information in the passage. **(E)** is the best response. In the first sentence of the second paragraph, the author distinguishes a "quite-different paradigm" (that is, the case of Reynolds) from the conceptions of Cartier-Bresson and Avedon in that the Reynolds paradigm "has its roots not in confrontation or consultation but in active collaboration between artist and sitter." It is rather obvious from the third sentence of the passage that Cartier-Bresson conceives the encounter as "confrontational"; thus, the author seems to be characterizing an Avedon sitting as a "consultation."

TIP

Determining the best answer usually requires comparing the accuracy of the two (or three) best choices.

Common Reading Comprehension Problems

Here are some of the most common problems you might encounter with the Reading Comprehension passages:

- Your concentration may be poor
- Your reading speed may be too slow
- You may need to search the passage again and again for the information needed to respond to each question
- You may have difficulty narrowing down the answer choices to one answer that is clearly the best

All these problems result from the same bad habit: passive reading. To overcome this habit you must develop an active approach. You can begin by keeping the following goal in mind as you read each passage: Try to understand the passage well enough so that you can briefly explain the main point and line of reasoning to someone who has not read the passage.

Techniques to Help You Overcome the Common Problems

Avoid the passive reading mode. Don't take a passive approach toward the Reading Comprehension passages. In other words, don't give equal time and attention to every sentence in the passage. And, don't read the passage from beginning to end without thought as to what information is needed to respond to the questions. Reading passively might enable you to remember some scattered factual information and ideas, but it won't help you with questions that require some insight and assessment of the passage's information.

Pause midway through the passage to sum up and anticipate. After reading the first logical "block" of the passage (perhaps the first third or half of the passage), pause for a moment to evaluate that material. Try to summarize, answering the following questions for yourself:

12

- How would I sum up the passage to this point?
- At what point is the discussion now?
- What basic points is the author trying to get across in this portion?
- Do the ideas in this portion continue a line of thought, or do they begin a new one?
- Where is the discussion likely to go from here?

Consider the first question as you read the passage the first time. Don't wait until you've read the entire passage to begin considering the first question posed. If the first question relates to the beginning of the passage, try answering it, at least tentatively, as soon as you can. The initial part of the passage will often provide enough information for you to answer (tentatively) any question that asks about the author's overall thesis, topic, or purpose. Return to the passage and read the next logical "chunk" still keeping the first question in mind. Reconsider the first question in light of this additional information. Have you changed your mind about your tentative response after reading it? Or has it confirmed that your initial answer was correct?

Always read the entire passage before confirming your response to the first question. Even if the first question seems clearly to involve the initial portion of the passage, do not confirm your response to that question without first reading the entire passage. It is always possible that information relevant to the first question will appear at the end of the passage.

Try to summarize the passage after reading it. After reading the entire passage, take a few seconds to recap the passage in your mind. What was the author's main point and what were the major supporting points? Just think about the flow of the discussion; don't be concerned with remembering all the detailed factual information.

Try to minimize vertical scrolling. Some vertical scrolling will be necessary to read an entire passage. Try to minimize scrolling by taking notes and by responding to the first question posed as you read. Also, do not dwell on questions too long; otherwise, you might be tempted to reread the passage in its entirety, thereby using up valuable time and adding to the eye strain associated with scrolling up and down text on the screen. (CBT only)

Don't preview before reading the passage. You might think that you should preview the passage by reading the first (and perhaps last) sentence of each paragraph before reading a passage straight through (from beginning to end). Presumably, doing this would provide clues about the passage's scope, the author's thesis or major conclusions, and the argument's structure and flow. Although this technique makes sense in theory, it is rarely helpful in practice on the GRE.

DO's and DON'Ts to Help You Read More Effectively

Here's a useful list of DO's and DON'Ts to help you remember the key points of the previous discussion.

Do	**DON'T**

DO read actively — not passively.

DON'T give equal time and attention to every sentence in the passage.

DON'T read the passage from beginning to end without thinking about what information is needed to respond to the questions.

DON'T read the passage without one of the test questions in mind.

DO read the entire passage before selecting your answer.

DON'T read the first and last sentences of the passage before reading it from beginning to end.

DO try to minimize vertical scrolling. (CBT only)

Techniques To Help You Follow the Author's Train of Thought

Look for Common Organization Patterns

The organization of the passage reveals the flow of the author's argument. Focusing on structure will help you to do the following:

- Understand the author's main idea and primary purpose
- Identify major evidence in support of the thesis
- Understand the author's purpose in mentioning various details
- Distinguish main points from minor details

You can often answer questions regarding the main idea, the primary purpose, and the author's attitude just by recognizing the passage's basic organization. Three general organizational patterns appear most often among the Reading Comprehension passages: theory and critique, historical influence, and classification. Familiarizing yourself with these common patterns will help you to anticipate the flow of the discussion in a passage.

12

As you study these patterns, keep in mind that not all passages fall neatly into one of these common patterns. A particular passage might reflect two patterns, present a variation of one of the three common patterns, or reflect some other less common pattern.

Pattern 1: Theory and Critique. The author identifies the conventional (older, established, or traditional) view, theory, or explanation of a phenomenon and either implies or states that it is flawed.

Pattern 2: Historical Influence. The author describes a current or recent state of affairs and claims that this state of affairs resulted from certain previous historical events.

Pattern 3: Classification. The author identifies two or three basic types, categories, or classes of a phenomenon.

 The sample passage at the beginning of this hour is a good example of the classification pattern.

Don't Be Overly Concerned with the Details as You Read

Most GRE Reading Comprehension passages are packed with details. If you try to absorb all the details as you read, you will lose sight of the main points and sacrifice reading speed. Don't get bogged down in the details. Instead, just make a note of where such things as examples, lists, and other details are located. Then, if a particular question involves those details, you can quickly and easily locate them and read them in more detail.

Develop Notes and Outlines

As you're reading make shorthand notes to summarize paragraphs or to indicate the flow of the passage's discussion. Notes can also help you locate details more quickly and recap the passage more effectively. Keep your notes as brief as possible—two or three words are enough in most cases to indicate a particular idea or component of the passage. For complicated passages, a "mini-outline" is a good way to organize information and to keep particular details straight in your mind. The following situations are ideal for a mini-outline:

- If the passage categorizes or classifies various things, use an outline to help you keep track of which belong in each category.

- If the passage mentions several individual names (for example, of authors, artists, political figures, and so on), use an outline to link them according to influence, agreement or disagreement, and so forth.

- If the passage describes a sequence of events, use a time-line outline to keep track of the major features of each event in the sequence.

Make outlines as brief as possible. Don't write complete sentences, just focus on key words.

Workshop

Additional Reading Comprehension questions are available on-line at the authors' Web site: *http://www.west.net/~stewart/gre*

12

Quiz

(Answers and explanations begin on page 244.)

Questions 1-3 are based on the following passage:

Dorothea Lange was perhaps the most notable of the photographers commissioned during the 1930s by the Farm Security Administration (FSA), part of a
(5) federal plan to revitalize the nation's economy and to communicate its human and social dimensions. The value of Lange's photographs as documents for social history is enhanced by her techni-
(10) cal and artistic mastery of the medium. Her well-composed, sharp-focus images reveal a wealth of information about her subjects and show historical evidence that would scarcely be known but for her camera. Her
(15) finest images, while according with conditions of poverty that prompted political response, portray people who appear indomitable, unvanquished by their reverses. "Migrant Mother," for example,
(20) portrays a sense of the innocent victim, of perseverance, of destitution as a temporary aberration calling for compassion, solutions, and politics to alter life for the better. The power of that photograph,
(25) which became the symbol of the photographic file of the FSA, endures today.

The documentary book was a natural genre for Lange and her husband Paul Taylor, whose narrative accompanied
(30) Lange's FSA photographs. In *An American Exodus*, produced by Lange and Taylor, a sense of the despair of Lange's subjects is heightened by the captioned quotations of the migrants. Taken from
(35) 1935 to 1940, the *Exodus* pictures became the accepted vision of the migration of Dust Bowl farm workers into California.

1. According to the passage, the photograph entitled "Migrant Mother"

   (A) appeared in the documentary book *An American Exodus*.
   (B) was accompanied by a caption written by Lange's husband.
   (C) was taken by Lange in 1935.
   (D) portrays the mother of a Dust Bowl farm worker.
   (E) is considered by the author to be one of Lange's best photographs.
   (Hint: This is an explicit detail question. As you read the passage for the first time try to find the relevant details to answer the question.)

2. The passage provides information for responding to all the following questions EXCEPT:

(A) What was the FSA's purpose in compiling the photographic file to which Lange contributed?

(B) How did the FSA react to the photographs taken by Lange under its commission?

(C) In what areas of the United States did Lange take the photographs that appear in *An American Exodus*?

(D) Why did Lange agree to work for the FSA?

(E) What qualities make Lange's photographs noteworthy?

(Hint: This is an explicit detail question. Look for specific information that would provide answers to each of the questions. If you made a mini-outline of the passage during your first reading you probably have all the information you need to respond.)

3. Among the following characterizations, the passage is best viewed as

(A) a survey of the great photographers of the Depression era.

(B) an examination of the photographic techniques of Dorothea Lange.

(C) an argument for the power of pictures to enact social change.

(D) a discussion of the goals and programs of the FSA's photographic department.

(E) an explanation of Lange's interest in documenting the plight of Depression victims.

(Hint: This is a primary purpose question. Think about what the author spends most time discussing.)

Questions 4 and 5 are based on the following passage:

Radiative forcings are changes imposed on the planetary energy balance; radiative feedbacks are changes induced by climate change. Forcings can arise from natural

(5) or anthropogenic causes. For example, the concentration of sulfate aerosols in the atmosphere can be altered by volcanic action or by the burning of fossil fuels. The distinction between forcings and feed-

(10) backs is sometimes arbitrary; however, forcings are quantities normally specified in global climate model simulations, whereas feedbacks are calculated quantities. Examples of radiative forcings are

(15) greenhouse gases (such as carbon dioxide and ozone), aerosols in the troposphere, and surface reflectivity. Radiative feedbacks include clouds, water vapor in the troposphere, and sea-ice cover.

(20) The effects of forcings and feedbacks on climate are complex and uncertain. For example, clouds trap outgoing radiation and thus provide a warming influence. However, they also reflect incoming solar

(25) radiation and thus provide a cooling influence. Current measurements indicate that the net effect of clouds is to cool the Earth. However, scientists are unsure whether the balance will shift in the

(30) future as the atmosphere and cloud formation are altered by the accumulation of greenhouse gases. Similarly, the vertical distribution of ozone affects both the amount of radiation reaching the Earth's

(35) surface and of reradiated radiation that is trapped by the greenhouse effect. These two mechanisms affect the Earth's temperature in opposite directions.

12

4. According to the passage, radiative forcings and radiative feedbacks can usually be distinguished in which of the following ways?

   (A) Whether the radiative change is global or more localized

   (B) The precision with which the amounts of radiative change can be determined

   (C) That altitude at which the radiative change occurs

   (D) Whether the amount of radiative change is specified or calculated

   (E) Whether the radiative change is directed toward or away from the Earth

   (Hint: This is an explicit detail question. As you read the passage for the first time try to locate the relevant details to answer the question. Be sure to read the entire passage before you confirm your answer choice.)

5. The author discusses the effect of clouds on atmospheric temperature probably to show that

   (A) radiative feedbacks can be more difficult to isolate and predict than radiative forcings.

   (B) the climatic impact of some radiative feedbacks is uncertain.

   (C) some radiative feedbacks cannot be determined solely by global climate model simulations.

   (D) the distinction between radiative feedbacks and radiative forcings is somewhat arbitrary.

   (E) the effects of radiative forcings on planetary energy balance are both complex and uncertain.

   (Hint: This is a purpose of detail question. Locate the relevant part of the passage and ask yourself why the author discusses the effect of clouds on atmospheric temperature.)

Answers and Explanations

1. **(E)** This is an example of an explicit detail question. The author cites "Migrant Mother" as an example of "(h)er finest images"-that is, as an example of her best photographs. Answer (A) calls for speculation. The photograph might have appeared in Lange's book; however, the passage does not explicitly say so. (B) calls for speculation. Lange's husband wrote narrative captions for the photographs appearing in *Exodus*. However, the passage does not indicate that "Migrant Mother" was accompanied by a caption or even that the photograph appeared in the book. (C) provides information not mentioned in the passage. Although it is reasonable to assume that Lange took the photograph during the 1930s, the passage neither states nor implies what year she took the photo. (D) calls for speculation. According to the passage, the photographs appearing in *Exodus* "became the accepted vision of the migration of Dust Bowl farm workers to California." However, the author does not indicate either that "Migrant Mother" appeared in the

book or that the woman portrayed in the photograph was indeed the mother of a Dust Bowl farm worker.

2. **(D)** This is another explicit detail question. The passage provides absolutely no information about Lange's motives or reasons for accepting her FSA commission. The passage's first sentence answers (A) implicitly: " . . . the FSA, part of a federal plan to revitalize the economy and to communicate its human and social dimensions." Thus, the photographic file was compiled in furtherance of that purpose. The first paragraph's last sentence answers (B) implicitly. The FSA thought highly enough of one of Lange's photographs to use it as a symbol for its photographic file. The second paragraph answers (C) implicitly. According to the passage, the *Exodus* pictures recorded the migration of Dust Bowl farm workers into California. Thus, some (and probably all or nearly all) of these photographs were taken in the Dust Bowl region of the U.S. or in California. The passage answers (E) in the first paragraph, where the author mentions Lange's "well-composed, sharp-focus" images.

3. **(C)** This is a main point or primary purpose question.

   Admittedly, (C) is not an ideal characterization of the passage, which seems more concerned with Lange's work than with making a broader argument about the power of pictures. Nevertheless, the author does allude to Lange's ability to convey a need for social change through her photographs. Accordingly, the passage

can be characterized as presenting one example (Lange) to support the broader point suggested by choice (C). Response (A) is far too broad. Lange is the only photographer that the passage discusses. (B) is too narrow. Although the author mentions some of Lange's techniques (for example, her "well-composed, sharp-focus images"), the author does not examine them in any detail.(D) distorts the passage and is too broad. First, the passage does not indicate that a distinct photographic department within the FSA existed; in this sense, (D) distorts the passage's information. Second, although the first sentence alludes to the FSA's overall purpose, the passage offers no further discussion of the agency's goals or program, other than the discussion of Lange's involvement in compiling its photographic file; in this sense, (D) is far too broad. (E) distorts the passage. The author does not discuss Lange's motive or reasons for photographing Depression victims other than that the FSA commissioned her to do so.

4. **(D)** This is an explicit detail question. According to the passage, radiative "forcings are quantities normally specified in global climate model situations, whereas feedbacks are calculated quantities." Answer (A) is wholly unsupported by the passage. The author never discusses the geographic extent of radiative changes in any context. The passage does not support (B). The fact that feedbacks are "calculated quantities" whereas forcings are "specified" quantities does not in itself suggest that one can be more precisely determined than the other. (C) and (E)

12

confuse the information in the passage in a similar way. The second paragraph discusses altitude as a factor influencing the relative effects on ozone changes (a radiative forcing) of radiation directed toward Earth and radiation directed away from Earth. This area of discussion involves forcings only, not feedbacks.

5. **(B)** This is a purpose of detail question. (B) restates the author's point in the first sentence of the second paragraph. Immediately thereafter, the author discusses clouds as an example of this point-it is difficult to predict the impact of greenhouse gases on clouds and thus on temperature. The passage does not support (A). In the second paragraph, the author discusses two particular examples of radiative changes: one involving radiative forcings and the other involving radiative feedbacks. The author's purpose in discussing these two phenomena is to illustrate the author's previous point that "(t)he effects of some forcings and feedbacks on climate are complex and uncertain." However, the author makes no attempt to compare the relative complexity or uncertainty of these two effects.(C) confuses the information in the passage and is somewhat nonsensical. The global climate model simulations specifies (do not determine) forcings (not feedbacks). Moreover, (C) is wholly unsupported by the information in the second paragraph; nowhere does the author discuss or mention global climate simulations in relation to the effects of clouds on atmospheric temperatures. The passage supports (D), but (D) does not respond to the question. In the first paragraph, the author attempts to distinguish between forcings and feedbacks and does indeed mention that the distinction can be somewhat arbitrary. However, this point is completely unrelated to the discussion in the second paragraph. (E) is the second-best response. The passage's first sentence defines radiative forcings as "changes imposed on the planetary energy balance." (E) is indeed one of the author's points in the second paragraph. However, (E) does not respond to the question, which deals with feedbacks rather than forcings.

Hour 13

Teach Yourself Reading Comprehension II

Now that you know what to look for in GRE reading passages, it's time to focus on the questions themselves. In this hour you'll teach yourself to recognize the GRE's basic Reading Comprehension question types and the most common wrong answer ploys. Here are your specific goals for this hour:

- Teach yourself to identify the six basic question types and the eight common wrong-answer types
- Teach yourself how to deal with the six basic question types
- Teach yourself some DOs and DON'Ts for responding to GRE Reading Comprehension questions
- Review the skills you learned this hour by attempting a GRE-style quiz

Six Reading Comprehension Question Types

Here are the six basic types of reading questions you'll see on the GRE.

 NOTE Your particular test might not include each of these question types. Question types 1-4 are the most common.

Question Type 1. Main Idea or Primary Purpose

This type tests your ability to recognize the central idea of a passage or to determine the author's purpose. Main-idea and primary-purpose questions are typically worded as follows:

- The author's aim in the passage is to
- The author is primarily concerned with
- Which of the following is the best title for the passage?
- Which of the following questions does the passage answer?

Question Type 2. Explicit Detail

This type tests your ability to recall explicit information in the passage. Detail questions are typically worded as follows:

- Each of the following is mentioned in the passage *except:*
- The passage includes all of the following as examples of ... *except*:
- According to the passage all of the following are true *except*:
- The author mentions ... as examples of

Question Type 3. Inference

This type tests your ability to go beyond the author's explicit statements and determine what these statements imply. Inference questions are typically worded as follows:

- The author implies that
- It can be inferred from lines X-X that ...
- In discussing ... the author suggests which of the following?
- Which of the following does the passage imply ...

Question Type 4. Purpose Of Details

This type tests your ability to recognize the function of specific information stated in the passage. Purpose-of-detail questions are typically worded as follows:

- The author discusses ... in order to
- The reason the author mentioned ... was to
- The author quotes ... in order to
- The function of ... in the passage is to

Question Type 5. Author's Tone Or Attitude

This type tests your ability to sense how the author feels about the subject of the passage. Attitude-recognition questions are typically worded as follows:

- The author would most likely agree with which of the following?
- Which of the following best describes the author's attitude towards
- The author's tone in the passage can best be described as
- The author's presentation is best characterized as

Question Type 6. Application

This type tests your ability to apply the author's ideas to new situations. Application questions are typically worded as follows:

- Which of the following statements would be most likely to begin the next paragraph after the passage?
- Given the information in the passage how would the author likely respond to ...
- It is most likely that in the paragraph immediately preceding this passage the author discussed
- The passage would be most likely to appear in

13

Eight Favorite Wrong-Answer Types

Think about it! In most cases, four of the five answers to any question are wrong. This means that knowing how to recognize the various ways the test-makers try to make bad answers look good is just as important as knowing how to get the right answer. Here's a list of the eight most common wrong-answer types you will see. Keep these wrong-answer types in mind when you're narrowing down the choices to the best answer choice. By eliminating obvious wrong answers the best choices will pop out at you.

Wrong-Answer Type 1. Distort the author's position or distort information in the passage. An answer choice distorts the information in the passage if it understates, overstates, or twists the passage's information or the author's point in presenting that information. An answer choice distorts the author's position if it misrepresents the author's attitude, argument, main concern, tone, perspective, or opinion.

Wrong-Answer Type 2. Inappropriate response to question. This is an answer choice that uses information from the passage, but does not respond to the question. This type of response can be tempting because the information from the passage will appear familiar to you. If you fail to keep the question in mind as you read the answer choices you will fall for it.

Wrong-Answer Type 3. Unwarranted or unsupported inference. This is an answer choice that relies on speculation on your part or an inference on your part that is not supported by the passage. This type of response will leap to a conclusion not supported by the passage. Typically, such a response will bring in material that is outside of the passage or will exaggerate or generalize a relatively narrow inference that is warranted by the passage.

Wrong-Answer Type 4. Contrary response. This is an answer choice that is contrary to the passage, contradicts information in the passage, or is stated backward. For example a backward answer might confuse cause with effect or author agreement with author disagreement. You'd be surprised how easily you can turn around certain facts or confuse cause with effect. The test-maker knows this and typically includes an answer choice that is contradicted by, runs contrary to, or states backward some information in the passage.

Wrong-Answer Type 5. Confused response. This is an answer choice that confuses one opinion, position, or detail with another. Typically, such a response incorrectly represents the position or opinion of one person or group as that of another, or it might mention details from the passage that are not relevant to the question at hand.

Wrong-Answer Type 6. Too narrow in scope. An answer choice is too narrow in scope if it focuses on one element of the passage, ignoring other important elements. An answer choice is also too narrow if it focuses on particular information in the passage that is too specific or narrowly focused in terms of the question posed. If the passage discusses a particular topic in only one of three or four paragraphs, you can pretty safely conclude that the author's primary concern is not with that specific topic.

Wrong-Answer Type 7. Too broad in scope. An answer choice is too broad (general) if it embraces information or ideas that are too general or widely focused in terms of the question posed. An answer choice is also too broad in scope if it encompasses the author's main concern or idea but extends that concern or idea beyond the author's intended scope.

Wrong-Answer Type 8. Inappropriate or extraneous information. This is an answer choice that relies on information that the passage does not mention. Such a response brings in extraneous information not found anywhere in the passage.

A Sample Question Set

Before examining the question types in greater detail, take 5-6 minutes to read the following passage and try to answer the questions that follow. As you read the questions try to identify the question type. As you read the answer choices try to identify the wrong-answer types. (We'll use this question set as well as the sample set from Hour 12 (page 233) to illustrate many of the ideas that follow.)

The decline of the Iroquois Indian nations began during the American Revolution of 1776. Disagreement as to whether they should become involved in the war (5) began to divide the Iroquois.

Because of the success of the revolutionaries and the encroachment upon Iroquois lands that followed, many Iroquois resettled in Canada, while those (10) who remained behind lost the respect they had enjoyed among other Indian nations. The introduction of distilled spirits resulted in widespread alcoholism, leading in turn to the rapid decline of both the (15) culture and population. The influence of the Quakers impeded, yet in another sense contributed, to this decline. By establishing schools for the Iroquois and by introducing them to modern technology (20) for agriculture and husbandry, the Quakers instilled in the Iroquois some hope for the future yet undermined the Iroquois' sense of national identity.

Ironically, it was Handsome Lake who (25) can be credited with reviving the Iroquois culture. Lake, the alcoholic half-brother of Seneca Cornplanter, perhaps the most outspoken proponent among the Iroquois for assimilation of white customs and in-(30) stitutions, was a former member of the Great Council of Iroquois nations. Inspired by a near-death vision in 1799, Lake established a new religion among the Iroquois which tied the more useful as-(35) pects of Christianity to traditional Indian beliefs and customs.

1. The passage mentions all the following events as contributing to the decline of the Iroquois culture EXCEPT:

(A) New educational opportunities for the Iroquois people

(B) Divisive power struggles among the leaders of the Iroquois nations

(C) Introduction of new farming technologies

(D) Territorial threats against the Iroquois nations

(E) Discord among the nations regarding their role in the American Revolution

13

2. It can be inferred from the second paragraph that the author considers Handsome Lake's leading a revival of the Iroquois culture to be "ironic" because

(A) he was a former chief of the Great Council.

(B) he was not a full-blooded relative of Seneca Cornplanter.

(C) he was related by blood to a chief proponent of assimilation.

(D) Seneca Cornplanter was Lake's alcoholic half-brother.

(E) his religious beliefs conflicted with traditional Iroquois beliefs.

3. Assuming that the reasons asserted by the author for the decline of the Iroquois culture are historically representative of the decline of cultural minorities, which of the following developments would most likely contribute to the demise of a modern-day ethnic minority?

(A) A bilingual education program in which children who are members of the minority group learn to read and write in both their traditional language and the language prevalent in the present culture

(B) A tax credit for residential-property owners who lease their property to members of the minority group

(C) Increased efforts by local government to eradicate the availability of illegal drugs

(D) A government-sponsored program to assist minority-owned businesses in using computer technology to improve efficiency

(E) The declaration of a national holiday commemorating a past war in which the minority group played an active role

This sample question set (referred to later as the "Iroquois" set) includes examples of three of the six types of questions (question types 2, 3, and 6 respectively) and five of the eight wrong-answer types (wrong-answer types 1,3,4,5, and 7). Were you able to identify them correctly? (Detailed explanations of these questions will be given in the discussion that follows.)

How to Deal With the Six Basic Question Types

Now you'll take a closer look at each of the six question types. Your focus will be on the proper approach to take in each case as well as to become familiar with the wrong-answer types commonly used with each type. To illustrate each type you'll look at the Iroquois question set as well as the "portrait" question set on page 233 in Hour 12.

Main Idea Questions

Main-idea and primary-purpose questions test your ability to detect the author's central idea or theme, or the primary purpose of the passage. Basically, you're expected to be able to differentiate between the forest and the trees — in other words, to distinguish broader and larger ideas and points from supporting evidence and details. Here's a 3-step approach to these questions:

1. **Read the entire passage and formulate your own statement of the main idea of the passage or of author's primary purpose—*before* you look at the answer choices.**

2. **Eliminate answer choices that are too narrow in scope, too broad in scope, or distort the author's position.**

3. **If, after step 2, you are left with two viable answer choices check for the following:**

    *   **consistency between the passage's main idea and the author's primary purpose**

    *   **consistency with the author's attitude (tone, opinion, perspective, and so on)**

CAUTION

> Every passage has a main idea and a primary purpose. In many cases you'll find a sentence at the beginning or end of the passage that states the main idea or primary purpose. However, don't expect every passage to be so helpful; many passages do not include explicit concluding statements or primary-purpose statements.

It's time to go back to the sample question set involving portraits on page 233 (Hour 12). Read the passage once again and try tackling the first question in this set using the approach you just learned. Then read the brief explanation that follows.

QUESTION   1. Which of the following best expresses the passage's main idea?

(A) The success of a portrait depends largely on the relationship between artist and subject.

(B) Portraits, more than most other art forms, provide insight into the artist's social relationships.

(C) The social aspect of portraiture sitting plays an important part in the outcome of the sitting.

(D) Photographers and painters differ in their views regarding their role in portrait photography.

(E) The paintings of Reynolds provide a record of his success in achieving a social bond with his subjects.

13

ANALYSIS The best answer is **(C)**. Answer choices (A), (B) and (D) distort the passage's information. Answer choice (E) is too narrow in scope.

For a more detailed analysis of this question, see Hour 12, page 236.

Explicit Detail Questions

Explicit-detail questions are designed to measure your ability to assimilate details — more specifically, your ability to process detailed information accurately as well as your efficiency in looking up information. The question might either ask which choice (among the five) is mentioned or which choice (among the five) is not mentioned. Here's a 3–step approach to this type of question.

 ACTION PLAN
1. **Make a mini-outline of the passage.**
2. **Use your-mini outline to zero in on the key words in the question.**
3. **Eliminate answer choices that**
   - **confuse information in the passage by referring to unrelated details**
   - **bring in details not mentioned in the passage**
   - **contradict information stated in the passage**

 TIP

> Effective notes or a mini-outline will help you locate the relevant information quickly. Wherever some sort of list is included in the passage—a list of characteristics, a list of examples, or some other list—take note of it. You can be sure that there will be an explicit detail question that focuses on that list.

Now go back once again to the Iroquois question set you looked at earlier. This time try tackling the first question using the 3-step approach you just learned. Then read the explanation that follows.

QUESTION 1. The passage mentions all the following events as contributing to the decline of the Iroquois culture EXCEPT:

(A) new educational opportunities for the Iroquois people.

(B) divisive power struggles among the leaders of the Iroquois nations.

(C) introduction of new farming technologies.

(D) territorial threats against the Iroquois nations.

(E) discord among the nations regarding their role in the American Revolution.

ANALYSIS   This is a variation of question type 2. In this version the answer choice that
confuses, brings in extraneous information or contradicts information stated in
the passage is the best answer. **(B)** is the best answer choice. Nowhere in the passage
does the author mention any power struggles among the leaders of the Iroquois nations.

Inference Questions

Inference questions require you to draw simple conclusions or to recognize somewhat
broader points by going beyond specific passage information. In these questions you must
go beyond what the author explicitly states, and look for other information that would
most likely be true given what is explicitly stated. Inference questions usually require only
that you piece together (logically speaking) no more than two consecutive sentences. To
analyze the question, locate the relevant line or lines in the passage, read around those
lines—the sentence preceding and the sentence following. The inference should be clear
enough to you. The question stem typically refers to specific lines or a specific paragraph
in the passage. In any event, you will discover that, based on the information in the
question stem, you can usually locate the relevant portion of the passage within 5 to 10
seconds (which is quite helpful if you are short of time). Here's a 3–step approach to this
question type.

ACTION PLAN
1. **Locate and read the relevant lines (if given) or paragraph in the passage.**
2. **Ask yourself what other information would most likely be true given what
    is stated in the relevant lines or paragraph.**
3. **Eliminate answer choices that**
    - **require you to make unwarranted assumptions or reach unsup-
      ported conclusions**
    - **require you to bring in extraneous information**
    - **are contrary to or contradict information stated in the relevant lines
      or paragraph**
    - **confuse information stated in the relevant lines or paragraph**
    - **distort or over-generalize information stated in the relevant lines or
      paragraph**

13

CAUTION   Don't overlook the obvious! Inference questions often require you to make
only very "tight" inferences; in other words, the passage will suggest the
conclusion so strongly that no other interpretation is really reasonable. Don't
fight the passage by looking for a more subtle or deeper interpretation.

Now go back to the Iroquois question set and try tackling question 2 using the 3-step method you just learned. Then look at the explanation that follows.

QUESTION 2. It can be inferred from the second paragraph that the author considers Handsome Lake's leading a revival of the Iroquois culture to be "ironic" because

(A) he was a former member of the Great Council. (*This answer choice confuses details from the passage.*)

(B) he was not a full-blooded relative of Seneca Cornplanter. (*This answer choice confuses details from the passage.*)

(C) he was related by blood to a chief proponent of assimilation. (*This is the correct answer.*)

(D) Seneca Cornplanter was Lake's alcoholic half-brother (*This answer choice states information from the passage backward.*)

(E) his religious beliefs conflicted with traditional Iroquois beliefs. (*This answer choice is contrary to the passage's information.*)

ANALYSIS (C) is the best answer choice. The passage states that Cornplanter was an outspoken proponent of assimilation and that Handsome Lake was related to Cornplanter as a half-brother. The fact that Lake was responsible for the Iroquois reasserting their national identity is ironic, then, in light of Lake's blood relationship to Cornplanter.

Purpose-of-detail Questions

Purpose-of-detail questions are designed to determine whether, in immersing yourself in the details, you lost sight of the author's reason for including the details. Basically, what you have to figure out is the aim or function of certain material in the passage. When you come across detailed information in the passage, ask yourself what role these details play in the discussion. As you read, keep in mind that it is more important for you to understand why the author mentions details than to remember the details themselves (you can always look them up later). Here's a 3–step approach to this question type.

ACTION PLAN 1. **Locate the relevant detail (quote, example, discussion) in the passage.**

2. **Read the sentences immediately preceding and following the detail and ask yourself what role it plays in the discussion.**

3. **Eliminate answer choices that**
   - **involve inferences the passage does not support**
   - **distort the author's purpose**
   - **confuse information in the passage**
   - **are contrary to or contradict information in the passage**

Here's an example of this question type taken from the portrait question set you looked at last hour (Hour 12, page 233).

 QUESTION   2. The author quotes Cartier-Bresson in order to

(A) refute Avedon's conception of a portrait sitting.

(B) provide one perspective of the portraiture encounter.

(C) support the claim that portrait sittings are, more often than not, confrontational encounters.

(D) show that a portraiture encounter may be either brief or extended.

(E) distinguish a sitting for a photographic portrait from a sitting for a painted portrait

ANALYSIS   **(B)** is the best answer. Answer choices (A) and (C) distort the passage's information. (D) confuses the information, and (E) is not supported by the passage.

Author's Attitude Questions

Attitude-recognition questions are designed to test your ability to sense the author's emotional involvement with the topic of the passage. In other words, you're trying to figure out how the author feels about the subject. To determine the mood, tone, or attitude of the author you must pay close attention to words in the passage that convey the author's emotions. Generally speaking, a lack of emotional terms or images in a passage would tend to indicate a neutral, academic, or indifferent attitude toward the subject on the part of the author. Words, images, and descriptive phrases that convey a light mood would likely indicate an optimistic, enthusiastic, positive mood or attitude, whereas those that convey a dark or brooding mood would likely indicate a negative, critical, resigned attitude. Here's a 3-step approach to this question type.

ACTION PLAN   1. **Scan the passage looking for emotion-laden words, descriptions, or images.**

2. **Assess the author's overall emotional tone by deciding whether these words, descriptions, or images are emotionally positive, neutral, or negative**

3. **Eliminate answer choices that**
   - **run contrary to the author's emotional tone**
   - **distort or exaggerate the author's emotional tone**
   - **confuse the author's emotional tone**
   - **are too negative, too positive, or too extreme**

13

TIP

> Since most of the passages that appear on the GRE are taken from academic journals or magazines, it is unlikely that the author's of these articles will display strong emotions or political incorrectness in their writing. Answer choices that are extremely negative, positive or politically incorrect can be eliminated immediately.

Here's an example of this question type based on the Iroquois passage you looked at earlier. Try tackling this question using the approach you just learned. Then read the brief explanation that follows.

QUESTION   4. The author's attitude toward the influence of the Quakers on the Iroquois nations is best described as which of the following?

(A) critical

(B) laudatory

(C) congratulatory

(D) enthusiastic

(E) defensive

ANALYSIS   (A) is the best answer. (B) and (C) are too positive and distort the author's attitude. While the author does indicate that Quaker's influence "impeded" the decline of the Iroquois nation and "instilled in the Iroquois some hope for the future," thereby approving and congratulating their influence, the author also points out that their influence "contributed to" the decline and "undermined the Iroquois' sense of national identity." (D) and (E) run contrary to the author's emotional tone. There are no indications in the passage that support these interpretations of the author's attitude.

Application Questions

Application questions are not as common as the other types. Basically you are asked to apply the author's ideas to new situations or to speculate as to how the passage would continue. Like inference questions, application questions require you to go beyond what the author explicitly states. The major difference between these types, however, is that these questions usually involve making much broader inferences. In some cases you will be asked to interpret how the author's ideas might apply to other situations, or be affected by them. To do this requires you to make logical connections between the author's stated ideas and other ideas not explicitly discussed in the passage. In other cases you will be asked to assess the author's attitude or feeling toward some new situation. To do this requires you to project the author's attitude and feelings into new situations and determine how the author would likely react to them. Here's a 3-step approach to this question type.

Action Plan 1. Read the passage to determine the author's main idea, reasons for it, and attitude towards it.

2. Put yourself in the author's place and ask yourself one of the following questions (the question stem will tell you which one is relevant):

- what would I say next?
- what would I say to introduce my idea?
- what would I say in this situation?
- how would I feel in this case?
- what would make my view stronger (or weaker)?
- who am I trying to convince?

3. Eliminate answer choices that

- require you to make an inference that is not supported by the passage
- are contrary to or contradict the author's main idea or attitude
- distort the author's attitude
- are based on information that is not stated in the passage

Here's an example of this question type taken from the Iroquois question set you looked at earlier. Try tackling this question using the approach you just learned. Then read the brief explanation that follows.

Question 3. Assuming that the reasons asserted by the author for the decline of the Iroquois culture are historically representative of the decline of cultural minorities, which of the following developments would most likely contribute to the demise of a modern-day ethnic minority?

(A) A bilingual education program in which children who are members of the minority group learn to read and write in both their traditional language and the language prevalent in the present culture.

(B) A tax credit for residential-property owners who lease their property to members of the minority group.

(C) Increased efforts by local government to eradicate the availability of illegal drugs.

(D) A government-sponsored program to assist minority-owned businesses in using computer technology to improve efficiency.

(E) The declaration of a national holiday commemorating a past war in which the minority-group played an active role.

13

ANALYSIS (D) is the best answer. According to the author, the Quakers' introduction of new technology to the Iroquois was partly responsible for the decline of the Iroquois culture in that it contributed to the tribe's loss of national identity. (D) presents a similar situation.

DO's and DON'Ts For Reading Comprehension Questions

Do	Don't

DON'T second-guess the test-maker.

DO read every answer choice in its entirety.

DON'T over-analyze questions or second-guess yourself.

DON'T overlook the obvious.

DO eliminate responses that run contrary to the main idea of the passage.

DO keep in mind the 8 common wrong-answer types to avoid falling into the test-maker's traps.

Workshop

 ONLINE   Additional Reading Comprehension questions are available on-line at the authors' Web site: *http://www.west.net/~stewart/gre*

Quiz

(Answers and explanations begin on page 264.)

Questions 1-5 are based on the following passage.

The origin of the attempt to distinguish early from modern music and to establish the canons of performance practice for each lies in the eighteenth century. In the
(5) first half of that century, when Telemann and Bach ran the *collegium musicum* in Leipzig, Germany, they performed their own and other modern music. In the German universities of the early twenti-
(10) eth century, however, the reconstituted *collegium musicum* devoted itself to performing music from the centuries before the beginning of the "standard repertory," by which was understood music from
(15) before the time of Bach and Handel.

Alongside this modern *collegium musicum*, German musicologists developed the historical subdiscipline known as "performance practice," which included
(20) the deciphering of obsolete musical notation and its transcription into modern notation, the study of obsolete instruments, and the re-establishment of lost oral traditions associated with those forgotten
(25) repertories. The cutoff date for this study was understood to be around 1750, the year of Bach's death, since the music of Bach, Handel, Telemann and their contemporaries did call for obsolete instruments

(30) and voices and unannotated performing traditions-for instance, the spontaneous realization of vocal and instrumental melodic ornamentation. Furthermore, with a few exceptions, late baroque music had
(35) ceased to be performed for nearly a century, and the orally transmitted performing traditions associated with it were forgotten as a result. In contrast, the notation in the music of Haydn and Mozart
(40) from the second half of the eighteenth century was more complete than in the earlier styles, and the instruments seemed familiar, so no "special" knowledge appeared necessary. Also, the music of
(45) Haydn and Mozart, having never ceased to be performed, had maintained some kind of oral tradition of performance practice.

Beginning around 1960, however, the
(50) early musicians—the performers of early music—began to encroach upon the music of Haydn, Mozart, and Beethoven. Why? Scholars studying performance practice had discovered that the living oral
(55) traditions associated with the Viennese classics frequently could not be traced back to the eighteenth century and that there were nearly as many performance mysteries to solve for music after 1750 as
(60) in earlier repertories. Furthermore, more

13

and more young singers and instrumentalists became attracted to early music, and
as many of them graduated from student
and amateur status to become fully pro-
(65) fessional, the technical level of early-
music performances took a giant leap
forward.

   As professional early-music groups,
building on these developments, expanded
(70) their repertories to include later music, the
angry cries from the mainstream could be
heard on five continents. The differences
between the two camps extended beyond
the already fascinating question of which
(75) instruments to use and how (or whether)
to ornament to the more critical matter of
style and delivery. At the heart of their
disagreement is whether historical knowledge about performing traditions is a pre-
(80) requisite for proper interpretation of music or whether it merely creates an obstacle
to inspired musical tradition.

   1. It can be inferred that the "standard reper-
      tory" mentioned in line 13 might have in-
      cluded music

      (A) composed before 1700
      (B) of the early twentieth century
      (C) written by the performance-practice
          composers
      (D) written before the time of Handel
      (E) that called for the use of obsolete
          instruments
      *(Hint: This is an inference question
      (type 3). Locate the relevant lines and
      ask yourself which of the answer choices
      is most likely true on the basis of the
      information stated.)*

   2. The author mentions the improved tech-
      nical level of early-music performances
      (lines 65–67) in order to

      (A) call into question the fairness of the
          mainstream's objections to the
          expansion of performance practice
          to include later works
      (B) explain why an increasing number
          of young musicians were being
          attracted to early music
      (C) refute the mainstream's claim that
          historical knowledge about per-
          forming traditions creates an
          obstacle to inspired musical
          tradition
      (D) explain the expansion of perfor-
          mance practice to include later
          works of music
      (E) support the argument that the
          Viennese classics were more
          difficult to perform than earlier
          works
      *(Hint: This is a purpose of detail
      question (type 4). Locate the relevant
      lines and read the sentences immedi-
      ately preceding and following. Ask
      yourself what role the targeted informa-
      tion plays in this context.)*

3. According to the passage, performance practice in the early twentieth century involved all of the following EXCEPT:

   (A) deciphering outdated music notation

   (B) varying the delivery of music to suit the tastes of the particular audience

   (C) determining which musical instrument to use

   (D) reestablishing unannotated performing traditions

   (E) transcribing older music into modern notation

   {Hint: This is an explicit detail question (type 2). Make a mini-outline of the passage zeroing in on the key words in the question.)

4. Which of the following statements, if true, would best support the author's explanation for the encroachment by the early-musicians upon the music of Mozart, Haydn, and Beethoven?

   (A) The mainstream approved of the manner in which the early-musicians treated the music of Bach and Handel.

   (B) Unannotated performing traditions associated with these composers were distinct from those associated with pre-1750 works.

   (C) Most instrumentalists are attracted to early music because of the opportunities to play obsolete instruments.

   (D) The music of these composers is notated more completely than is the music of Bach and Handel.

   (E) The early-musicians and the mainstream both prefer the same style and delivery of music.

   (Hint: This is an application-of-ideas question (type 6).)

5. Which of the following is the most appropriate title for the passage?

   (A) Performance Practice: The Legacy of the German *Collegium musicum*

   (B) How Far Should Early Music Extend?

   (C) Unannotated Performing Traditions of the Eighteenth and Twentieth Centuries

   (D) Performance Practice and New Interpretations of the Viennese Classics

   (E) Competing Views Regarding the Necessity of Historical Knowledge for Inspired Musical Tradition

   (Hint: This is a primary-purpose question (type 1). Formulate your own statement of the main idea of the passage, then look for the title that best expresses that idea.)

13

Answers and Explanations

1. **(E)** It is reasonably inferable from the first paragraph as a whole that the "standard repertory" mentioned in line 13 refers to the music of Bach and Telemann as well as to other ("modern") music from their time (first half of the eighteenth century). In the second paragraph, the author mentions that the music of Bach, Telemann, and their contemporaries called for obsolete instruments (line 22). Thus, the standard repertory might have included music that called for the use of obsolete instruments, as (E) indicates.

2. **(D)** At the beginning of the third paragraph, the author states that, beginning around 1960, early-musicians began to encroach upon the works of Haydn, Mozart and Beethoven. The remainder of the third paragraph is devoted to explaining the reasons for this encroachment. One of the contributing reasons given is that the technical level of early-music performances had improved.

3. **(B)** Although performance practice did indeed involve varying the performance of a work of music from one time to the next (by including spontaneous vocal and instrumental ornamentation), the passage neither states nor implies that how the delivery of music varied from time to time depended upon the particular tastes of the audience. Thus, (B) is unsupported by the passage.

4. **(B)** According to the passage, one reason for the encroachment was that some of the oral traditions associated with the Viennese classics (the works of Mozart, Haydn, and Beethoven) could not be traced back to the eighteenth century. (B) supports this point by providing specific evidence that this was indeed the case.

5. **(B)** The author's primary concern in the passage is to trace the scope of works included in performance practice from the early twentieth century to the latter half of the century. The author identifies and explains the reasons for the trend of including later works within the scope of so-called "early music" (second and third paragraphs), then refers (in the final paragraph) to a controversy surrounding this trend. (B) reflects the author's primary concern as well as embracing the controversy.

Part IV

Learn to Answer GRE Analytical Questions

HOUR 14

Teach Yourself Analytical Reasoning I

This hour you'll familiarize yourself with the Analytical Reasoning question format, learn strategies for handling these questions, and examine one type of *logic game* (set of Analytical Reasoning questions) appearing frequently on the GRE. In this hour you will learn:

- What logic games look like
- Strategies for handling a logic game
- How to analyze a typical "logic game"
- All you need to know about formal logic for these questions
- How to recognize and handle GRE "selection" games

Analytical Reasoning questions are grouped into sets which we'll call *logic games* from now on.

Analytical Reasoning at a Glance

How Many:

Paper-based test: 19 questions (grouped into 3–5 games, 4–7 questions per game)

CBT: 26 questions (grouped into 6 games, 4–5 questions per game)

Where: In the Analytical section(s), mixed in with Logical Reasoning questions

What's Covered:

Logic games test your ability to:

- understand a system of relationships
- draw deductive conclusions about those relationships
- assimilate and organize information quickly and accurately
- visualize spatial relationships

Directions:

Here are the directions for Analytical Reasoning questions:

DIRECTIONS: This group of questions is based on a passage and a set of rules. In answering the questions, you might find it helpful to draw rough diagrams. For each question, select the best answer from the five lettered choices.

What GRE Logic Games Look Like

Let's take a look at a typical GRE logic game. This is a good example of a *sequencing* game—a type that appears frequently on the GRE. Take about 10 minutes to assimilate the rules of this game and to attempt the questions. Get out some scratch paper; you'll need it. We'll analyze this game just a few pages ahead.

QUESTION An amusement park roller coaster includes five cars, numbered 1 through 5 from front to back. Each car accommodates up to two riders, seated side by side. Six people—Tom, Gwen, Laurie, Mark, Paul, and Jack—are riding the coaster at the same time.

> Laurie is sharing a car.
>
> Mark is not sharing a car and is seated immediately behind an empty car.
>
> Tom is not sharing a car with either Gwen or Paul.
>
> Gwen is riding in either the third or fourth car.

1. Which of the following groups of riders could occupy the second car?

    (A) Laurie only

    (B) Tom and Gwen

    (C) Laurie and Mark

    (D) Jack and Tom

    (E) Jack, Gwen, and Paul

2. If Gwen is riding immediately behind Laurie's car and immediately ahead of Tom's car, all of the following must be true EXCEPT:

    (A) Gwen is riding in the fourth car.

    (B) Paul is riding in the third car.

    (C) Tom is riding in the fifth car.

    (D) Laurie is riding in the third car.

    (E) The first car is empty.

3. Which one of the following statements CANNOT be true?

    (A) Neither Tom nor Gwen is sharing a car with another rider.

    (B) Neither Mark nor Jack is sharing a car with another rider.

    (C) Tom is sharing a car, and Jack is sharing a car.

    (D) Gwen is sharing a car, and Paul is sharing a car.

    (E) Tom is sharing a car, and Gwen is sharing a car.

4. If Paul is riding in the second car, how many different combinations of riders are possible for the third car?

    (A) 1

    (B) 2

    (C) 3

    (D) 4

    (E) 5

14

5. Assume that a seventh rider is riding with Jack in the first car, but that all other conditions remain unchanged. Which of the following is a complete and accurate list of the riders who might be riding in the fifth car?

(A) Mark

(B) Tom, Paul

(C) Tom, Laurie, Paul

(D) Tom, Laurie, Mark

(E) Mark, Paul, Tom, Laurie

What You Should Know About GRE Logic Games

Logic games can be categorized, according to your primary task. The test-makers design logic games to fit into certain basic molds. The primary difference between these molds involves the nature of the relationship among the game's subjects. So we've categorized GRE logic games accordingly. Here are the basic categories you're most likely to see on your exam (you'll examine in each in turn during the next three hours):

type of game:	Your task:
selection	You select subjects from among a pool
linear sequencing	You line up the subjects in order (in sequence)
attribute	You assign characteristics—or attributes—to each subject
grouping	You divide the subjects into three or more groups
non-linear spatial	You determine how the subjects are arranged spatially
logical	You determine cause-and-effect relationships among the subjects

 Not all logic games fit squarely into one mold. Many are hybrids in which you must perform two or more of the tasks listed above. It's impossible for us to cover every possible variation. So be flexible; try to develop skills that you can apply to any game.

Each question in a game refers to the same *premise*. The *premise* establishes the setting for the game, lists the subjects involved (e.g., roller-coaster riders), and describes generally how the subjects are related to one another (e.g., roller coaster riders are seated ahead of, next to, or behind other riders).

Each question in a game refers to the same *rules*. These are the statements listed below the premise. They impose specific constraints upon the relationships among the subjects. In other words, *rules limit the number of possible combinations*. You might see as few as two or as many as eight rules in a set, but the number typically ranges from four to six.

You consider each question independently of the others. Additional information provided by the questions themselves is *not* cumulative. No information, other than what is provided in the original premise and conditions, should be carried over from one question to another.

In comparing answer choices, you won't find any shades of gray. In each question, one and only one answer choice can be proven beyond a doubt to be the correct one. In this respect, Analytical Reasoning questions are like Quantitative questions (and unlike all other types of GRE questions, in which you weigh the quality of the answer choices).

On the paper-based test, the first game in each Analytical section will probably be your easiest one. But don't assume that each successive game will be more difficult. In fact, most test-takers do *not* find the last game to be the most difficult one. (On the CBT, of course, the difficulty level adjusts to your level of ability as you go, so there's no set pattern.)

On the paper-based test, the first one or two questions in each game are usually simpler than the others. Earlier questions generally involve the more basic and obvious relationships established by the rules of the game. Some might require no analysis other than recognizing rule violations among the answer choices. Others might focus on just one or two of the rules, without requiring more than one or two deductive steps. In fact, you might be able to respond to the first one or two questions without resorting to pencil and paper. (On the CBT, of course, the difficulty level adjusts to your level of ability as you go, so there's no set pattern.)

On the paper-based test, each game fits on one page of the test booklet. For each game, all of the questions will appear on the same page as the premise and rules. You'll use the blank space below the questions (typically the bottom third of the page) to draw diagrams.

On the CBT, the screen splits vertically for each logic game. The premise and rules appear to the left; the question appears to the right. You may have to scroll to view all of the rules.

Every rule will come into play at some point in the game. By the time you've attempted all the questions, expect to apply each of the game's rules at least once. The test-makers do *not* inject superfluous information just to throw you off track.

14

You won't get very far on logic games without your pencil. Among ETS' "official" tips is the suggestion that although some test-takers find drawing diagrams useful in solving Analytical Reasoning problems, you shouldn't be concerned if a particular problem seems to be best approached without using diagrams. Take it from us: Although you'll encounter the occasional *question* that doesn't require pencil work, you'll definitely need to draw a diagram at some point during every game.

> Learning to construct useful diagrams for logic games is in large part what the next three hours in this book are about.

Time is a big factor for most test-takers. GRE logic games can be tough and time-consuming, even for smart test-takers who have prepared for them. So don't worry if you have trouble handling every question in every game within the allotted time. Nearly every other test-taker is in the same position.

How to Approach a GRE Logic Game

Here's a 5-step approach that will help you to handle any GRE logic game.

1. **Size up the game.**
2. **Create a simple roster of subjects and a template that you can use for every question.**
3. **Incorporate each specific rule into (or around) your template.**
4. **Based on the rules, draw useful conclusions if possible.**
5. **Attempt the first two questions, then "regroup" if you need to.**

Let's Apply the 5-Step Action Plan to a Logic Game

It's time to go back to the roller coaster game you looked at a few pages back. Let's walk through the game using the 5-step approach you just learned.

1. Reading the premise and rules quickly tells you that the game involves two simultaneous tasks: *sequencing* the subjects from front to back and *grouping* riders in the cars. This type of game is usually easy, so on the paper-based test you won't want to skip this one. On the paper-based test, you can also glance quickly at all of the

questions themselves for clues. Key words such as *behind*, *ahead*, and *group*, help confirm your initial assessment.

2. Every possibility falls into one of two scenarios, based on the last rule—*Gwen is riding in either the third or fourth car.* So you can draw two distinct diagrams, one for each scenario. These are the templates you'll use throughout the game.

SCENARIO #1	SCENARIO #2
1	1
2	2
3 G	3
4	4 G
5	5

3. Now consider the other rules. If you try to incorporate any of these rules directly into the template, you'd have to add several different diagrams to account for all of the additional possibilities. What if you overlook a possibility? Run out of space on our paper? Run out of time? Instead of complicating the diagram, simply indicate the remaining rules either as pictures or symbols near the template (we've used the "not equals" symbol to signify that two riders are not sharing the same car):

SCENARIO #1	SCENARIO #2
1	1
2	2
3 Ⓖ	3
4	4 Ⓖ
5	5

[L_]   ⊠
                  M

T ≠ $^G/_P$

TGLMPJ

4. What else can you deduce from the premise and rules? Can you "fit" any other riders into the diagram? Not without adding restrictions. But you can draw certain conclusions about the number of riders in each car. The game's premise states that each car can accommodate up to two riders, but one of the rules states that Mark is seated alone behind an empty car. That leaves three other cars to accommodate the other five riders. Thus, accommodating all six riders requires this distribution:

14

- one and only one car (the car immediately ahead of Mark's car) is empty
- of the other four cars, two (including Mark's car) are occupied by one rider each
- two riders share each of the remaining two cars

This additional information is important in analyzing the questions. In fact, by drawing these conclusions prior to answering the questions, you've already done much of the work required to answer the questions.

5. Let's walk through each of the five questions of our roller coaster game.

ANALYSIS 1. The correct answer is (**D**). As is typical for the first question in a game, you don't need a diagram to handle this one. Each answer choice other than (D) violates the premise or one of the rules. (A) violates the rule that Laurie is sharing a car. (B) violates the rule that Gwen is riding in either the third or fourth car; (B) also violates the rule that Tom is not sharing a car with Gwen (although either rule violation suffices to eliminate this answer choice). (C) violates the rule that Mark is not sharing a car. (E) violates the premise that each car can accommodate up to two riders.

TIME SAVER The most efficient way to handle questions such as this one is consider one rule at a time, scanning the answer choices for violations of the rule.

---

2. The correct answer is (**B**). Consider the question stem in light of our two templates on page 273. You can eliminate scenario #1. Why? In scenario #1, Laurie, Gwen, and Tom would occupy the second, third, and fourth cars, respectively. But this arrangement would not accommodate Mark seated alone immediately behind an empty car (as required by one of the game's rules). So scenario #2 is the only one that applies to this question. Given the additional information in the question stem, Laurie must occupy the third car while Tom occupies the fifth car. Accordingly, Mark must occupy the second car, and the first car must be empty:

SCENARIO #1	SCENARIO #2
1	1 ⊠
2 [L_]	2 M
3 Ⓖ	3 [L_]
4 T	4 Ⓖ
5	5 T

However, Paul may occupy either the third or fourth car. Thus, Statement (B) is not necessarily true.

3. The correct answer is **(A)**. This question focuses on the additional information inferable from the conditions. So if you've done Step 4, you've already done the work needed to answer this question, and you won't need your diagram to handle it. Mark and only one other rider must each be seated alone; otherwise, the coaster could not accommodate all six riders. (Remember, each car can accommodate no more than two riders.) Thus, Tom and Gwen cannot both be seated alone.

4. The correct answer is **(C)**. Question 4, like Question 2, provides additional information that allows you to eliminate one of the two templates (page 273). In Question 4, however, it's scenario #2 that you can eliminate. If Paul and Gwen occupy the second and fourth cars, respectively, Mark cannot sit alone immediately behind an empty car (as required by one of the game's rules). Focusing, then, on scenario #1 (Gwen occupies the third car), given that Paul occupies the second car, Mark must occupy the fifth car, and the fourth car must be empty:

SCENARIO #1	SCENARIO #2
1	1
2 P	2 P
3 Ⓖ	3
4 ⊠	4 Ⓖ
5 M̄	5

Considering the four remaining riders, the rules expressly prohibit Tom from riding with Gwen (in the third car). Accordingly, Gwen must occupy the third car either alone or with Laurie or Jack. Thus, one of exactly three combinations of riders could be riding in the third car: Gwen only, Gwen and Laurie, or Gwen and Jack.

5. The correct answer is **(D)**. Consider the two alternative scenarios on page 273. In scenario #1 (Gwen in the third car), given that Jack and the seventh rider (R) occupy the first car, Mark must occupy the fifth car alone. Next, consider scenario #2 (Gwen in the fourth car). Given that Jack and the seventh rider occupy the first car, Mark must occupy the third car (while the second car is empty). Since Tom cannot share a car with Gwen, Tom must occupy the fifth car. Since Tom cannot share a car with Paul, Paul must share the fourth car with Gwen. Accordingly, Laurie must share the fifth car with Tom.

.14

SCENARIO #1

1 J R
2
3 G
4 ⊠
5 M

SCENARIO #2

1 J R
2 ⊠
3 M
4 G P
5 T L

Thus, either Mark alone (under scenario #1) or both Tom and Laurie (under scenario #2) must occupy the fifth car.

NOTE
Notice that Question 5 alters the original premise slightly. This is unusual. You might see one or two questions like this on the entire exam—at the most.

DO's and DON'Ts (Before You Answer the Questions)

Do   **DON'T**

DON'T be fooled by the apparent length of a game. There's no automatic correlation between the number of questions or rules and the difficulty level of a game.

DON'T let the wording of the rules trip you up. If you carelessly misread a rule, you might respond incorrectly to numerous questions.

DON'T list all possible combinations; instead, use templates that encompass all the possibilities.

DO look for a key rule around which the other rules can be organized. In all likelihood, only one or two games on your exam will include such a key rule; but always look for it!

DO skip one of the games if your optimal pace calls for it (paper-based test only).

DO's and DON'Ts (Answering the Questions)

Do	DON'T

DO ask yourself what you can deduce from information provided by a question, *then* scan the answer choices.

DON'T do more work than necessary; stop when you've done enough to zero in on the correct answer.

DO preserve your template from question to question; no pens are allowed, so earmark information that applies to all questions (circle it, or draw it larger or darker).

DON'T spend more than 10 minutes on any one game. Let those toughies go; on the paper-based test, return to them only if you've finished the section and have extra time (you probably won't).

DO take reasoned guesses, if you're running out of time. A quick glance at a question stem and at one or two rules may suffice to zero in on the correct answer—or at least eliminate a few incorrect ones.

Formal Logic—Everything You Need to Know for Logic Games

You don't need a formal college-level logic course to handle GRE logic games. Much of what you'd learn in such a course—particularly the terminology and symbols—is of little practical use in handling GRE logic games. But there's one particular concept in formal logic that is crucial for success in handling logic games. So we'll cover it right here.

The concept involves so-called *conditional statements* and the *contrapositive*. The conclusion of a conditional statement is such that the "then" clause is always inferable from the "if" clause. Consider this premise:

Premise: If a shirt is red, then it must have long sleeves.

Given this premise, only one of the following statements is inferable (Can you spot which one?):

1. If a shirt does not have long sleeves, then it cannot be red.

2. If a shirt has long sleeves, then it is red.

3. If a shirt is not red, then it does not have long sleeves.

Only statement 1 is inferable. Notice that it reverses the "if" clause and the "then" clause, and negates both. Logicians would refer to this inferable statement as the *contrapositive of*

14

the conditional. Neither statement 2 nor 3 is inferable. Why not? Because a long-sleeved shirt can be a color other than red. To restate all of this more generally:

Premise:

   If *A*, then *B*.

Conclusion:

1. If not *B*, then not *A*. (contrapositive—valid)
2. If *B*, then *A*. (not inferable)
3. If not *A*, then not *B*. (not inferable)

Conditional rules make a logic game more complex and more confusing because you must:

- remember that the rule applies only under certain circumstances
- be alert to the contrapositive inference as you work through the questions
- be careful to avoid the two invalid inferences identified above

You can be sure that in at least one game on your exam, one or two conditional statements will show up among the rules. Conditional statements are especially common in *selection* games, as you're about to discover.

TIP

> Conditional statements don't always include the words *if* and *then*. For example, here are three other ways of expressing our original premise about shirts:
> - All red shirts have long sleeves.
> - Only long-sleeved shirts are red.
> - A shirt is red only if it has long sleeves.
>
> If you see one of these forms on the exam, convert it to an "if-then" statement. The if-then form is generally easier to work with.

Selection Games

Now that you've got the idea of a logic game, let's look at one of the most common type of games on the GRE: the *selection* game. Selection games involve dividing subjects into *exactly two* groups. The term "selection" is used here because your task is to select particular subjects from a *roster*, or *pool*, while the remaining subjects remain deselected. Two groups result: those subjects that are selected, and those subjects that are not selected.

In other words, for each subject you must make a yes-or-no decision. For example, is the subject

- included or excluded?
- going or staying?
- on or off?

The Simple Selection Game

A simple (relatively easy) selection game is one that involves a *fixed number* of selected subjects—as in the following game.

> **NOTE**
>
> During the next three hours you'll examine sample games with only one question each—because what's most important is learning how to set up a game. Remember: Each game on the GRE will include several questions.

QUESTION A particular two-story apartment building includes ten units. Apartments A, B, C, D, and E are located on the second floor. Apartments F, G, H, I, and J are located on the first floor. Each apartment is either vacant or occupied.

Six of the apartments are occupied.

Apartments B and C are not both occupied.

Either Apartment D or I, or both, are vacant.

Apartments G and H are either both vacant or both occupied.

Either Apartment E or Apartment J, but not both, is vacant.

If there are more vacant apartments on the first floor than on the second floor, all of the following must be true EXCEPT:

(A) Apartment F is vacant.

(B) Apartment I is vacant.

(C) Apartment B is vacant.

(D) Apartment D is occupied.

(E) Apartment E is occupied.

ANALYSIS The correct answer is (C). As in any logic game, ask yourself what you can deduce from the rules. Since a total of six apartments must be occupied, four must be vacant. Either E or J is vacant, either D or I must be vacant, and either B or C must be vacant. Thus, G and H cannot both be vacant; otherwise, at least five apartments would be

14

vacant. Accordingly, G and H must both be occupied. The best diagramming approach to a game such as this involves the use of a simple roster, along with a shorthand restatement of the rules. Circle both G and H in the diagram:

(6 OCCUPIED)

* $^D/_I$ (OR BOTH) VACANT

A B C D E   * J ≠ E

F Ⓖ Ⓗ I J   * $^B/_C$ (OR BOTH) VACANT

Then, as you respond to the questions, indicate that an apartment is occupied by circling it on your roster, and indicate that an apartment is vacant by crossing it out on your roster. A total of four apartments must be vacant (because six are occupied). Since G and H are both occupied, the other three apartments on the first floor must be vacant, while only one apartment on the second floor is vacant. Since B and C cannot be occupied, either B or C must be the one second-floor apartment that is vacant. Accordingly, A, D, and E must all be occupied:

Ⓐ B C Ⓓ Ⓔ   (4)

F̸ Ⓖ Ⓗ I̸ J̸   (2)

The Complex Selection Game

A complex (relatively difficult) selection game involves an *unfixed number* of selected subjects. Selection games can be further complicated by conditional statements, which you can easily misinterpret if you're not careful.

QUESTION Nine people—P, Q, R, S, T, U, V, W, and X—all wish to go on a particular fishing trip.

Either V or S must go, but V and S cannot both go.

Among P, T, and X, exactly two must go.

If either T or U goes, both T and U must go.

X will not go unless R goes.

If either P or Q goes, but if P and Q do not both go, then either V or W, but not both, must go.

If fewer people go on the trip than do not go, how many different distinct groups can be assembled to go on the trip?

(A) 1

(B) 2

(C) 3

(D) 4

(E) 5

ANALYSIS The correct answer is **(B)**. As with the simple selection game you just examined, the best diagramming approach here is to use a simple roster, along with a shorthand restatement of the rules. Arrange the subjects in your roster to reflect particular rules. Rephrase conditional statements that are expressed in a confusing manner, being very careful to interpret the statements correctly. For example, the rule that X cannot go unless R goes can properly be restated as "If X goes, then R must go" and expressed in shorthand form.

$$(1)\ \text{V S} \qquad \text{[TU]}$$
$$(2)\ \text{P T X} \qquad \text{X} \rightarrow \text{R}$$
$$\text{Q R U W} \qquad {}^{P}\!/_{Q}\,(\text{BNB}) \rightarrow {}^{V}\!/_{W}\,(\text{BNB})$$

As you respond to the questions, select subjects by circling them on your roster, and eliminate subjects by crossing them out on your roster.

Now on to the question. In order to satisfy the additional information in the question stem, no more than four people can go. According to the rules, among P, T, and X, exactly two must go. Assume first that P and T (but not X) go. Since T goes, U must go. According to the rules, either S or V must go. In this case, it must be V that goes, because P is going without Q. (One of the rules requires either V or W to go in this situation.) So one possible combination of four is: P, T, U, V. Next, assume instead that P and X (but not T) go. Since X goes, R must go. Again, V (not S) must also go. So a second possible combination of four is: P, X, R, V. Finally, assume instead that T and X (but not P) go. Since X goes, R must go. Since T goes, U must go. However, the rules require either S or V to go as well, which renders this scenario impossible, given that only four people go. So we're left with two possible combinations altogether.

Workshop

14

In this hour's Workshop, you'll apply what you just learned about handling selection games to a 7-question game.

ONLINE   Additional Analytical Reasoning sets are available on-line, at the authors' Web site: *http://www.west.net/~stewart/gre*

Quiz

DIRECTIONS: Attempt the following GRE-style logic game. Try to limit your time to 10 minutes. We've included a few hints to help you if you're having trouble.

(Answers and explanations begin on page 283.)

Questions 1–7

A school principal must select at least four of eight parents—A, B, C, D, E, F, G, and H—to serve on a particular committee. The principal's selections are bound by the following restrictions:

If A serves, B must serve.

If either C or D serves, both C and D must serve.

If E serves, D cannot serve.

Either E or G must serve, but E and G cannot both serve.

H and B cannot both serve if G serves.

(Hint: One of the rules suggests two alternative scenarios. In one of the two scenarios, you'll be able to cross out C and D.)

1. Which of the following could be a complete and accurate list of the committee members?

   (A) H, G, A, F
   (B) H, D, C, F
   (C) B, D, G, F, H
   (D) E, A, B, F, H
   (E) G, C, D, B, H

2. If G is NOT selected to serve on the committee, all of the following must be true EXCEPT:

   (A) B will be selected.
   (B) A will be selected.
   (C) E will be selected.
   (D) C will not be selected.
   (E) D will not be selected.

3. If the committee includes G and exactly four other parents, which of the following parents must be one of those four?

   (A) B
   (B) C
   (C) F
   (D) A
   (E) H

4. If the committee includes the maximum number of parents, which of the following is a complete and accurate list of the parents NOT included on the committee?

   (A) E
   (B) G
   (C) E, A
   (D) E, H
   (E) G, C, D

5. If A and H both serve on the committee, with respect to how many parents can it be determined whether or not the parent serves on the committee?

   (A) 4
   (B) 5
   (C) 6
   (D) 7
   (E) 8

6. If the committee includes A and exactly three other parents, how many distinct combinations of committee members are possible?

   (A) 1
   (B) 2
   (C) 3
   (D) 4
   (E) 5

7. G must serve on the committee if which of the following does NOT serve?

   (A) A
   (B) B
   (C) C
   (D) F
   (E) H

Answers and Explanations

Questions 1-7

You can use two alternative rosters as a template. The left-hand roster below assumes that E, but not G, is selected, while the right-hand roster assumes that G, but not E, is selected. According to the rules, if E is selected, D cannot be selected, and C and D must both be selected if either is selected. Thus, you can cross out (deselect) C and D in the left-hand roster.

```
A B C̸ D̸ | A B C D
Ⓔ F G̸ H | C̸ F Ⓖ H

       A→B
      [C D]
   G→ Ⓗ B̸
```

The rules are represented in symbolic form below the two rosters. As you respond to the questions, circle parents on the roster whenever you determine that they must be selected, and cross out parents whenever you determine that they cannot be selected. Use this approach for every question except question 1.

1. **(D)** The most efficient way to approach this question is to consider one rule at a time, scanning the answer choices to eliminate violators. For example, consider the rule that H and B cannot both be selected if G is selected. A quick glance at the answer choices reveals that (C) and (E) both violate this rule. Answer choice (A) violates the rule that if A serves,

B must also serve. Answer choice (B) violates the rule that either G or E must serve.

2. **(B)** If G is not selected, then E must be selected. Accordingly, we need to consider only the left-hand diagram, in which G, C, and D are all deselected. At least three parents among A, B, F, and H must be selected. One of those three must be B; otherwise, A, but not B, would be selected, which would violate the rule: *If A serves, then B must serve*. Thus, all answer choices except (B) must be true.

3. **(B)** Only the right-hand diagram, in which G is selected, applies here. According to the question, exactly four other parents must be selected. If neither C nor D were selected, then A, B, F, and H would all be selected; this result, however, would violate the rule: *H and B cannot both serve if G serves*. Thus, C and D must both be selected. (Remember that if either C or D is selected, both must be selected.)

4. **(D)** A bit of intuition helps determine the maximum number of committee members. Intuitively, it would seem that the largest possible committee would include C and D, since either both or neither must be selected. Proceeding from this assumption, G, but not E, will be selected. Of the remaining four parents, the most that can be selected together is three—A, B and F

may all be selected together. H cannot be selected under this scenario since B and G are both selected.

5. **(D)** Since A is selected, B must also be selected. Since G cannot be selected if B and H are both selected, G cannot be selected. Accordingly, E must be selected (only the left-hand diagram applies), and neither C nor D may be selected. F is the only parent with respect to whom it is uncertain whether the parent is selected.

6. **(C)** First consider the left-hand diagram (E, but not G, is selected). Since A is selected, B must also be selected. Either of the two remaining parents—F and H— could be included in the four-member committee. Thus, two possible combinations result: A, B, E, and F or A, B, E, and H. Next, consider the right-hand diagram (G, but not E, is selected). Again, since A is selected, B must also be selected. B and H cannot both be selected. The only remaining parent is F, resulting in only one possible combination: A, B, F, and G. The total number of possible combinations, considering both diagrams, is three.

7. **(B)** If B is not selected, A cannot be selected. Considering the left-hand diagram, only three parents—E, F, and H—would be available. Thus, only the right-hand diagram (G is selected) applies.

HOUR 15

Teach Yourself Analytical Reasoning II

Now that you know the basic strategies for logic games, it's time to take a closer look at two of the game types that appear most frequently on the GRE: *sequencing* and *attribute* games. In this hour you will learn:

- How to recognize and handle different types of GRE sequencing games
- How to recognize and handle different types of GRE attribute games
- What to do with games that combine sequencing and attributes
- How to apply what you learn to a GRE-style quiz

Just as in hour 14, each sample game here includes only one question. Remember, though, that on the GRE each game will include several questions.

Linear Sequence Games

Linear sequencing involves lining up the game's subjects in order *in a row*—or sequence—either from left to right or from top to bottom. The nature of the order might be spatial, chronological, or quantifiable (e.g., size, weight). In any case, your task is the same—line them up in order! Each subject in a sequencing game occupies *one position only*. Expect to see any of the following variations on the GRE (we'll look at one example of each type in the pages ahead):

- The fill-in-the-blank sequence game
- The double-decker sequence game
- The cluster sequence game
- The sequence formula game

Sequencing is sometimes combined with another task to create a hybrid game. You'll look at an example of a hybrid later this hour.

The Fill-in-the-Blank Sequence Game

A *fill-in-the-blank sequence* game involves nothing more than arranging the subjects linearly in a string of blank spaces, using a fill-in-the-blank approach. Make sure that you keep straight which end of the sequence is which, and you should not have much trouble with this type of game.

QUESTION A night club features a different performer—either P, Q, R, S, or T—each night of the week that the club is open for business. P and Q are comedians. R, S, and T are musicians. The club's weekly schedule begins on Sunday and ends on Saturday. The club is never closed for two consecutive nights during the week.

The same type of act—comedy or music—is never featured on two consecutive nights during the week.

Q and P are always featured later in the week than S.

R is always featured either on Monday or on Thursday.

P is always featured the night immediately after the night of the same week that T is featured.

15

Which of the following is an acceptable assignment at the club?

(A) P is featured on Tuesday.

(B) Q is featured on Monday.

(C) R is featured on Wednesday.

(D) S is featured Thursday.

(E) T is featured on Friday.

ANALYSIS The correct answer is **(E)**. First, create a template. The rule that "R is always featured on either Monday or Thursday" suggests two alternative scenarios. You can display the other rules below the two sequences.

Notice how the "snapshot" below the sequences suggests that Q must appear later than (to the right of) S, but might appear either before T and P or after T and P. Also notice that we're using brackets to indicate that no other performer can be featured between T and P.

Can you fill in any of the blanks in either diagram, based just on the rules? A bit of trial and error, along with some intuition, should tell you that you can't—at least not without thinking long and hard about it. That's a good clue that you should move on to the question.

Scan the answer choices, looking for any that you can easily eliminate. Answer choice (C) is obviously unacceptable; it violates the rule that R must be featured either on Monday or Thursday. Answer choice (D) is obviously unacceptable as well. Q, P, and T must all be featured later in the week than S, so S cannot be featured on Thursday. You've narrowed the candidates to (A), (B), and (E). You can take each one in turn, and test it against both scenarios.

Consider answer choice (A). If P is featured on Tuesday, you can easily rule out scenario 1, in which R appears on Monday. In scenario 2, S and T would appear on Sunday and Monday, respectively, violating the rule that the same type of act cannot be featured on consecutive nights. Eliminate answer choice (A). Next, consider answer choice (B). If Q appears on Monday, scenario 1 can obviously be ruled out since R is featured that night. In scenario 2, T and P would have to be featured on Tuesday and Wednesday to avoid musician appearances on consecutive nights. But this result would violate the premise, because the club cannot be closed on two consecutive nights. Eliminate answer choice (B). Answer choice (E) is acceptable under scenario 1, and is therefore the correct answer.

The Double-Decker Sequence Game

Your task in a *double-decker sequence* game is to pair each subject with another subject *and* sequence the pairs. One typical scenario involves teams (of two subjects) competing in a race or other contest.

 In a two-man bobsled race, ten athletes—A, B, C, D, E, F, G, H, I, and J—each finished in one of five places in the standings. There were no ties.

H and I were teamed together.

C and F were not teamed together.

E and G were teamed together and did not place last in the standings.

B placed immediately ahead of F in the standings.

If H and B placed second and third, respectively, which of the following must be true?

(A) C placed fourth.

(B) G placed first.

(C) F placed fifth.

(D) A placed fourth.

(E) D placed third.

ANALYSIS The correct answer is (B). First, create a template such as the one below, which assigns each subject (athlete) to one of five positions:

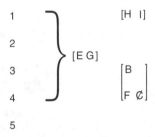

10 ABCDEFGHIJ

Notice that we've placed the [EG] and [HI] teams to the right of the sequence, ready to be pasted into the sequence as needed to respond to the question. The relationship between B and F is also indicated in picture form. Also notice the use of the strike-through symbol (/) to indicate that a team including C and F is not permitted. In working with this diagram, keep in mind that left-right orientation between team members is irrelevant.

Next, ask yourself what else you know based upon the additional information in the question. Since B placed third, F must have placed fourth. According to one of the rules, E and G did not place last. Therefore, the only place in which E and G could finish is first, and the correct answer is (B).

1 [E G] ⌉
2 [H I] |
         ⎬ [E G]
3 B |
4 F   ⌋
5

TIP

> In the bobsled game, we could have used a horizontally-oriented sequence instead. Use whichever orientation is easiest for you to work with.

The Cluster Sequence Game

As with any sequence game, your task here is to assign each subject to one position in a sequence. In a *cluster sequence* game, however, any number of subjects (perhaps none, perhaps all) might occupy a given position. You've already seen one example of this game type: last hour's roller coaster game. Now look at another example.

QUESTION Each of five detectives—Arkin, Billings, Cobart, Dansen, and Eckles—has been assigned to search one floor of a house. The house includes five floors—the basement, the first floor, the second floor, the third floor, and the attic.

Cobart has been assigned to a higher floor than any other detective.

Billings has been assigned to a lower floor than Dansen.

At least two detectives have been assigned to the second floor.

Exactly one detective has been assigned to the first floor, and exactly one detective has been assigned to the third floor.

If exactly one floor separates the floor to which Eckles is assigned from the floor to which Arkin is assigned, which of the following CANNOT be true?

(A) Arkin is assigned to the basement.

(B) Billings is assigned to the first floor.

(C) Dansen is assigned to the second floor.

(D) Cobart is assigned to the third floor.

(E) Eckles is assigned to the third floor.

ANALYSIS The correct answer is (E). First, create a template. The key to working through this game quickly is to determine alternative scenarios based upon the number of detectives assigned to each floor. Given that exactly one detective is assigned to the first floor and one to the third floor, the three others must be allocated among the second floor, the basement, and the attic. Since at least two detectives are assigned to the second floor, three basic possibilities emerge. Because Cobart is assigned to a higher floor than any other detective, and because Dansen is assigned to a higher floor than Billings, the three alternative diagrams may be partially completed as follows ("X" indicates a floor to which no detective is assigned):

Floor			
A	X	C	X
3	C	–	C
2	– –	– –	ADE
1	–	–	B
B	–	X	X

(Left side: Ⓒ ↑ Ⓓ ↑ Ⓑ)

Be careful in this game not to confuse the *first* floor with the *bottom* floor, which is the basement.

Next, consider the additional information provided by the question. You can eliminate the second alternative diagram, because it would assign Eckles and Arkin to the first and third floors (in either order), restricting both Dansen and Billings to the second floor, thereby violating the rule that Billings is assigned to a lower floor than Dansen. You can also eliminate the third alternative diagram because it would require that Arkin and Eckles be assigned to the same floor. So only the first diagram applies to the question. Dansen and Billings must be assigned to the second and first floors, respectively, while Arkin and Eckles are assigned to the second floor and to the basement (in either order):

```
        Floor
         A  |  X
            |
         3  |  C
            |
         2  |  D A  ⟵
            |        )
         1  |  B    )
            |       )
         B  |  E  ⟵
```

In neither scenario can Eckles be assigned to the third floor; thus, statement (E) must be false.

The Sequence Formula Game

Sequence formula games will strike you as a bit like the kind of games you've played at the kitchen table with a special board, some dice, and different colored tokens. The "players" in a sequence formula game begin in a certain sequence and are then manipulated according to a designated set of simple rules.

QUESTION A chess tournament among five boys involves one match at a time in which each player in turn elects to challenge the player either immediately above him or below him in the current rankings. At the outset of the tournament, Rodney, Kyle, Gary, Vladimir, and Peter are ranked first through fifth, in that order. The players must take turns making challenges in the order of their initial rankings.

   If the challenger wins the match, his opponent is demoted to fifth in the rankings.

   If the challenger loses the match, the challenger is demoted to fifth in the rankings.

   If the match results in a stalemate, the challenger is demoted one position in the rankings.

Each time a player is demoted, the rankings of the other four players in relation to one another remain unchanged.

If the first two matches both result in stalemates, any of the following might represent the players' rankings, from first to fifth, after the first three matches EXCEPT:

(A) Rodney, Gary, Vladimir, Peter, Kyle

(B) Rodney, Kyle, Gary, Peter, Vladimir

(C) Rodney, Kyle, Vladimir, Peter, Gary

(D) Rodney, Gary, Kyle, Vladimir, Peter

(E) Rodney, Kyle, Vladimir, Gary, Peter

ANALYSIS The correct answer is **(D)**. In sequence formula games such as this one, take the extra time to internalize the rules and visualize the game as it is played. The only written diagram you're likely to find useful for every question is a list of the subjects in their initial order or ranking.

Since Rodney is initially ranked first, he makes the first challenge and must challenge Kyle (because a player may challenge another player only if they are positioned consecutively in the current rankings). Given that the first match results in a stalemate, Rodney is demoted one position, and the rankings after the first match are as follows:

   R challenges K: K, R, G, V, P

The next match involves a challenge by Kyle since he was initially ranked second. Kyle must challenge Rodney, and a stalemate would return the players to their initial rankings:

   K challenges R: R, K, G, V, P

The third match involves a challenge by Gary since he was initially ranked third. Gary may challenge either Kyle or Vladimir. In each case, one of three different rankings would result:

   G challenges K:
      G wins: R, G, V, P, K
      G loses: R, K, V, P, G
      stalemate: R, K, V, G, P
   G challenges V:
      G wins: R, K, G, P, V
      G loses: R, K, V, P, G
      stalemate: R, K, V, G, P

Only answer choice (D) is not among the possible rankings listed above.

 NOTE Sequence formula games are unusual in that you won't need a template or other diagram. Instead, just start with the initial sequence.

Attribute Games

Attribute games involve assigning to each subject in the game *one or more characteristics*. You should know how to handle these common variations:

- the dual attribute game
- the multiple attribute game
- the matrix game
- the hybrid attribute-sequence game

15

The Dual Attribute Game

The *dual attribute* game involves assigning two characteristics—or *attributes*—to each of the game's subjects. More complex games (such as the one below) incorporate conditional rules.

QUESTION A certain basketball team consists of seven members—J, K, L, M, N, P, and Q. Each team member plays one of three positions—guard, forward, or center. At least two of the players are forwards, and at least one player is a center. Each player is on either the injured list or the active list.

> K, N, and P are guards. J and L are not guards.
>
> No forward is on the injured list.
>
> At least two guards are on the active list.

Assume that the team can play only if at least two guards, two forwards, and one center are on the active list. Which of the following statements, if true, would permit the team to play?

(A) Only M and Q are on the injured list.

(B) Only J and L are on the injured list.

(C) Only K and N are on the injured list.

(D) Only L and M are on the injured list.

(E) Only J and Q are on the injured list.

ANALYSIS The correct answer is (**C**). First, create a template. The following diagramming approach works well for this game type. Notice that the rules are depicted affirmatively in the grid. For example, the rule that "J and L are not guards" has been inverted (each is either a forward or a center) so that the choice between forward and center can be made by circling the appropriate letter. Also notice how the rule that "no forward is on the injured list" is depicted visually. The picture indicates the rule affirmatively (a forward must be on the active list) with a directional arrow that leads from F to A.

	J	K	L	M	N	P	Q
G, F, C	F/C	G	F/C		G	G	
A, I							

≥ 2 F	G	G	F
≥ 1 C	A	A	↓ A

Next, consider the question. You can determine the correct response by inserting the information from each answer choice, in turn, into the diagram. The following diagram for response (C) easily allows for two active guards (P and either M or Q), two active forwards (among J, L, M, and Q), and one active center (among J, L, M, and Q).

	J	K	L	M	N	P	Q
G, F, C	F/C	G	F/C		G	G	
A, I	A	I	A	A	I	A	A

You can also derive the solution more intuitively. In each answer choice, only two of the players are on the injured list. At least one of those two players must be either K, N, or P (the three players that must be guards); otherwise, two of the four remaining players would be on the injured list. Since those four remaining players must include a center and two forwards, it would not be possible to assemble an active playing team that includes two forwards and one center. Thus, you can eliminate all answer choices that fail to include either K, N, or P.

The Multiple Attribute Game

For some attribute games, it may not be feasible to construct a single grid or template to accommodate all of the rules. An attribute game involving *more than two attributes* generally calls for a more flexible approach. These games may not appear especially difficult at first glance. But if you're not ready for them, they can be very confusing once you get into them.

QUESTION Four children—W, X, Y, and Z—are the only patients in the children's ward of a particular hospital. Each child has either red or brown hair. Each child is assigned to either a private room of his or her own or a semi-private room which is shared with either one or two other children. No two children are the same age.

X, a girl, is assigned to a private room.

The youngest child is assigned to a semi-private room.

At least one child is a red-haired boy.

Z is not the oldest child and does not share a room with the oldest child.

W and X both have brown hair.

If two of the children have red hair and if each of these two children is assigned to a semi-private room, then it CANNOT be true that

(A) W is the youngest child

(B) Y is the oldest child

(C) W is the oldest child

(D) Z is the youngest child

(E) X is the oldest child

ANALYSIS The correct answer is (B). This game involves no fewer than four attributes for each child: hair color (red or brown), gender (male or female), room assignment (private or semi-private), and roommate (if any). Also at issue are the relative ages of the children. With this many variables, don't try to use a grid-type diagram. Instead, *take organized notes*, listing the four children and noting those attributes that can be determined for each child:

W   Brown

X   Brown/Girl/Private

Red Boy ⤳ Y

Z   Doesn't share w/oldest

*Youngest shares

What else can be deduced from the rules? Since W and X both have brown hair, either Y or Z must be a red-haired boy, as indicated in the diagram.

Now consider the question. W and X both have brown hair. Thus, Y and Z must be the two red-haired children who are assigned to semi-private rooms. Y and Z must share a room with each other; otherwise, one of them would have to share a room with X, which would violate the rule that X is assigned to a private room. Since Z cannot share a room with the oldest child, Y cannot be the oldest child.

TIP In games involving multiple attributes, drawing a grid probably won't help much. Instead, jot down a roster of the subjects along with some shorthand notes about the characteristics of each subject.

The Matrix Game

The *matrix* game requires you to make the same series of *yes-or-no* decisions for each of the game's subjects. The term "matrix" refers to the suggested diagram approach.

QUESTION During the high school summer session, six different subjects—art, biology, calculus, driver education, English, and French—are offered. An academic day includes five class periods, and each subject must be offered exactly three times during the day.

> Only calculus and driver education are offered during the first period.
>
> French and three other classes are offered during the second period.
>
> Only biology is offered during the third period.
>
> More subjects are offered during the fourth period than during the fifth period.

Two subjects that must be offered during the same three periods are

(A) art and biology

(B) art and French

(C) driver education and calculus

(D) driver education and French

(E) English and calculus

ANALYSIS The correct answer is **(B)**. First, create a template. In this matrix game, you must decide which of *six* subjects will be offered during each of *five* periods. Thus, the game potentially involves *thirty* "yes-or-no" decisions, which can all be displayed in a checkerboard or matrix.

In any matrix game, *focus on the totals* for each column and for each row of your matrix; these totals will probably be crucial to handling the game. List information about these totals around the perimeter of the matrix. In the game at hand, each of the six subjects is offered exactly three times; thus, three check-marks must appear in each column—a total of 18 check-marks in the entire matrix. Display the number of check-marks in each row to the right of the matrix.

Here's the key to this game: Since rows 1, 2, and 3 must include a total of seven check-marks, rows 4 and 5 must include a total of eleven check-marks. (Remember: the matrix must include 18 check-marks altogether.) The only way to include eleven check-marks between rows 4 and 5 is to assign six to one and five to the other. Since the rules specify that more subjects are offered during fourth period than during fifth period, six check-marks must appear in row 4, and five check-marks must appear in row 5. Next, evaluating the number of check-marks in each column, you can determine that art, English, and

French must each be offered during the second, fourth, and fifth periods; otherwise, each of these three subjects would not be offered exactly three times.

	A	B	C	D	E	F	
1	✗	✗	✓	✓	✗	✗	(2)
2	✓				✓	✓	(4)
3	✗	✓	✗	✗	✗	✗	(1)
4	✓	✓	✓	✓	✓	✓	(6)
5	✓				✓	✓	(5)
	(3)	(3)	(3)	(3)	(3)	(3)	

Now consider the question, which calls for you to compare columns in order to identify an identical pair. Art and French must both be offered during second, fourth, and fifth periods. Thus, the correct answer is (B).

CAUTION

> Many test-takers misuse this checkerboard diagram for other types of attribute games. Remember: The only scenario in which a checkerboard is appropriate is when you need to make yes-or-no decisions for a matrix of combinations. If the game doesn't fit this mold, don't use the checkerboard.

The Hybrid Attribute-Sequence Game

Now that you've looked at different types of sequencing games and attribute games, let's look at a hybrid game that combines the two types.

QUESTION At a pet store, five cats—A, B, C, D, and E—are displayed in a row of five cages, one cat in each cage. Three of the cats are male, and two of the cats are female.

B is male.

The female cats are not kept in adjacent cages.

C is separated from E by one cage.

A is kept in one of the three middle cages.

If all three male cats are kept in adjacent cages, which of the following is a complete and accurate list of the cats whose gender—male or female—can be determined?

(A) A and B

(B) B and D

(C) A, B, and D

(D) A, B, C, and E

(E) B, C, D, and E

ANALYSIS The correct answer is (C). Your initial diagram for this game might include a sequence along with a shorthand restatement of the rules:

Now consider the question. The three males must be in cages 2, 3, and 4 in order to satisfy the rule that the two females must be separated. Thus, although you have not constructed a sequence for the five cats, you do know the gender of the cat in each cage. B is a male and thus must be in one of the three middle cages. A is in one of the three middle cages and thus must be a male. That leaves D, C, and E. C and E cannot be in cages 2 and 4 (in either order), because either A or B must occupy one of those cages. (In the diagram below, A and B could be reversed.) C and E must therefore be either in cages 1 and 3 (in either order) or in cages 3 and 5 (in either order):

In either event, you cannot determine the gender of either C or E (although they are not of the same gender). Finally, D must be in either cage 1 or 5, and thus must be female. The correct response is (C).

Workshop

In this hour's Workshop, you'll tackle two GRE-style logic games.

 Additional Analytical Reasoning sets are available on-line, at the authors' Web site: *http://www.west.net/~stewart/gre*

Quiz

DIRECTIONS: Attempt the following two GRE-style logic games. Try to limit your time to 20 minutes altogether. You'll see a few hints to help you if you're having trouble.

(Answers and explanations begin on page 301.)

Questions 1–6

A law firm occupies five of the six floors in a new office building. The remaining floor is still vacant. The law firm consists of four departments—civil litigation, tax, antitrust, and securities. Each of the four departments occupies a separate floor, and the antitrust department occupies two adjacent floors.

The securities department occupies the floor either immediately above or immediately below the tax department.

At least two floors separate the floor occupied by the tax department from each floor occupied by the antitrust department.

(Hint: You can construct alternative diagrams based on the two floors occupied by the antitrust department, but it's probably easier to use one master diagram instead.)

1. Which of the following lists, in order from the first floor to the sixth floor, is acceptable?

(A) securities, tax, vacant floor, antitrust, antitrust, civil litigation

(B) vacant floor, antitrust, civil litigation, antitrust, securities, tax

(C) vacant floor, tax, civil litigation, securities, antitrust, antitrust

(D) antitrust, antitrust, civil litigation, tax, securities, vacant floor

(E) civil litigation, antitrust, antitrust, vacant floor, securities, tax

2. Which of the following is a complete and accurate list of the floors that may be vacant?

(A) first, third, fifth

(B) third, fourth, sixth

(C) second, third, fourth, sixth

(D) first, third, fourth, sixth

(E) first, third, fifth, sixth

3. The antitrust department CANNOT occupy which two floors?

    (A) first and second
    (B) second and third
    (C) third and fourth
    (D) fourth and fifth
    (E) fifth and sixth

4. Which of the following is a complete and accurate list of the departments that may occupy the fifth floor?

    (A) antitrust, tax
    (B) securities, antitrust, civil litigation
    (C) civil litigation, securities, tax
    (D) antitrust, tax, securities
    (E) securities, antitrust

5. If the antitrust department occupies the third floor, how many different department arrangements are possible?

    (A) 1
    (B) 2
    (C) 3
    (D) 4
    (E) 5

6. If the civil litigation department occupies the sixth floor, which of the following must be true?

    (A) The third floor is vacant.
    (B) The securities department occupies the second floor.
    (C) The tax department occupies the fifth floor.
    (D) The antitrust department occupies the first floor.
    (E) The securities department occupies the fourth floor.

Questions 7–11

Five classic cars—three hardtop models and two convertible models—appear consecutively in a parade. Each car is either a Ford or a Chevy, and each car is either gray, red, or white. Each car is one color only, and each of the three colors is represented at least once among the five cars.

The first and fifth cars to appear are both hardtops.

No Ford is white.

Only one of the hardtops is a Chevy.

(Hint: Don't try to incorporate a sequence into your initial diagram. The game includes too many factors. Also, restate conditional rules so they're easier to work with.)

7. Which of the following could appear in the parade?

    (A) two white hardtops
    (B) three Ford convertibles
    (C) three gray Chevys
    (D) two Chevy hardtops
    (E) three white Chevys

8. If exactly three of the cars are Chevys, which of the following must be true?

    (A) A convertible immediately follows another convertible.
    (B) A hardtop immediately follows another hardtop.
    (C) A Ford immediately follows another Ford.
    (D) A Chevy immediately follows another Chevy.
    (E) A white car immediately follows another white car.

9. If both convertibles are gray, which of the following must be false?

(A) All Fords are hardtops.
(B) All Fords are gray.
(C) All Chevys are white.
(D) All gray cars are convertibles.
(E) All red cars are hardtops.

10. If the first three cars are white, all of the following must be true EXCEPT:

(A) The first car is a Chevy.
(B) The fourth car is a Ford.
(C) The second car is a convertible.
(D) The fourth car is a hardtop.
(E) The fourth car is gray.

11. If all Ford hardtops appear consecutively in the parade, which of the following must be true?

(A) The first car is a Ford.
(B) The second car is a hardtop.
(C) The third car is a convertible.
(D) The fourth car is a Chevy.
(E) The fifth car is a Ford.

15

Answers and Explanations

Questions 1–6

This is a simple fill-in-the-blank sequencing game. You could construct alternate diagrams—for example, representing all possible positions of the antitrust department (eliminating those that are inconsistent with the rules). A simpler and more elegant approach, however, is to draw one master diagram, depicting the rules near the diagram for reference:

$$\boxed{T\ S\ A\ A\ C\ X}$$

$$\overline{1}\ \overline{2}\ \overline{3}\ \overline{4}\ \overline{5}\ \overline{6}$$

$$[A\,A] \neq [\overset{\frown}{T\,S}]$$

* ≥ 2 floors *between* A & T

In the explanations below, letters are used to signify departments (e.g., "A" for antitrust department).

1. **(E)** Consider one rule at a time, eliminating answer choices that violate the rule. (A) and (D) violate the rule that T must be separated from A by at least two floors. (B) violates the rule that A must occupy adjacent floors. (C) violates the rule that T and S occupy adjacent floors.

2. **(D)** If either floor 2 or floor 5 were vacant, then A and T could not be separated by at least two floors. However, any one of the remaining floors might be vacant.

3. **(C)** A cannot occupy floors 3 and 4; otherwise, A and T would be separated by no more than one floor (floor 2 or floor 5), resulting in a rule violation.

4. **(D)** Try positioning each department on floor 5 to see whether a rule violation results. C cannot occupy floor 5 without violating the rule that A and T must be separated by at least two floors.

5. **(B)** If A occupies floor 3, then it must also occupy floor 2. Otherwise, A and T could not be separated by at least two floors. Accordingly, T must occupy floor 6, and S must occupy floor 5. C must occupy either floor 1 or floor 4; the remaining floor—either 1 or 4—is vacant. Thus, two possible sequences result:

$$C[A\ A]X[S\ T]$$
$$\underline{X}[\underline{A}\ \underline{A}]\underline{C}[\underline{S}\ \underline{T}]$$
$$1\ 2\ 3\ 4\ 5\ 6$$

6. **(A)** If C occupies floor 6, only two arrangements will ensure that A and T are separated by at least two floors:

$$[A\ A]\ [S\ T]\ C$$
$$\underline{[T}\ \underline{S]}\ \underline{[A}\ \underline{A]}\ \underline{C}$$
$$1\ 2\ 3\ 4\ 5\ 6$$

In either case, the third floor must be vacant.

Questions 7–11

In this multiple attribute game, each car includes three attributes: top, make, and color. Two conditional rules (the last two rules) and a sequencing feature add to the game's complexity. In order to work through this game efficiently, it's best to construct a diagram in which attributes are matched in roster form without regard to sequence:

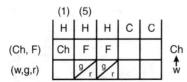

The conditional rule that "Only one of the hardtops is a Chevy" has been incorporated into the diagram. The conditional

rule that "No Ford is white" has been restated as "All white cars must be Chevys" and expressed symbolically near the diagram.

7. **(E)** Two of the three hardtops must be Fords since only one of the hardtops is a Chevy. Fords cannot be white. Thus, no more than one hardtop (the Chevy) can be white, and (A) must be false. (B) violates the statement in the premise that there are two convertibles (not three). (C) is not possible. If three of the cars were gray Chevys, both remaining cars would be Fords; however, no Ford can be white, and so there could be no white car in the parade. This result would violate the statement in the premise that each color must be represented at least once. (D) violates the rule that only one of the hardtops is a Chevy. (E) is possible. One of the two Fords could be red, and the other could be gray.

8. **(D)** The two convertibles must both be Chevys. In order to disprove statement (D), the three Chevys would have to be first, third, and fifth. If so, hardtops could not appear both first and fifth. This result would violate one of the rules, and so statement (D) must be true.

9. **(B)** Either of the two convertibles could be a Chevy or a Ford. The Chevy hardtop must be white, since each color must be represented at least once. The roster in the diagram above can be filled in as follows:

H	H	H	C	C
Ch	F	F	?	?
w	g/r	g/r	g	g

Either convertible could be a Ford; thus, statement (A) could be true. At least one of the five cars must be red, and that car must be one of the two Fords; thus, statement (B) must be false. Both convertibles could be Fords; thus, statement (C) could be true. The second and third cars could both be red; thus, statement (D) could be true. Only cars 2 and 3 can be red, and these two cars are both hardtops; thus, statement (E) must be true.

10. **(E)** If a car is white, it must be a Chevy; thus, the first three cars are all white Chevys. The fourth and fifth cars must be the two Ford hardtops. The first car must be the Chevy hardtop, and the second and third cars must be Chevy convertibles:

(1)	(5)	4	2	3
H	H	H	C	C
Ch	F	F	Ch	Ch
w	$^9/_r$	$^9/_r$	g	g

Statement (E) is not necessarily true; the fourth car could either be gray or red.

11. **(C)** The two Ford hardtops must appear either first and second or fourth and fifth; otherwise, the first and fifth cars could not both be hardtops. If the two Ford hardtops appear first and second, then the Chevy hardtop must appear fifth. On the other hand, if the two Ford hardtops appear fourth and fifth, then the Chevy hardtop must appear first. Two alternative sequences result:

1	2	3	4	5
H	H	C	C	H
F	F	?	?	Ch

1	2	3	4	5
H	C	C	H	H
Ch	?	?	F	F

In either sequence, the third car must be a convertible; thus, statement (C) must be true.

15

HOUR **16**

Teach Yourself Analytical Reasoning III

In addition to the selection games, sequencing games and attribute games you learned about during hours 14 and 15, there are three other types of logic games you're likely to encounter on the GRE. These are grouping games, spatial games and logic tree games. This hour you'll focus on these last three types, examining sample questions and analyzing sample answers. Here are your goals for this hour:

- Learn to recognize and handle grouping games
- Learn to recognize and handle non-linear spatial games
- Learn to recognize and handle logic tree games
- Apply what you learn by attempting a GRE-style quiz

Just as in hours 14 and 15, each sample game here includes only one question. Remember, though, that on the GRE each game will include several questions.

Grouping Games

Grouping games involve dividing a game's subjects into *at least three* different groups. Of course, any sequencing or attribute game also involves dividing up the subjects—according to position or characteristic. But so-called "grouping" games call for a distinct diagramming approach. Once you've seen a few, you'll recognize a grouping game immediately.

The Simple Grouping Game

Simple (easier) grouping games limit the game's parameters and possibilities in one or more of the following ways:

- the number of subjects allocated to each group is fixed
- the groups are distinct and identifiable
- the subjects are distinct and identifiable

 The town of Smallville includes ten residents—A, B, C, D, E, F, G, H, I, and J. Each resident lives on one of three streets—Maple Street, Pine Street, or Elm Street. Either three or four residents live on each of these three streets.

C, E, and J all live on different streets.

B and I both live on Pine Street.

D, F, and H all live on the same street.

If J lives on the same street as A, how many distinct combinations of residents could live on Maple Street?

(A) 1

(B) 2

(C) 3

(D) 4

(E) 5

ANALYSIS The correct answer is **(C)**. First, create a template; then and ask yourself what else you can deduce. If you try to employ one of the diagramming techniques for attribute games to this one, you'll discover that an "attribute" approach simply will not accommodate the rules here. Instead, create three distinct spaces, or *groups*, each representing a different street. You can deduce several important pieces of information from the rules. First, since the ten residents must be allocated into groups of either three or four, three residents must live on each of two streets, while four residents live on the remaining street. Second, since D, F, and H all live on the same street, either C, E, or J must also live on that street (because C, E, and J all live on different streets). Thus, that street includes four residents. Accordingly, B, I, and exactly one other resident live on Pine Street, while A, G, and exactly one other resident live on the remaining street.

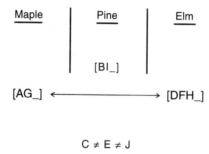

Now consider the question. If J and A live on the same street, that street (either Maple or Elm) must include exactly three residents—A, G, and J. Alternatively, Maple Street could include D, F, H, and either C or E. Thus, three distinct combinations of residents could live on Maple Street.

 Don't think of groups as attributes. Otherwise, you might use an inappropriate diagramming approach.

The Complex Grouping Game

Grouping games are not always as simple as the one you just looked at. Any of the following features would result in a more challenging grouping game:

- the number of subjects allocated to each group is variable
- the groups are indistinguishable
- the subjects are indistinguishable

More "unknowns" in a grouping game generally make for a more complex and time-consuming game.

QUESTION Three jars contain a total of twelve jellybeans. Five jellybeans are pink, three are green, two are yellow, and two are black. Each jar contains at least two jellybeans of different colors.

No two jars contain the same number of jellybeans.

No jar contains both pink and green jellybeans.

No jar contains both yellow and black jellybeans.

One of the three jars could contain any of the following assortments of jellybeans EXCEPT:

(A) two black jellybeans and one pink jellybean

(B) two yellow jellybeans and three green jellybeans

(C) one yellow jellybean and two pink jellybeans

(D) one pink jellybean and one black jellybean

(E) one green jellybean and two yellow jellybeans

ANALYSIS The correct answer is (E). Two important pieces of information can be determined from the rules. First, although the precise number of jellybeans in each jar cannot be determined, certain parameters can be established. Each jar must contain at least two jellybeans, and no two jars may contain the same number of jellybeans. Thus, only three possible assortments result (excluding the issue of color):

2 - 3 - 7

2 - 4 - 6

3 - 4 - 5

Second, two and only two different colors may be represented in each jar; otherwise, either pink and green jellybeans or yellow and black jellybeans would be included in the same jar. (Either result would violate a rule.) Because visualization is important in a grouping game, your diagram here should include a roster of jellybeans to the side of three distinct spaces representing the three jars. Indicate grouping parameters below the jars. Keep in mind that the jars are indistinguishable, and so you may arbitrarily establish the left jar, for example, as that which will contain the fewest jellybeans:

Y ≠ B	2/3/7	YY
G ≠ P	2/4/7	BB
	3/4/5	GGG
		PPPPP

In responding to the question, as you place jellybeans in the jars, simultaneously cross them off the roster. For example, to analyze answer choice (A), try placing two "B"s and one "P" in the first jar. Since each jar may include jellybeans of two and only two different colors, the remaining jellybeans fall logically into their respective groups as follows:

BB	GGG	PPPP
P	Y	Y

Using the same approach for the remaining answer choices, you can quickly deduce that the correct response to the question is (E). By placing both yellow jellybeans together in the same jar, a rule violation is inevitable. Either one jar will contain only one color, or colors will be commingled in violation of a rule.

 TIME SAVER | If a grouping game doesn't fix the number of subjects in each group, you can bet that this issue is the key to the game; so establish parameters right up front. Doing so will save you time when it comes to answering the questions.

Spatial Games

Spatial games involve positioning the game's subjects as they would appear on a two-dimensional plane. Here you'll examine the two most common types:

- The line-and-node game
- The multiple row game

The Line-and-Node Game

Line-and-node games involve *spatial connections* between the subjects of the game. Your task is to determine how to get from one subject (or node) to the other subjects following the connecting lines. Some lines may be two-way streets, while others may be one-way streets. Also, some subjects might be impossible to reach from certain other subjects. The rules tend to be permissive in nature rather than mandatory; that is, the rules speak in terms of where you *can* go from any given point of departure, rather than compelling you to go.

QUESTION A commuter-subway schedule for a particular city lists all of the routes between seven stations—A, B, C, D, E, F, and G. Subways must stop as they pass through every station. Examining the schedule, a commuter made the following observations:

He may ride from A directly to B and D only.

He may ride from B directly to only one station.

He may ride from C directly to E and F only.

He may ride from D directly to C only.

He may ride from E directly to only one station.

He may ride from F directly to A, C, and G only; he may ride to F directly from C only.

He may ride from G directly to A only.

He may ride from B to E by stopping at two other stations first.

He may ride from C to D by stopping at one other station first.

If the commuter departs from F and makes five stops, which of the following is a complete and accurate list of the stations which might be the fifth stop?

(A) C, D, E, F, G

(B) A, B, D, E, G

(C) A, B, C, E, F, G

(D) B, C, D, E, F, G

(E) A, B, C, D, E, F, G

ANALYSIS The correct answer is **(E)**. Construct a line-and-node, or flow, chart. It isn't important how the stations are arranged. The key is to connect them in a way that accurately reflects the rules of the game. All of the rules, with the exception of the last two rules (involving interim stops), can be charted as follows:

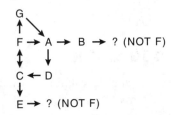

Next, consider the two rules involving interim stops in light of this flowchart. First, if a commuter can ride from B to E by stopping at two other stations during the interim, a route must run directly from B to D. The commuter cannot ride from B through G and D to E because from G he may ride to A only. A commuter cannot ride from B through F and C to E because the only direct route to F is from C. A commuter cannot ride from B through A and D to E because he may ride from D to C only. Second, if a commuter can ride from C to D by stopping at one other station during the interim, a route must run directly from E to D because E is the only station to which the commuter can ride directly from C:

16

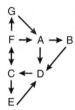

Now consider the question. From F, the commuter might end at any of the seven stations after five stops. The commuter may ride back and forth between F and C as often as necessary to end at the desired fifth stop:

$$F \rightarrow C \rightarrow F \rightarrow C \rightarrow F \rightarrow A$$
$$F \rightarrow C \rightarrow F \rightarrow G \rightarrow A \rightarrow B$$
$$F \rightarrow G \rightarrow A \rightarrow B \rightarrow D \rightarrow C$$
$$F \rightarrow C \rightarrow F \rightarrow G \rightarrow A \rightarrow D$$
$$F \rightarrow C \rightarrow E \rightarrow D \rightarrow C \rightarrow E$$
$$F \rightarrow G \rightarrow A \rightarrow D \rightarrow C \rightarrow F$$
$$F \rightarrow C \rightarrow F \rightarrow C \rightarrow F \rightarrow G$$

> **TIP**
> Don't be intimidated by a line-and-node game just because the game looks lengthy. These games tend to be relatively easy.

The Multiple Row Game

Multiple row games involve arranging the game's subjects spatially among two or more rows. A diagram is usually provided to identify rows and columns.

QUESTION A debating team is traveling by airplane to a tournament. The team consists of six students—K, L, M, N, O, and P. The team is accompanied by two teachers—X and Y. Each student and each teacher has been assigned a seat in either row 1 or row 2 of the airplane. Three executives have also each been assigned a seat in row 1 or row 2. Each row includes six seats, three on each side of the aisle:

```
SEAT:   A B C   D E F
row 1   _ _ _| |_ _ _
row 2   _ _ _| |_ _ _
```

L and M must sit next to each other, and M must occupy a window seat.

N and O must sit next to each other, and N must occupy an aisle seat.

P and K must sit next to each other, and P must occupy a window seat.

Passengers seated across the aisle from each other are not considered to be seated "next to" each other.

A passenger is seated directly ahead of or behind another passenger only if the two passengers share the same seat letter but in adjacent rows.

If X and Y both occupy window seats, and if N is seated directly in front of one of the three executives, any of the following could be true EXCEPT:

(A) O is seated next to an executive.

(B) Y is seated next to an executive.

(C) L and P occupy seats on different sides of the aisle.

(D) O is seated directly in front of K.

(E) M and O occupy seats on the same side of the aisle.

ANALYSIS The correct answer is **(A)**. Before responding to the question, it's helpful to realize that two pairs of students (a "pair" includes two students that must sit next to each other) must sit on one side of the aisle while the third pair sits on the other side. The diagrams below indicate two of several acceptable arrangements (notice in the diagrams that P and M are each occupying window seats, while N is occupying an aisle seat, all conforming to the rules of the game):

One possible arrangement:

```
[P  K] _ | |[N  O] _
[M  L] _ | |_ _ _
```

Another possible arrangement:

$$[M \quad L] \_ \; \bigg| \bigg| \; \_ \quad \_ \quad \_$$
$$\_ \; [O \quad N] \; \bigg| \bigg| \; \_ \; [K \quad P]$$

The question is really rather easy to analyze in light of the foregoing scheme. The question stem stipulates that X and Y both occupy window seats. According to the original rules, P and M also each occupy window seats. Two basic alternatives emerge: either X and Y sit on the same side of the aisle (with [PK] and [ML] all on the other side) or X and Y sit on different sides of the aisle (with [PK] and [ML] on different sides). For example:

One possible arrangement:

$$[P \quad K] \_ \; \bigg| \bigg| \; [N \quad O] \_$$
$$[M \quad L] \_ \; \bigg| \bigg| \; E \; \_ \; Y$$

Another possible arrangement:

$$[M \quad L] \_ \; \bigg| \bigg| \; [N \quad O] \; Y$$
$$X \; \_ \; \_ \; \bigg| \bigg| \; E \; [K \quad P]$$

In considering the diagrams immediately above, bear in mind that these do not represent the only possible positions for X and Y. For instance, the positions of X and Y could be reversed. Similarly, [PK] and [ML] could be reversed. Finally, the horizontal "mirror image" of each diagram would also be valid. In any event, however, [NO] must sit in row 1, and O must sit next to either X or Y. Why? Because the question stem stipulates that N sits directly in front of one of the executives. Thus, N must sit in row 1 as indicated in the diagrams above. O must sit between N and one of the two teachers and therefore cannot sit next to an executive.

The Logic Tree Game

The rules of a *logic tree* game can be characterized as the building blocks of logic trees. Your primary task is to construct the tree through repeated application of a *formula* or alternative formulas. Because these games deal with abstract relationships and conditional statements, they tend to be difficult.

QUESTION Gremlins are always either white, orange, or brown in color.

Any mating involving an orange gremlin produces only brown gremlins.

Any mating involving a white gremlin produces only white gremlins.

No mating between two brown gremlins ever produces a brown gremlin.

Any of the following could be among the four grandparents of a brown gremlin EXCEPT:

(A) exactly four brown gremlins

(B) exactly three brown gremlins

(C) exactly two orange gremlins

(D) exactly one orange gremlin

(E) exactly three orange gremlins

ANALYSIS The correct answer is **(E)**. This is typical of a logic tree game in that several alternative formulas result from the rules. For example, a brown gremlin can result only from the mating of either two orange gremlins or one orange and one brown gremlin. That is, there are two alternative formulas for producing a brown gremlin. An orange gremlin can result only from the mating of two brown gremlins (because an orange parent produces only brown offspring and a white parent always produces white offspring). That is, there is only one formula for producing an orange gremlin. As long as an orange gremlin does not participate in a mating, the mating might produce a white gremlin. Thus, there are three alternative formulas for producing a white gremlin. But, listing each and every different formula could result in confusion. Instead, indicate general formulas as follows:

$$O \rightarrow B$$
$$W \rightarrow W$$
$$(B\ B) \rightarrow {}^O\!/_W$$

The arrows in this diagram are significant in that they suggest a rule of condition (an if/then statement), and so the contrapositive rule of logic is likely to come into play (see "Formal Logic—Everything You Need to Know for Logic Games" in Hour 14).

Now consider the question. Neither parent of a brown gremlin can be white (a white gremlin produces only white gremlins). Both parents of a brown gremlin cannot be brown. Thus, two possibilities exist with respect to the parents of a brown gremlin—one must be orange while the other is either brown or orange:

$$(O\ O) \rightarrow B$$
$$(O\ B) \rightarrow B$$

Orange offspring can be produced only by two brown parents. Thus, in the first scenario, all four grandparents must be brown. Brown offspring can be produced only from either two orange parents or one orange parent and one brown parent (the identical formula as that in the diagram immediately above). Adding this information to the diagram above:

(1) $\begin{matrix} (B\ B) \rightarrow \\ (B\ B) \rightarrow \end{matrix} \begin{pmatrix} O \\ O \end{pmatrix} \rightarrow B$

(2) $\begin{matrix} (B\ B) \rightarrow \\ (O\ ^B\!/\!_O) \rightarrow \end{matrix} \begin{pmatrix} O \\ B \end{pmatrix} \rightarrow B$

At most, then, two of the grandparents can be orange. Thus, answer choice (E) is the correct response. Notice that analyzing the question required repeated application of one or more formulas. Remember that these formulas are the blocks with which you must construct a logic tree for a question.

 In logic tree games, be on the lookout for conditional statements. The contrapositive is sure to come into play. Simply put, remember that if X results in Y, then if you don't end up with Y, you didn't start with X.

Workshop

In this hour's Workshop, you'll tackle two GRE-style logic games.

 Additional Analytical Reasoning games are available on-line, at the authors' Web site: *http://www.west.net/~stewart/gre*

Quiz

DIRECTIONS: Attempt the following two GRE-style logic games. Try to limit your time to 20 minutes altogether. You'll see a few hints to help you if you're having trouble.

(Answers and explanations begin on page 318.)

Questions 1–6

In a series of chemistry experiments, each experiment involves combining the contents of two different beakers. A beaker may contain one of three chemical compounds—X, Y, or Z—in either a gaseous or liquid medium. Two beakers containing the same chemical compound must never be combined, and gaseous Z must never be combined with liquid Y. The results of the series of experiments are as follows:

Each experiment produces exactly one chemical compound—X, Y, or Z—in exactly one medium—gas or liquid.

Combining X and Y produces Z.

Combining X and Z produces X.

Combining Y and Z produces Y.

A gas may result only by combining a liquid and a gas.

Combining a gas and a liquid produces a liquid if and only if X is used.

(Hint: The rules boil down to four basic logic trees. Start by considering the last two rules together.)

1. An experiment in which gaseous Y and liquid Z are combined produces:

    (A) liquid X
    (B) liquid Y
    (C) liquid Z
    (D) gaseous X
    (E) gaseous Y

2. Liquid X will be produced by combining:

    (A) gaseous X and liquid Y
    (B) liquid X and gaseous Z
    (C) liquid Y and liquid Z
    (D) gaseous Z and gaseous Y
    (E) gaseous Y and liquid Z

3. How many different results are possible from a single experiment?

    (A) 2
    (B) 3
    (C) 4
    (D) 5
    (E) 6

4. If each chemical compound is used exactly four times in six simultaneous experiments, which of the following statements must be true?

    (A) Exactly one of the experiments produced Z.
    (B) Exactly two of the experiments produced X.
    (C) Exactly three of the experiments produced Y.
    (D) Exactly two of the experiments produced a gas.
    (E) Exactly two of the experiments produced a liquid.

5. Two and only two possible different experiments will produce which of the following?

    (A) liquid X
    (B) liquid Y
    (C) liquid Z
    (D) gaseous X
    (E) gaseous Y

6. If the results of two simultaneous experiments are combined in a third experiment to produce a gas, any of the following might have been used in at least one of the three experiments EXCEPT:

    (A) gaseous X
    (B) gaseous Y
    (C) gaseous Z
    (D) liquid X
    (E) liquid Y

Questions 7–12

Six commuters—C, D, E, F, G and H—participate in a van pool together. The seating capacity of the van is eight; two of the seats are empty. The seats are arranged in three rows as follows:

```
              (front of van)
    row 1:   1      2
    row 2:   3   4   5
    row 3:   6   7   8
```

Seat 1 is the driver's seat. Seats 4 and 7 are the only two seats that are considered "middle" seats. Two commuters can converse with each other only if they are sitting either immediately next to each other or diagonally from each other. However, the driver cannot converse with any other commuter. A commuter is seated "diagonally" from another commuter if the commuter is in an adjacent row and one seat to the left or right from the other commuter. The commuters' seating arrangement is subject to the following rules:

Either E, F, or G always drives the van.

Neither C nor D will sit in a middle seat.

G will not sit in row 3.

H and D must sit next to each other.

(Hint: The key to this game involves the position of H. So before you tackle the questions, ask yourself what you can deduce about H's position.)

7. Which of the following is an acceptable seating arrangement, in order, for seats 1, 2, 3, and 4?

   (A) G, D, empty seat, empty seat
   (B) F, C, E, H
   (C) G, empty seat, F, C
   (D) E, F, C, empty seat
   (E) C, G, F, E

8. Among the following pairs of commuters, with respect to which pair is it always true that the two commuters cannot converse with each other?

   (A) G and H
   (B) F and C
   (C) C and D
   (D) E and F
   (E) D and E

9. If seat 6 and seat 8 are empty, which of the following must be true?

   (A) H occupies seat 4.
   (B) G occupies seat 1.
   (C) F occupies seat 2.
   (D) E occupies seat 7.
   (E) D occupies seat 3.

10. The fewest number of commuters that can converse is

   (A) 0
   (B) 1
   (C) 2
   (D) 3
   (E) 4

16

11. If D converses with G during a commute, which of the following must be true?

    (A) E is driving the van.
    (B) Seat 3 is empty.
    (C) H occupies seat 7.
    (D) D occupies seat 5.
    (E) Seat 2 is empty.

12. If H can converse with exactly two other commuters, with respect to which of the following seats is it NOT possible to determine whether the seat is occupied?

    (A) seat 1
    (B) seat 2
    (C) seat 4
    (D) seat 6
    (E) seat 7

Answers and Explanations

Questions 1–6

In approaching this logic tree game, begin by listing the formulas suggested by the rules. In doing so, you can deduce several important additional facts. Considering the last two rules together, if either two liquids or two gases are combined, the result must be a liquid, while if a liquid and a gas are combined, the result is a gas if Y and Z are used or a liquid if either X and Y or X and Z are used. Since a gas may be produced only if Y and Z are combined, any experiment combining X and Y or X and Z must produce a liquid. This additional information is necessary to analyze the questions.

```
                        (LL)
                  (GL)  (GG)
        XY    XZ    YZ    YZ
        ↓     ↓     ↓     ↓
       Z(L)  X(L)  Y(G)  Y(L)
```

1. **(E)** Combining Y and Z produces Y. Combining a liquid and a gas produces a gas if X is not used. Thus, the experiment produces gaseous Y.

2. **(B)** According to the rules, combining X and Z in any form produces liquid X.

3. **(C)** Without restriction, a total of six different results would be possible—X, Y, or Z each in either liquid or gaseous form. However, any experiment using X must produce a liquid rather than a gas (see general comments above). Thus, an experiment combining X and Y or X and Z must produce liquid Z and liquid X, respectively. Gaseous Z and gaseous X are impossible results.

4. **(B)** A bit of intuition or experimenting reveals that three experiments—combining X with Y, X with Z, and Y with Z— must each be performed twice if each chemical compound is to be used four times in six experiments. Thus, Z, X, and Y must each be produced twice. Accordingly, statement (B) must be true, while statements (A) and (C) must be false. A liquid may result from a minimum of four to a maximum of six of the experiments (see general comments above). Accordingly, statement (D) is not necessarily true, while statement (E) must be false.

5. **(B)** In an experiment combining Y and Z, the rules stipulate that gaseous Z must not be combined with liquid Y. Thus, Z and Y are either both liquid, both gas, or Z is liquid while Y is gas. In each of the first two cases, liquid Y results. In the last case, gaseous Y results (because X is not used). Thus, Y may result from only one of two different experiments—combining liquid Y and liquid Z or combining gaseous Y and gaseous Z. Answer choices (A) and (C) are incorrect—liquid X and liquid Z may each result from any one of four different experiments. Answer choice (D) is incorrect because gaseous X is an impossible result (see question 3). Answer choice (E) is incorrect because only one experiment—combining gaseous Y and liquid Z—will produce gaseous Y.

6. **(C)** If either X or Z results from an experiment, it must be in liquid form (see general comments above). Thus, since the end result in this experiment is a gas, it must be gaseous Y. Gaseous Y can be produced only by combining gaseous Y and liquid Z. Liquid Z can be produced only by combining X and Y, although X and Y may each be in either gas or liquid form. Thus, the only answer choice that cannot be used in any of the three experiments is gaseous Z.

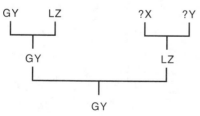

Questions 7–12

The key to working through this multiple-row game efficiently is to realize that H must occupy either seat 4 or seat 7. Why? D and H must sit next to each other. They cannot sit in row 1, since neither of them can drive the van. D cannot occupy a middle seat (that is, seat 4 or seat 7). Thus, H must occupy one of the two middle seats. Every question in this game includes this logical link as part of the analysis.

7. **(D)** In response (A), D occupies seat 2; this is unacceptable, however, because D must sit immediately next to H (H cannot drive). In response (B), H occupies seat 4. Since D must sit next to H, D must occupy seat 5 (seat 3 is occupied by E). This leaves no seat for G in either row 1 or row 2, violating the rule that "G will not sit in row 3." The arrangement indicated by response (C) would place C in seat 4, which is one of the middle seats, violating the rule that C will not occupy a middle seat. In response (E), C drives the van (the driver occupies seat 1), violating the rule that "either E, F, or G always drives the van."

8. **(C)** Since D will not sit in a middle seat, H must sit in one of the two middle seats (either seat 4 or seat 7), with D immediately next to H (in seat 3, 5, 6, or 8). Since C cannot sit in a middle seat, it is impossible for C and D to either sit next to each other or diagonally from each other.

16

9. **(A)** If seat 6 and seat 8 are empty, D and H (who must sit next to each other) must occupy row 2. Since D will not sit in a middle seat, H must occupy seat 4, while D occupies either seat 3 or seat 5.

10. **(D)** This question requires a bit of intuition or experimentation. To minimize the number of commuters who can converse, seat 4 must be empty—any commuter occupying seat 4 could converse with commuters in seats 2, 3, 5, 6, and 8. Assuming, then, that seat 4 is empty, H must sit in seat 7 with D in either seat 6 or 8. H can converse with D as well as with the commuter in either seat 3 or seat 5 (or both). Assuming that one of those two seats is empty, H can still converse with two other commuters (who in turn can converse with H). Therefore, at a minimum, three commuters (H, D, and one other under this "minimum conversation" scenario) can converse.

11. **(C)** Where is G sitting? G is not driving, since the rules prohibit the driver from conversing with another commuter. The rules also prohibit G from sitting in row 3. Thus, G must sit in seat 2, 3, 4, or 5. However, if G were to occupy seat 2 and converse with D, D would be in seat 4, which violates the rule that D cannot occupy a middle seat. Accordingly, G must sit in row 2. D, then, must sit in row 3, in either seat 6 or 8. In either case, H sits next to D in seat 7.

12. **(D)** H must occupy either seat 4 or seat 7 (see general comments above). If H were to occupy seat 4, then D would occupy either seat 3 or seat 5, and of course H could converse with D. However, H could not be limited to conversing with only one additional commuter. Thus, H must occupy seat 7 (and D must occupy either seat 6 or seat 8). Given that H occupies seat 7, the only way to limit H to conversing with only two others is to position the two empty seats among seats 3, 5, and 6. Accordingly, seats 1, 2, and 4 must be occupied (of course, seat 1 must be occupied in any event).

HOUR 17

Teach Yourself Logical Reasoning I

This hour (as well as next) you'll teach yourself how to handle the Logical Reasoning questions that appear in the Analytical section of the GRE. Here are your goals for this hour:

- Learn what Logical Reasoning questions look like and how to deal with them
- Learn how to identify the conclusion of an argument
- Learn how to identify inferences from given premises
- Learn how to identify assumptions needed to make an argument correct
- Review the skills you learn this hour by attempting a GRE-style quiz

Logical Reasoning at a Glance

Where: In the GRE Analytical section, mixed in with Analytical Reasoning questions

How Many:

Paper-based test: 6 out of the 25 questions in the Analytical section (3 midway through the section and 3 at the end of the section)

CBT: 9 out of the 35 questions in the Analytical section

Ground Rules:

- Scratch paper is allowed and provided
- Each question is considered independently
- No penalty (deduction) is assessed for incorrect answers

What's Covered: You will be tested on the following Logical Reasoning skills:

- Identifying the main point or conclusion of an argument
- Making inferences or drawing conclusions from given premises
- Identifying assumptions in an argument
- Assessing the effect of additional information on an argument
- Identifying the method of reasoning employed in an argument
- Detecting reasoning errors
- Recognizing arguments that employ a similar method

What's Not Tested: You won't have to know formal logic or the terminology of formal logic

What's Assumed: You will have to be familiar with the following ideas:

- Argument
- Issue
- Premise
- Conclusion
- Assumption

Directions: There are no specific directions for Logical Reasoning questions—just the following instruction:

For each question select the best answer choice given.

What Logical Reasoning Questions Look Like

Logical Reasoning questions consist of a brief *passage* containing an argument followed by a *question* about the passage (called the *question stem*) and five *answer choices*. Here's an example of a typical Logical Reasoning question.

QUESTION Captive animals exhibit a wider range of physical and behavioral traits than animals in the wild. That's why researchers who study captive animals are able to study a wider range of genetic possibilities than researchers who study wild animals.

For this argument to be logically correct, it must make which one of the following assumptions?

(A) Animals in zoos exhibit a wider range of physical and behavioral traits than wild animals.

(B) Animals that permit researchers to study a wide range of genetic possibilities are better research subjects than animals that do not.

(C) The wider the range of the physical and behavioral traits in a population of animals, the greater the range of their genetic possibilities.

(D) Captive animals are studied more than wild animals.

(E) Wild animals exhibit a narrow range of physical and behavioral traits.

What You Should Know About GRE Logical Reasoning Questions

Logical Reasoning passages vary considerably in writing style and content from question to question. The passages may be drawn from the physical sciences, humanities, social sciences, and historical and contemporary sources.

There are only seven basic question types. However, there is extensive variation in the way in which each type is phrased. Don't worry: most of the question variations will be covered in the lessons that follow.

Prior knowledge of the topic at hand is never required to answer the question. All of the information you need to answer the question is contained in the passage. Logical Reasoning questions test your ability to recognize correct and incorrect reasoning; they do not test your knowledge of the topic under discussion.

GRE Logical Reasoning questions do not assume that you know the terminology of formal logic or that you have taken a course in logic. You won't need to know specialized terms such as "syllogism," "valid," and "modus ponens," but you will be expected to understand certain ideas. To understand and critique the reasoning contained in argument requires, at a minimum, that you be familiar with ideas such as argument, topic, issue, premise, conclusion, main point, and assumption. Before you go any further, take a few moments to review these basic ideas.

Argument: The word "argument" is used in two different ways. When we say that two or more people are "having an argument" or "are arguing," we mean merely that there is a discussion going on in which the participants disagree about some topic. This is not the sense of "argument" intended in GRE Logical Reasoning questions. In this context, to argue is to offer reasons in support of the truth of some claim or the correctness of some action. An argument, in this sense, is a sequence of statements some of which are given as reasons or evidence for the truth or correctness of some claim.

Premise: A premise is a reason that is offered to support the truth or correctness of a claim. An argument may have any number of premises, but it must have at least one. Some of the premises of an argument might be unstated. Unstated premises in arguments are commonly referred to as assumptions.

Assumption: Assumptions are unstated premises that fill logical gaps in the stated argument. They are left unstated in most cases because the author believes that they are obvious or that they express claims that the audience already accepts as true or correct.

Conclusion: A conclusion is any claim that is supported by reasons. An argument may have any number of conclusions, but it must have at least one. In complex arguments that have more than one conclusion, some will be intermediate conclusions and one will be the final conclusion.

Intermediate conclusion: A claim that is supported by reasons and that, in turn, becomes a reason to support another conclusion in the argument.

Final conclusion: The final conclusion is a claim that is supported by reasons but does not support any other claim in the argument. The final conclusion isn't always explicitly stated. In such cases, however, the author usually presents the reasons in such a way that there is really only one obvious conclusion that can be drawn from them. This implicit conclusion, even though unstated in the argument, is the main point or final conclusion of the argument.

How to Tackle a Logical Reasoning Question

It's important to have a plan in mind before you begin any new task. This is especially true when dealing with the Logical Reasoning questions on the GRE. Knowing in advance how you will approach each problem is just as important as having the skills to solve the problem. Here's a 3-step approach that will help you to handle any Logical Reasoning question.

ACTION PLAN
1. **Read the question stem carefully**
2. **Read the passage carefully**
3. **Read the answers carefully**

DO's and DON'Ts for Handling Logical Reasoning Questions

Do	Don't

DO identify the skill being tested before you read the passage.

DON'T let yourself get bogged down on a question.

DO pay attention only to the skill that is being tested.

DO focus your attention on the argument's logic.

DON'T choose an answer simply because you believe it is true or because you agree with it.

DON'T reject an answer because you believe it is false or because you disagree with it.

17

How to Identify the Main Point or Conclusion of an Argument

One of the most important Logical Reasoning skills you'll learn this hour is how to identify the premises and conclusions of arguments. Even though you'll be tested only on your ability to correctly identify conclusions, figuring out which statements are premises as well as identifying which are conclusions is essential to answering most of the Logical Reasoning questions on the GRE.

GRE questions that ask you identify the conclusion of an argument are typically worded as follows:

- Which of the following best expresses the main point of the passage?
- The conclusion of the argument is best expressed by which of the following?

Here is a list of words and phrases that are commonly used to indicate that the sentence that follows is a conclusion:

therefore	proves that
entails that	implies that
allows us to infer that	so
as a result	it is likely that
hence	suggests that
consequently	demonstrates that
it follows that	that's why

In cases where such words and phrases are absent, you can identify the conclusion by first identifying the premises and then looking for the sentence that they are intended to support. Here are some words and phrases commonly used to indicate that the sentence that follows is a premise:

since	for the reason that
for	is entailed by
because	assuming that
inasmuch as	is substantiated by
follows from	is shown by
given that	as a result
is suggested by	on the supposition that
is proved by	can be concluded from

CAUTION The words 'since' and 'because' are not always used to indicate premises. For example, in the sentence 'Since my baby left me, I've been miserable,' the word 'since' is not used to indicate a reason. Rather, it indicates a particular period of time. In the sentence 'The house burned down because the iron overheated,' the word 'because' does not indicate a reason, it indicates the cause of the fire.

Using Indicator Words to Identify Premises and Conclusions

Now let's look at a few examples to see how these indicator words and phrases can help you identify the premises and conclusion of an argument.

Einstein is as great a cult figure as Madonna, *so* T-shirts with Einstein's picture on them will sell as well as shirts with Madonna's picture.

Since Einstein is as great a cult figure as Madonna, T-shirts with Einstein's picture on them will sell as well as shirts with Madonna's picture.

In the first example, the word *so* indicates the conclusion; in the second example, the word *since* indicates the premise. The argument in each of these examples is identical and can be rewritten as follows:

Premise: Einstein is as great a cult figure as Madonna.

Conclusion: T-shirts with Einstein's picture on them will sell as well as shirts with Madonna's picture.

Here's a more complicated example:

Inasmuch as Einstein is as great a cult figure as Madonna, *it is likely that* T-shirts with Einstein's picture on them will sell as well as shirts with Madonna's picture, *so* we should add them to our inventory.

Each of the three italicized expressions in this example is an indicator. The first indicates a premise, the other two indicate conclusions. The word *so* indicates the final conclusion. The phrase *it is likely that* indicates the intermediate conclusion.

 CAUTION

Recall that in arguments that contain more than one conclusion, the final conclusion is the statement that is supported by other statements but does not itself support any other statement; intermediate conclusions are statements that are supported by other statements and that, in turn, support further statements.

17

Using a Rhetorical Question to Signal a Conclusion

In addition to the use of indicator words and phrases, another common way to signal an argument's conclusion is to express it as a rhetorical question or as an answer to a rhetorical question. The purpose of such questions is not to solicit information, but rather to emphasize a particular point or to raise a particular issue. Rhetorical questions typically (but not always) appear at the beginning of the passage. The remaining sentences in the passage typically state reasons that support the position on the issue that the rhetorical question encompasses. Look at the following example:

Can anyone really deny that abortion is morally wrong? After all, killing humans is wrong, and abortion is just another way of killing a human.

The rhetorical question in this argument leaves little doubt about the author's position on this issue. The way in which the question is posed clearly indicates that, at least for the author, this is not an open question. Generally, the more sarcastic the tone of the question, the more obvious the author's position on the issue that the question encompasses. The converse of this is generally the case as well. The conclusion of the argument in this example is simply a restatement of the rhetorical question expressed in the first sentence—namely, that abortion is morally wrong. The remaining sentences in this passage are premises that support this conclusion.

Identifying the Main Point or Conclusion of an Argument

Here's a 3-step approach that will help you identify the main point or conclusion of any argument:

> The steps in this and all of the following procedures in this and next hour's lessons assume that you have already identified the problem type and have read and understood any specific directions pertaining to the question as outlined in the Action Plan for Logical Reasoning questions on page 325.

1. **Scan the passage looking for conclusion or premise indicator words or phrases.**
2. **If there are no indicator words or phrases in the passage, scan the passage looking for a rhetorical question.**
3. **If the passage has no indicator expressions or rhetorical questions, look at the first and last statements in the passage.**

How to Identify Inferences from Given Premises

Inference questions test your ability to draw conclusions from given information. To be more precise, inference questions test your ability to determine what conclusion must be true, or is most likely true, given that the statements in the passage are true. In problems of this type, the information in the passage functions as the premises of the argument and the candidate conclusions are among the answer choices.

> In a variation of this type of question a blank space is left at the end of the passage and you are asked to choose the conclusion that best completes the reasoning of the argument from among the answer choices.

Types of Inference Questions

Inference questions are worded in a variety of ways. Here are examples of the three basic types:

1. If all the statements in the passage are true, which one of the following must also be true?

2. Which one of the following conclusions is most strongly supported by the statements in the passage?

3. Which of the following statements can be properly inferred from the passage?

The difference between the first two of these types of questions is important. The conclusion that *must be true* given the information stated in the passage is the one that cannot conceivably be false, given this information. The conclusion that is *most strongly supported* by the information stated in the passage is the one that is most unlikely to be false (in other words, most likely true), given this information. Questions that ask for what can be "properly inferred" or "properly drawn" from the passage are somewhat tricky. Without getting too technical, the bottom line is that questions asking for the conclusion you can "properly" infer or draw from the statements in the passage can be understood in two ways. They can be asking either for the conclusion that *must be true*, or for the conclusion that the passage *most strongly supports*.

NOTE

> For an inference to be "proper," it must be made in accordance with acceptable inference rules or meet certain standards of acceptable inference. In deductive reasoning, these rules and standards are designed to ensure that the truth of the premises guarantees the truth of the conclusion, whereas in inductive reasoning, the rules and standards are designed to ensure that the truth of the premises makes it highly likely that the conclusion is true.

Degrees of Support

In the context of Logical Reasoning, the word "support" means "increases the likelihood that the conclusion is true." Thus, to say that the premises support the conclusion is to say that they increase the likelihood that it is true. Given this, you can see that premises can provide varying *degrees* of support for conclusions, ranging from very little to maximum support. The premises provide maximum support if the conclusion cannot conceivably be false given that the information stated by the premises is true. Obviously, maximum support is the highest degree of support possible. Lesser degrees of support will reflect the degree of likelihood that the conclusion is true given that the premises are true. Thus, some premises will provide a *stronger* degree of support for a conclusion than others.

What this boils down to is that inference questions are aimed at testing your ability to make correct judgments about the *degree of support* premises provide for conclusions. As the previous example illustrates, the way in which this is typically done on the GRE is to provide you with some information in a passage and a list of possible conclusions in the answer choices, and have you select the answer that is most strongly supported by this information.

Dealing With "Must Be True" Inference Questions

Here's a 2-step approach to help you deal with questions that ask you to find the statement that *must* be true given the information stated in the passage:

ACTION PLAN

1. **Read the passage very carefully. If necessary, jot down the premises on your scratch paper parsing out key information and deleting unnecessary verbiage.**

2. **Read each of the answers. Ask yourself whether it can conceivably be false given that the sentences in the passage are true.**

   The correct answer is the one that cannot conceivably be false given the information stated in the passage.

Here's a simple example to illustrate this approach:

QUESTION Cheating on your taxes is lying, and lying, as we all know, is morally wrong.

If the statements in the passage are true, which one of the following *must* also be true?

(A) Cheating on your taxes is illegal.

(B) Cheating is morally wrong.

(C) Cheating on your taxes is morally wrong.

(D) Lying is cheating.

(E) Cheating is immoral.

 1. Jot down the premises as follows:

Premise: Cheating on your taxes is lying.

Premise: Lying is morally wrong.

2. Read each answer in turn and determine whether it can conceivably be false given the information stated in the premises.

Remember, the correct answer is the one that *cannot conceivably be false*, given that the information in the passage is true.

Now let's look at each of the answer choices. Look at answer choice (A). Can it conceivably be false given the stated information? The answer is yes, because the given information does not explicitly mention anything about what is legal or illegal.

Don't make any superfluous assumptions. Focus only on the information *explicitly* stated in the passage.

Look at answer choice (B). Can it conceivably be false given the stated information? Again, the answer is yes, because the given information does not state that all kinds of cheating are lying. It states only that a particular kind of cheating (cheating on your taxes) is lying. Now look at answer choice (B). Can it conceivably be false given the stated information? In this case, the answer is no, because if all tax cheating is lying, and all lying is morally wrong, then all tax cheating must be morally wrong. Response (C) is the correct answer.

Once you have found an answer that must be true given the information, you need not continue with other answer choices. This type of question has only *one* correct answer.

Dealing With "Most Strongly Supported" Inference Questions

Here's a 2-step approach to help you deal with questions that ask you to find the statement that is *most strongly supported* given the information stated in the passage:

1. **Read the passage very carefully. If necessary, jot down the premises on your scratch paper parsing out key information and deleting unnecessary verbiage.**

2. **Read each answer choice. Determine how likely it is true given the information stated in the passage. Use a simple four-point scale to score each of the answers. For example, 1 = very unlikely, 2 = not very likely, 3 = somewhat likely, 4 = very likely. Using this scale the correct answer is the one that gets the *highest score*.**

NOTE   You can also use this procedure to deal with questions that ask you to find
the conclusion that can be *properly inferred* from the information in the
passage. The only change you need to make is to expand the four-point scale
to a five-point scale, assigning 5 to answers that must be true.

Here's an example of this approach:

Dogs taken to humane shelters are routinely checked for rabies. The dog that bit James
was obtained from the humane shelter the day before it bit him.

QUESTION   If the statements in the passage are true, which of the following is most strongly
supported?

   (A) Humane shelter technicians never make mistakes when testing dogs for rabies.

   (B) The dog contracted rabies after it was released from the shelter but before it bit
James.

   (C) The dog does not have rabies.

   (D) James has rabies.

   (E) The humane shelter technicians are incompetent.

ANALYSIS   **1.** Here's the key information stated in the passage:

     Premise: Dogs taken to humane shelters are routinely checked for rabies.

Premise: The dog that bit James was obtained from the humane shelter.

Premise: The dog was obtained from the humane shelter the day before it bit James.

2. Using the 4-point scale, here's the score for each of the answer choices:

The score for (A) is 2. (A) is not very likely true, because the information in the passage
really doesn't address itself to the issue of whether the testing procedures are reliable.

The score for (B) is (2). (B) is not very likely true. Although it is possible that the dog
contracted rabies during this brief period, without additional information regarding the
dog's whereabouts during this period, it is difficult to assess the likelihood that this is the
case. Given the information in the premises.

The score for (C) is 4. (C) is very likely true. The fact that the dog was tested for rabies
just a short time before the incident makes it very likely that the dog was not rabid at the
time of the incident.

The score for (D) is 1. (D) is very unlikely true. The likelihood that (D) is true is a function of the likelihood that (C) is true, so if it is very likely that the dog does not have rabies, then it's very likely that James does not have rabies.

The score for (E) is 2. (E)is not very likely true. Although it is possible that the technicians are incompetent, the information stated in the premises does not support that claim..

Reviewing the scores, response (C) gets the highest score. (C) is the most strongly supported, and thus **(C)** is the correct answer.

 CAUTION   When using this approach you must read and score *all* of the answer choices.

17

How to Identify Assumptions

An assumption is an unstated premise that fills in a logical gap in the stated argument. In other words, it's is a missing piece of information that is required to support the conclusion. Assumption questions test your ability to supply the unstated information that is required to support the conclusions of arguments.

Assumption questions are typically worded as follows:

- The conclusion of the argument is properly drawn if which one of the following is assumed?
- For the argument to be logically correct, it must make which of the following assumptions?
- Which of the following is an assumption on which the argument depends?

Notice that the above questions ask you for the assumption that makes the argument *logically correct* or that allows the conclusion to be *properly drawn*. The exact conditions that must be satisfied for an argument to be "logically correct," or for the conclusion to be "properly drawn," differ depending on the argument type. As a general rule, however, the more unlikely it is for the conclusion to be false given that the premises are true, the more "logically correct" the argument and the more "properly drawn" is the conclusion. Therefore, the assumption that will make the argument logically correct, or the conclusion "properly drawn", is a statement that, when taken with the stated premises, significantly increases the likelihood that the conclusion is true. Moreover, given several choices, the statement that increases this likelihood most is the best choice.

Starting With the Answer Choices

When dealing with assumption questions, one approach is to use the answer choices to help you figure out the assumption. To do this, first identify the premises and the conclusion. Next, look at the answer choices and ask yourself which most increases the likelihood that the conclusion is true.

Here's a simple example to illustrate this approach:

 Fred is a philosophy major, that's why I'm sure he'll score high on the GRE.

For the argument to be logically correct, it must make which of the following assumptions?

(A) Philosophy majors have good verbal skills.

(B) Philosophy majors have good Logical Reasoning skills.

(C) Philosophy majors score high on the GRE.

ANALYSIS First, jot down the argument to reveal its structure as follows:

Assumption: _____.

Stated Premise: Fred is a philosophy major.

Conclusion: Fred will score high on the GRE.

Second, look at each of the answer choices and ask which *most* increases the likelihood that the conclusion is true?

Look at answer (A). Having good verbal skills is necessary to score high on the GRE, but you need additional skills as well. So, while (A) increases the likelihood that the conclusion is true, there remains a significant likelihood that the conclusion is false.

Look at answer (B). Having good Logical Reasoning skills is necessary to score high on the GRE, but you need additional skills as well. So, while (B) increases the likelihood that the conclusion is true, there remains a significant likelihood that the conclusion is false.

Look at answer (C). This claim increases the likelihood that the conclusion is true. Moreover, given (C), the likelihood that the conclusion is false is completely eliminated. **(C)** is the best choice because it increases the likelihood that the conclusion is true more than the other two choices.

Starting With the Argument

Another approach is to try to figure out the assumption *before* you look at the answer choices. In this approach you use the stated information in the argument as a guide to the unstated assumption. Typically, assumptions in arguments serve to connect key ideas in the author's reasoning or fill logical gaps in the pattern of the reasoning. Consequently, this approach focuses on either identifying the argument's key ideas or the logical pattern of the argument. To do this, first identify the premises and the conclusion. Next, identify the key ideas in the argument or the pattern of the argument. The assumption required to make the argument logically correct is one that either links key ideas that are not linked in the premises and conclusion or that completes the argument's logical pattern.

 CAUTION

> Determining whether to identify the keys ideas or to identify the pattern of the argument depends upon the argument at hand. Don't worry; careful study of the examples and exercises in this lesson will give you a good idea of which to do in each case.

17

Here's a simple example to illustrate this approach:

People enjoy stories written by Mark Twain because they enjoy humorous stories.

Here's the argument:

Assumption: _____.

Premise: People enjoy humorous stories.

Conclusion: People enjoy stories written by Mark Twain.

The key ideas in the argument are (1) things people enjoy, (2) humorous stories, and (3) stories written by Mark Twain. The stated premise links ideas (1) and (2). The conclusion links ideas (1) and (3). Since ideas (2) and (3) are not linked in the argument, the assumption required to make the argument logically correct must link these two ideas. The statement that does this is: Stories written by Mark Twain are humorous.

Here's another example to illustrate this approach:

If there's really an energy crisis in this country, the government can't be lying. So, the government must be telling the truth.

Here's the argument:

Assumption: _____.

Premise: If there is an energy crisis in this country, the government is not lying.

Conclusion: The government is not lying.

The pattern of this argument is:

Assumption: _____.

Premise: If A, then B.

Conclusion: B

The statement required to complete this pattern is *A.* So, in this example the assumption is: There is an energy crisis in this country.

Dealing With Assumption Questions

Combining the approaches discussed above, here's a 4-step plan to help you identify the assumption that makes an argument logically correct:

1. **Identify the stated premises and the conclusion of the argument.**

2. **Read each answer choice. Look for the one that most increases the likelihood that the conclusion is true.**

   As an alternative to step 2, do steps 3 and 4:

3. **Identify the key ideas in the argument or identify the argument's logical pattern.**

4. **Look for an answer choice that links key ideas that are not linked in the stated premises and conclusion, or that completes the argument's logical pattern.**

Workshop

In this workshop, you'll review the skills you learned this hour by attempting a GRE-style quiz.

ONLINE   Additional Logical Reasoning questions are available on-line at the authors' Web site: *http://www.west.net/~stewart/gre*

Quiz

DIRECTIONS: Try these 5 GRE-style Logical Reasoning questions. Limit your time to 80 seconds per question.

(Answers and explanations begin on page 339)

1. If our society continues to have large numbers of homeless people living on the streets, then we will continue to have street crime. But, there is no immediate prospect of ending the problem of homeless people living on the streets, because that would be an extremely difficult undertaking even if there were great public support, which there clearly isn't.

   Which of the following conclusions can be properly inferred from the statements in the passage?

   (A) The number of homeless people in our society will increase.
   (B) Most people are interested in solving the problem of street crime.
   (C) The main victims of street crime are homeless people.
   (D) Our society will continue to have street crime.
   (E) The problem of homelessness cannot be solved.

   (Hint: Look for the answer choice that is most likely true given the information in the passage.)

2. Can anyone seriously deny that unrestricted immigration will harm hundreds of thousands of American workers? If the United States allows unrestricted immigration, there will soon be a surplus of cheap labor. This will inevitably lead to lower wages. And if wages fall, it's only a matter of time until the standards of living of other workers are adversely affected.

   The conclusion of the argument is best expressed by which of the following?

   (A) Unrestricted immigration will result in a surplus of cheap labor.
   (B) A surplus of cheap labor will lead to lower wages for all workers.
   (C) A decrease in worker's wages should be avoided at all costs.
   (D) Unrestricted immigration will be detrimental to the standards of living of all workers.
   (E) Hundreds of thousands of American workers will be harmed by unrestricted immigration.

   (Hint: Look for a paraphrase of the rhetorical question in the passage.)

17

3. Wearing seatbelts in a car is like getting a vaccine to prevent measles. In both cases it's good for our health and wellbeing, but it's a hassle and lots of people wouldn't do it unless they were forced to. All in all, however, it's good that we have a law requiring people to get vaccinated for measles. Likewise, it's good to have a law that requires people to wear seat belts in cars.

The conclusion of the argument is best expressed by which of the following?

(A) Wearing seat belts in cars is good for our health and wellbeing.
(B) People will not wear seat belts unless they are forced to.
(C) The law that requires people to get vaccinated for measles is a good idea.
(D) The law that requires people to wear seat belts in cars is a good idea.
(E) Wearing seat belts in cars is a hassle.

(Hint: Ask yourself what point the author is trying to make.)

4. Non-human primates are excellent animal models for the study of human disease because of their close genetic relationship to humans. Indeed, comparisons of the chromosomes and DNA of non-human primates and humans reveals a startling similarity in their structure and primitive origin, and testifies to the commonality of the genetic material between these phylogenetically related species.

Which one of the following is an assumption upon which the argument depends?

(A) Animals that are related genetically to humans make good models for studying human disease.
(B) The genetic makeup of humans and non-human primates is very similar.
(C) The more similar in structure and primitive origin of the chromosomes and DNA of species, the more commonalities in their genetic material.
(D) Phylogenetically related species make good models for studying one another.

Non-human primates are closely related to humans.

(Hint: Look for an unstated link between key ideas.)

5. Since the transitional government has declared that they are not terrorists and will not use terrorist tactics to remain in power after the transition, we can be assured that they do not condone terrorist acts.

For the argument to be logically correct, it must make which of the following assumptions?

(A) Only terrorists condone acts of terrorism.
(B) Governments that don't condone acts of terrorism can be trusted to keep their word.
(C) Few transitional governments condone acts of terrorism.
(D) All terrorists engage in acts of terrorism.
(E) Terrorism is a tactic that many governments use to remain in power.

(Hint: Look for an unstated link between key ideas.)

Answers and Explanations

1. **(D)** Here's the key information in the passage:

   Premise: If our society continues to have homeless people living on the streets, then we will continue to have street crime.

   Premise: We will continue to have homeless people living on the streets.

   Here's the score for each answer choice:

   The score for (A) is 2. The information given in the passage does not support this claim. The score for (B) is 2. The information given in the passage does not support this claim.
   The score for (C) is 2. The information given in the passage does not support this claim. The score for (D) is 5. Given the information in the passage (d) must be true. The score for (E) is 2. The information given in the passage does not support this claim.

2. **(E)** The conclusion of this argument is expressed by the rhetorical question at the beginning of the passage. The sarcastic tone of the question indicates that the author believes that unrestricted immigration will harm hundreds of thousands of American workers. Answer choice (E) is a restatement of this idea.

3. **(D)** In this argument an analogy is drawn between wearing seat belts and getting vaccinated. On the basis of several similarities between them, the author reasons

that they are also similar in an additional way. The conclusion is signaled by the word '*likewise*', which indicates the additional feature they share.

4. **(A)** Here's the argument:

   Assumption: _____.

   Premise: Non-human primates are closely related genetically to humans.

   Conclusion: Non-human primates are excellent animal models for the study of human disease.

   The key ideas in this argument are (1) non-human primates, (2) animals that are related genetically to humans, and (3) animals that are models for the study of human disease. The stated premise links ideas (1) and (2). The conclusion links ideas (1) and (3). The assumption in the argument must relate ideas (2) and (3). Among the answer choices, only answer (A) links these two ideas.

5. **(A)** Here's the argument:

   Assumption: _____.

   Premise: The transitional government has declared that they are not terrorists.

   Conclusion: The transitional government does not condone terrorist acts.

   The key ideas in the argument are (1) the transitional government (2) terrorists, and (3) groups that condone acts of terrorism.

17

The stated premise links ideas (1) and (2). The conclusion links ideas (1) and (3). The assumption required to make the argument logically correct must link ideas (2) and (3). Of the answer choices only (A) links ideas (2) and (3).

HOUR 18

Teach Yourself Logical Reasoning II

This hour you'll teach yourself four new Logical Reasoning skills that you'll need for the GRE. In this hour you will learn:

- How to assess the effect additional information has on an argument's conclusion
- How to identify the method of an argument
- How to recognize some common reasoning errors
- How to recognize similarities between arguments
- How to apply the skills you learn this hour to a GRE-style quiz

How to Assess the Effect of Additional Information

Questions that test your ability to assess the effect new information has on an argument are the most common type on the GRE. The passage states an argument. The answer choices state additional information. Your task is to assess the effect this additional information has on the argument.

There are just two types of additional information questions:

1. Those that ask you to choose the answer that strengthens the argument.
2. Those that ask you to choose the answer that weakens the argument.

But on the GRE these questions are worded many different ways.

Weaken questions are commonly worded as follows:

- Which one of the following, if true, casts the most doubt on the argument?
- Which one of the following, if accepted by the authors, would require them to reconsider their conclusion?
- Which of the following, if true, most seriously calls the preceding conclusion into question?
- Which of the following, if true, most seriously undermines the author's contention?

Strengthen questions are commonly worded as follows:

- Which of the following, if true, most strengthens the argument?
- Which of the following would provide the most support for the conclusion?
- Which of the following supports the conclusion in the passage?
- The conclusion in the argument would be more reasonable if which one of the following were true?

Determining Argument Strength and Weakness

The strength of an argument is determined by the degree of likelihood that the conclusion is true given that the premises are true. The higher this degree of likelihood, the stronger the argument. Conversely, the lower this degree of likelihood, the weaker the argument.

For example, compare the following arguments:

1. 90% of all men are forgetful, Adam is a man, therefore Adam is forgetful.
2. 50% of all men are forgetful, Adam is a man, therefore Adam is forgetful.

The first argument is stronger than the second. In the first, the likelihood that the conclusion is true given that the premises are true is 90%. If you had to make a bet whether Adam is forgetful and you knew the information stated in the premises, you'd probably wager a lot on it. In the second, the likelihood that the conclusion is true given that the premises are true is 50%. In this case you'd wager a lot less.

Of course, in both cases you could lose your wager. For example, if it turned out that Adam was a mnemonist (a memory expert), then both wagers would be bad bets. In other words, this *additional information* about Adam would weaken both arguments considerably. You can see that it would do this by considering how much less you'd be willing to wager if you knew this. On the other hand, if it turned out that Adam had advanced Alzheimer's disease (a result of which is severe memory loss), then both wagers would be good bets. In other words, this additional information about Adam would strengthen both arguments considerably. Again, you can see that it would do this by considering how much more you'd be willing to bet if you knew this.

The bottom line is arguments can be strengthened or weakened by additional information. Arguments are strengthened by the new information if the likelihood that the conclusion is true (given that the premises are true) is increased by the addition of the new information. Arguments are weakened by the new information if the likelihood that the conclusion is true (given that the premises are true) is decreased by the addition of the new information.

18

Weakening an Argument

There are basically three ways to weaken an argument: (1) undermine a major assumption of the argument, (2) attack one of the premises of the argument, or (3) suggest an alternative conclusion that you can infer from the given premises. When dealing with problems that ask you to choose a statement that weakens an argument, the correct answer does one of these three things.

Here's a 3-step approach to help you deal with questions that ask you to find the statement that weakens an argument:

1. **Identify the argument's premises and conclusion.**
2. **Identify the argument's major assumption.**
3. **Look for an answer choice that does one of the following:**
   - **undermines the major assumption**
   - **attacks a stated premise**
   - **suggests an alternative conclusion that you can infer from the stated premises**

   The correct answer is one that does any one of these.

Here's a simple example that illustrates this approach:

 The current regime is oppressive since it is holding thousands of people in jail without due process of law.

Which of the following, if true, most weakens this argument?

(A) The current regime has only been in power for two weeks.

(B) Most of the prisoners are political prisoners.

(C) Many non-oppressive regimes hold people in jail without due process of law.

ANALYSIS 1. Here's the argument:

Premise: The current regime is holding thousands of people in jail without due process of law.

Conclusion: The current regime is oppressive.

2. Here's the major assumption:

All regimes that hold people in jail without due process of law are oppressive.

3. Here's the reason (C) is the best choice:

Answer **(C)** undermines the argument's major assumption.

Strengthening an Argument

There are two ways to strengthen an argument, (1) offer support for the argument's major assumption, or (2) provide additional evidence for the conclusion (that is, evidence beyond what the given premises state). When dealing with problems that ask you to choose a statement that strengthens an argument, the correct answer does one of these two things.

Here's a 3-step approach to help you deal with questions that ask you to find the statement that strengthens an argument:

ACTION PLAN 1. **Identify the argument's premises and conclusion.**

2. **Identify the argument's major assumption.**

3. **Look for an answer choice that does either of the following:**

   • **provides support for the major assumption**

   • **provides additional evidence for the conclusion**

   The correct answer is one that does either of these.

Here's a simple example that illustrates this approach:

 Since we need to improve our minds in order to live full and happy lives, it follows that we cannot just play all the time.

Which of the following, if true, most strengthens the argument?

(A) People who play all the time lead empty, unfulfilling lives.

(B) The only way to improve your mind is through study and hard work.

(C) Most people do not live full and happy lives.

ANALYSIS   **1.** Here's the argument:

> *Premise:* We need to improve our minds in order to live full and happy lives.
>
> *Conclusion:* We cannot just play all the time.

2. Here's the major assumption:

Play does not improve our minds.

3. Here's the reason (B) is the best choice:

Answer **(B)** provides support for the argument's major assumption.

How to Recognize Reasoning Errors

18

Reasoning error questions test your ability to recognize various flaws or mistakes in reasoning. There are many different types of reasoning mistakes, but all of them involve practices that fail to meet the standards of good reasoning. Basically, these standards require that the premises of arguments provide grounds for believing that the conclusion is true, and they also require that criticisms or refutations of arguments focus on showing that the premises somehow fail to do this. Arguments that employ devices aimed at getting you to accept conclusions that are unwarranted by the premises, as well as refutations of arguments that employ devices that are aimed at getting you to reject the conclusion for reasons other than that it is unwarranted by the premises violate the standards of good reasoning. The word "fallacy" is used to describe the error or mistake such arguments contain. Because there are so many different fallacies to keep track of each has been given a name. The good news is that you won't be required to identify the fallacy by its traditional name; instead, you must simply select the best description of the reasoning error from the answer choices.

Reasoning error questions are typically worded as follows:

- Which of the following is the best statement of the flaw in the argument?
- Which one of the following indicates an error in the reasoning leading to the conclusion in the argument?
- Which one of the following questionable argumentative techniques does this passage employ?

Unfortunately, there is no magic pill you can take to learn all of the reasoning errors – there are just too many. The best way to study for these questions is to familiarize yourself with several of the most common errors. To help you do this, read the following discussion of the errors and study the examples.

NOTE

For purposes of clarity, in the following discussion each fallacy will be given a name. Remember, however, that you are *not* required to identify fallacies by name on the test, so try to focus on the mistake in each case rather than on trying to memorize the name.

Statistical Reasoning Errors

Fallacies of "hasty generalization." The two most common statistical reasoning errors are the fallacy of the biased sample and the fallacy of the small or insufficient sample. The fallacy of the biased sample is committed whenever the data for a statistical inference are drawn from a sample that is not representative of the population under consideration. The fallacy of the small or insufficient sample is committed whenever too small a sample is used to be representative of the population or whenever greater reliability is attributed to the conclusion than the sample size warrants. These two fallacies are commonly referred to as fallacies of "hasty generalization."

Example 1 (Biased sample):

In a recent survey conducted on the Internet, 80 percent of the respondents indicated their strong disapproval of government regulation of the content and access of web-based information. This survey clearly shows that legislation designed to restrict the access or to control the content of Internet information will meet with strong opposition from the electorate.

This argument draws the data for its inference from a sample that is not representative of the entire electorate. Because the survey was conducted on the Internet, not all members of the electorate have an equal chance of being included in the sample. Moreover, people who use the Internet are more likely to have an opinion on the topic than people who do not. For these reasons, the sample is obviously biased.

Example 2 (Insufficient sample):

I met my new boss at work today and she was very unpleasant. Twice when I tried to talk with her, she said that she was busy and told me not to interrupt her again. Later, when I needed her advice on a customer's problem, she ignored me and walked away. It's obvious that she has a bad attitude and is not going to be easy to work with.

The data for this argument's inference are insufficient to support the conclusion. Three observations of a person's behavior are not necessarily representative of that person's behavior in general. Obviously, the boss could just have been having a bad day or been engrossed in other things.

> To recognize statistical reasoning errors, look for an argument in which the author reaches a general conclusion on the basis of a small number of cases, or from information that is biased in favor of the conclusion.

Causal Reasoning Errors

The "after this, therefore because of this" fallacy. This reasoning error is by far the most common causal fallacy, and the one most likely to appear on the GRE. This is the fallacy of concluding that because event Y occurred after some other event X, X must have caused Y. Many common superstitions are examples of this fallacy (for example, believing that the cause of your misfortune is the fact a black crossed your path just before it occurred.). The reasoning error in arguments of this type is that the evidence stated in the premises is insufficient to warrant the conclusion. Moreover, typically in these arguments the causal connection between the two events is implausible given our general understanding of the world.

Example 1:

Ten minutes after walking into the auditorium, I began to feel sick to my stomach. There must have been something in the air in that building that caused my nausea.

Example 2:

The stock market declined shortly after the president's election, thus indicating the lack of confidence that the business community has in the new administration.

Both examples conclude that there is a causal connection between two events simply on the basis of one occurring before the other. In the first example the only reason given for claiming that the air in the auditorium caused the feeling of nausea is that the feeling of nausea happened shortly after entering the auditorium. In the second example the only evidence offered to support the claim that the president's election caused the decline in the stock market is the fact that the election preceded the decline. Although the election might have been a causal factor in the stock market's decline, to argue that it is the cause merely because the election preceded the decline is to commit the "after this, therefore because of this" fallacy.

To recognize this error, look for an argument in which the author's *only* reason for concluding that one event is the cause of another is that it occurred before the other.

Unwarranted Assumption Errors

Unwarranted assumptions are assumptions that have no merit or independent justification. In other words, they are assumptions that are gratuitous, unfounded, or that lack plausibility.

The "black-and-white" fallacy. This is one of the most common unwarranted-assumption fallacies. This error occurs when one assumes, without warrant, that there are only two alternatives, then reasons that because one of the alternatives is false or unacceptable, the other must be true or accepted. Typically, arguments that suffer from this reasoning error offer no evidence to support the claim that only two alternatives are available, and a little thought reveals that this assumption is not self-evident.

In cases where there are in fact only two alternatives, and this fact is obvious or justifiable, this pattern of reasoning is highly effective and acceptable.

Example:

> Either we put convicted child molesters in jail for life or we risk having our children become their next victims. We certainly can't risk this, so we had better lock up these criminals for the rest of their lives.

The argument assumes that only two alternatives are possible. The passage presents no evidence to support this claim, and a little thought reveals that the claim obviously has no validity. Although child molestation is a difficult problem to deal with, it is unlikely that the only solution to the problem is the one that the argument mentions. It is also unlikely that the advocated solution is the only way that we can protect children from becoming the victims of convicted offenders.

To recognize this error, look for an argument in which the author reasons that we are forced to choose between alternatives (usually two), and that since one of them is clearly unacceptable we must accept the other.

Irrelevant Appeals Fallacies

Irrelevant appeals attempt to persuade us to accept a conclusion by appealing to matters that are not relevant to the truth or correctness of the conclusion. Such appeals are considered reasoning errors because they violate the requirement that the reasons offered in support of a claim provide evidence that the claim is true or correct. In other words, such appeals mistakenly view the goal of argumentation to be simply persuasion rather than the attainment of the truth.

Appeal to ignorance. This appeal is commonly used to get us to accept a claim. The basic form of this error is to argue that a claim is true (or false) solely on the grounds that no one has demonstrated or can demonstrate that the claim is false (or true).

Example:

> Scientists have not established any causal link between smoking and lung cancer, hence we must simply accept the fact that smoking does not cause lung cancer.

Inability to prove that something is true (or false) cannot, by itself, be taken as evidence that it is false (or true). If this were accepted as a principle of reasoning, it would follow, for example, that our inability to prove that UFOs don't exist would lead immediately to the conclusion that UFOs exist.

18

| TIP | To recognize this error, look for an argument in which the author reasons that our lack of knowledge that some claim is true (or false) is grounds for accepting the claim as false (or true). |

Appeal to authority. Another device used to gain acceptance of a claim is to cite an authority. In place of evidence that supports the claim, authors resort to the testimony or expertise of others to support the claim. Appealing to an authority is not always incorrect. As a matter of fact, people often rely on other people or sources when accepting claims. We do this, for example, when appealing to scientists, textbooks, doctors, and other experts to support our beliefs. This practice becomes incorrect when the competence, reliability, qualifications, motives, prejudices, and so on, of the persons or sources who are cited as experts or authorities is questionable.

Example:

> Geena Goodlooks is one of this country's most respected and honored actresses. You can be certain that when she says welfare reform is needed, it has to be true.

In this argument, you have to wonder about the relevance of Geena's testimony to the truth of the claim that it supports. The argument offers no evidence that justifies its reliance on her testimony on this topic. Obviously, the fact that she is a "respected and honored" actress hardly qualifies her as an expert on the need for welfare reform.

 TIP

> To recognize this error, look for an argument in which the *only* reason given for accepting the conclusion is that some individual, group, or publication that is not qualified, or is biased, claims that it is true.

Reasoning Errors Involving the Use of Language

The fallacy of equivocation. This reasoning error occurs when a key word or phrase that has more than one meaning is employed in different meanings throughout the argument. Because the truth of the premises and the conclusion is in part a function of the meanings of the words in the sentences that express them, a shift in meaning of key terms in the argument leads the audience to draw conclusions that are not supported by the premises.

Example:

> Logic is the study of arguments, and since arguments are just disagreements, it follows that logic is just the study of disagreements.

In this example the word "argument" is used in two different meanings. In the first premise, "argument" means a discourse in which reasons are offered in support of a claim; the second premise defines "argument" as "a disagreement." If you adopt the second meaning, the first premise is false; if you adopt the first meaning, the second premise is false. Either way, the premises simply fail to support the conclusion.

 TIP

> To recognize this reasoning error look for an argument in which the author uses a key term or phrase in different meanings in the premises and conclusion.

Common Fallacies of Refutation

Fallacies of refutation are committed in criticizing the arguments of others. Refutation reasoning errors occur whenever the critic focuses on aspects of the argument that are irrelevant to the reasoning employed in the argument or the truth of the claims that make up the argument. The basic tactic in criticisms that commit errors of this type is to avoid attacking the argument, and instead attack the author, or a deliberately weakened version of the author's argument.

Attacking the author. Attacks that focus on the argument's author rather than the author's argument take three forms. The attack focuses either on the character, the motives, or the behavior of the person presenting the argument. The aim of the attack in all three cases is to discredit the conclusion of the person's argument. Assaults of this type are rarely, if ever, relevant to the reasoning employed in the argument or the truth or correctness of the conclusion. They are irrelevant for the simple reason that an arguer's personal character, motives, or behavior are rarely relevant to the correctness of his or her reasoning or the truth of the statements employed in the reasoning. Criticisms that employ attacks of these types are commonly known as *ad hominem* arguments (which means "against the person").

Example 1 (Attack on author's character):

When you realize that the man who is trying to convince you that he would be the best president this country has ever seen is in fact a womanizer and an illegal drug user, it's not difficult to draw the conclusion that his arguments are completely unacceptable.

This attack criticizes the presidential candidate's arguments by attacking the character of the candidate. No attempt is made to consider or attack the candidate's arguments.

Example 2 (Attack on author's motives):

The radio and television industry has been lobbying against proposed changes in the laws governing the use of publicly owned transmission frequencies. But just keep this in mind: No matter how good the industry's arguments might be, broadcasters stand to lose a great deal if the proposed changes become law.

In this case the radio and television industry's arguments are dismissed out of hand on the grounds that broadcasters have a vested interest in the outcome. The tactic exhibited in this example is commonly called "poisoning the well" because it condemns the argument's source to discredit the argument.

Example 3 (Attack on author's behavior):

My esteemed colleague accuses me of misappropriating taxpayers' funds for my own personal use. Well, it might interest you to know that he has the unenviable distinction of having spent more on so-called fact-finding trips to exotic locations all around the world than anyone else in Congress.

In this example, the politician makes no attempt to attack the colleague's argument; rather, the focus of the attack is to accuse the person of similar questionable behavior or wrong-doing. Because of this the reasoning error in this example is commonly called the "you too!" or "two wrongs don't make a right" fallacy.

18

TIP

To recognize refutation errors of this type, look for an argument in which the focus of the criticism is the author of the argument rather than the argument.

How to Identify the Method of Arguments

The method of an argument is simply the way in which the author goes about establishing the conclusion, or in the case of a critical answer to an argument, the way in which the author attempts to defeat the conclusion. Method questions test your ability to recognize various reasoning strategies or techniques. You're not required to identify the method by name, but only to select from the answer choices the best description of the argument's general reasoning strategy.

Method questions are typically worded as follows:

- The argument proceeds by:
- Which one of the following argumentative techniques is used in the passage?
- The method of the argument is to:
- The argument employs which one of the following reasoning techniques?

As with the reasoning errors you studied earlier this hour, the best way to study for method questions is to familiarize yourself with several of the most common reasoning techniques and strategies. To help you do this, read the following brief discussions and study the examples.

CAUTION

The following methods of establishing or defeating conclusions are not necessarily effective or logically correct. Don't get confused. The issue in questions dealing with the method of an argument is merely to *identify* the method that the author employs, not to determine whether the method is effective or logically correct.

Reasoning by Analogy

A common method to establish a conclusion is to use an analogy. Starting with a claim or situation that is familiar and unproblematic, the author argues that the issue in question is very much like the familiar case, and hence that what is true of it is probably true of the case in question.

Example:

> The mushrooms we saw in the forest yesterday are the same color, size, and shape as those we saw in the grocery store today. Obviously, the mushrooms sold in the grocery store aren't poisonous, so it's likely that the ones we saw in the forest aren't poisonous either.

Statistical Reasoning

Many arguments use statistics to establish claims. These arguments usually begin with a statistical claim to the effect that some percentage of a certain group has a certain characteristic. The argument typically concludes that because a given individual is in the group, the individual is likely (or unlikely) to have the selected characteristic.

Example 1:

> Only two percent of all vegetarians contract colon cancer. Because Sally is a vegetarian, it is unlikely that she'll get colon cancer.

Example 2:

> Eighty percent of all logic students scored high on the GRE. Fred is a logic major, so he probably scored high on the GRE.

18

Reasoning from Experience

People often use past experience as a reason for believing that something is the case or will be the case. This method of reasoning typically begins with an experience that the author or someone else has had. This experience then functions as a premise from which the author argue that some, as yet unobserved, event or situation will occur.

Example:

> We have observed the sun rising countless times in the past, hence we can be assured that the sun will rise tomorrow.

A variation of this method is to argue that some general claim is true on the basis of the observation of several instances of the claim. Arguments that employ this method of reasoning typically begin with premises that state the observed instances; the conclusion typically asserts that what is true of the observed instances is true of all or most instances.

Example:

> Don't worry! All the lettuce that we checked in the shipment was in excellent condition, so you can be assured that all the lettuce is okay.

Causal Reasoning

Authors typically attempt to establish causal conclusions (conclusions that assert a causal relation between two events) by using eliminative reasoning. Arguments that employ this method usually proceed by isolating a common feature shared by a number of events by a process of elimination. The premises typically describe testing procedures aimed at determining which, if any, of a set of properties are causally related to the event in question. Through experiment or observation, the author attempts to eliminate each of these features as a causal candidate. The feature that resists these attempts is concluded to be the cause of the event under consideration.

Example:

Six customers of a fast-food restaurant developed food poisoning shortly after eating lunch there. An investigation revealed that they had all drunk different beverages but not all had eaten salads, soups, or french fries. However, they had all eaten chicken sandwiches prepared with different breads. The health department concluded that the cause of the food poisoning was poorly cooked chicken.

How to Recognize Similarities Between Arguments

Parallel argument questions test your ability to recognize similarities between arguments. There are basically two kinds of questions. Some ask you to find the argument that employs the same method of reasoning, and others ask you to find the argument that contains the same reasoning error as the argument in the passage.

Questions that ask you to find the argument that employs the *same method of reasoning* as the argument in the passage are typically worded as follows:

In which of the following is the method of reasoning most parallel to that in the preceding argument?

Questions that ask you to find the argument that contains the *same reasoning error* as the argument in the passage are typically worded as follows:

Which one of the following arguments contains a flaw that is most similar to the one in the preceding argument?

Dealing with Parallel Method and Parallel Reasoning Error Questions

Here's a simple 2-step approach to help you deal with parallel argument questions that ask you to find an argument that has the same method or same reasoning error as the argument in the passage.

 ACTION PLAN   **1. Identify the method or the reasoning error in the passage's argument.**

2. Read the answer choices looking for an argument that employs a similar method or has a similar reasoning error.

Here's an example:

QUESTION   Shortly after James visited his friend in the hospital he became ill. This proves that going to the hospital when your not sick is a bad idea because you never know what you're going to catch there.

Which one of the following arguments contains a flaw that is most similar to the one in the preceding argument?

(A) I have no idea what George did, but moments after he came into the room Joyce got up and ran out in a big hurry. He must have done something terribly wrong to make her act that way.

(B) 90% of those who smoke heavily also drink heavily. This proves that heavy smoking leads to heavy drinking.

(C) Whenever Sam drinks alcohol, he's a pain to be around. He's unhappy, wants to quit school, and says going to be a beach bum. Once he stops drinking, everything is fine again. That's why I'm sure it's the booze that makes him act this way.

ANALYSIS   **1.** The reasoning error in the passage is the "after this, therefore because of this" fallacy. The only reason given for the claim that James' illness was caused by his visit to the hospital is that his visit preceded his illness.

2. Answer choice (A) commits the same fallacy. The only reason given for the claim that George's entrance into the room caused Joyce to leave in a hurry is that she left moments after George came in.

18

Workshop

In this Workshop, you'll review the skills you learned this hour by attempting a GRE-style quiz.

 ONLINE Additional Logical Reasoning questions are available on-line at the authors' Web site: *http://www.west.net/~stewart/gre*

Quiz

DIRECTIONS: Try these 5 Logical Reasoning questions. Limit your time to 80 seconds per question.

(Answers and explanations begin on page 358.)

1. All of the lawyers I've ever met were pushy, money hungry, and self-centered. Since your blind date is a lawyer, you can bet he'll be aggressive, cheap, and inattentive.

   The argument proceeds by:

   (A) reaching a general conclusion on the basis of a biased sample
   (B) reaching a conclusion on the basis of previous experience
   (C) isolating a feature through a process of elimination and concluding that this feature is causally related to the event under consideration
   (D) attacking the motive of the argument's author
   (E) attacking the character of the argument's author

   (Hint: Ask yourself what method the author employs to reach the conclusion.)

2. Does having a large amount of money guarantee happiness? Results of a recent survey overwhelmingly confirm that having a sizable quantity of money is the key to happiness. In the survey, 78 percent of those who responded who also claimed that they possessed a large amount of money said that they were happy.

   Which of the following, if true, most seriously calls the survey finding into doubt?

   (A) No clear quantitative definition of large amount of money was provided to the respondents.
   (B) No clear qualitative definition of *happiness* was provided to the respondents.
   (C) Most of the respondents who claimed to have a large amount of money in fact did not.

(D) Many people are happy even though they do not possess a great deal of money.

(E) Many people who have a great deal of money are not happy.

(Hint: This is a weaken question. Look for an answer choice that attacks a premise of the argument.)

3. Whether we like it or not we must either become energy self-efficient or resign ourselves to the threat of international blackmail. Given these alternatives, it's obvious that we have no choice but to become energy self-efficient.

The conclusion in the argument would be more reasonable if which one of the following were true?

(A) At the current rate of use, global energy sources will be depleted within the next century.

(B) We have the required natural energy sources to be energy self-sufficient.

(C) We have the required technological knowledge to develop our energy resources.

(D) There are no other countries that we can rely upon, without fear of threat, to meet our future energy needs.

(E) Our current natural energy sources are insufficient to meet our present energy needs.

(Hint: This is a strengthen question. Look for an answer choice that provides support for a major assumption of the argument.)

4. Failure to comply with the directions contained in this chain letter will result in bad consequences. Jane received this letter and passed it on in the required 72-hour period. A week later, she won $6 million in the lottery. Sam received it but did not comply with the directions. Within a week after receiving it, he was trampled to death by a renegade elephant at the circus.

The faulty reasoning in which one of the following is most parallel to that in the preceding argument?

(A) The portrayal of violence on television and in the movies is the main cause of violence in our nation. Hence, to get rid of violence in our nation, we must censor television shows and movies.

(B) Mandatory life sentences for three-time felons is a bad idea. People who think that such sentences are a good idea think that they will stop violent crime. But if we really want to stop violent crime, instead of locking people up we should eliminate the root cause of violent crime by ceasing to glamorize violence in movies and on television.

(C) It has been well established that smoking marijuana leads to heroin use, and that heroin use leads to drug addiction. Drug addiction, in turn, leads to crime to support the drug habit. The epidemic of drug-related crime is threatening the very core of our existence as a nation. Hence, to stop this threat, we must not legalize marijuana use.

18

(D) Parents are wrong to criticize their children for coming home late, smoking, watching too much television, and getting poor grades. After all, they do all these things and besides they're not all that smart themselves.

(E) Statistics show that nearly every heroin user started out by using marijuana. This is convincing proof that smoking marijuana is the main cause of heroin addiction.

(Hint: Look for a causal reasoning error in the passage, then find the answer choice that has the same error.)

5. I'm well aware that the very idea of deliberately injuring a laboratory animal is extremely repulsive. But if we don't experiment on living animals, then we won't be able to learn how to treat humans with injuries. So, like it or not, it must be done.

Which of the following is the best statement of the flaw in the argument?

(A) The author assumes without justification that there are only two alternatives open to us.

(B) The author assumes that humans are like laboratory animals.

(C) The author reasons that our lack of knowledge of human injuries is grounds for injuring laboratory animals.

(D) The author employs the term "injury" in two different meanings.

(E) The author's conclusion is a restatement of the premise.

(Hint: Look for an unwarranted assumption in the argument.)

Answers and Explanations

1. **(B)** In this argument the author reasons from their previous experience with lawyers that other lawyers will have similar characteristics.

2. **(C)** Here's the argument:

    Premise: 78 percent of the respondents said that they were happy.

    Premise: The same 78 percent of the respondents claimed that they possessed a large amount of money.

    Conclusion: Having a sizable quantity of money is the key to happiness.

    Answer choice (C) directly attacks the second premise listed above thereby seriously calling survey finding into doubt. If (C) is true, the second premise listed above is false. As a consequence, the argument falls apart because the connection between having money and being happy in the argument is completely severed. Answer choices (A) and (B) state possible problems that could have an adverse effect on the reliability of the survey, but neither of these answers directly attacks the truth of a stated premise, nor do they undermine the major assumption or suggest an alternative conclusion that could be inferred from the premises. Answer (D) is consistent with the conclusion of the argument. The conclusion does not state that everyone who is happy has a large amount of money; it states that persons who have a large amount of money are happy. Answer (D) doesn't weaken the argument because it does not suggest an alternative conclusion that could be inferred from the premises nor does it undermine the major assumption of the argument or attack a stated premise. Answer (E) contradicts the conclusion of the argument. The conclusion states that persons who have a large amount of money are happy; answer (E) states the opposite of this claim.

3. **(D)** Here's the argument:

   Premise: We must either become energy self-efficient or resign ourselves to the threat of international blackmail.

   Conclusion: We must become energy self-efficient

   In this argument there are two underlying assumptions:

   (1) The only alternatives available to us are the two stated in the premise.

   (2) We don't want to resign ourselves to the threat of international blackmail.

Answer choice (D) provides support for the first assumption by ruling out a third possible alternative.

4. **(E)** The reasoning error in the passage is to conclude that the Jane's good fortune and Sam's misfortune were caused by the ways they responded to the chain letter. The only reason offered in support of this conclusion is that their manner of response to the letter preceded what happened to them. The argument in answer choice (E) suffers from the same error. The only reason offered in (E) for the claim that smoking marijuana causes heroin addiction is that statistics show marijuana use precedes heroin use.

5. **(A)** The unwarranted assumption in this argument is that there are only two alternatives available. Either we experiment on living animals or we fail to learn how to treat humans with injuries.

18

Part V

Practice with Sample Exams

HOUR 19

Sample Test 1 (Quantitative Ability— Paper-based Format)

This hour you'll begin taking a sample paper-based GRE. You'll start with a full-length Quantitative Ability section that looks just like each of the two on the paper-based test. Then you'll go on to complete the paper-based GRE in Hours 20 and 21. Here are your goals for this hour:

- Take the test section under timed conditions
- Check the answer key on page 370
- Assess your performance by checking the score conversion chart on pages 455–456
- Review the explanations for the test (they begin on page 423)

Quantitative Ability Test

Time—30 Minutes

30 Questions

All numbers used are real numbers.

All figures lie on a plane unless otherwise indicated.

All angle measures are positive.

All lines shown as straight are straight.

Figures are intended to provide useful information for answering the questions. However, except where a figure is accompanied by a "Note" stating that the figure is drawn to scale, solve the problems using your knowledge of mathematics, *not* by visual measurement or estimation.

DIRECTIONS: *Questions 1–15* each consists of two quantities, one in Column A and one in Column B. You are to compare the two quantities and select:

(A) if the quantity in Column A is greater

(B) if the quantity in Column B is greater

(C) if the quantities are equal

(D) if the relationship cannot be determined from the information given

Notes:

There are only four answer choices, so NEVER MARK (E) as the best choice.

In some questions, additional information pertaining to one or both of the quantities to be compared is centered above the two columns.

Any symbol appearing in both columns represents the same thing in one column as in the other.

	Column A	Column B
1.	The number of prime numbers between 1 and 25	9
2.	The average (arithmetic mean) of 48, 75, and 95	The average (arithmetic mean) of 46, 76, and 97

$$a \blacksquare b = (a + b)(a - b)$$

	Column A	Column B
3.	$2 \blacksquare 2$	$-2 \blacksquare -2$

On the xy-coordinate plane appear four points—A, B, C, and D—which have (x,y) coordinates of $(-2,-1)$, $(4,-1)$, $(-2,3)$, and $(3,4)$, respectively.

	Column A	Column B
4.	The distance from A to B	The distance from C to D
5.	The ratio of p to $(p + 1)$ if $5 < p < 10$	The ratio of p to $(p + 1)$ if $10 < p < 15$

In the series $\{N_1, N_2, N_3, \ldots\}$, $N_1 = -1$, and $N_{(x+1)} = -|N_x + x|$.

	Column A	Column B
6.	$N_2 - N_3$	$N_4 - N_5$

p is a positive integer.

	Column A	Column B
7.	The remainder when $3p + 5$ is divided by 3	The remainder when $7p + 8$ is divided by 7

$R > r$

	Column A	Column B
8.	Circumference of circle with radius r	Area of circle with radius R

$s > 1$

	Column A	Column B
9.	The volume of a cube with a side of s	The volume of a rectangular solid with sides of s, $s + 1$, and $s - 1$

$2x^2 + 9x = 5$

	Column A	Column B
10.	x	-5

19

	Column A	Column B		Column A	Column B

As two wheels—*A* and *B*—
roll across the ground, they both
rotate at a rate of 60 revolutions per
second. The radius of wheel *A* is 3.
The radius of wheel *B* is 150.

11. | The distance wheel *A* travels per minute | The distance wheel *B* travels per second |

$$0 < |a| < 1$$
$$0 < |b| < 1$$

12. | $a^3 + b^3$ | $a^2 + b^2$ |

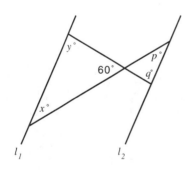

$l_1 \parallel l_2$

13. | $x - y$ | $q - p$ |

14. | $\dfrac{(-6)^7}{(-6)^3}$ | $\dfrac{(-11)^6}{(-11)^3}$ |

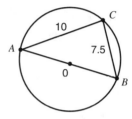

The circle's center is at *O*.

15. | The diameter of the circle | 12.5 |

DIRECTIONS: *Questions 16–30* each includes five answer choices. For each question, select the best answer choice.

16. Which of the following has the largest numerical value?

    (A) $\dfrac{3}{5}$

    (B) $\dfrac{\frac{2}{3}}{\frac{11}{9}}$

    (C) $\sqrt{.25}$

    (D) $.81^2$

    (E) $\dfrac{.2}{.3}$

17. The sum of Alan's age and Bob's age is 40. The sum of Bob's age and Carl's age is 34. The sum of Alan's age and Carl's age is 42. What is Bob's age?

    (A) 12
    (B) 16
    (C) 18
    (D) 20
    (E) 24

18. If the legislature passes a particular bill by a ratio of 5 to 4, and if 900 legislators voted in favor of the bill, how many voted against it?

    (A) 400
    (B) 500
    (C) 720
    (D) 760
    (E) 800

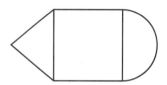

19. Three carpet pieces—in the shapes of a square, a triangle, and a semicircle—are attached to one another, as shown in the figure above, to cover the floor of a room. If the area of the square is 144 feet and the perimeter of the triangle is 28 feet, what is the perimeter of the room's floor, in feet?

    (A) $32 + 12\pi$
    (B) $40 + 6\pi$
    (C) $34 + 12\pi$
    (D) $52 + 6\pi$
    (E) $52 + 12\pi$

20. M is $P\%$ of what number?

    (A) $\dfrac{MP}{100}$

    (B) $\dfrac{100P}{M}$

    (C) $\dfrac{M}{100P}$

    (D) $\dfrac{P}{100M}$

    (E) $\dfrac{100M}{P}$

19

Questions 21–25 refer to the following graph.

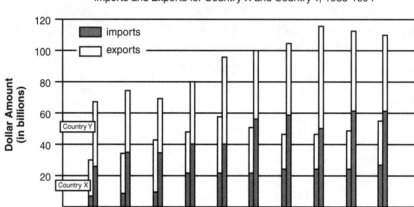

Imports and Exports for Country X and Country Y, 1985-1994

21. In which of the years shown did Country Y's imports exceed Country X's imports by the greatest percentage?

    (A) 1985
    (B) 1986
    (C) 1992
    (D) 1993
    (E) 1995

22. During how many of the years shown did Country Y's exports exceed its own imports by at least $10 billion?

    (A) One
    (B) Two
    (C) Three
    (D) Four
    (E) Five

23. During the year that Country X's exports exceeded its own imports by the greatest dollar amount, Country Y's imports exceeded Country X's imports by approximately

    (A) $22 billion
    (B) $75 billion
    (C) $90 billion
    (D) $110 billion
    (E) $160 billion

24. During the year that the total imports for Country X and Country Y combined was nearest to $85 billion, the exports for the two countries combined totaled approximately

    (A) $65 billion
    (B) $75 billion
    (C) $90 billion
    (D) $110 billion
    (E) $160 billion

25. With respect to the two-year period during which Country Y's imports increased by the greatest amount from one year to the next, the ratio of Country Y's exports to its own imports during the second of those two years was approximately

    (A) 3:5
    (B) 4:5
    (C) 1:1
    (D) 6:5
    (E) 4:3

26. If $m = n$ and $p < q$, then

    (A) $m - p < n - q$
    (B) $p - m > q - n$
    (C) $m - p > n - q$
    (D) $mp > nq$
    (E) $m + q < n + p$

27. Two competitors battle each other in each match of a tournament with nine participants. What is the minimum number of matches that must occur for every competitor to battle every other competitor?

    (A) 27
    (B) 36
    (C) 45
    (D) 64
    (E) 81

28. If q workers can paint a house in d days, how many days will it take $q + 2$ workers to paint the same house, assuming all workers paint at the same rate?

    (A) $d + 2$ (D) $\dfrac{qd + 2d}{q}$

    (B) $d - 2$ (E) $\dfrac{qd}{q + 2}$

    (C) $\dfrac{q + 2}{qd}$

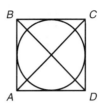

29. If the circumference of the circle above is 16π, and if the length of AC equals the length of BD, what is the length of AC?

    (A) $4\sqrt{2}$
    (B) 16
    (C) $16\sqrt{2}$
    (D) 32
    (E) 16π

30. Dan drove home from college at an average rate of 60 miles per hour. On his trip back to college, his rate was 10 miles per hour slower and the trip took him one hour longer than the drive home. How far is Dan's home from the college?

    (A) 65 miles
    (B) 100 miles
    (C) 200 miles
    (D) 280 miles
    (E) 300 miles

19

STOP.

End of Quantitative Section

Answer Key

1. C	11. A	21. B
2. B	12. B	22. C
3. C	13. D	23. A
4. A	14. A	24. B
5. B	15. C	25. B
6. C	16. E	26. C
7. A	17. B	27. B
8. D	18. C	28. E
9. A	19. B	29. C
10. D	20. E	30. E

Hour **20**

Sample Test 1 (Verbal Ability— Paper-based Format)

This hour you'll continue your sample paper-based GRE by completing a full-length Verbal Ability section that looks just like each of the two on the paper-based test. Here are your goals for this hour:

- Take the test under timed conditions
- Check the answer key on page 380
- Assess your performance by checking the score conversion chart on pages 455–456
- Review the explanations (they begin on page 428)

Verbal Ability Test

Time—30 Minutes

38 Questions

DIRECTIONS: Each of the following numbered sentences contains either one or two blanks. A blank indicates that a word or brief phrase has been omitted. Select among the five choices the word or phrase for each blank that *best* fits the meaning of the sentence as a whole.

1. Any person who has observed working conditions on the factory floor could ------- the ------- argument set forth by the company's management, an argument which might convince those less familiar with the strikers' plight.

   (A) refute .. specious
   (B) support .. protracted
   (C) repeat .. recumbent
   (D) review .. cogent
   (E) elicit .. prodigious

2. The Eighteenth Amendment, often called the Prohibition Act, ------- the sale of alcoholic beverages.

   (A) prolonged
   (B) preempted
   (C) sanctioned
   (D) proscribed
   (E) encouraged

3. He was incongruous in his approach to the problem, at once ------- and -------.

   (A) surly .. stubborn
   (B) sincere .. earnest
   (C) clandestine .. foolhardy
   (D) principled .. insouciant
   (E) careless .. refractory

4. Traveling by automobile was ------- to him, but he thought nothing of bobsledding, which had been his ------- for many years.

   (A) tiresome .. profession
   (B) tiring .. outlet
   (C) harrowing .. hobby
   (D) a threat .. relief
   (E) exciting .. diversion

5. Advances in women's rights during the early twentieth century, albeit sporadic, set into motion certain sociological forces that culminated in what can be described based on historical perspective as the ------- feminist movement of the 1960s and 1970s.

   (A) resplendent
   (B) controversial
   (C) incumbent
   (D) inexorable
   (E) sporadic

6. The wealthy mogul appeared to be ------- about the charitable cause to which he generously contributed, and his appointment to the board of directors of the charitable organization served to confirm that he was a(n) ------- person.

(A) dedicated .. venerable
(B) indifferent .. benevolent
(C) philanthropic .. parsimonious
(D) sympathetic .. incongruous
(E) hypocritical .. depraved

7. Many child psychologists believe that a playground bully's ------- demeanor is mere bravado—an attempt to compensate for insecurities—and that this ------- juvenile malevolence portends trouble coping with responsibilities as an adult.

(A) imperturbable .. vapid
(B) truculent .. feigned
(C) stringent .. credulous
(D) supercilious .. blatant
(E) parsimonious .. contentious

DIRECTIONS: In each of the following questions, a numbered word pair is followed by five lettered pairs. Select the lettered pair that expresses a relationship most similar to the relationship expressed in the numbered pair.

8. SHIP : ARMADA : :
(A) sail : wind
(B) gun : cannon
(C) atom : molecule
(D) chemical : reaction
(E) violin : viola

9. TREMBLE : FEAR : :
(A) scream : envy
(B) smile : rage
(C) demand : anger
(D) follow : adoration
(E) weep : grief

10. GEM : SETTING : :
(A) diamond : gold
(B) painting : milieu
(C) ring : necklace
(D) building : scaffold
(E) portrait : subject

11. FEEL : HANDLE : :
(A) caress : abrade
(B) read : peruse
(C) laugh : giggle
(D) burgeon : grow
(E) lift : heave

12. ROBUST : VIGOR : :
(A) massive : strength
(B) sick : illness
(C) farsighted : glasses
(D) satiated : appetite
(E) sanguine : hope

13. INNOVATION : PRECEDENT : :
(A) inception : reality
(B) illusion : veracity
(C) conservation : simplicity
(D) renovation : antiquity
(E) invention : production

20

14. DELETERIOUS : PERNICIOUS : :

(A) delightful : delicious
(B) blithe : exuberant
(C) painful : sore
(D) helpful : useful
(E) mercurial : indefatigable

15. JOCULAR : SOLEMNITY : :

(A) latent : visibility
(B) pompous : spectacle
(C) razed : demolition
(D) vindictive : enmity
(E) lonely : insularity

16. DIATRIBE : BITTERNESS : :

(A) dictum : indolence
(B) recapitulation : brevity
(C) polemic : consonance
(D) encomium : reproach
(E) concordance : contrariety

DIRECTIONS: Each passage in this group is followed by questions or incomplete statements about its content. After reading a passage, select the best answer to each question from the five lettered choices. Answer all the questions following a passage on the basis of what the passage states or implies.

A free radical is a highly reactive molecule that contains at least one unpaired electron in its outer orbital shell. Once it is "free" in living tissues, the unbalanced
(5) molecule causes cellular damage until it is "neutralized" by a scavenging antioxidant enzyme. Free radicals are extremely detrimental to cellular quality and length of cellular life. When a cell membrane is
(10) damaged by a free radical, the cell loses the capacity to transport nutrients, oxygen, water, or waste matter. As a result, cell membranes may rupture, spilling their contents into surrounding tissues, and
(15) thereby damage surrounding cells. The worst of these destructive reactions occur in the chromosomes and nucleic acids of the cell. The resulting damage causes changes in the cell replication rate and is
(20) the major cause of cancer cell mutations. Moreover, the origin of most cardiovascular disease is closely tied to unrestrained free radical damage to the cell membranes lining the blood vessels. Free radicals are
(25) also the implicated "villains" in the cholesterol plaque accumulations that have been linked to the causes of cardiovascular heart disease, advances in the rate of aging, adult onset diabetes, athero-
(30) sclerosis, and coronary artery disease.

17. According to the passage, each of the following is true of free radicals EXCEPT:

    (A) free radicals are unbalanced molecules

    (B) free radicals are the major cause of high cholesterol

    (C) free radicals damage a cell's ability to transport oxygen

    (D) free radicals cause damage to blood vessels

    (E) free radicals can be canceled out by antioxidant enzymes

18. It can be inferred from lines 9–15 that cell membranes may rupture as a result of free radical damage because

    (A) the cell membrane is punctured by the free radical

    (B) the contents of the cell exceed the capacity of the cell membrane

    (C) the free radical displaces the contents of the cell

    (D) the cell membrane is dissolved by the free radical

    (E) the cell membrane is torn by the free radical

19. Which of the following best expresses the passage's main idea?

    (A) Free radicals are the major cause of disease.

    (B) Free radicals are the major cause of cell damage.

    (C) Free radicals can be neutralized by antioxidant enzymes.

    (D) Unrestrained free radicals can cause cell damage.

    (E) Free radicals are harmful to cells in living tissue.

20. The author mentions the reactions that occur in the chromosomes and nucleic acids of the cell as a result of free radical damage in order to

    (A) show that unrestrained free radical damage to cells is the origin of most cardiovascular disease.

    (B) show how free radical damage to cells causes adult onset diabetes.

    (C) show how antioxidant enzymes neutralize free radicals.

    (D) describe in detail the damage free radicals cause in the cell membranes that line the blood vessels.

    (E) show how damage to cells by free radicals is linked to cancer cell mutations.

Christina Rossetti's potent sensual imagery—the richest since Keats—compelled Edmond Gosse, perhaps the most influential literary critic in late Vic-
(5) torian England, to observe that this Victorian poetress "does not shrink from strong delineation of the pleasures of life even when denouncing them." In the face of Rossetti's virtual canonization by critics
(10) at the end of the nineteenth century, however, Virginia Woolf ignores her apparent conservatism, instead seeing in her curiosity value and a model of artistic purity and integrity for women writers. In 1930,
(15) the centenary of Rossetti's birth, Woolf identified her as "one of Shakespeare's more recent sisters" whose life had been reclusively Victorian but whose achievement as an artist was enduring.
(20)   Woolf remembers Rossetti for her four volumes of explosively original poems

loaded with vivid images and dense emotional energy. "A Birthday," for instance, is no typical Victorian poem and is (25) certainly unlike predictable works of the era's best known women poets. Rossetti's most famous poem, "Goblin Market," bridges the space between simplistic fairy tale and complex adult allegory—at once (30) Christian, psychological, and pro-feminist. Like many of Rossetti's works, it is extraordinarily original and unorthodox in form. Its subject matter is radical and therefore risky for a Victorian poetess (35) because it implies castigation of an economic (and even marital) marketplace dominated by men, whose motives are, at best, suspect. Its Christian allusions are obvious but grounded in opulent images (40) whose lushness borders on the erotic. From Rossetti's work emerge not only emotional force, artistic polish, frequently-ironic playfulness, and intellectual vigor but also an intriguing, enigmatic quality. (45) "Winter: My Secret," for example, combines these traits along with a very high (and un-Victorian) level of poetic self-consciousness.

"How does one reconcile the aesthetic (50) sensuality of Rossetti's poetry with her repressed, ascetic lifestyle?" Woolf wondered. That Rossetti did indeed withhold a "secret" both from those intimate with her and from posterity is Lona Packer's (55) thesis in her 1963 biography of Rossetti. Packer's claim that Rossetti's was a secret of the heart has since been disproved through the discovery of hundreds of letters by Rossetti, which reinforce the (60) conventional image of her as pious, scrupulously abstinent, and semi-reclusive. Yet the passions expressed in her love poems do expose the "secret" at the heart of both Rossetti's life and art: a willingness to (65) forego worldly pleasures in favor of an aestheticized Christian version of transcendent fulfillment in heaven. Her sonnet "The World," therefore, becomes pivotal in understanding Rossetti's (70) literary project as a whole—her rhymes for children, fairy tale narratives, love poems, bleak verses of spiritual desolation, and devotional commentaries. The world, for Rossetti, is a fallen place. Her work is (75) pervasively designed to force upon readers this inescapable Christian truth. The beauty of her poetry must be seen therefore as an artistic strategy, a means toward a moral end.

21. Based upon the information in the passage, Virginia Woolf would most likely agree that Rossetti's work

   (A) exposes a secret about Rossetti's life
   (B) describes yet at the same time denounces life's pleasures
   (C) has an enigmatic quality
   (D) affirms that Rossetti was pious and reclusive
   (E) serves as a model of artistic integrity

22. All of the following are mentioned in the passage as qualities that emerge from Rossetti's work EXCEPT:

   (A) lush imagery
   (B) ironic playfulness
   (C) stark realism
   (D) unorthodox form
   (E) intellectual vigor

23. The author implies that Rossetti's style was similar to that of

(A) Keats
(B) Shakespeare
(C) Gosse
(D) Woolf
(E) Packer

24. Which of the following statements is most reasonably inferable from the passage?

(A) "Winter: My Secret" is Rossetti's best-known poem.
(B) Rossetti was not among the best-known poets during her era.
(C) The accounts of Rossetti's life contained in Packer's biography of Rossetti differ from those included in Woolf's biography of Rossetti.
(D) Rossetti's display of poetic self-consciousness drew criticism from her contemporaries.
(E) "Goblin Market" was published later than "A Birthday."

25. The author discusses Packer's thesis and its flaws in order to

(A) contrast the sensuality of Rossetti's poetry with the relative starkness of her devotional commentary
(B) reveal the secret to which Rossetti alludes in "Winter: My Secret"
(C) call into question the authenticity of recently discovered letters written by Rossetti
(D) compare Woolf's understanding of Rossetti with a recent, more enlightened view
(E) provide a foundation for the author's own theory about Rossetti's life and work

26. The author implies that Rossetti's "The World"

(A) combines several genres of poetry in a single work
(B) was Rossetti's last major work
(C) is the most helpful expression of Rossetti's motives
(D) was Rossetti's longest work
(E) reflects Rossetti's shift away from her earlier feminist viewpoint

27. Which of the following best expresses the main idea of the passage?

(A) Newly discovered evidence suggests that Rossetti's works were misinterpreted by earlier critics and scholars.
(B) Rossetti can be compared to Shakespeare both in her private life and in the enduring quality of her work.
(C) Victorian poetry can be properly interpreted only by considering the personal life of the particular poet.
(D) The apparent inconsistency between Rossetti's personal life and literary work are explained by Rossetti's poems themselves.
(E) Rossetti's artistic integrity served as a model for later women poets.

20

DIRECTIONS: For each of the following questions, select the word or phrase among the five choices that is most nearly *opposite* in meaning to the numbered word. *Note*: This question might require you to distinguish fine shades in meaning, so you should carefully consider all five choices.

28. CURSORY:

   (A) essential
   (B) polite
   (C) charmed
   (D) comprehensive
   (E) interested

29. INSOLVENT:

   (A) liquefied
   (B) obedient
   (C) clever
   (D) rapid
   (E) wealthy

30. REPROVE:

   (A) invalidate
   (B) dissuade
   (C) agree
   (D) compliment
   (E) encourage

31. INGRATIATE:

   (A) distance
   (B) move on
   (C) obstruct
   (D) command
   (E) thank

32. CORNUCOPIA:

   (A) humility
   (B) darkness
   (C) affirmation
   (D) lack
   (E) purity

33. ACCESSION:

   (A) aloofness
   (B) usurpation
   (C) severance
   (D) donation
   (E) return

34. SALUTARY:

   (A) abrupt
   (B) complicating
   (C) injurious
   (D) evasive
   (E) peremptory

35. RANCOR:

   (A) tranquillity
   (B) happiness
   (C) impartiality
   (D) humor
   (E) affection

36. ITINERANT:

    (A) motionless
    (B) mutable
    (C) completely satisfied
    (D) sensitive
    (E) straight

37. VERDANT:

    (A) complete
    (B) wan
    (C) forbidding
    (D) exposed
    (E) desolate

38. AMICABLE:

    (A) extreme
    (B) precocious
    (C) perfunctory
    (D) contumacious
    (E) potent

20

STOP.
End of Verbal Section

Answer Key

1. A	14. B	27. D
2. D	15. A	28. D
3. D	16. B	29. E
4. C	17. B	30. D
5. D	18. B	31. A
6. A	19. E	32. D
7. B	20. E	33. C
8. C	21. E	34. C
9. E	22. C	35. E
10. D	23. A	36. A
11. B	24. B	37. E
12. E	25. E	38. D
13. B	26. C	

HOUR 21

Sample Test 1 (Analytical Ability— Paper-based Format)

This hour you'll complete your sample paper-based GRE by taking a full-length Analytical Ability section. The paper-based GRE includes two Analytical Ability sections of 25 questions each. Here are your goals for this hour:

- Take the test under timed conditions
- Check the answer key on page 389
- Assess your performance by checking the score conversion chart on pages 455–456
- Review the explanations (they begin on page 432)

Analytical Ability Test

Time—30 Minutes

25 Questions

Questions 1–4

A director is casting a movie about twins, and must select the cast from among nine actors—A, B, C, D, E, F, G, H, and I. B is A's twin, C is D's twin, and E is F's twin. G, H and I may each be included only as "extras." A, B, E, G, and H are members of the actors' union; C, D, F, and I are non-union members.

The director must include at least two pairs of twins in the cast.
The director cannot assemble a cast that includes more union members than non-union members.
A and B must both be included in the cast if either is included.
C and D must both be included in the cast if either is included.
At least one extra must be included in the cast.

1. Which of the following is an acceptable complete cast for the movie?

   (A) A, B, E, F, I
   (B) C, D, F, G, H, I
   (C) B, C, D, E, H, I
   (D) A, B, C, D, E, F, G
   (E) C, D, E, F, G, H, I

2. The cast must include which of the following?

   (A) D
   (B) I
   (C) F
   (D) H
   (E) E

3. If the director assembles the largest possible cast, all of the following must be included in the cast EXCEPT:

   (A) A
   (B) D
   (C) F
   (D) H
   (E) I

4. If G and only one other extra are selected for a cast of six actors, how many distinct casts are possible?

   (A) 1
   (B) 2
   (C) 3
   (D) 4
   (E) 5

5. It is commonly held in discussions of capital punishment that there is no evidence that the death penalty deters. This is simply untrue. We have an enormous amount of both informal and formal evidence—from everyday experience and from such "experiments" as increasing the fees for parking violations—that, as a general rule, the greater the punishment, the fewer people will behave in the punished way. Thus, it is perfectly reasonable to expect that the death penalty would have a more dissuasive effect than would life imprisonment.

Which of the following must be assumed for the above argument to be logically correct?

(A) Everyday experience shows that the death penalty deters.
(B) Life imprisonment does not act as a deterrent to murder.
(C) The death penalty is a greater punishment than life imprisonment.
(D) Potential murderers consciously weigh the alternatives beforehand and decide that the crime is worth life in prison, but not death.
(E) The more severe the punishment, the more it acts as a deterrent.

6. Given that the stated goal of environmentalists is to reduce the amount of carbon dioxide in the atmosphere while at the same time preserving existing plant life on earth, there are two very good reasons for harvesting living trees from old-growth forests. First, doing so would reduce the amount of carbon dioxide in the atmosphere for the simple reason that when old trees die they decompose, thereby releasing their stored carbon dioxide. Second, it would make room for more young trees which absorb carbon dioxide thereby further reducing the amount of carbon dioxide in the atmosphere.

Which one of the following, if true, most seriously weakens the above argument?

(A) Levels of carbon dioxide in the atmosphere have remained relatively constant over the past 100 years.
(B) Reduction in the amount of carbon dioxide in the atmosphere is necessary to reduce the "greenhouse effect."
(C) The amount of carbon dioxide released into the atmosphere through the decomposition of old trees is insignificantly small when compared to the amount released by agricultural waste.
(D) Old-growth forests are the habitat of many species which will not survive if these forests are destroyed.
(E) A reduction in the amount of carbon dioxide in the atmosphere is detrimental to plant life.

21

7. Recent clinical tests clearly demonstrate that Psor-Be-Gone is an effective treatment to reduce the recurrence of psoriasis. Of 23 patients who previously had severe recurrent cases of psoriasis (a bacterial infection of the skin), only two had a recurrence after regular treatment with Psor-Be-Gone. This is a recurrence rate of less than ten percent. In contrast, in a double-blind experiment 15 control subjects who were treated with a placebo in place of Psor-Be-Gone had a recurrence rate of eighty percent.

Which of the following, if true, would provide the most support for the conclusion in the above argument?

(A) Numerous independent studies have shown the active ingredient in Psor-Be-Gone to be an effective antibacterial agent for a wide spectrum of skin disorders.

(B) Most of the ingredients in Psor-Be-Gone are completely inert.

(C) None of the patients treated with Psor-Be-Gone had any adverse skin reactions.

(D) Psor-Be-Gone has been scientifically proven to be an effective treatment for numerous common skin diseases.

(E) The placebo used in the control group experiment did not contain the active ingredient found in Psor-Be-Gone.

Questions 8–12

On a particular day at a warehouse, each of five workers—Jackson, Klein, Lawry, Manning, and North—performs two different tasks. Each worker performs one task in the morning and one task in the afternoon.

Three tasks—assembling, boxing, and gluing—are performed in the morning.

Three tasks—gluing, stacking, and loading—are performed in the afternoon.

North and two other workers glue.

Three of the workers stack.

Jackson does not perform either task that Klein performs.

Lawry does not perform either task that Manning performs.

The five workers listed above are the only workers at the warehouse on that particular day.

8. Which of the following CANNOT be true?

(A) Jackson assembles.
(B) Klein glues.
(C) Lawry stacks.
(D) Manning loads.
(E) North boxes.

9. If Jackson loads, which of the following must be true?

(A) Jackson glues.
(B) Klein stacks.
(C) Lawry boxes.
(D) Manning glues.
(E) North assembles.

10. If Lawry loads, which of the following must be true?

  (A) Either Klein or Manning boxes.
  (B) Either Jackson or Manning glues.
  (C) Either Klein or Lawry glues.
  (D) Either Lawry or Manning boxes.
  (E) Either Jackson or Klein assembles.

11. If Klein is the only worker who assembles, all of the following must be false EXCEPT:

  (A) Manning glues in the morning.
  (B) Jackson loads in the afternoon.
  (C) Lawry glues in the afternoon.
  (D) Klein loads in the afternoon.
  (E) Jackson glues in the morning.

12. If Klein and North perform the same two tasks, all of the following must be true EXCEPT:

  (A) Jackson does not glue.
  (B) Klein does not assemble.
  (C) Lawry does not load.
  (D) Manning does not stack.
  (E) North does not box.

Questions 13–18

  Of nine members on a baseball team, four bat right-handed, three bat left-handed, and two are switch hitters. Each of the nine players bats once and only once in the batting order.

  Exactly two left-handed batters bat consecutively.
  The switch hitters do not bat consecutively.
  No two right-handed batters bat consecutively.
  A right-handed batter bats fourth.

13. Any of the following are possible batting assignments, in order from the first to the third batter, EXCEPT:

  (A) right-handed batter, switch hitter, left-handed batter
  (B) right-handed batter, left-handed batter, switch hitter
  (C) switch hitter, left-handed batter, right-handed batter
  (D) switch hitter, right-handed batter, left-handed batter
  (E) left-handed batter, right-handed batter, switch hitter

14. Which of the following is an acceptable batting order for the fifth, sixth, and seventh positions, respectively?

  (A) right-handed batter, left-handed batter, left-handed batter
  (B) left-handed batter, switch hitter, switch hitter
  (C) switch hitter, right-handed batter, left-handed batter
  (D) left-handed batter, right-handed batter, right-handed batter
  (E) switch hitter, left-handed batter, left-handed batter

15. If a right-handed batter bats second, which of the following must be true?

  (A) A right-handed batter bats ninth.
  (B) A left-handed batter bats fifth.
  (C) A switch hitter bats seventh.
  (D) A right-handed batter bats sixth.
  (E) A left-handed batter bats eighth.

21

16. If left-handed batters bat second and eighth, all of the following must be true EXCEPT:

    (A) A right-handed batter bats first.
    (B) A switch hitter bats fifth.
    (C) A right-handed batter bats sixth.
    (D) A switch hitter bats seventh.
    (E) A right-handed batter bats ninth.

17. If all left-handed batters bat after all switch hitters, all of the following must be false EXCEPT:

    (A) A left-handed batter bats seventh.
    (B) A switch hitter bats second.
    (C) A left-handed batter bats ninth.
    (D) A right-handed batter bats eighth.
    (E) A switch hitter bats fifth.

18. If both switch hitters bat after all left-handed batters, which of the following must be true?

    (A) A switch hitter bats seventh.
    (B) A left-handed batter bats fifth.
    (C) A left-handed batter bats first.
    (D) A switch hitter bats sixth.
    (E) A right-handed batter bats eighth.

Questions 19–22

Eight voters—Perez, Quinn, Raffi, Sperry, Trager, Utley, Villar, and Wieser—are voting in two elections. Each voter must vote for either Able or Berman, and each voter must vote for either Cargis or Dorsey. The election results are as follows:

Berman received exactly four votes.
Raffi, Sperry, and Trager voted for Able.
Villar did not vote for the identical two candidates as either Wieser or Utley.
Wieser did not vote for the identical two candidates as Utley.

19. The elections must have resulted in

    (A) a tie between Able and Berman
    (B) a tie between Cargis and Dorsey
    (C) Berman defeating Able
    (D) Cargis defeating Dorsey
    (E) Dorsey defeating Cargis

20. With respect to which of the following pairs of voters is it possible that the two voters voted for the same two candidates?

    (A) Raffi and Sperry
    (B) Trager and Perez
    (C) Villar and Trager
    (D) Utley and Quinn
    (E) Wieser and Perez

21. The greatest number of voters who could have voted for Cargis is

    (A) 4
    (B) 5
    (C) 6
    (D) 7
    (E) 8

22. If Perez and Quinn voted for different candidates in the election between Cargis and Dorsey, which of the following CANNOT be true?

    (A) Exactly two voters voted for both Berman and Cargis.
    (B) Exactly three voters voted for both Berman and Dorsey.
    (C) Exactly four voters voted for both Able and Dorsey.
    (D) Exactly one voter voted for both Able and Cargis.
    (E) Exactly three voters voted for both Able and Dorsey.

23. There is no such thing as one single scientific method. Instead, there is a jumble of methods ranging from careful observation and collection of data from which hypotheses are advanced to mere conjecture of the underlying causes. Moreover, no attempts to rationally justify the various methods of science as sources of truth have as yet proven fruitful. For these reasons it can be concluded that science is not preferable to religion or mythology when it comes to finding out the basic truths of the universe.

Which one of the following claims, if true, would most weaken the author's position in the passage?

(A) Science is based on reason, whereas religion and mythology are based on faith.

(B) Unlike religion and mythology, the various methods of science all yield accurate predictions, and yielding accurate predictions is an indicator of truth.

(C) Religion and mythology are based on superstition and ignorance.

(D) There is widespread agreement among scientists about the nature of the universe but little agreement among the practitioners of religion and mythology.

(E) More technological advances have been made in the past two centuries, during which science has reigned, than in the preceding twenty centuries, in which mythology and religion reigned.

24. Unless a settlement can be reached, the truce will be violated by one of the parties to the dispute. But a settlement can be reached only if the border issues can be resolved, and the border issues can be resolved only if both parties are willing to give up the territory they captured during the hostilities.

If the statements above are true, but both parties are not willing to give up the territory they captured during the hostilities, then each of the following must also be true EXCEPT:

(A) A settlement can't be reached and the truce will be violated by one of the parties to the dispute.

(B) The border issues cannot be resolved.

(C) The truce will not be violated by either of the parties to the dispute.

(D) A settlement cannot be reached.

(E) The border issues cannot be resolved, nor can a settlement be reached.

21

25. Flagrant violations of human rights were cited by the Astonian government as the official reason for ceasing to provide military support to the embattled country of Cretia. But, at the same time, military support continues to be provided to countries with far worse human-rights records than Cretia. Hence, despite the official explanation for this change in policy, this reversal cannot be accounted for solely by the Astonian government's commitment to human rights.

Which of the following, if true, would most strengthen the conclusion in the above argument?

(A) Cretia's neighboring countries recently entered into a non-aggression pact with one another.

(B) Astonia recently entered into long-range trade agreements with Cretia's neighboring countries.

(C) The newly elected head of the Cretian government is an avowed anti-Astonian.

(D) Cretia has a longer record of human-rights abuse than other countries to which military support is provided by Astonia.

(E) The Astonian government's decision to provide military support to a country is made mainly on the basis of the country's capability of defending itself from outside aggression.

STOP.
End of Analytical Section

Answer Key

1. E	9. B	17. A
2. A	10. E	18. B
3. D	11. A	19. A
4. C	12. D	20. B
5. C	13. C	21. D
6. E	14. C	22. B
7. A	15. A	23. B
8. E	16. D	24. C
		25. E

HOUR 22

Sample Test 2 (Quantitative Ability— CBT Format)

This hour you'll begin taking a sample computer-based GRE. You'll start with a full-length Quantitative Ability section that follows the format of the CBT. Then you'll go on to complete the computer-based GRE in Hours 23 and 24. Here are your goals for this hour:

- Take the test section under timed conditions
- Check the answer key on page 399
- Assess your performance by checking the score conversion chart on pages 456–457
- Review the explanations (they begin on page 438)

NOTE

> The difficulty level of questions here is evenly distributed across various levels. Keep in mind, though, that the CBT does not necessarily follow this pattern, but instead will determine the difficulty level of each question based on your responses to prior questions.

Quantitative Ability Test

Time—45 Minutes

28 Questions

All numbers used are real numbers.

All figures lie on a plane unless otherwise indicated.

All angle measures are positive.

All lines shown as straight are straight.

Figures are intended to provide useful information for anwering the questions. However, except where a figure is accompanied by a "Note" stating that the figure is drawn to scale, solve the problems using your knowledge of mathematics, *not* by visual measurement or estimation.

DIRECTIONS (PROBLEM SOLVING): For each question that includes five lettered answer choices, select the best of the five choices provided.

DIRECTIONS (QUANTITATIVE COMPARISONS): Each question that does NOT include five lettered answer choices consists of two quantities, one in Column A and one in Column B. Compare the two quantities and select:

(A) if the quantity in Column A is greater
(B) if the quantity in Column B is greater
(C) if the quantities are equal
(D) if the relationship cannot be determined from the information given

Notes (Quantitative Comparisons):

There are only four answer choices, so NEVER INDICATE (E) as the best answer.

In some questions, additional information pertaining to one or both of the quantities to be compared is centered above the two columns.

Any symbol appearing in both columns represents the same thing in one columns as in the other.

NOTE The additional directions for Quantiative Comparisons and for Problem Solving questions will appear on your computer screen before the test presents to you the first question of each type.

22

1. A certain five-member committee must be assembled from a pool of five women— A, B, C, D, and E—and three men—X, Y, and Z. What is the probability that the committee wil include B, C, E, Y, and Z?

(A) $\dfrac{1}{30}$

(B) $\dfrac{1}{25}$

(C) $\dfrac{2}{35}$

(D) $\dfrac{1}{15}$

(E) $\dfrac{3}{32}$

2. | Column A | Column B |
    |---|---|

    $$3x + 4 = y$$

    x is a positive integer less than or equal to 7.

The number of values for y that are prime numbers	2

3. | Column A | Column B |
    |---|---|
    | 39% of 67,000 | 67% of 39,000 |

4. | Column A | Column B |
    |---|---|

    Of 40 pairs of socks in a drawer, x pairs are solid white, y pairs are solid gray, and more than 19 of the pairs are striped.

$x - y$	The number of striped pairs of socks in the drawer

5. A certain purse contains 30 coins, and each coin is either a nickel or a quarter. If the total value of all coins in the purse is $4.70, how many nickels does the purse contain?

(A) 12
(B) 14
(C) 16
(D) 20
(E) 22

6. | Column A | Column B |
    |---|---|

    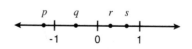

$q - p$	$r + s$

7.   *Column A*   *Column B*

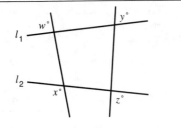

$l_1 \parallel l_2$

$w - y + x - z$	0

8. A county animal shelter houses two different types of animals—dogs and cats. If d represents the number of dogs, and if c represents the number of cats, which of the following expresses the portion of animals at the shelter that are dogs?

(A) $\dfrac{d+c}{d}$

(B) $\dfrac{d+c}{c}$

(C) $\dfrac{d}{c}$

(D) $\dfrac{c}{d}$

(E) $\dfrac{d}{d+c}$

Questions 9 and 10 refer to the following chart.

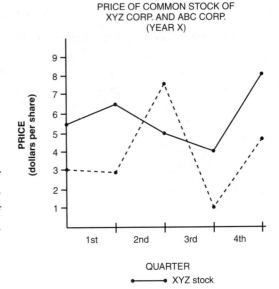

PRICE OF COMMON STOCK OF
XYZ CORP. AND ABC CORP.
(YEAR X)

PRICE (dollars per share)

QUARTER

●——● XYZ stock
●- - - -● ABC stock

9. At the time during year X when the difference between the price of *ABC* common stock and the price of *XYZ* common stock was at its greatest, the price of *ABC* common stock was approximately what percent of the price of *XYZ* common stock and *ABC* common stock combined?

(A) 16%
(B) 30%
(C) 36%
(D) 42%
(E) 103%

10. At the time during year X when the aggregate price of ABC and XYZ stock was the greatest, the price of XYZ stock was approximately what percent of the price of ABC stock?

   (A) 25
   (B) 60
   (C) 70
   (D) 140
   (E) 170

11.

Column A	Column B
The arithmetic mean (average) of the numbers in the set {16, 18, 20, 22, 24, 26, 28}	The arithmetic mean (average) of the numbers in the set {17, 19, 21, 23, 25, 28}

12.

Column A	Column B
The volume of a solid cube whose total surface area is 24	The volume of a 3-dimensional rectangular solid whose total surface area is 25

13. Which of the following fractions is smallest in value?

   (A) $\dfrac{3}{4}$

   (B) $\dfrac{5}{6}$

   (C) $\dfrac{7}{8}$

   (D) $\dfrac{19}{24}$

   (E) $\dfrac{13}{15}$

14. If $x + y = 16$, and if $x^2 - y^2 = 48$, then $x - y =$

   (A) 3
   (B) 4
   (C) 6
   (D) 32
   (E) 36

15.

Column A	Column B

A buyer pays a $1.00 tax on an item that costs $10.00 after the tax is added.

The percentage rate of the tax	11%

22

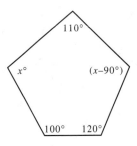

16. In the figure above, what is the value of x?

(A) 100
(B) 110
(C) 125
(D) 135
(E) 150

17.

Column A	Column B
$\dfrac{a^2 + b^2}{ab}$	$\dfrac{a}{b} + \dfrac{b}{a}$

18. If a portion of $10,000 is invested at 6% and the remaining portion is invested at 5%, and if x represents the amount invested at 6%, what is the annual income in dollars from the 5% investment?

(A) $5(x - 10,000)$
(B) $.05(x + 10,000)$
(C) $.05(10,000 - x)$
(D) $5(10,000 - x)$
(E) $.05(x - 10,000)$

19.

Column A	Column B
The ninth number in the following sequence: {3, 3, 4, 6, 9, 13,…}	31

20.

Column A	Column B

Point O lies at the circle's center

$x = 60$

The area of the shaded region	The combined area of the two triangles

Questions 21 and 22 refer to the following chart.

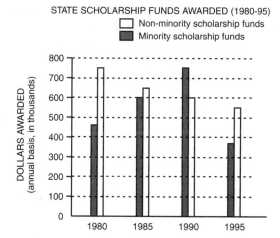

STATE SCHOLARSHIP FUNDS AWARDED (1980-95)

☐ Non-minority scholarship funds
■ Minority scholarship funds

21. Based on the years respresented in the chart, during the greatest 10-year change in non-minority scholarship funds awarded, what was approximately the greatest five-year percentage change in minority scholarship funds awarded?

(A) 15
(B) 25
(C) 27
(D) 33
(E) 43

22. Among the years shown in the chart, during the year in which the total amount of non-minority and minority funds awarded was the greatest, the difference between the two amounts was approximately

(A) $130,000
(B) $160,000
(C) $220,000
(D) $270,000
(E) $400,000

23.

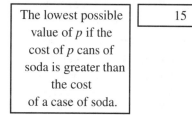

Column A	Column B

A case of soda costs $16.75. The cost of p individual cans of soda is $1.20 per can.

The lowest possible value of p if the cost of p cans of soda is greater than the cost of a case of soda.	15

24. If $0 < x < 1$, which of the following expressions is smallest in value?

(A) $\sqrt{x}$

(B) $\sqrt{\dfrac{1}{x}}$

(C) $\sqrt[3]{x^2}$

(D) x^4

(E) $\dfrac{1}{x^2}$

25. Two buses are 515 miles apart. At 9:30 a.m., they start traveling toward each other at rates of 48 and 55 miles per hour. At what time will they pass each other?

(A) 1:30 p.m.
(B) 2:00 p.m.
(C) 2:30 p.m.
(D) 3:00 p.m.
(E) 3:30 p.m.

26.

Column A	Column B

$$\boxed{u} = u^2 - u$$

$$\dfrac{\boxed{3}+1}{\boxed{-3}+1}$$

$$\dfrac{\boxed{-3}-1}{\boxed{3}-1}$$

27.

Column A	Column B
The distance on the *xy*-plane from the point defined by the (*x,y*) coordinates (−2,−1) to the point defined by the (*x,y*) coordinates (1,3)	The distance on the *xy*-plane from the point defined by the (*x,y*) coordinates (3,2) to the point defined by the (*x,y*) coordinates (1,−3)

28. An investor wants to sell some of the stock that he owns in MicroTron and Dynaco Corporations. He can sell MicroTron stock for $36 per share, and he can sell Dynaco stock for $52 per share. If he sells 300 shares altogether at an average price per share of $40, how many shares of Dynaco stock has he sold?

(A) 52
(B) 75
(C) 92
(D) 136
(E) 184

STOP.
End of Quantitative Section

Answer Key

1. A	10. E	19. C
2. A	11. B	20. A
3. C	12. D	21. D
4. D	13. A	22. B
5. B	14. A	23. B
6. D	15. A	24. D
7. C	16. E	25. C
8. E	17. C	26. B
9. B	18. C	27. B
		28. B

22

HOUR 23

Sample Test 2 (Verbal Ability— CBT Format)

This hour you'll continue taking your sample computer-based GRE by completing a full-length Verbal Ability section in the CBT format. Here are your goals for this hour:

- Take the test under timed conditions
- Check the answer key on page 410
- Assess your performance by checking the score conversion chart on pages 456–457
- Review the explanations (they begin on page 442)

NOTE   The difficulty level of questions here is evenly distributed across various levels. Keep in mind, though, that the CBT does not necessarily follow this pattern, but instead will determine the difficulty level of each question based on your responses to prior questions.

Verbal Ability Test

Time—45 Minutes

30 Questions

Directions for Sentence Completion Questions

(Directions similar to these will appear on your screen before your first Sentence Completion question.)

This sentence has one or more blank spaces, each one indicating an omitted word or phrase. Following the sentence are five words or sets of words. From these answer choices, select the word or set of words that, when inserted in the sentence, best fits the meaning of the sentence as a whole.

Directions for Antonym Questions

(Directions similar to these will appear on your screen before your first Antonym question.)

For this question, select the word or phrase among the five choices that is most nearly *opposite* in meaning to the numbered word. *Note:* the question might require you to distinguish fine shades in meaning, so you should carefully consider all five choices.

Directions for Analogy Questions

(Directions similar to these will appear on your screen before your first Analogy question.)

In this question, a word pair printed in capital letters is followed by five other word pairs printed in lower case letters. Select the word pair that expresses a relationship most similar to the relationship expressed by the word pair in capital letters.

Directions for Reading Comprehension Questions

(Directions similar to these will appear on your screen before your first Reading Comprehension question set.)

The questions in this group are based on the reading passage shown. For each question, select the best answer from the five choices given. Answer all the questions following a passage on the basis of what the passage *states* or *implies*.

1. During a campaign, politicians often engage in ------- debate, attacking each other's proposals in a torrent of ------- words.

   (A) acerbic .. amiable
   (B) acrimonious .. angry
   (C) intensive .. nebulous
   (D) garrulous .. inarticulate
   (E) impassioned .. vapid

2. FLAGRANT :

   (A) vile
   (B) ingratiating
   (C) imaginative
   (D) formidable
   (E) innocuous

3. DENIGRATE :

   (A) come after
   (B) exonerate
   (C) substantiate
   (D) laud
   (E) recommend

4. INCREDULITY :

   (A) abasement
   (B) faith
   (C) solvency
   (D) loyalty
   (E) coherence

5. COTTON : SOFT : :

   (A) wool : warm
   (B) iron : hard
   (C) nylon : strong
   (D) wood : polished
   (E) silk : expensive

6. It is clearly in the public's best interest for news agencies to admonish their journalist employees to ------- all information tantamount to hearsay through independent scrutiny.

   (A) embellish
   (B) corroborate
   (C) query
   (D) endorse
   (E) impede

23

7. AUSTERE :

   (A) blustering
   (B) obtuse
   (C) calm
   (D) inviting
   (E) gratifying

8. FISH : AQUARIUM : :

   (A) lions : den
   (B) insects : ground
   (C) automobile : garage
   (D) stew : cauldron
   (E) birds: aviary

9. WALK : AMBLE : :

   (A) work : tinker
   (B) play : rest
   (C) run : jump
   (D) jog : trot
   (E) disperse : leave

10. SILVER : METAL : :

    (A) gold : alloy
    (B) plastic : container
    (C) helium : gas
    (D) sand : glass
    (E) sediment : rock

11. FOMENT :

(A) speak in a terse manner
(B) praise
(C) pacify
(D) conform to established custom
(E) impede

12. Because she thought her younger brother's behavior was ------- , the fact that he was the cynosure of the family's attention and, ostensibly, of their affection, ------- her.

(A) consequential .. pleased
(B) putative .. baffled
(C) laconic .. encouraged
(D) insipid .. demeaned
(E) impertinent .. annoyed

Questions 13 and 14 are based on the following passage.

Economists and other social scientists have demonstrated that the research and development activities of private firms generate widespread benefits enjoyed by
(5) consumers and society at large. As a result, the overall economic value to society often exceeds the economic benefits enjoyed by innovating firms as a result of their research efforts. This excess of the
(10) social rate of return over the private rate of return enjoyed by innovating firms is described by economists as a positive externality or spillover. These spillovers imply that private firms will invest less
(15) than is socially desirable in research, with the result that some desirable research projects will not be undertaken, and others will be undertaken more slowly, later, or on a smaller scale than would be
(20) socially desirable.

Spillovers occur for a number of reasons. First, spillovers occur because the workings of the market or markets for an innovative product or process create
(25) benefits for consumers and non-innovating firms. Second, spillovers occur because knowledge created by one firm is typically not contained within that firm, and thereby creates value for other firms
(30) and other firms' customers. Finally, because the profitability of a set of interrelated and interdependent technologies may depend on achieving a critical mass of success, each firm pursuing one or more
(35) of these related technologies creates economic benefits for other firms and their customers.

13. Which of the following statements about spillovers finds the least support in the passage?

(A) Research and development projects undertaken by innovating firms provide benefits to non-innovating firms.
(B) Socially desirable research projects may not be undertaken by private firms.
(C) Knowledge gained by the research and development efforts of private firms will benefit only those firms.
(D) Innovative technologies produced by innovating firms create benefits for other firms engaged in related technologies.
(E) The economic value to society of private firms research and development activities is often greater than the economic benefit to the innovating firm.

14. The passage provides information for responding to all of the following questions EXCEPT:

(A) What are the underlying causes of spillovers?

(B) What benefits do non-innovating firms enjoy from the research and development efforts of innovating firms?

(C) What is a "positive externality?"

(D) Why do private firms invest less in research and development than is socially desirable?

(E) Why is knowledge that is acquired by an innovating firm typically not contained within that firm?

Questions 15–18 are based on the following passage.

Late Victorian and modern ideas of culture are indebted to Matthew Arnold, who, largely through his *Culture and Anarchy* (1869), placed the word at the center of
(5) debates about the goals of intellectual life and humanistic society. Arnold defined culture as "the pursuit of perfection by getting to know the best which has been thought and said." Through this
(10) knowledge, Arnold hoped, we can turn "a fresh and free thought upon our stock notions and habits." Although Arnold helped to define the purposes of the liberal arts curriculum in the century following the
(15) publication of *Culture*, three concrete forms of dissent from his views have had considerable impact of their own.

The first protests Arnold's fearful designation of "anarchy" as culture's enemy,
(20) viewing this dichotomy simply as another version of the struggle between a privileged power structure and radical challenges to its authority. Arnold certainly tried to define the arch—the legitimizing
(25) order of value—against the an-arch of existentialist democracy, yet he himself was plagued in his soul by the blind arrogances of the reactionary powers in his world. The writer who regarded the contemporary
(30) condition with such apprehension in *Culture* is the poet who wrote "Dover Beach," not an ideologue rounding up all the usual modern suspects.

Another form of opposition saw
(35) Arnold's culture as a perverse perpetuation of classical and literary learning, outlook, and privileges in a world where science had become the new arch and from which any substantively new order of
(40) thinking must develop. At the center of the "two cultures" debate were the goals of the formal educational curriculum, the principal vehicle through which Arnoldian culture operates. However, Arnold himself
(45) had viewed culture as enacting its life in a much more broadly conceived set of institutions.

Today, however, Arnoldian culture is sustained by multiculturalism, a movement
(50) aimed largely at gaining recognition for voices and visions that Arnoldian culture has implicitly suppressed. In educational practice, multiculturalists are interested in deflating the imperious authority that
(55) "high culture" exercises over curriculum while bringing into play the principle that we must learn what is representative, for we have overemphasized what is exceptional. The multiculturalists' conflict with

(60) Arnoldian culture has clear affinities with the radical critique; yet multiculturalism affirms Arnold by returning us more specifically to a tension inherent in the idea of culture rather than to the culture- *(65)* anarchy dichotomy.

The social critics, defenders of science, and multiculturalists insist that Arnold's culture is simply a device for ordering us about. Instead, it is designed to register *(70)* the gathering of ideological clouds on the horizon. There is no utopian motive in Arnold's celebration of perfection. Perfection mattered to Arnold as the only background against which we could form a just *(75)* image of our actual circumstances, just as we can conceive finer sunsets and unheard melodies. This capacity which all humans possess, Arnold made the foundation and authority of culture.

15. The author of the passage is primarily concerned with

   (A) arguing against those who have opposed Arnold's ideas
   (B) describing Arnold's conception of culture
   (C) explaining why Arnold considered the pursuit of perfection to be the essence of culture
   (D) tracing Arnold's influence on the liberal arts educational curriculum
   (E) examining the different views of culture that have emerged since the mid-18th century

16. Based upon the author's interpretation of Arnoldian culture, with which of the following statements would Arnold most likely disagree?

   (A) The capacity to conceive perfection is the foundation of culture.
   (B) Culture operates in a wide array of social institutions.
   (C) Existential democracy is culture's enemy.
   (D) The educational curriculum should de-emphasize what is representative.
   (E) The anarchy-culture dichotomy embraces the struggle against the privileged power structure.

17. It can be inferred from the passage that the two-cultures debate

   (A) emerged as a reaction to the multiculturalist movement
   (B) developed after 1869
   (C) influenced Arnold's thinking about culture
   (D) was carried on by American as well as European scientists
   (E) led to a schizophrenic educational system

18. In criticizing Arnold's dissenters, the author employs all of the following methods EXCEPT:

    (A) pointing out the paradoxical nature of an argument against Arnoldian culture
    (B) presenting evidence that conflicts with a claim made by Arnold's dissenters
    (C) asserting that a claim made by the dissenters is an oversimplification
    (D) drawing an analogy between one of the dissenters' claims and another insupportable theory
    (E) suggesting that the focus of one of the dissenters' arguments is too narrow

19. PALLID :

    (A) tumultuous
    (B) impetuous
    (C) verbose
    (D) vibrant
    (E) hostile

20. NAIL : PUNCTURE : :

    (A) sword : laceration
    (B) drill : screw
    (C) saw : sawdust
    (D) bludgeon : bruise
    (E) wheel : track

21. Displeased with the ------- of his novel, the author withdrew from the television project.

    (A) adaptation
    (B) compilation
    (C) translation
    (D) outcome
    (E) resurgence

22. SPARK : CONFLAGRATION : :

    (A) match : light
    (B) oxygen : combustion
    (C) drizzle : torrent
    (D) sugar : sweetness
    (E) mountain : hillock

23. INTERLOPER : MEDDLE : :

    (A) misanthrope : usurp
    (B) rogue : repent
    (C) advocate : espouse
    (D) dilettante : proselytize
    (E) ombudsman : refine

24. Understandably, the host country's dignitaries treated the powerful statesman with unmistakable -------, while they afforded his spouse, who accompanied him, a commensurate degree of -------.

    (A) courtesy .. deference
    (B) impunity .. respect
    (C) curiosity .. capriciousness
    (D) regalia .. liturgy
    (E) formality .. acrimony

23

Questions 25 and 26 are based on the following passage.

The German empire was largely a creation of the political genius of Bismarck. Not since Napoleon had Europe seen such a dominant and effective leader. In 1847 he
(5) had entered politics and found it to his liking and quickly rose up the ranks. Upon becoming Minister-President of Prussia, he made a famous pronouncement: "The great questions of the day will not be
(10) decided by speeches and the resolutions of majorities . . . but by iron and blood." He quickly went about showing what he meant by using war to unify the German states. There were victorious wars against
(15) Denmark and Austria. These victories threatened France, and another war ensued in 1870. Napoleon III and his army, which was thought to be the finest fighting machine in Europe, surrendered in
(20) humiliation. The Franco-Prussian war brought the German states together, and Bismarck took full advantage of the opportunity this afforded, arguing for the creation of a new German empire with the
(25) Prussian king, Wilhelm I (Wilhelm II's grandfather), as emperor. The states agreed and made their proclamation on French soil in the Hall of Mirrors at Versailles. This, combined with a heavy
(30) war indemnity and the loss of the rich iron-mining and manufacturing territory of Alsace and Lorraine, was a grievous insult to the people of France.

25. The passage mentions all of the following events as leading to the creation of the new German empire EXCEPT:

(A) the defeat of Napoleon III in the Franco-Prussian war
(B) Bismarck's election to the post of Minister-President of Prussia
(C) France's loss of the territory of Alsace and Lorraine
(D) the defeat of Denmark and Austria by the unified German states
(E) Bismarck's pronouncement that "iron and blood" would settle the great questions of the day

26. Each of the following can be inferred from the passage EXCEPT:

(A) Wilhelm II's father was not named Wilhelm
(B) the German states were unified for military purposes
(C) the people of France were insulted by Bismarck
(D) Napoleon III and his army were not the finest fighting machine in Europe
(E) the wars against Austria and Denmark were fought by Prussia

27. As it turns out, the new administration ------- by failing to ------- the reforms it promised as the cornerstones of its campaign platform.

(A) vouchsafed .. promulgate
(B) ensconced .. abdicate
(C) egressed .. augment
(D) reneged .. implement
(E) equivocated .. parlay

28. MUNIFICENT : GENEROSITY : :

   (A) dolorous : sorrow
   (B) domineering : perspicacity
   (C) indisputable : doubt
   (D) fortunate : haplessness
   (E) beguiled : judiciousness

29. BRAGGART : DIFFIDENCE : :

   (A) benefactor : generosity
   (B) pariah : esteem
   (C) partisan : partiality
   (D) savant : wisdom
   (E) sycophant : flattery

30. RESOLUTION :

   (A) introduction
   (B) vacillation
   (C) revocation
   (D) denunciation
   (E) revulsion

23

STOP.
End of Verbal Section

Answer Key

1. B	11. C	21. A
2. E	12. E	22. C
3. D	13. C	23. C
4. B	14. E	24. A
5. B	15. A	25. D
6. B	16. E	26. C
7. D	17. B	27. D
8. E	18. D	28. A
9. A	19. D	29. B
10. C	20. A	30. B

Hour 24

Sample Test 2 (Analytical Ability— CBT Format)

This hour you'll complete your sample computer-based GRE by taking a full-length Analytical Ability section in the CBT format. Here are your goals for this hour:

- Take the test under timed conditions
- Check the answer key on page 422
- Assess your performance by checking the score conversion chart on pages 456–457
- Review the explanations (they begin on page 445)

NOTE The difficulty level of questions here is evenly distributed across various levels. Keep in mind, though, that the CBT does not necessarily follow this pattern, but instead will determine the difficulty level of each question based on your responses to prior questions.

Analytical Ability Test

Time—60 Minutes

35 Questions

DIRECTIONS: For each question, select the best of the five answer choices. Some groups of questions are based on the same passage and set of rules. In answering these questions, you might find it helpful to draw rough diagrams.

1. Unequal pay for men and women is a completely indefensible practice and one that must be stopped immediately. After all, can anyone seriously doubt that women have as much right to self-esteem as men? Surely this fact alone is reason enough to justify their right to earn as much money as men.

   Which of the following is an assumption on which the above argument depends?

   (A) A person who has less money than another has less self-esteem.
   (B) People who do not have jobs lack self-esteem.
   (C) Women and men who perform similar jobs should earn similar salaries.
   (D) Equal pay for equal work is a constitutionally guaranteed right of all workers.
   (E) High self-esteem is as important to women as it is to men.

Questions 2–5

Five movie patrons—Alice, Bill, Charles, David and Erma—are waiting in a single-file line to buy popcorn at the theater. Popcorn is available in four different box sizes—small, medium, large, and jumbo. Each of the five patrons may buy one and only one box of popcorn.

Alice is farther ahead in line than Erma and will buy a smaller box of popcorn than David.

Bill will buy a smaller box of popcorn than Alice.

Charles is farther ahead in line than Bill and will buy a larger box of popcorn than both David and Erma.

Either Bill or Erma, but not both, is farther ahead in line than David.

2. Which of the following represents the order, from first to fifth, in which the five movie patrons could be waiting in line?

   (A) Alice, Bill, Charles, David, Erma
   (B) Alice, David, Charles, Erma, Bill
   (C) Alice, Erma, Charles, David, Bill
   (D) Charles, Alice, Erma, Bill, David
   (E) Charles, Alice, David, Erma, Bill

3. If the last two movie patrons in line each buys a medium box of popcorn, the second person in line is:

   (A) Alice
   (B) Bill
   (C) Charles
   (D) David
   (E) Erma

4. All of the following must be false EXCEPT:

   (A) The first person and the last person in line both buy a small box of popcorn.
   (B) The first person and the last person in line both buy a large box of popcorn.
   (C) The first two people in line both buy a medium box of popcorn.
   (D) The first two people in line both buy a large box of popcorn.
   (E) The last two people in line both buy a small box of popcorn.

5. If the first movie patron in line buys the same size box of popcorn as the fifth patron, both the position in line and the size of box purchased may be determined with respect to how many of the five patrons?

   (A) 1
   (B) 2
   (C) 3
   (D) 4
   (E) 5

6. New genetic testing procedures have been developed that can detect the presence or absence of dirolin in foods. Dirolin is the toxin that causes food poisoning in humans. While rarely fatal if identified and treated in its early stages, food poisoning causes severe intestinal illness and vomiting. It is for this reason that the Department of Public Health and Safety should require that all processed foods be subjected to the new testing procedures.

Which one of the following, if true, would require the author to reconsider the conclusion?

   (A) A recent Disease Control Agency report states that reported cases of food poisoning have declined steadily over the past decade.
   (B) Death as a result of food poisoning is extremely rare in modern first-world countries.
   (C) Current processing procedures employed in preparing foodstuffs are extremely effective in preventing and detecting dirolin contamination.
   (D) The bacillus that produces dirolin can be easily treated with modern antibiotics.
   (E) Improper preserving and processing procedures are responsible for the presence of dirolin in prepared foods.

24

7. In Los Alamos the majority of residents are professionals whose incomes exceed $120,000. Moreover, they always elect conservative candidates in their elections. Los Brunos is also populated with professionals who earn high incomes; therefore it is likely that _____.

   Which of the following best completes the argument?

   (A) Los Brunos residents have incomes above $120,000

   (B) Los Brunos residents always elect conservative candidates

   (C) poor people do not live in Los Brunos

   (D) people who earn high incomes are usually conservative

   (E) the majority of residents of Los Brunos are doctors and lawyers

8. Residential water use has been severely restricted in response to the current drought in our state. However, current reservoir levels are at the same height as during the drought that occurred here eight years ago. Because residential water use was not restricted then, it should not be restricted now.

   Which of the following, if true, would most seriously undermine the author's contention?

   (A) No new reservoirs have been constructed in the state since the last drought.

   (B) The population of the state has grown at a steady rate of over two million people a year since the last drought.

   (C) Residential water use makes up over fifty percent of the total water use.

   (D) The restrictions on residential water use are projected to last for only two months during the summer.

   (E) Since the last drought, water-conserving devices are required by law to be installed in all new residential construction.

9. Contrary to popular belief, there are cases in which wearing a seat belt can actually endanger one's life rather than protect it. In one recent accident, for example, a car hit a tree and, except for a small space on the floor, was completely crushed. Luckily, the driver was not wearing a seat belt and was thrown to the floor on impact. Had he been wearing a seat belt he would surely have been killed. Cases like this lead me to conclude that we should not be required by law to wear seat belts.

   Which of the following is an assumption on which the above argument depends?

   (A) Laws should not require an individual to engage in an act that may endanger his or her life.

   (B) Most people believe that the mandatory seat-belt law saves lives.

   (C) Obeying the mandatory seat-belt law will not necessarily protect the wearer in automobile accidents.

   (D) The mandatory seat-belt law should not be obeyed.

   (E) Obeying the seat-belt law isn't always a good idea.

Questions 10–13

Each student in an art class has used at least one of six different colors of paint—green, white, red, yellow, blue, and black—for a watercolor assignment. Each color was used by at least one student. The instructor has made the following observations about her students' use of colors:

Some students who used green also used white.

None of the students used both green and black.

All students who used white also used either blue or yellow, but not both.

All students who used red also used yellow.

Some students who used white also used red.

All students who used yellow also used green.

10. If a particular student used only two colors, which of the following is a complete and accurate list of the possible pairs of colors used by that student?

(A) blue and green; green and yellow; white and blue

(B) black and blue; green and yellow; blue and white

(C) white and blue; green and blue; blue and black; yellow and green

(D) green and blue; yellow and red; white and blue; black and blue

(E) blue and white; yellow and green; black and blue; white and green

11. What is the greatest number of colors that one student could have used?

(A) 2
(B) 3
(C) 4
(D) 5
(E) 6

12. If a student used one color only, which of the following is a complete and accurate list of the possible colors that student could have used?

(A) blue
(B) black
(C) black or blue
(D) green or black
(E) green, black, or blue

13. Which of the following CANNOT be a complete list of the colors used by one student?

(A) white, black, blue
(B) white, blue, green
(C) yellow, green, blue
(D) red, yellow, green, white
(E) white, blue, green, yellow

24

14. There is clear evidence that the mandated use of safety seats by children under age four has resulted in fewer child fatalities over the past five years. Compared to the five-year period prior to the passage of laws requiring the use of safety seats, fatalities of children under age four have decreased by 30 percent.

Which one of the following, if true, most substantially strengthens the argument above?

(A) The number of serious automobile accidents involving children under age four has remained steady over the past five years.

(B) Automobile accidents involving children have decreased sharply over the past five years.

(C) The use of air bags in automobiles has increased by 30 percent over the past five years.

(D) Most fatal automobile accidents involving children under age four occur in the driveway of their home.

(E) The number of teenage drivers has increased by 30 percent over the past five years.

Questions 15-19

A particular television program has nine sponsors—A, B, C, D, E, F, G, H, and I—each with its own commercial. The program is interrupted by five commercial breaks. Two commercials appear at each break, except for the fifth break, at which only one commercial appears. Each of the nine different commercials appears exactly once during the program.

E's commercial appears at an earlier break than C's commercial.

D's commercial appears at a later break than both F's commercial and B's commercial.

A's commercial appears at the same break as C's commercial.

B's commercial does not appear at the same break as E's commercial.

G's commercial appears during the same break as H's commercial.

15. Which of the following CANNOT be true?

(A) C's commercial appears at the second break.

(B) E's commercial appears at the fifth break.

(C) D's commercial appears at the second break.

(D) F's commercial appears at the third break.

(E) G's commercial appears at the fourth break.

16. Any of the following pairs of commercials may appear at the same break together EXCEPT:

(A) I's commercial and F's commercial

(B) B's commercial and I's commercial

(C) F's commercial and B's commercial

(D) E's commercial and D's commercial

(E) I's commercial and E's commercial

17. If two complete commercial breaks separate B's commercial from F's commercial, for how many commercials is it possible to determine the break during which the commercial appears?

(A) 1

(B) 2

(C) 3

(D) 4

(E) 5

18. If C's commercial appears at the second break, how many different pairs of commercials could appear at the first break?

    (A) 1
    (B) 2
    (C) 3
    (D) 4
    (E) 5

19. If G's commercial appears at the third break, which of the following statements is sufficient to determine the break at which each and every commercial appears?

    (A) A's commercial appears at the fourth break.
    (B) B's commercial appears at the first break.
    (C) C's commercial appears at the second break.
    (D) E's commercial appears at the first break.
    (E) F's commercial appears at the fourth break.

Questions 20–23

The students in a music class must take turns changing a melody by making one and only one of the following alterations to the melody created by the previous student:

Each student may add one note at the end of the melody.
Each student may delete one note from the melody.
Each student may replace one note of the melody with a different note.
Each student may exchange one note with another in the melody, but the two exchanged notes must be different.

The initial melody consists of four notes. In order from first to last, the notes are: C, D, E, and F. In changing a melody, each student must also comply with the following restrictions:

Note D must neither immediately precede nor immediately follow note F.
Note E may be exchanged with note C only if neither note occurs as the first or last note of the melody.
Each of the four notes—C, D, E, and F—must occur in the melody at least once, and the melody must not include any notes of the musical scale other than these four.

20. Which of the following melodies can be created by the first student?

    (A) C F D E
    (B) E D C F
    (C) C F E D
    (D) E D E F C
    (E) C D E F D

21. The fewest number of students that must take a turn in order to create a melody consisting of notes E, D, C, F, C, and D, in sequence, is:

    (A) 2
    (B) 3
    (C) 4
    (D) 5
    (E) 6

22. If a student wishes to exchange one note with another, which of the following melodies offers the greatest number of possible changes of this kind?

   (A) D C E F
   (B) C F E D
   (C) E D C F C
   (D) C D D E F
   (E) E F F C D

23. Which of the following could be the second and third notes, respectively, of the melody created by the first student?

   (A) D and E
   (B) F and E
   (C) D and C
   (D) E and E
   (E) E and D

24. Recent reports from waste management companies indicate that disposable plastic containers make up an increasingly large percentage of the waste they collect. As a result, landfills and incineration sites now deal almost exclusively with the disposal of plastics, whereas glass and metal containers previously made up the bulk of their refuse. It is evident from this radical change in disposal patterns that the use of plastic containers has virtually replaced the use of glass and metal containers.

Which of the following, if true, would most seriously call into question the conclusion above?

   (A) Metal and glass containers are more expensive to manufacture than plastic containers.
   (B) An increasing proportion of metal and glass containers is now being recycled.
   (C) Plastic containers can be used over and over again before being discarded.
   (D) Plastic containers decompose faster than metal and glass containers.
   (E) Environmentalists have been unsuccessful in their attempts to decrease the production of plastic containers.

Questions 25–29

Bob is planning a backpacking trip in Pine National Park. The park contains seven camps—A, B, C, D, E, F, and G. Bob must begin and end his trip as well as spend each interim night only among these seven camps. His trip is subject to the following restrictions:

   From Camp A, campers may hike directly to Camp B only.
   From Camp B, campers may hike directly to Camps A and D only.
   From Camp C, campers may hike directly to Camps B and F only.
   From Camp D, campers must not hike to any other camp.
   From Camp E, campers may hike directly to Camp C only.
   From Camp F, campers may hike directly to Camps A and C only.
   From Camp G, campers may hike directly to Camps E and F only.

Except where a round trip between two camps is possible, the elevation of each camp is higher than that of the next camp visited.

25. If Bob plans to visit all seven camps without visiting the same camp twice, which of the following routes can he follow, from first to last camp visited?

   (A) E, G, F, C, A, B, D
   (B) G, E, C, F, A, B, D
   (C) F, G, E, C, D, B, A
   (D) G, F, E, C, A, B, D
   (E) G, E, C, B, D, F, A

26. If Bob plans to begin and end his trip at the same camp, spending one interim night in the park, how many distinct routes may he follow?

   (A) 2
   (B) 3
   (C) 4
   (D) 5
   (E) 6

27. Which of the following CANNOT be true?

   (A) Camp C is higher in elevation than Camp A.
   (B) Camp E is lower is elevation than Camp D.
   (C) Camp C is higher in elevation than Camp F.
   (D) Camp E is neither higher nor lower in elevation than Camp A.
   (E) Camp F is neither higher nor lower in elevation than Camp D.

28. If Bob visits at least two camps in addition to the camp at which he begins his trip, with respect to how many different departure points is it certain that Bob will descend from each camp to the next?

   (A) 0
   (B) 1
   (C) 2
   (D) 3
   (E) 4

29. Assume that Bob visits a total of three different camps, including the camp at which he begins his trip. If he makes exactly two interim overnight stops between the beginning and the end of his trip, he could begin his trip at any of the following camps EXCEPT:

   (A) Camp A
   (B) Camp B
   (C) Camp C
   (D) Camp E
   (E) Camp G

30. The budget deficit will continue to grow unless taxes are raised soon. However, that's not going to happen in the foreseeable future. The upshot is that if the budget deficit continues to grow, the next generation of taxpayers will be burdened by an almost unbearable debt.

If the above statements are true, which of the following must be true?

   (A) Taxes will be raised soon.
   (B) The budget deficit will not continue to grow.
   (C) The political climate will not change in the foreseeable future.
   (D) The budget deficit will continue to grow but the next generation of taxpayers will not be burdened with an almost unbearable debt.
   (E) The next generation of taxpayers will be burdened with an almost unbearable debt.

24

Questions 31–34

Gary has assembled a basket of fruit as a holiday gift for each of his four friends—Susan, Todd, Ursula, and Vadim. A total of fifteen pieces of fruit—five guavas, five mangos, and five kiwis—are distributed among the four baskets according to the following conditions:

Susan, Todd, and Ursula will each receive exactly two different types of fruit.

Vadim will receive only guavas.

Todd will receive more pieces of fruit than Susan.

Each basket includes at least three pieces of fruit.

31. Which of the following distributions could represent the total number of fruit pieces that Gary can give to Susan, Todd, Ursula, and Vadim, respectively?

(A) 3, 6, 3, 3
(B) 3, 3, 5, 4
(C) 4, 5, 4, 3
(D) 3, 3, 3, 6
(E) 3, 4, 3, 4

32. All of the following statements must be false EXCEPT:

(A) Todd will receive exactly three pieces of fruit.
(B) Todd will receive exactly six pieces of fruit.
(C) Susan will receive exactly five pieces of fruit.
(D) Vadim will receive exactly six pieces of fruit.
(E) Ursula will receive exactly six pieces of fruit.

33. If Ursula's basket contains more pieces of fruit than Todd's basket, all of the following must be false EXCEPT:

(A) Only Vadim will receive guavas.
(B) Vadim will receive exactly four guavas.
(C) Todd will receive exactly four kiwis.
(D) Susan will receive exactly three mangos.
(E) Ursula will receive exactly two guavas.

34. If Susan's basket contains two guavas and two kiwis, but no other pieces of fruit, how many different combinations of fruit could Todd's basket contain?

(A) one
(B) two
(C) three
(D) four
(E) five

35. The overall demand for used computers has risen dramatically in the past few years. Most of this increase is due to the explosion of entertainment software products aimed at young first-time computer users. As is to be expected, this demand has exerted an upward pressure on prices of used computers. As a result, we can expect that an increasing number of computer owners will be selling their old computers in order to buy the latest models.

Which of the following, if true, would most help to support the conclusion in the argument above?

(A) Computer technology is progressing so rapidly that computers purchased a year ago are now virtually obsolete.

(B) Exciting new software is being developed that can only run on the latest computer models.

(C) Most computer users do not know how to upgrade their old computers to accommodate the latest software products.

(D) It is less expensive to buy a new computer than to buy the components and build one yourself.

(E) The primary reason computer owners have not bought new computers or used computers that are newer models is that their old computers have little or no resale value.

24

STOP.
End of Analytical Section

Answer Key

1. A	13. E	25. B
2. C	14. A	26. C
3. B	15. B	27. B
4. C	16. A	28. A
5. E	17. E	29. A
6. C	18. B	30. E
7. B	19. E	31. A
8. B	20. C	32. B
9. A	21. C	33. E
10. C	22. A	34. B
11. C	23. A	35. E
12. E	24. B	

APPENDIX A

Explanations and Solutions to Sample Tests 1 and 2

Sample Test 1

Quantitative Ability Test (Hour 19)

1. **(C)** The prime numbers between 1 and 25 are 2, 3, 5, 7, 11, 13, 17, 19, and 23.

2. **(B)** There's no need to add the two series of numbers or compute their averages. Instead, compare 48 to 46, and compare 95 to 97. These terms cancel out, so the comparison is simply between 76 and 75.

3. **(C)** To determine quantity A, substitute the number 2 for a and for b in the centered equation: $(2 + 2)(2 - 2) = (4)(0) = 0$. Follow the same procedure for the quantity in Column B: $(-2 + -2)(-2 - -2) = (-4)(0) = 0$. The quantities in both columns are equal to 0.

4. **(A)** It is obvious that the length of AB is 6. The length of CD is $\sqrt{5^2 + 1^2} = \sqrt{26}$, or approximately 5.1. Therefore, AB is longer.

5. **(B)** Quantity A must be a fraction (ratio) between $\frac{5}{6}$ and $\frac{10}{11}$. Quantity B must be a fraction (ratio) between $\frac{10}{11}$ and $\frac{15}{16}$.

6. **(C)** $N_2 = -|-1+1| = 0$
$N_3 = -|0+2| = -2$
$N_4 = -|-2+3| = -1$
$N_5 = -|-1+4| = -3$

7. **(A)** The question can be simplified. When you divide 5 by 3 the remainder is 2. When you divide 8 by 7, the remainder is 1.

8. **(D)** The circumference of a circle with radius r is $2\pi r$. The area of a circle with radius R is πR^2. Cancel out π from both quantities, and compare $2r$ to R^2. Their relative number values can vary. For example, if $r = \frac{1}{2}$ and $R = 1$, the two quantities are equal; but if $r = 1$ and $R = 2$, quantity B is greater.

9. **(A)** This is easily solved by substitution. Let s equal 2. The volume of a cube with a side of 2 is 8. The volume of the rectangular block in Column B is $2 \times 1 \times 3 = 6$.

10. **(D)** The question provides a factorable quadratic equation. Determine the possible values of x by setting the quadratic expression equal to 0 (zero), factoring that expression, then setting each factor equal to zero:

$$2x^2 + 9x = 5$$
$$2x^2 + 9x - 5 = 0$$
$$(x + 5)(2x - 1) = 0$$
$$x + 5 = 0, \ 2x - 1 = 0$$
$$x = -5, \ \frac{1}{2}$$

There are two possible values of x: -5 and $\frac{1}{2}$. Thus, you cannot determine the relationship between x and -5 (x could be either equal to or greater than -5).

11. **(A)** Wheel B's radius, as well as circumference, is 50 times greater than wheel A's ($3:150 = 1:50$). In order to travel as far each second as wheel A travels per minute, wheel B's circumference would have to be 60 times greater (since there are 60 seconds per minute). Thus, wheel A travels further in one second than wheel B does in one minute. (The number of revolutions per second is not relevant, as long as the rotation rate is the same for both wheels.)

12. **(B)** Given the centered information, $a^2 + b^2$ will always be positive. If a and b are both negative, $a^3 + b^3$ will result in a negative sum. If a and b are both positive, $a^3 + b^3$ will result in a positive sum. Any fraction between 0 and 1, raised to the third power, is less than the same fraction squared. Thus, even if $a^3 + b^3$ results in a positive sum, that sum must be less than $a^2 + b^2$.

13. **(D)** Because the two lines are parallel, the two triangles are the same shape, and their corresponding angles are equal in size ($x = p$ and $y = q$), and therefore $x - y = p - q$. However, the quantity

$x - y$ is being compared here to $q - p$, not $p - q$. The two quantities are equal in size only if all four angles are equal (60°). It is not possible to determine whether all four angles are the same size, regardless of the fact that the third angle of each triangle is 60°.

14. **(A)** Both quantities can be simplified by applying the rule $\frac{a^x}{a^y} = a^{(x-y)}$. The quantity in Column A equals -6^4. The quantity in Column B equals -11^3. Any negative number raised to an even power is always positive, while a negative number raised to an odd power is always negative. Thus, $-6^4 > -11^3$.

15. **(C).** If one side of a triangle inscribed in a circle passes through the circle's center (the length of the side equals the circle's diameter), the triangle must be a right triangle. The angle opposite that side is 90°. Thus, $\triangle ABC$ is a right triangle, and $\angle ACB = 90°$. Since sides AC and CB are given, you can use the Pythagorean Theorem to determine AB. A shortcut is to recognize that ratio $CB : AC$ is 7.5 : 10, or 3 : 4. Thus, the ratio $CB : AC : AB$ must be 3 : 4 : 5, or 7.5 : 10 : 12.5. $AC = 12.5$, so the correct answer is (C).

16. **(E)** Convert all expressions to decimal form:

(A) $\dfrac{3}{5} = .6$

(B) $\dfrac{\frac{2}{3}}{\frac{11}{9}} = \dfrac{2}{3} \cdot \dfrac{9}{11} = \dfrac{2}{1} \cdot \dfrac{3}{11} = \dfrac{6}{11} \approx .55$

(C) $\sqrt{.25} = .5$

(D) $.81^2 = (.81)(.81) = .65^+$

(E) $\dfrac{.2}{.3} = .66^+$

17. **(B)** To solve this problem, set up three equations:

$$A + B = 40$$
$$B + C = 34$$
$$A + C = 42$$

To solve for B, you can first subtract the second equation from the third equation:

$$A + C = 42$$
$$\underline{B + C = 34}$$
$$A - B = 8$$

Then subtract this resulting equation from the first equation:

$$A + B = 40$$
$$\underline{A - B = 8}$$
$$2B = 32$$
$$B = 16$$

18. **(C)** $\frac{5}{9}$ of the legislators voted for the bill. Determine the total number of legislators by setting up and solving the following equation, then subtract 900 from the total:

$$900 = \tfrac{5}{9}x$$
$$8100 = 5x$$
$$1620 = x$$
$$1620 - 900 = 720$$

19. **(B)** Each side of the square equals 12 feet. The length of the remaining two sides of the triangle totals 16. The curved length of the semicircle $= \frac{1}{2}\pi d = \frac{1}{2}\pi(12) = 6\pi$. The length of the two sides of the square included in the overall

perimeter totals 24. The total perimeter of the floor = 16 + 6π + 24 = 40 + 6π.

20. **(E)** Convert the question into an algebraic equation, and solve for x:

$$M = \frac{P}{100} \cdot x$$

$$100M = Px$$

$$\frac{100M}{P} = x$$

21. **(B)** For each year, you need to compare the relative heights of the two gray bars. 1986 was the only year that Country Y's imports ($35B) more than tripled Country X's imports ($10B). Be careful: In 1993, the dollar amount difference was the greatest. But the percentage difference in 1993 was clearly less than in 1986.

22. **(C)** Compare the white and gray portions of the Country Y bar for each year. Do a quick visual inspection for each year's bar. Eliminate any year in which it appears that Country Y's import bar is at least half the height of Country Y's export bar. (Eliminate 1987, 1988, 1990, 1991, 1993, and 1994.) That leaves four years to consider. Here are the export and import amounts (in billions) during these remaining four years:

1985: $\dfrac{\$42}{\$27}$ (a difference of $15)

1986: $\dfrac{\$39}{\$35}$ (a difference of $4)

1989: $\dfrac{\$57}{\$40}$ (a difference of $17)

1992: $\dfrac{\$65}{\$50}$ (a difference of $15)

Only during 1985, 1989, and 1992 did Country Y's exports exceed its imports by at least $10B.

23. **(A)** This question involves two steps. First, visually compare the difference in height between Country X's white bar and gray bar for each year. (Be careful to look at County X's bar, *not* Country Y's!) You don't need to determine amounts at this point. A quick inspection reveals that 1987 was the year Country X's exports exceeded its own imports by the greatest amount. Now go on to the second step. During 1987, Country Y's imports were approximately $35B and Country X's imports were approximately $13B. The difference is $22B.

24. **(B)** This is another two-step question. First, notice the general upward trend in imports (as well as exports) over the 10-year period. Try to zero in on the appropriate year by eliminating *early* years, during which the import totals were clearly too low to be in the running. (You can eliminate 1985–1992.) That leaves only two years: 1993 and 1994. Of these two, only the import total for 1993 comes close to $85B ($24B for Country

X plus $62B for Country Y). Now for the second step. Estimate both export amounts for 1993. Be careful! You need to measure the white portions only. The total exports for 1993 amount to about $75B ($25B for Country X plus $50B for Country Y).

25. **(B)** First, find the greatest increase in Y's imports from one year to the next. 1989 to 1990 saw the greatest increase in Country Y's imports—from $40B to $56B. Now go on to the second step. During the second of these two years (1990), Country Y's imports were $44B and its exports were $56B. The ratio is 44:56. You can eliminate answer choices (C), (D), and (E) since each of them indicate a 1:1 ratio *or higher*. Of the two remaining choices 4:5 is closer to 44:56.

26. **(C)** In answer choice (C), unequal quantities are subtracted from equal quantities. The differences are unequal, but the inequality is reversed since unequal numbers are being subtracted from rather than added to the equal numbers.

27. **(B)** Competitor 1 must engage in eight matches. Competitor 2 must engage in seven matches not already accounted for (the match between competitors 1 and 2 has already been tabulated). Similarly, competitor 3 must engage in six matches other than those accounted for, and so on. The minimum number of total matches = 8 + 7 + 6 + 5 + 4 + 3 + 2 + 1 = 36.

28. **(E)** The number of days (d) that it takes q workers to paint a house varies inversely with the number of days that it takes $q + 2$ workers to paint a house. You can express the relationship with the following equation: $(q)(d) = (q + 2)(x)$, where x = the number of days that it takes $q + 2$ workers to paint a house. Dividing both sides of the equation by $(q + 2)$ gives you: $x = \frac{qd}{q+2}$.

29. **(C)** AC is a diagonal of the square $ABCD$. To find the length of any square's diagonal, multiply the length of any side by $\sqrt{2}$. So first you need to find the length of a side here. Half the length of a side equals the circle's radius, and the circumference of any circle equals $2\pi r$, where r is the radius. Thus, the radius here is 8, and the square's sides are 16 each. Therefore, the diagonal $AC = 16\sqrt{2}$.

30. **(E)** You can express the distance both in terms of Dan's driving time going home and going back to college. Letting x equal the time (in hours) it took Dan to drive home, you can express the distance between his home and his workplace both as $60x$ and as $50(x + 1)$. Equate the two distances (because distance is constant) and solve for x as follows:

$$60x = 50(x + 1)$$
$$60x = 50x + 50$$
$$10x = 50$$
$$x = 5$$

It took Dan five hours at 60 miles per hour to drive from college to home, so the distance is 300 miles.

Verbal Ability Test (Hour 20)

1. **(A)** Arguments that seem convincing but are actually insupportable are *specious*. Anyone familiar with the workers' conditions could *refute* (disprove) the management's argument.

2. **(D)** A law known as the "Prohibition Act" would naturally be expected to *proscribe* (outlaw) certain activity. None of the other choices make sense here. *Prolonged* means "continued or sustained"; *preempted* means "seized or usurped"; *sanctioned* means "approved."

3. **(D)** An incongruous approach suggests an internal inconsistency, so the two missing words should run contrary in meaning to each other. Only (D) clearly fits the bill. *Principled* (conscientious) and insouciant (unconcerned or carefree) describe opposing characteristics. (*Surly* means "irascible or irritable"; *clandestine* means "secret" or "surreptitious"; *refractory* means "stubborn.")

4. **(C)** The phrase "but he thought nothing of" suggests irony or paradox. It is ironic that automobile travel should be *harrowing*, or frightening, to someone who engages in the dangerous sport of bobsledding as a *hobby*.

5. **(D)** *Inexorable* means "inevitable." The sentence describes the feminist movement as a result of forces already "set into motion," suggesting inevitability. None of the other choices make as much sense in context here. *Resplendent*

means "grand or glorious"; *incumbent* means "currently holding an official position or office"; *sporadic* means "intermittent."

6. **(A)** Because his appointment confirmed his character, the two missing words must be consistent in meaning. Thus, you can eliminate (B) and (C). *Benevolent* means "generous"; *philanthropic* (charitable) and *parsimonious* (selfish) are antonyms. In (D), the use of the word *incongruous* (inconsistent) makes no sense here, and it is used improperly to describe a person in any event. As for (E), *hypocritical* makes sense considered alone in the first clause; but *depraved* means "wicked or evil," and it makes no sense to conclude that the wealthy mogul must be evil because he was appointed as a member of the board. The only reasonable choice is (A). *Venerable* means "worthy of respect" or "honorable."

7. **(B)** A bully's demeanor (manner) usually appears *truculent* (cruel or vicious). *Bravado* means "pretense," *malevolence* means "hatred or malice," and *feigned* means "pretended." So by pretending to be malicious, a bully hides his insecurities.

8. **(C)** A *ship* is part of an armada, and an *atom* is part of a *molecule*. None of the other pairs exemplify a part-to-whole relationship. (A) is a red herring; it involves boating, just like the original.

9. **(E)** *Trembling* is a physiological symptom—or manifestation—of *fear*, just as *weeping* is a physiological manifestation of *grief*. Neither (A), (B), nor (C) exemplify this type of relationship. (D) is the second-best answer; an *adoring* person might follow the object of his or her adoration. But this manifestation is not physiological, nor is it as inexorable as trembling or weeping (as manifestations of fear and grief, respectively).

10. **(D)** A *gem* is placed within a *setting* (framework) in jewelry, just as a *building* is constructed within the framework of a *scaffold*. (B) is a red herring. *Milieu* means "environment, background, or setting." But the word does not suggest spatial constraints as do a gem's setting or a building's scaffold. (A) and (C) are also red herrings; both involve gems and jewelry, just like the original.

11. **(B)** To *handle* is to examine by *feel*; similarly, to *peruse* is to examine or *scrutinize*—usually by reading. None of the other pairs exemplify this relationship. *Caress* and *abrade* are essentially antonyms. (C) is probably the second-best answer. The word *giggle* describes a peculiar form of *laughing*—but not a studied form. To *burgeon* is to begin to grow or blossom. To *heave* is to *lift* with great exertion.

12. **(E)** *Robust* means full of *vigor*, just as *sanguine* means full of *hope*. (B) is the second-best answer, because *sickness* and *illness* are synonymous. However,

sickness does not suggest a fullness (of illness).

13. **(B)** An *innovation* is a new idea that lacks *precedent* (an earlier instance or example). Similarly, an *illusion* by definition lacks *veracity* (truthfulness). (D) is the second-best answer. To *renovate* is to renew or improve something older—such as an antique. Yet something renovated can still be antique. *Conservation* bears no relationship to *simplicity*. (E) is a red herring; *invention* is synonymous with *innovation*.

14. **(B)** *Deleterious* means "harmful or unhealthy." *Pernicious* means "fatal," a greater degree of harm. *Blithe* means "cheerful." *Exuberant* means "uninhibited or high-spirited," denoting a higher degree of joy. Neither (A), (C), nor (D) clearly exemplify a relationship of degree. The two words in each pair are essentially synonyms. As for (E), *mercurial* means "inconstant" or "fluctuating," while *indefatigable* means "persistent" or "determined." So these two words are essentially antonyms.

15. **(A)** To be *jocular* is to lack *solemnity*. To be *latent* is to lack *visibility*. Thus, in each pair, the two words are essentially antonyms. None of the other pairs exemplify this type of relationship. In fact, in each other pair, the two words are essentially synonyms.

16. **(B)** A *diatribe* is a speech characterized by bitterness. A *recapitulation* is a summary or synopsis—and thus is characterized by *brevity*. In both cases,

the second word describes the first. A *dictum* is a pronouncement or affirmation and bears no relationship to *indolence*, which means "laziness." An *encomium* is speech characterized by praise—just the opposite of reproach (blame or criticism). A *polemic* is a debate, controversy, or disagreement—just the opposite of *consonance*, which means agreement and accord. Similarly, *concordance* means agreement or consensus, just the opposite of *contrariety*.

17. **(B)** While free radicals' effect on cholesterol is mentioned in the passage (lines 24–30), their effect is related to "cholesterol plaque accumulations," and not high cholesterol. (A) is mentioned explicitly in line 4. (C) is mentioned explicitly in lines 9–12. (D) is mentioned explicitly in lines 23–24. (E) can be inferred from the claim that a free radical causes cellular damage "until it is "neutralized" by a scavenging antioxidant enzyme" (line 6).

18. **(B)** The author states, "When a cell membrane is damaged by a free radical, the cell loses the capacity to transport nutrients, oxygen, water, or waste matter. As a result, cell membranes may rupture, spilling their contents into surrounding tissues, and thereby damage surrounding cells." The clear implication of this information is that the cell membrane ruptures because it can no longer contain the various materials. In other words, the contents of the cell exceed the capacity of the cell membrane.

19. **(E)** The passage deals mainly with the various ways in which free radicals harm cells. The second line of the passage indicates that the damage occurs in "living tissues."

20. **(E)** In lines 18–20 the passage states that damage resulting from the "destructive reactions" in the chromosomes and nucleic acids of the cell causes "changes in the cell replication rate and is the major cause of cancer cell mutations."

21. **(E)** In lines 13–14, the author states that Woolf saw in Rossetti "a model of artistic purity and integrity for women writers."

22. **(C)** In describing Rossetti's work, the author never uses the words "stark" or "realism," nor does the author describe her work in any way that might be expressed by either of these terms.

23. **(A)** The author claims that Rossetti's potent sensual imagery was "the richest since Keats" (line 2). Thus, it can be inferred that Rossetti's style was similar to that of Keats in that both writers used potent sensual imagery.

24. **(B)** In the first sentence of the second paragraph, the author states that "'A Birthday' is no typical Victorian poem and is certainly unlike predictable works of the era's best-known women poets." It is reasonably inferable that Rossetti was not among the era's best-known women poets, at least during her time.

25. **(E)** The author's threshold purpose in discussing Packer's biography is to

affirm that Rossetti's style of writing was not a reflection of her personal lifestyle. Having dismissed the theory that Rossetti was keeping secrets about her life, the author goes on (in the final paragraph) to offer a better explanation for the apparent contradiction between Rossetti's lifestyle and the emotional, sensual style of her poetry.

26. **(C)** In the final paragraph, the author states that "'The World'" is "pivotal in understanding Rossetti's literary project as a whole." Based upon the remainder of the final paragraph, the author seems to understand Rossetti's "literary project as a whole" as an attempt to convey an inescapable Christian truth to her readers (see lines 74–76). It is reasonably inferable, then, that "The World" provides significant insight into Rossetti's motives.

27. **(D)** The author's primary concern in the first two paragraphs is to point out that Rossetti's work conflicts with her apparently conservative personal life. The author's own impressions of Rossetti's work are corroborated by those of Woolf and Gosse. The third paragraph begins by asking how to reconcile this apparent conflict. (The newly discovered letters discussed in the third paragraph only reinforce the inconsistency between her personal life and literary work.) In the last paragraph, the author attempts to explain the inconsistency by examining Rossetti's love poems (particularly, her sonnet "The World").

28. **(D)** *Cursory* means "a brief examination"; a *comprehensive* examination is "detailed and extensive."

29. **(E)** To be *insolvent* is to be "without money"; the opposite is to be *wealthy*.

30. **(D)** To *reprove* is to "scold"; to *compliment* is to "give approval."

31. **(A)** To *ingratiate* oneself is to "work one's way into another's confidence"; to *distance* oneself is to "deliberately keep apart from another."

32. **(D)** *Cornucopia* means "abundance"; the opposite of abundance is *lack* (absence).

33. **(C)** *Accession* is "the taking on of responsibilities or titles;" *severance* is "the breaking off of a tie or bond," as in the giving up of responsibilities.

34. **(C)** Something *salutary* is "beneficial"; something *injurious* is "dangerous."

35. **(E)** *Rancor* is a feeling of "hostility" or "antagonism" toward another; *affection* is a feeling of "fondness" toward another.

36. **(A)** *Itinerant* means "traveling from place to place"; *motionless* means just the opposite.

37. **(E)** *Verdant* means "lush and overgrown;" *desolate* means "bare of any living thing."

38. **(D)** An *amicable* person is "friendly" or "agreeable"; a *contumacious* person is "stubborn."

A

Analytical Ability Test (Hour 21)

Questions 1–4

For this selection game, create a roster which incorporates the rules, at least to the extent possible. Indicate union members with upper-case letters and non-union members with lower-case letters. List the three extras separately to avoid confusion. As in any logic game, ask yourself what else you can deduce from the original rules. In a selection game, determine whether any of the subjects must be selected and whether any of the subjects cannot be selected. Here, given that at least two sets of twins must be selected, C and D must both be selected. Why? If C and D were not selected, then A, B, E, and F (three of whom are union members), would all be selected; as a result, only two non-union members (F and I), at most, could be selected. However, the rules stipulate that at least as many non-union members as union members must be selected; thus, C and D must both be selected:

[A B] [ⓒ ⓓ] [E / f]
G H i   (≥ 1)

non-union ≥ UNION

1. **(E)** Consider one rule at a time and eliminate answer choices that violate that rule. For example, considering the rule that at least two sets of twins must be selected, answer choices (B) and (C) can be eliminated. Answer choices (A) and (D) violate the rule that at least as many non-union members as union members must be selected.

2. **(A)** C and D must both be selected (see general comments above).

3. **(D)** Since union members cannot outnumber non-union members, the maximum number of actors that can be selected is eight. A bit of experimenting is required to determine who must be included in that group of eight. Assume first that all three sets of twins are selected. Since there are three union members and three non-union members among the six twins, I (a non-union member) and one other extra (either G or H) must be selected to complete the maximum cast. G and H cannot both be selected, since union members would thereby outnumber non-union members. Assume next that all twins except E are selected; to maximize the total number of actors selected, all three extras may be selected. Considering both scenarios, E, G, and H are the only three actors that need not be selected for a cast of eight. Among these three, only H appears among the answer choices.

4. **(C)** First, remember that C and D must both be selected in any event. So your task here is to determine the number of possibilities for the remaining four members. Assuming first that G and H (but not I) are selected, E and F must both be selected for a cast of six, while neither A nor B can be selected. Why? If A and B are selected, or if E but not F is selected, the number of union members in a six-member cast would exceed the

number of non-union members. Thus, if G and H (but not I) are selected, the director can assemble only one possible six-member cast: {C, D, E, F, G, H}. Next, assuming that G and I (but not H) are selected, two distinct six-member casts are possible: {C D G I A B} or {C D G I E F}. The total number of distinct casts is three.

5. **(C)** The argument stated in the passage is basically as follows:

   Premise: The greater the punishment, the fewer people will behave in the punished way.

   Conclusion: The death penalty will have a more dissuasive effect than would life imprisonment.

   The assumption required to fill the gap in the above argument is that the death penalty is a greater punishment than life imprisonment. This is exactly what response (C) asserts.

6. **(E)** The task in this problem is to find the answer that weakens the argument; that is, one that undermines the major assumption of the argument, attacks a stated premise, or that suggests an alternative conclusion that could be inferred from the premises. The major assumption of the argument is that the two elements of the stated goal of environmentalists are compatible with one another; that is, that preserving existing plant life and at the same time reducing the amount of carbon dioxide in the atmosphere are not conflicting aims. Response (E) directly contradicts this assumption, and as a result weakens the argument.

7. **(A)** The task in this problem is to find an answer that strengthens the argument; that is, one that offers support for the major assumption of the argument or that provides additional evidence for the conclusion. Response (A) provides additional evidence for the conclusion. The fact that the active ingredient in Psor-Be-Gone has been demonstrated to be an effective wide-spectrum anti-bacterial agent in independent tests adds credence to the claim that it is an effective treatment of the specific bacterium that causes psoriasis.

Questions 8–12

This game can be troublesome unless you recognize that additional key facts can be deduced from the rules. Because three workers stack in the afternoon, North must stack; otherwise, either Jackson and Klein would both stack or Lawry and Manning would both stack, resulting in a violation either of the rule that Jackson does not perform either of the two tasks that Klein performs or of the rule that Lawry does not perform either of the two tasks that Manning performs. Accordingly, either Jackson or Klein (but not both) must stack, and either Lawry or Manning (but not both) must stack. As a result, during the afternoon, only one worker may glue (otherwise, no workers would load, which would violate one of the rules), and, in the morning, two workers must glue. One of the two workers who glue in the morning must be North, since the rules specify that North glues, and since we have determined that North must stack in the afternoon. Based upon this additional information, we can construct the following diagram:

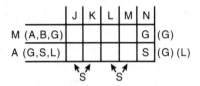

$(J \neq K)(L \neq M)$
*each worker does
2 different tasks

Given that each worker must perform two different tasks, that Jackson cannot perform either of the two tasks that Klein performs, and that Lawry cannot perform either of the two tasks that Manning performs, it is helpful to consider Jackson's and Klein's four tasks as a unit, bearing in mind that each task in that unit must be different (and the same for Lawry and Manning).

8. **(E)** As noted in the general comments above, N must glue in the morning and stack in the afternoon. Accordingly, N cannot box.

9. **(B)** As noted in the general comments above, either J or K must stack in the afternoon. Thus, if J loads (in the afternoon), K must stack (in the afternoon).

10. **(E)** Either L or M must stack; thus, if L loads, then M must stack. At least one of the workers must glue in the afternoon;

thus, that worker must be either J or K (while the other stacks). Because J and K (in either order) glue and stack in the afternoon, J and K must (in either order) assemble and box in the morning; otherwise, either one would perform the same task in the morning and afternoon or both would perform the same task. As a result, either L or M must glue, while the other either assembles or boxes. Thus, the only statement among the answer choices that must be true is (E).

11. **(A)** Among J, L, and M, two workers must box in the morning. Thus, either L or M must glue in the morning (otherwise, L and M would both box), and J must box in the morning. Since either L or M must glue in the morning, neither can glue in the afternoon, and so L and M (in either order) must stack and load in the afternoon. Finally, J and K (in either order) must glue and stack in the afternoon. Since M may either box or glue in the morning, Statement (A) could be true.

12. **(D)** N must glue in the morning and stack in the afternoon. Thus, K must also glue in the morning and stack in the afternoon. Since J and K do not perform the same tasks, J must load in the afternoon and either assemble or box in the morning. As a result, L and M must (in either order) glue and stack in the afternoon and (in either order) assemble and box in the morning. Thus, of the five answer choices, only Statement (D) could be false.

Questions 13–18

One viable approach to this game is to jot down the possible sequences, considering together that a right-handed batter bats fourth and that no right-handed batters bat consecutively. First consider a right-handed batter batting first (sequences 1-3 below), then consider a right-handed batter batting second (sequences 4-6 below). Also consider that unless a sequence contains at least two adjacent empty slots, it can be eliminated, since two left-handed batters bat consecutively. (Eliminate sequence 4 below.) Finally, insert those two left-handed batters wherever you can. The result is five alternative scenarios:

```
  1.  R  L  L  R  _  R  _  R  _
  2.  R  _  _  R  _  R  _  _  R
  3.  R  _  _  R  _  _  R  _  R
X 4.  _  R  _  R  _  R  _  R  _
  5.  _  R  _  R  _  R  L  L  R
  6.  _  R  _  R  L  L  R  _  R
```

Another (and probably more efficient) approach is to simply construct one initial diagram which indicates that a right-handed batter must bat fourth, while indicating the other rules near that diagram:

```
                   Ⓡ
_   _   _   _   _   _   _   _   _
1   2   3   4   5   6   7   8   9
```

```
┌────────┐
│  RRRR  │   [LL]≠L
│  LLL   │   S≠S
│   SS   │   R≠R
└────────┘
```

13. **(C)** The quickest way to locate the correct answer here is to consider, one at a time, each restriction regarding the first three batters. Then scan the answer choices for violations. If you consider that a right-handed batter cannot bat third, a quick glance down the list of third batters reveals the correct answer immediately—only in answer choice (C) does a right-handed batter bat third.

14. **(C)** Narrow down the choices by considering the conditions one at a time and scanning the answer choices for violations. Considering that a right-handed batter bats fourth and that right-handed batters cannot bat consecutively, (A) can be eliminated. Considering that the two switch hitters cannot bat consecutively, (B) can be eliminated. (D) and (E) each require that two or more right-handed batters bat consecutively. (C) is the only choice that does not violate any rule.

15. **(A)** Given that a right-handed batter bats second, then the remaining two right-handed batters must bat either sixth and ninth or seventh and ninth. (In either case, a right-handed batter must bat ninth.) Otherwise, either no two left-handed batters would bat consecutively or two right-handed batters would bat consecutively. Either result would violate a rule.

16. **(D)** Given that left-handed batters bat second and eighth, a bit of experimenting reveals that only two viable sequences result:

R L L Ⓡ S R S L L
R L S Ⓡ S R L L R
1̲ 2̲ 3̲ 4̲ 5̲ 6̲ 7̲ 8̲ 9̲

Thus, either a switch hitter or a left-handed batter can bat seventh.

17. **(A)** A bit of intuition and experimenting reveals that the first left-handed batter in the order must bat fifth, and no later, resulting in two possible sequences:

S R S Ⓡ L R L L R
S R S Ⓡ L L R L R
1̲ 2̲ 3̲ 4̲ 5̲ 6̲ 7̲ 8̲ 9̲

The foregoing sequences make clear that statement (A) could be true, while each of the other four statements must be false.

18. **(B)** Given that both switch hitters bat after all left-handed batters, a bit of experimenting reveals that a switch hitter can bat sixth at the earliest. Two possible sequences result:

R L L Ⓡ L S R S R
R L L Ⓡ L R S R S
1̲ 2̲ 3̲ 4̲ 5̲ 6̲ 7̲ 8̲ 9̲

In either case, a left-handed batter must bat fifth.

Questions 19–22

In this game, your task is to allocate eight subjects (the voters) among four different groups (who they voted for):

- the group who voted for Able and Cargis
- the group who voted for Able and Dorsey
- the group who voted for Berman and Cargis
- the group who voted for Berman and Dorsey

According to the rules, Berman receives exactly four votes. As a result, Able must also receive exactly four votes (from Raffi, Sperry, Trager and one other voter). Considering together the last two conditions, Utley, Villar, and Wieser must all be included in different groups. Accordingly, one of those three voted for Able, while the other two, along with Perez and Quinn, voted for Berman. The rules can now be incorporated into a group-oriented diagram as follows:

$$(RST\_) \begin{cases} [AC] \\ [AD] \end{cases}$$

$$(PQ\_\_) \begin{cases} [AC] \\ [AD] \end{cases}$$

$$U \neq V \neq W$$

In the following explanations, voters and candidates are identified by the first letter of their last name, as in the diagram above.

19. **(A)** Because A received exactly four votes, B must also have received exactly four votes.

20. **(B)** R, S, T, and one other voter voted for A. That other voter must be either U, V, or W. Therefore, T and P could not both have voted for A.

21. **(D)** V, U, and W must all be included in different groups. Thus, at least one voter among these three must have voted for D rather than for C.

22. **(B)** P and Q both voted for B (see general comments above). If one voted for C while the other voted for D, then P and Q must each be joined by exactly one other voter (among V, U and W) in their respective groups (see diagram above). Otherwise, among V, U, and W, two would be in the same group together, resulting in a rule violation.

23. **(B)** The task in this problem is to find an answer that weakens the argument-that is, one that undermines the major assumption of the argument, attacks a stated premise, or that suggests an alternative conclusion that could be inferred from the premises. The major assumption of the argument is that there are no additional reasons for preferring science over religion and mythology as a source of truth. Response (B) under-mines this assumption by pointing out that science differs from religion and mythology in that its methods yield accurate predictions and that this is a reliable indicator of truth.

24. **(C)** The information in the passage and the question stem can be restated as follows:

Premise 1: Either a settlement can be reached or the truce will be violated by one of the parties in the dispute.

Premise 2: If a settlement is reached, the border issues can be resolved.

Premise 3: If the border issues can be resolved, then both parties are willing to give up the territory they captured during the hostilities.

Premise 4: Both parties are not willing to give up the territory they captured during the hostilities.

(C) is the best response. From premise 4 and premise 3 it follows necessarily that the border issues cannot be resolved. From this claim and premise 2 it follows necessarily that a settlement cannot be reached, and from this claim and premise 1 it follows necessarily that the truce will be violated by one of the parties to the dispute. This latter claim contradicts response (C); consequently (C) cannot be true given the information in the passage.

25. **(E)** The task in this problem is to find an answer that strengthens the argument; that is, one that offers support for the major assumption of the argument or that provides additional evidence for the conclusion. Of the answer choices, response (E) is the best choice because it does the latter; that is, it provides a convincing rationale for the seemingly inconsistent action on the part of the Astonian government.

Sample Test 2

Quantitative Ability Test (Hour 22)

1. **(A)** There are a total of 30 distinct combinations of three women and two men. Thus, the probability that any one specific combination will be selected is 1 in 30.

2. **(A)** x can range in value from 1 to 7. Plugging in each of those values, y can be 7, 10, 13, 16, 19, 22, or 25. Of these, 7, 13, and 19 are prime numbers.

3. **(C)** In both quantities, you're multiplying 39 by 67, then shifting the decimal point to the right one place. (There's no need to do the math.)

4. **(D)** The drawer must include at least 20 pairs of striped socks. That leaves a maximum of 20 pairs of solid socks. If the drawer contains exactly 20 solid white pairs, then $x = 20$, the drawer contains no solid grey pairs ($y = 0$), and $x - y = 20$. Accordingly, quantity A equals quantity B in this case. However, if the drawer contains fewer than 20 solid white pairs, then $x < 20$ and $x - y < 20$, and quantity A is less than quantity B.

5. **(B)** Let x = the number of nickels. $30 - x$ = the number of quarters. Convert both expressions to cents:

   $5x$ = the value of nickels in cents.

   $750 - 25x$ = value of quarters in cents

The total of these two expressions is 470. Set up the equation, then solve for x:

$$5x + (750 - 25x) = 470$$
$$-20x = -280$$
$$x = 14$$

6. **(D)** Because $p < q < 0$, $q - p$ must be positive. However, whether $q - p > r + s$ depends on the values of each of the four variables.

7. **(C)** Given that $l_1 \parallel l_2$, w and x are supplementary—the sum of their angle measures is 180°. Similarly, y and z are supplementary. Thus, $(w + x) - (y + z) = 0$.

8. **(E)** The shelter houses $d + c$ animals altogether. Of these animals, d are dogs. That portion can be expressed as the fraction $\frac{d}{d+c}$.

9. **(B)** The price difference was at its maximum at the end of the 1st quarter, when the price of *ABC* stock was about \$2.80 and the price of *XYZ* stock was about \$6.60. The total price of both was about \$9.40. \$2.80 is $\frac{28}{94}$ of \$9.40. To estimate the percentage, round 28 up to 30 and round 94 up to 100: $\frac{30}{100} = 30\%$. (Be sure to round off a numerator and denominator in the same direction!)

10. **(E)** First, narrow down the viable data points by looking for pairs that are high up on the chart. The only two viable

points in time are end of second quarter and end of fourth quarter. Compare these two pairs. Remember: your task is to find that pair whose aggregate (combined) price is greater. It's a close call, but the total for the final pair (end of fourth quarter) is a bit larger than the total for the other pair.

At the end of the fourth quarter, the price of *XYZ* stock was approximately $8.25, and the price of *ABC* stock was approximately $4.75. The question asks for *XYZ* price as a percentage of the *ABC* price.

$$100\% + \frac{8.25 - 4.75}{4.75} = 100\% + \frac{3.50}{4.75}.$$

Round 4.75 up to 5.00, then determine a percentage:

$$100\% + \frac{3.50}{5.00} = 100\% + \frac{7}{10} = 170\%$$

11. **(B)** Compare the patterns in the two sets. Column A lists even integers from 16 to 28. Column B lists consecutive odd integers, except that the last integer is 28 instead of 27. If the last integer in Column B were 27, the two quantities would be equal. Thus, the average of the integers in Column B must be greater.

12. **(D)** Quantity A is 8 (the length of each side is 2). The rectangular solid's shape can vary considerably. At one extreme, the solid could be a cube, in which case its volume would be greater than that of the cube described in Column A. At the other extreme, the rectangular solid could be relatively "flat," approaching a volume of 0, yet still have a surface area

of 25. You don't have to prove this with numbers to recognize that the correct answer must be (D).

13. **(A)** To compare (A), (B), (C), and (D), use a common denominator of 24:

$$\frac{3}{4} = \frac{18}{24}$$

$$\frac{5}{6} = \frac{20}{24}$$

$$\frac{7}{8} = \frac{21}{24}$$

$$\frac{19}{24}$$

Of these four numbers, $\frac{3}{4}$ is the smallest. To compare $\frac{3}{4}$ with $\frac{13}{15}$, compare "cross-products." Since $(3)(15) < (4)(13)$, $\frac{3}{4} < \frac{13}{15}$.

14. **(A)** $x^2 - y^2 = (x + y)(x - y) = 48$

Substituting 16 for $x + y$:

$$16(x - y) = 48$$

$$x - y = 3$$

15. **(A)** The tax ($1.00) is based on a $9.00 price. Thus, the tax is $\frac{1}{9}$, which is greater than 11%.

16. **(E)** Since the figure has 5 sides, it contains 540°:

$$180(5 - 2) = 540$$

The sum of the five angles is 540, so solve for *x*:

$$540 = x + 110 + (x - 90) + 120 + 100$$

$$540 = 2x + 240$$

$$150 = x$$

17. **(C)** In quantity A, distribute the denominator to each term in the numerator, then cancel where possible:

$$\frac{a^2 + b^2}{ab} = \frac{a^2}{ab} + \frac{b^2}{ab} = \frac{a}{b} + \frac{b}{a}$$

18. **(C)** The amount invested at 5% is $10,000 - x$ dollars. Thus, the income from that amount is $.05(10,000 - x)$ dollars.

19. **(C)** Each successive increase from term to term in the sequence is greater than the previous increase by 1 $\{x, x + 0, x + 1, x + 2,...\}$. Given that 13 is the sixth term and exceeds the previous term by 4, the seventh, eighth, and ninth terms are $13 + 5$, $18 + 6$, and $24 + 7$, respectively.

20. **(A)** Given that $x = 60$, the area of each of the two triangles must be less than $\frac{60}{360}$, or $\frac{1}{6}$ the area of the circle (the difference is the region between each triangle and the circle's circumference). So the combined area of the two triangles is less than $\frac{1}{3}$ the area of the circle. Given that $x = 60$, $\angle AOC$ measures 120°, and the area of the shaded region is exactly $\frac{120}{360}$, or $\frac{1}{3}$ that of the circle.

21. **(D)** Be careful with the first part of the question. It specifies a 10-year change, not a 5-year change. (There are only two 10 year periods covered in the chart.) Also, be sure to look at the white bars, not the dark ones. The greatest 10-year change in nonminority scholarship funds awarded occurred from 1980 to 1990:

$750,000 to $600,000 (approximately). During this period, the greatest percentage change in minority funds awarded occurred from 1980 to 1985—an increase from $450,000 to $600,000 (approximately). This increase of approximately $150,000 is 33% of $450,000 (the amount in 1980).

22. **(B)** A quick visual inspection should reveal that the aggregate amount awarded in 1990 exceeded that of any of the other 3 years shown. During that year, minority awards totaled approximately $760,000 and non-minority awards totaled approximately $600,000. The difference between the two amounts is $160,000.

23. **(B)** Multiply quantity B by $1.20 to determine whether (and by how much) the cost of p cans exceeds the cost of a case. $(\$1.20)(15) = \$18$, which exceeds the cost of a case by $1.25, *more* than the cost of one can. Accordingly, quantity A is 14.

24. **(D)** From largest to smallest, the order is: (E), (B), (A), (C), (D). Let $x = \frac{1}{2}$. Using this value in each of the five expressions:

(A) $\sqrt{\dfrac{1}{2}} \approx .71$

(B) $\sqrt{\dfrac{1}{\frac{1}{2}}} = \sqrt{2} \approx 1.4$

(C) $\sqrt[3]{\left(\dfrac{1}{2}\right)^2} = \sqrt[3]{\dfrac{1}{4}} \approx \dfrac{1}{1.6}$, or .625

(D) $\left(\dfrac{1}{2}\right)^4 = \dfrac{1}{16}$

(E) $\dfrac{1}{\frac{1}{4}} = 4$

25. **(C)** The total distance is equal to the distance that one bus traveled plus the distance that the other bus traveled (to the point where they passeach other). Letting x equal the number of hours traveled, you can express the distances that the two buses travel in that time as $48x$ and $55x$. Equate the sum of these distances with the total distance and solve for x:

$$48x + 55x = 515$$
$$103x = 515$$
$$x = 5$$

The buses will pass each other five hours after 9:30 a.m.—at 2:30 p.m.

26. **(B)** Quantity A = $\dfrac{3^2 - 3 + 1}{(-3)^2 - (-3) + 1} = \dfrac{7}{13}$

Quantity B = $\dfrac{(-3)^2 - (-3) - 1}{3^2 - 3 - 1} = \dfrac{11}{5}$

27. **(B)** In quantity A, the vertical and horizontal distances (rise and run) are 4 and 3, respectively. In quantity B, the vertical and horizontal distances (rise and run) are 5 and 2, respectively. To determine each quantity, you apply the Pythagorean Theorem:

Quantity A: $3^2 + 4^2 = d^2$

Quantity B: $2^2 + 5^2 = d^2$

In the first equation, $d = 5$ (recall the 3:4:5 Pythagorean triplet). Now solve for d in the second equation:

$$4 + 25 = d^2$$
$$29 = d^2$$
$$\sqrt{29} = d$$
$$d = 5^+$$

There's no need to determine the precise value of Quantity B. You know it's greater than 5, and that's all you need to know to conclude that quantity B is greater than quantity A.

28. **(B)** The value of Dynaco shares sold plus the value of MicroTron shares sold must be equal to the value of all shares sold (that is, the "mixture"). Letting x represent the number of shares of Dynaco sold, you can represent the number of shares of MicroTron sold by $300 - x$. Set up an equation in which the value of Dynaco shares sold plus the value of MicroTron shares sold equals the total value of all shares sold, then solve for x:

$$\$52(x) + \$36(300 - x) = \$40(300)$$
$$52x + 10{,}800 - 36x = 12{,}000$$
$$16x = 1{,}200$$
$$x = 75$$

The investor has sold 75 shares of Dynaco stock. Checking your work:

$$\$52(75) + \$36(300 - 75) = \$12{,}000$$
$$\$3{,}900 + \$36(225) = \$12{,}000$$
$$\$3{,}900 + \$8{,}100 = \$12{,}000$$

Verbal Ability Test (Hour 23)

1. **(B)** The word *attacking* indicates the need for two strong negative words. Only choice (B) satisfies this requirement with *acrimonious*, meaning "harsh or bitter, and angry."

2. **(E)** Something *flagrant* is "obvious" or "conspicuous"; something *innocuous* is "barely perceptible."

3. **(D)** To *denigrate* is to "belittle"; to *laud* is to "praise."

4. **(B)** *Incredulity* means "disbelief" or "distrust"; *faith* means "trust."

5. **(B)** *Cotton* is *soft* to the touch, as an *iron* is *hard* to the touch. These are both inherent tactile characteristics. *Wool* keeps a person warm, but it is not necessarily *warm* to the touch. Strength is a characteristic of *nylon*, but its strength is not evident by touching it. *Wood* may or may not be *polished*. (A), (C), and (E) are red herrings; each one involves fabric, just like the original.

6. **(B)** *Corroborate* means "confirm, prove, or verify." Hearsay (second-hand information) tends to be unreliable, so it makes sense that in acting in the public's best interest journalists should scrutinize this information to verify its truthfulness.

7. **(D)** Something *austere* is "unfriendly" or "forbidding"; something *inviting* is "attractive" or "enticing."

8. **(E)** *Fish* are kept in an *aquarium*, an environment created by humans. *Birds* are kept in an *aviary*, also an environment created by humans. *Lions* live in *dens*, and *insects* live in the *ground*, but these environments are natural (not created by humans). An *automobile* can be kept in a *garage*, but an automobile has no natural environment. A *stew* cooks in a *cauldron* (large pot), but a stew has no natural environment.

9. **(A)** To *amble* is to *walk* unhurriedly without a predetermined destination. To *tinker* is to work aimlessly without a predetermined direction. None of the other pairs exemplify this type of relationship. (C) and (D) are red herrings; both involve pedestrian locomotion, just like the original.

10. **(C)** *Silver* is a type of *metal* and *helium* is a type of *gas*. An *alloy* is a mixture of metals; so *gold* can be a component of, not a type, of alloy. *Plastic* need not take the form of a *container*; it merely describes what some containers are made of. *Sand* is a raw material used to make *glass*. (E) is the second-best answer. *Sediment* is one of many physical forms that *rock* might take; but sediment is not a type or class of rock, but rather one form that rocks generally can take. Note: (A) is a red herring; it involves metals, just like the original.

11. **(C)** To *foment* is to "stir up" or "incite"; to *pacify* is to "calm."

12. **(E)** *Cynosure* means "center or focus." *Impertinent* means "rude or offensive." It makes sense in the context of the sentence that she would be annoyed that her brother receives not only more attention but also more affection in spite of his ill manners. None of the other word pairs make sense here. *Consequential* means "arrogant"; *putative* means "commonly accepted"; *laconic* means "concise"; *insipid* means "uninteresting."

13. **(C)** Statement (C) is totally unsupported and runs contrary to the passage. The author states that "spillovers occur because knowledge created by one firm is typically not contained within that firm, and thereby creates value for other firms." The clear implication of this statement is that other firms benefit from the knowledge gained by the research and development efforts of innovating firms. (A) is supported by the lines 23–27. (B) is supported by lines 13–15. (D) is supported by lines 30–37. (E) is supported by lines 5–9.

14. **(E)** While the passage indicates that knowledge created by one firm is typically not contained within that firm (lines 1–5), no explanation for this is stated.

15. **(A)** The author's threshold purpose, articulated in the final sentence of the first paragraph, is to identify the significant forms of dissent to Arnoldian culture. But the author proceeds to do more than merely identify and describe these forms of dissent; the author is also critical of the dissenters, for example,

because they have misunderstood Arnold. Response (A) embraces both the author's threshold and ultimate concerns.

16. **(E)** Admittedly, the author views "this dichotomy simply as another version of the old struggle between a privileged power structure and radical challenges to its authority" (lines 21–23). However, the author continues by suggesting strongly that the resemblance between Arnold's anarchy-culture dichotomy and the struggle against established authority is only an apparent one: in light of Arnold's "Dover Beach" and in light of the fact that Arnold was himself plagued by the "blind arrogances of the reactionary powers in the world" (lines 27–28), the interpretation of Arnold's dichotomy as "simply one more version of the old struggle . . . " misunderstands Arnold.

17. **(B)** Arnold's *Culture* was published in 1869. The three forms of opposition to Arnold's ideas as presented in this work, therefore, must have emerged later than 1869.

18. **(D)** The only analogy in the passage is found in the final paragraph, in which the author compares striving for perfection (i.e., culture) to conceiving "finer sunsets and unheard melodies" (line 76). Although the author uses this analogy to help the reader understand the author's final argument against Arnold's dissenters, this analogy is not in the nature of "an insupportable theory" which the author compares to a claim made by Arnold's dissenters, as response (D) suggests.

19. **(D)** *Pallid* means "colorless" or "lacking vitality or liveliness"; *vibrant* means "lively."

20. **(A)** A *nail* creates a *puncture*, and a *sword* creates a *laceration* (a cut or gash). Both actions create holes or openings. (B) is a red herring; a *drill* and a nail serve similar functions. However, a drill does not make a *screw*, but rather creates a hole in which a screw is inserted. In (C), (D), and (E), the first word describes an object that creates a result described by the second word. But in each case, the second word is not a hole or opening.

21. **(A)** The author probably withdrew from the project because he was displeased with the novel's *adaptation*, which is a change required to turn the novel into another form such as a television program. None of the other choices make as much sense in context.

22. **(C)** A *spark* is a very small fire, while a *conflagration* is a very large fire. The relationship is one of degree. Similarly, a *drizzle* is a very light rain, while a *torrent* is very heavy rain. The only other answer choice in which the relationship is one of degree is (E). But the relationship in (E) is backwards; a *mountain* is a large hill, and a *hillock* is a small hill. Note: (A) and (B) are red herrings; each involve fire, just like the original.

23. **(C)** An *interloper* seeks to *meddle* (interfere) in the affairs of another. An *advocate* (ally) seeks to *espouse* (support or defend) a particular viewpoint or cause. In both cases, the second word describes the inherent function (goal) of the first. None of the other pairs exemplifies this type of relationship. A *misanthrope* (one who hates humankind) does not seek to *usurp* (seize or capture). A *rogue* (outlaw or scoundrel) is generally unrepentant (so *rogue* and *repent* are contrary in meaning). A *dilettante* is someone who dabbles in the arts; the word bears no relationship to *proselytize* (to seek to convert others to one's own belief system). (E) is a red herring; an *ombudsman* is a consumer advocate who mediates disputes between a consumer and government or business. So there is some similarity in meaning between *ombudsman* and *interloper*. However, *ombudsman* bears no relationship to *refine*.

24. **(A)** The word *commensurate* means "proportionate"; so the two missing words should be essentially synonymous. (A) is the only choice that clearly fits the bill. *Courtesy* and *deference* both mean "respect," and both words make sense in context. (B) is the second-best choice; but *impunity* (privilege or exemption) carries a different meaning than *respect*. None of the remaining choices make sense in context. (*Capriciousness* means "whimsy or spontaneity"; *regalia* refers to formal or ceremonial attire and trappings, and *liturgy* means "ritual or ceremony"; *acrimony* means "anger or wrath.")

25. **(D)** Answer choice (D) is contradicted by the information in the passage. According to the passage the German states were brought together by the Franco-Prussian war. Since this war occurred after the wars against Denmark and Austria, the inference to be drawn is that the wars against Denmark and Austria were fought by Prussia, not the unified German states.

26. **(C)** Answer choice (C) is unsupported by the passage. There is no indication in the passage that Bismarck personally insulted the people of France. The insult mentioned in line 32 refers to the fact that the German states chose to proclaim the creation of a new German empire on "French soil in the Hall of Mirrors at Versailles." It was this decision and the loss of the territory of Alsace and Lorraine that "was a grievous insult to the people of France."

27. **(D)** The word renege means "abandon or quit"; implement means "accomplish or achieve"; this word pair makes sense in context—a failure to implement promised reforms amounts to reneging. None of the other pairs make sense here.

28. **(A)** Something *munificent* is characterized by great *generosity*. Similarly, something *dolorous* is characterized by great *sorrow*. A *domineering* person is overly assertive; but *perspicacity* means astuteness or insight. An *indisputable* claim is one that cannot be doubted. *Haplessness* describes an unfortunate person. *Beguiled* means "enchanted or charmed," but *judiciousness* means "common sense or good judgment."

29. **(B)** A *braggart* (a boastful person) generally lacks *diffidence* (modesty), just as a *pariah* (outcast) lacks esteem (regard). In all other answer choices, the second word characterizes the first. A *partisan* is by definition partial; a *savant* is by definition wise; and a *sycophant* is by definition a flatterer.

30. **(B)** *Resolution* means "determination" or "a clear sense of purpose"; *vacillation* is a state of "indecision" or "lack of clear purpose."

Analytical Ability Test (Hour 24)

1. **(A)** The argument in the passage is essentially that women have the right to earn as much money as men because they have as much right to self-esteem as men. The argument can be represented as follows:

Premise: Women have as much right to self-esteem as men.

Conclusion: Women have the right to earn as much money as men.

The logical gap in this argument that must be filled is the link between a person's self-esteem and the amount of money they earn. The suggestion is that a person's self-esteem is determined by the amount of money they have: the more money they have, the more self-esteem; the less money they have, the less self-esteem. Of the answer choices, response (A) best expresses this assumption.

(B) is off-focus. The argument is concerned only with unequal pay for men and women. This implies that they have jobs.

(C) is a paraphrase of the first sentence of the passage. In the first sentence it is stated that "unequal pay for men and women is a completely indefensible practice." (C) is just another way of saying this.

(D) brings in information not mentioned in the passage. The constitutionality of unequal pay for women and men is not discussed in the passage.

(E) is off-focus. The relative importance of self-esteem to men and women is not addressed in the argument. Response (E) does not express an assumption of the argument, but rather another plausible reason why women and men should receive equal pay.

Questions 2–5

This game involves a double sequence in which the two sequences must be considered together in order to answer all but the first two questions. Begin constructing the line-position sequence with the last rule, since it calls for two alternatives, either [B...D...E] or [E...D...B]. Two unfixed core sequences may be constructed to display line-position possibilities, and a single core

diagram may be used to order the people according to box size:

line position   *box size*

         A   E
         ←   ↙ ↓ ↘

(1) C B D E (5)   C   D   A   B   j l m s

            c
            ←
(1) A E D B (5)

The premise makes clear that Charles, David, Alice and Bill respectively buy jumbo, large, medium, and small boxes. Since Erma buys a smaller box than Charles, Erma must buy either a large, medium or small box.

2. **(C)** Referring to the two line-position diagrams above, only answer choice (C) [AECDB] is consistent with one of the two diagrams (the bottom diagram).

3. **(B)** Erma and Alice are the only people that can buy a medium box. If Erma and Alice are the last two people in line, only one line-position sequence is possible—CBDAE. Thus, Bill is second in line.

4. **(C)** Only Bill and Erma may buy a small box, but Bill and Erma cannot, in either order, appear first and last in line; thus, (A) is false. Only David and Erma may buy a large box, but David and Erma cannot, in either order, appear first and last in line; thus, (B) is false. Only Alice and Erma may buy medium boxes, and they may appear first and second in line; thus (C) could be true. David and Erma cannot be the first two people in line; thus, (D) is false. Bill and Erma cannot

be the last two people in line; thus, (E) is false.

5. **(E)** Erma must be either first or last in line, since Erma and only Erma buys the same size box as one of the others. Thus, the second line-position diagram above can be eliminated. Erma must buy the same size box as the first person in line, who must be either Charles or Alice. However, Charles must buy a jumbo box, while Erma must buy a smaller than jumbo box. Thus, the five people must be in line as follows: ACBDE. Since Alice and Erma must buy the same size box, the box sizes for all five people may also be determined.

6. **(C)** The task in this problem is to find an answer that weakens the argument; that is, one that undermines the major assumption of the argument, attacks a stated premise, or suggests an alternative conclusion that could be inferred from the premises. The major assumption in the argument is that current dirolin contamination detection methods are inadequate, ineffective, or completely lacking. Response (C) effectively undermines this assumption.

7. **(B)** The pattern of the argument is:

   Los Alamos has properties X, Y, and Z.

   Los Brunos has properties X and Y.

   Therefore it is likely that ____.

   Based on this comparison of Los Alamos and Los Brunos, the sentence that best completes the argument is: Los Brunos has property Z, which in this argument is the property of always electing conservative candidates. Based on this analysis, the unstated conclusion is: Los Brunos residents always elect conservative candidates.

8. **(B)** The major assumption of the argument in the passage is that there are no relevant differences between the conditions present during the previous drought and the current drought that would necessitate the water use restrictions imposed in response to the current drought. Response (B) undermines this assumption and, as a result, undermines the author's contention. The fact that there is a significant increase in the number of water users points to a relevant difference between the two situations that accounts for the difference in the restrictions.

9. **(A)** The argument in the passage is essentially that we should not be required by law to wear seat belts because wearing them may endanger our lives. The argument can be represented as follows:

   Premise: Wearing seat belts can endanger our lives.

   Conclusion: We should not be required by law to wear seat belts.

   The logical gap in this argument that must be filled is the link between acts that we are required by law to do and activities that may endanger us. Response (A) expresses the necessary link.

Questions 10–13

Because the subjects of this game are linked together by a series of conditional statements, a flow-chart approach is appropriate. In the diagram below, "some" statements are signified by double-arrowed dotted lines:

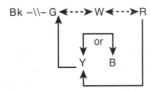

Since this game involves conditional rules, be aware of the contrapositive and related fallacies. For example, since all students using yellow also used green, it follows that if a student did not use green, he or she also did not use yellow (if not G, then not Y). However, it cannot be inferred that if a student used green, that student must have also used yellow (if G, then Y). In the diagram, the arrow flows only in one direction; it cannot be inferred that if a student did not use yellow, that student also did not use green (if not Y, then not G). Also be aware that the term "some" means at least one and possibly as many as all.

10. **(C)** Answer choices (A) and (B) are incomplete lists. Answer choice (D) is incorrect; a student using yellow and red must have used green as well (a total of three colors). Answer choice (E) is incorrect—a student using green and white must have used a third color as well—either blue or yellow.

11. **(C)** A single student could have used four colors at most—green, red, yellow and either blue or white.

12. **(E)** A student clearly could have used black only. In addition, a student could have used green only—although some students using green must also have used white, this student may have been one of those using green that did not use white as well. Finally, a student need not have used white in order to use blue, and so a student could have used blue only.

13. **(E)** A student using white could not have used both blue and yellow as well; thus, combination (E) is not possible.

14. **(A)** The task in this problem is to find an answer that strengthens the argument; that is, one that offers support for the major assumption of the argument or that provides additional evidence for the conclusion. The argument in the passage can be represented as follows:

Premise: Compared to the five-year period prior to the passage of laws requiring the use of safety seats by children, fatalities of children under age four have decreased by 30 percent.

Conclusion: The passage of laws requiring the use of safety seats by children under age four has resulted in fewer child fatalities over the past five years.

(A) is the best response. The major assumption of the argument is that there are no significant differences between the five-year period preceding the passage of the laws and the five-year period since their passage that could account for the decrease in fatalities. Response (A) supports this assumption.

(B) weakens the argument. The major assumption of the argument is that there are no significant differences between the five-year period preceding the passage of the laws and the five-year period since their passage that could account for the decrease in fatalities. Response (B) undermines this assumption.

(C), (D), and (E) do not offer support for the major assumption of the argument nor do they provide additional evidence for the conclusion of the argument.

Questions 15–19

As the diagram below suggests, each commercial break in the sequence includes two commercials. After displaying the information provided in the rules near your master diagram, you can deduce that either D or I must appear at the fifth break. Why? Only one commercial appears at the fifth break. C and A appear together, as do H and G. Thus, none of these four may appear at the fifth break. Also, since F and B both appear at an earlier break than D, neither F nor B may appear at the fifth break:

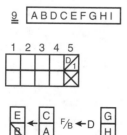

15. **(B)** Either D's commercial or I's commercial must appear at the fifth break (see general comments above); thus, statement (B) must be false.

16. **(A)** If I's commercial were paired with F's commercial, then B's commercial would have to be paired with E's commercial. This would result, however, in a rule violation. Thus, I's commercial cannot be paired with F's commercial.

17. **(E)** The condition in the question restricts the positions of B's commercial and F's commercial to the first and fourth breaks. Thus, the [GH] and [CA] pairs must appear at the second and third breaks, but in either order. Since E's commercial must precede C's commercial, E's commercial must appear at the first break. Since B's commercial and E's commercial cannot appear at the same break together, B's commercial must appear at the fourth break (and F's commercial must appear at the first break). Since D's commercial must appear at a later break than B's commercial, D's commercial must appear at the fifth break. Accordingly, I's commercial must appear with B's commercial at the fourth break.

18. **(B)** If C's commercial (together with A's commercial) appears at the second break, E's commercial must appear at the first break. B's commercial cannot appear with E's commercial, and so B's

commercial cannot appear at the first break. D's commercial must follow both B's and F's commercials, and so D's commercial cannot appear during the first break. Only F's commercial and I's commercial remain, either of which could appear at the first break with E's commercial.

19. **(E)** Given that G's commercial appears at the third break, H's commercial must also appear at that break. Now consider Statement (E). If F's commercial appears at the fourth break, D's commercial must appear at the fifth break, since the rules stipulate that D's commercial appears at a later break than the break at which F's commercial appears. The [AC] pair must therefore precede the [GH] pair. Because E's commercial appears at an earlier break than C's commercial, E's commercial must appear at the first break, and the [AC] pair must appear at the second break. B's commercial cannot appear at the first break with E's commercial, and so B's commercial must appear at the fourth break with F's commercial, while I's commercial appears with E's commercial at the first break:

Questions 20-23

This sequence formula game may appear intimidating at first due to its lengthy premise. Once you have internalized the rules of the game, analyzing the questions involves

applying the same formula repeatedly to the initial sequence. No initial diagram other than the original sequence or "melody" (C D E F) is necessary. Question 21 is more difficult than the others. It requires you to work backwards from a predetermined end result through unknown interim steps.

20. **(C)** The first student can create melody (C) by exchanging D and F in the initial sequence. Melody (A) violates the rule that F and D cannot occur in immediate succession; also, the first student cannot create (A) without also making another change. Melody (B) can be created by the first student only by exchanging C and E in the initial melody; however, this exchange would violate the rule that C and E can be exchanged only if neither occurs as the first or last note of the melody. Melody (D) can be created only by adding a note to the end of the initial melody as well as making some other change to the initial melody; the first student, however, is permitted to make one and only one change to the initial melody. Melody (E) violates the rule that F and D cannot occur in immediate succession.

21. **(C)** Notes D and F remain in their initial positions. Notes C and D have been added to the end of the melody by different students, and notes C and E (the first and third notes in the initial melody) have been exchanged. However, one student could not have effected an exchange between C and E since C initially occurred as the first note of the

melody. Thus, a third student changed the C to an E while a fourth student changed the E to a C. For example:

original	C D E F
student 1	C D E F C
student 2	C D E F C D
student 3	E D E F C D
student 4	E D C F C D

These four changes need not occur in the precise order indicated above.

22. **(A)** In melody (A), a student may make four different exchanges—D and C, C and E, E and F, or D and F. In melody (B), a student may make one of two different exchanges—C and F or F and D. In melody (C), a student may make one of three different exchanges—E and D, D and F, or F and the second C. In melody (D), a student may make one of two different exchanges—C and the first D or C and the second D. In melody (E), a student may make one of two different exchanges—E and the first F or E and the second F.

23. **(A)** The second and third notes (D and E) could remain unchanged by adding a note to the end of the melody; thus, (A) is a possibility. (B), (C), and (D) each require that a note be replaced; doing so, however, would result in a four-note melody with only three different notes (a rule violation). (E) requires that D and E be exchanged; the result, however, is that D would immediately precede F (a rule violation).

24. **(B)** The task in this problem is to find an answer that weakens the argument; that is, one that undermines the major assumption of the argument, attacks a stated premise, or that suggests an alternative conclusion that could be inferred from the premises. The major assumption in the argument is that glass and metal containers are not being disposed of in some way other than the way mentioned in the passage. Response (B) undermines this assumption, thereby calling into question the conclusion of the argument.

Questions 25–29

The most difficult aspect of this game is understanding the premise and constructing a proper diagram. Once this is done, analyzing the questions is not a difficult task. The rules suggest a line-and-node or flowchart approach; as you construct a diagram, you must bear in mind that unless Bob can make a round trip between two camps, he will descend in elevation from one camp to the next. For example, since Bob may hike directly from G to E but cannot hike directly from E to G, G must be higher in elevation than E. Continuing this analysis, E must be higher in elevation than C, since Bob can hike from E to C but not from C to E. Since Bob can hike from C to F as well as from F to C, it cannot be determined which camp (if either) is higher in elevation. Using this approach, a flow chart may be constructed as follows (a horizontal relationship indicates that relative elevation cannot be determined):

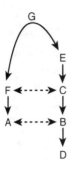

As you interpret this diagram, it is crucial to bear in mind that the elevations of F and A vis-a-vis E, C, B, and D cannot be determined. For example, it is possible that both F and A are actually lower in elevation than D.

25. **(B)** If Bob visits all seven camps, he must begin at Camp G and end at Camp D. To avoid visiting any camp more than once, only one route is available to Bob: G to E to C to F to A to B to D.

26. **(C)** In order for Bob to begin and end at the same camp, he must begin as well as end his trip at Camp A, B, C, or F. Four distinct routes are possible:

    A to B and back to A

    B to A and back to B

    C to F and back to C

    F to C and back to F

27. **(B)** Bob must descend in elevation from one camp to the next (except between camps where a round trip is possible); thus, Camp E must be higher in elevation than Camp D. Any of the other four statements could be true.

28. **(A)** Regardless of which camp Bob departs from, he might either move laterally or ascend in either direction across the dotted paths in the diagram. The only exception is Camp D; but the question stipulates that Bob must visit at least two camps, so he cannot depart from Camp D.

29. **(A)** In order to meet the conditions of the question, the route must include either F and C or A and B, and Bob must make a round trip between those two camps on either the first and second day of the trip or on the second and third day of the trip. Camp B is a possible departure point—B to A to B to D. Camp C is a possible departure point— for example, C to F to C to B. Camp E is a possible departure point—E to C to F to C. Camp F is a possible departure point—for example, F to A to B to A. However, if Camp A is Bob's departure point, he either makes two interim overnight stops but visits only two camps (A and B) or he visits three camps (A, B and D) but makes only one interim overnight stop (at Camp B).

30. **(E)** The task in this problem is to find the answer that must be true, that is, the one that cannot conceivably be false, given that the information stated in the passage is true. The premises in the passage can be represented as follows:

    Premise 1: Either the budget deficit will continue to grow or taxes will be raised soon.

    Premise 2: Taxes will not be raised soon.

Premise 3: If the budget deficit continues to grow, then the next generation of taxpayers will be burdened with an almost unbearable debt.

(E) is the best response. From premise 1 and premise 2 above it necessarily follows that:

Conclusion 1: The budget deficit will continue to grow.

From conclusion 1 and premise 3 it necessarily follows that:

Conclusion 2: The next generation of taxpayers will be burdened with an almost unbearable debt.

Since conclusion 2 necessarily follows from the information stated in the passage it cannot conceivably be false if this information is true.

Questions 31–34

The key to working through this grouping game efficiently is to establish at the outset the minimum and maximum number of pieces of fruit that each person may receive. Susan, Ursula, and Vadim must each receive at least three pieces, but Todd must receive at least four pieces (because Todd must receive more pieces than Susan). The maximum number of pieces that any person may receive is six (6 + 3 + 3 + 3 = 15), and only Todd may receive six pieces. (If any other person received six pieces, the total number of pieces would exceed fifteen because Todd must receive at

least four pieces.) Ursula and Vadim may each receive as many as five pieces, while Susan may receive only four pieces at maximum. (If Susan received five pieces, Todd would have to receive six, and the total number would exceed fifteen.) We can construct the following initial diagram:

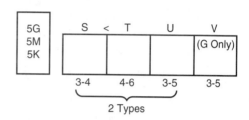

31. **(A)** Todd must receive more pieces that Susan, and the total number must be fifteen. (A) conforms to these conditions. (B) and (D) are not possible because Susan and Todd would receive the same number of pieces; (D) is not possible also because Vadim would receive six pieces, but there are only five guavas available, and the rules stipulate the Vadim receives only guavas. (C) provides for a total of 16 pieces, while (E) provides for a total of only 14 pieces.

32. **(B)** As noted in the comments above, Todd can receive six pieces while the other three each receive three pieces. All four other statements, however, must be false, as the comments above make clear.

33. **(E)** Ursula may receive no more than five pieces, and Todd may receive no fewer than four pieces (see general

comments above). As a result, if Ursula receives more pieces than Todd, then Ursula must receive five pieces, and Todd must receive four pieces. Accordingly, Susan and Vadim must each receive three pieces. Statements (A) and (B) must be false—Vadim will receive three pieces (all guavas), two guavas remaining for the other three friends. Statements (C) and (D) must be false because each friend (including Todd) must receive at least two different types of fruit. Only Statement (E) is possible.

34. **(B)** If Susan receives four pieces, then Todd must receive exactly five pieces while Vadim and Ursula both receive exactly three pieces (see general comments above). Given that Susan receives two guavas and two kiwis, three kiwis and five mangos remain to be allocated between Todd and Ursula. A bit of experimenting reveals that only two allocation schemes are possible—

either Todd receives one kiwi and four mangos while Ursula receives two kiwis and one mango, or Todd receives two kiwis and three mangos while Ursula receives one kiwi and two mangos.

35. **(E)** The task in this problem is to find an answer that strengthens the argument; that is, one that offers support for the major assumption of the argument or that provides additional evidence for the conclusion. The primary reason given in the argument for expecting an increasing number of computer owners to sell their old computers is that increased demand for used computers has exerted an upward pressure on prices of used computers. This suggests that the reason computer owners had not sold their old computers previously is that their old computers did not have sufficient resale value to enable them to purchase newer models. Response (E) explicitly states this reason and thus provides additional evidence for the conclusion.

APPENDIX B

Score Conversion Tables

Sample Test 1: Hours 19, 20, 21

Based on your raw score (your total number of correct responses), use the table below to determine your scaled score and corresponding percentile rank for each of the three sections.

Raw Score	Scaled Score / Percentile Rank		
	Verbal	Quantitative	Analytical
36-38	800/99		
35	770/99		
34	740/98		
33	720/96		
32	690/94		
31	670/91		
30	650/89	800/97	
29	630/85	800/95	
28	610/82	780/93	
27	590/78	750/88	

| Raw Score | Scaled Score / Percentile Rank | | |
	Verbal	Quantitative	Analytical
26	570/74	730/84	
25	550/69	700/79	800/99
24	530/63	680/75	800/99
23	510/58	650/70	790/98
22	490/52	630/65	770/97
21	470/47	600/59	750/95
20	450/43	580/53	720/92
19	430/36	560/49	690/86
18	410/31	540/44	660/81
17	400/25	520/39	630/75
16	380/22	500/34	600/67
15	370/18	470/29	570/58
14	350/15	450/24	540/50
13	340/12	430/19	510/42
12	320/9	400/14	480/33
11	310/7	380/11	450/26
10	290/5	360/9	420/20
9	270/3	330/6	390/14
8	250/1	310/4	360/9
7	240/1	280/3	330/6
6	220/1	250/2	290/3
5	200/1	210/1	260/1
4	200/1	200/1	230/1
0-3	200/1	200/1	200/1

Sample Test 2: Hours 22, 23, 24

Based on your raw score (your total number of correct responses), use the table below to determine your scaled score and corresponding percentile rank for each of the three sections.

Raw Score	Scaled Score / Percentile Rank		
	Verbal	Quantitative	Analytical
35			800/99
34			800/99
33			800/99
32			780/98
31			760/97
30	800/99		740/95
29	780/99		730/92
28	750/97	800/98	710/90
27	720/95	780/95	690/87
26	700/93	760/90	660/83
25	680/91	740/87	640/80
24	660/89	720/84	610/75
23	620/86	690/81	590/69
22	610/81	650/70	560/60
21	600/76	610/60	540/51
20	550/70	590/55	520/45
19	520/61	570/51	490/39
18	480/50	520/42	480/34
17	450/41	490/35	460/30
16	460/36	470/30	450/27
15	430/33	450/25	430/24
14	410/30	430/20	420/20
13	380/24	400/17	390/15
12	360/19	370/12	360/10
11	340/15	360/8	330/7
10	330/11	350/6	310/5
9	290/8	330/5	310/3
8	260/6	310/4	280/3
7	240/4	280/3	260/2
6	220/2	250/2	240/1
5	200/1	220/1	220/1
4	200/1	200/1	200/1
0-3	200/1	200/1	200/1

B